THE EMIL AND KATHLEEN SICK LECTURE-BOOK SERIES

IN WESTERN HISTORY AND BIOGRAPHY

THE EMIL AND KATHLEEN SICK LECTURE-BOOK SERIES
IN WESTERN HISTORY AND BIOGRAPHY

Under the provisions of a Fund established by the children of Mr. and Mrs. Emil Sick, whose deep interest in the history and culture of the American West was inspired by their own experience in the region, distinguished scholars are brought to the University of Washington to deliver public lectures based on original research in the fields of Western history and biography. The terms of the gift also provide for the publication by the University of Washington Press of the books resulting from the research upon which the lectures are based. This book is the eleventh volume in the series.

The Great Columbia Plain:
A Historical Geography, 1805–1910
by Donald W. Meinig

Mills and Markets: A History of the
Pacific Coast Lumber Industry to 1900
by Thomas R. Cox

Radical Heritage: Labor, Socialism, and Reform
in Washington and British Columbia, 1885–1917
by Carlos A. Schwantes

The Battle for Butte: Mining and Politics
on the Northern Frontier, 1864–1906
by Michael P. Malone

Nikkei in the Pacific Northwest

JAPANESE AMERICANS & JAPANESE CANADIANS
IN THE TWENTIETH CENTURY

Edited by Louis Fiset and Gail M. Nomura

CENTER FOR THE STUDY OF THE PACIFIC NORTHWEST

in association with

UNIVERSITY OF WASHINGTON PRESS

Seattle and London

Copyright © 2005 by the University of Washington Press
Printed in the United States of America
Designed by Pamela Canell
12 11 10 09 08 07 06 05   5 4 3 2 1

This book is published simultaneously in the United States and
Canada by the Center for the Study of the Pacific Northwest, P.O.
Box 353587, Seattle, WA 98195, in association with the University of
Washington Press, P.O. Box 50096, Seattle, WA 98145.

Library of Congress Cataloging-in-Publication Data
Nikkei in the Pacific Northwest : Japanese Americans and Japanese
Canadians in the twentieth century / edited by Louis Fiset
and Gail M. Nomura.— 1st ed.
p. cm. — (The Emil and Kathleen Sick lecture-book series
in western history and biography ; 11)
Papers from a conference held at the University of Washington
from May 4 to 6, 2000. Includes index.
ISBN 0-295-98461-9 (pbk. : alk. paper)
1. Japanese Americans—Northwest, Pacific—History—20th
century—Congresses.   2. Japanese—British Columbia—History—
20th century—Congresses.   3. Japanese Americans—Northwest,
Pacific—Ethnic identity—Congresses.   4. Japanese—British
Columbia—Ethnic identity—Congresses. 5. Immigrants—North-
west, Pacific—History—20th century—Congresses.   6. Northwest,
Pacific—History—20th century—Congresses.   7. Northwest,
Pacific—Ethnic relations—Congresses.   8. Regionalism—North-
west, Pacific—History—20th century—Congresses.
I. Fiset, Louis.   II. Nomura, Gail M.   III. Series.
F855.2.J3N55 2005   979.5'004956—dc22   2004021217

DEDICATED TO THE NIKKEI OF THE PACIFIC NORTHWEST,

PAST, PRESENT, AND FUTURE

FOR ROGER DANIELS, MENTOR AND FRIEND

L.F.

FOR GORDON HIRABAYASHI, "IDEALISM IS REALISM"

G.M.N.

CONTENTS

ACKNOWLEDGMENTS

Scholars from the United States, Canada, and Japan gathered on the University of Washington campus from May 4 to 6, 2000, to reflect on the century-long presence of Nikkei, persons of Japanese descent, in the Pacific Northwest, including British Columbia. The Nikkei Experience in the Pacific Northwest Conference, held in conjunction with the celebration of Gordon Hirabayashi as the 2000 Distinguished Alumnus of the College of Arts and Sciences, sought to bring together the latest research into the regional history of Nikkei outside the usual California-centered framework. Recognizing the fluidity of movement and contact across political borders, the Pacific Northwest was interpreted to encompass the Canadian Southwest of British Columbia, a region that had the heaviest concentration of Nikkei in Canada in the prewar era. Conference organizers also recognized that the history of the Nikkei has also been dominated by the events of World War II, and our goal was to place the incarceration years within the context of its history in the region. Conference participants represented an eclectic group, including sociologists, educators, attorneys, historians, and artists, whose backgrounds in architecture, anthropology, law, ethnic studies, literature, music, religion, documentary film making, oral history, and the visual arts informed their presentations.

The completion of this anthology owes much to the conference participants as well as other individuals and groups that enabled the conference to take place. John Findlay, past editor of *Pacific Northwest Quarterly,* provided early encouragement to pursue the conference and publish a collection of essays. Bruce Hevly, director of University of Washington's Center for the Study of the Pacific Northwest, provided valuable guidance for the conference and anthology project. Financial support was provided by the Emil G. and Kathleen T. Sick Fund and the Center for the Study of the Pacific Northwest; with additional funding from the King County Landmarks and

Heritage Commission†; the Henry M. Jackson School of International Studies, Canadian Studies Center; the Kenneth S. Allen Library Endowment; Friends of the UW Libraries; UW Libraries Manuscripts, Special Collections, and University Archives; and the Walter Chapin Simpson Center for the Humanities.

We thank our two anonymous reviewers of the manuscript whose insightful comments and suggestions helped us to improve the anthology. We also thank Patricia Roy for her help in furthering our understanding of Canadian history. We are grateful to the UW Department of American Ethnic Studies and its staff for providing assistance and support for the anthology. We also want to acknowledge Kim McKaig and Sara Early of *Pacific Northwest Quarterly* for their assistance in the production of the manuscript and to thank Kim McKaig for her essential organizational work on the conference. Additional thanks go to the University of Washington Press— Michael Duckworth, Naomi Pascal, and Marilyn Trueblood, for their guidance throughout the project. We appreciate the skillful copyediting by Mary Ribesky, who helped to improve the manuscript significantly. The editors are grateful to *Pacific Northwest Quarterly* for permission to republish Patricia Roy's essay. Finally, the editors wish to express our heartfelt appreciation to the contributing authors for their valuable research and contribution to the field of Nikkei history. We also thank our families for their patience and support throughout this long endeavor.

† King County
Landmarks & Heritage Commission
Hotel/Motel Tax Fund

Nikkei in the Pacific Northwest

I / INTRODUCTION

Nikkei in the Pacific Northwest

LOUIS FISET AND GAIL M. NOMURA

On June 28, 2003, the Vancouver Asahi baseball team was inducted into the Canadian Baseball Hall of Fame. A semi-professional team composed of Japanese Canadians from Vancouver and the Fraser Valley, the Asahis became both a top draw for pre–World War II white Vancouver baseball fans and community heroes for Japanese Canadians, beginning in 1926 with their first of many city league championships. Moreover, a string of five consecutive championships against Japanese American teams between 1937 and 1941 was a factor leading to their induction and continues to serve as a source of pride for surviving Asahi members.

Early rivalries from 1928 to 1935 matched the Vancouver Asahis against the Seattle Nippons and the Seattle Taiyos. From 1936 to 1941 the Canadian team played the champion of the Double A Courier League, which consisted of an amalgamation of Japanese American teams from throughout the Puget Sound region. The 1939 Courier League champion was the Fife Nippons, who that year also won the prestigious Northwest Fourth of July Baseball Tournament. From its founding in 1931, this tournament attracted the best Pacific Northwest regional Japanese American teams, such as the Boise Valley Asahis, Portland Fujis, Wapato Nippons, and the Green Lake (Seattle) and White River teams. The tournament evolved into the largest social gathering of Japanese Americans in the Pacific Northwest.

The sports-minded Seattle vernacular newspaper, *Japanese American Courier,* referred to the three-game, cross-border exchanges with the Vancouver Asahis as the "international series." The Asahis and Vancouver newspapers, on the other hand, named the same series the Pacific Northwest Championship.[1] Thus, the Nikkei, that is, the people of Japanese descent on both sides of the international boundary, found their own means to define the region.

Scholars have long debated the borders that define a region, which expand or contract depending upon political, physiographic, or cultural similarities that seem to draw an area into a single focus.[2] The states of Washington, Oregon, and Idaho, for example, represent the most commonly accepted political borders of the Pacific Northwest, with their northern extension stopping abruptly at the 49th parallel. Other definitions include Alaska, Montana, and sometimes Wyoming.

Physiographic borders tend to de-emphasize the 49th Parallel, "an imaginary line," writes Canadian historian Jeremy Mouat, "born of Euclidian geometry and geopolitics."[3] The vast Columbia River watershed is perhaps the most well known of the physiographic definitions of the Pacific Northwest, one that expands the Pacific Northwest into British Columbia and beyond Washington, Idaho, and Oregon.[4]

Regions defined by cultural characteristics take on yet other boundaries. The wetter and greener geography west of the Cascade range, sometimes called Cascadia, and the drier and browner places to the east coincide with two distinct anthropological "culture areas," defined as the Northwest Coast and the Columbia Plateau. The Indian peoples north and south of the 49th parallel on the moist side of the mountains, such as the Kwakiutl of the northern coast and the Makah of the Olympic Peninsula, shared more cultural characteristics with each other than they did with tribes on the drier lands to the east.

For Nikkei, like the Indians of the Pacific Northwest, the political border dividing the United States from British Columbia did not initially pose an obstacle. The largely unguarded border between Canada and the United States made crossings relatively easy.[5] Victoria and Vancouver were often used as entry points to the United States. In the minds of Japanese immigrants, the Issei, America often blended the North American countries of Canada and the United States. Nikkei crossed the border for baseball games, work, trade, shopping, meetings, vacations, and social events. Many social, cultural, political, and economic ties and connections developed between and among the Nikkei communities in the cross-border Pacific Northwest. Yet, national identities were distinct and clear.

The essays in this anthology begin to explore this regional history, and through them one can begin to make fruitful comparisons and distinctions in the histories of Japanese Americans and Japanese Canadians. However, to understand this regional history fully, readers should be aware of the historical context of the Japanese American and Japanese Canadian experience in the twentieth century.

In 1900, 5,617 Japanese resided in Washington State and 2,501 in Oregon, consisting of approximately 44 percent of all Nikkei living along the U.S. Pacific Coast at the time. An additional 4,597 resided in British Columbia, representing virtually all Japanese in the dominion. After 1890 most Issei immigrants arrived in the United States and the Canadian West as replacement workers for the Chinese, whose exclusion from immigration to the United States in 1882 and restrictions involving Canadian immigration in 1885 exacerbated an increasing demand for labor. While many migrant laborers returned to Japan, more replaced them, including workers who had first immigrated to Hawaii. The discovery of gold in the Klondike before the turn of the century brought prosperity to the region and additional demand for immigrant labor.

The Japanese migrant laborers, having inherited the legacy of the anti-Chinese movement, faced discrimination in employment, discovered urban housing difficult to find outside ethnic enclaves, and found adapting to their new culture difficult because of racist policies and actions taken against them by the majority community. Exclusionists in the United States, championed by organized labor who perceived the Japanese as an economic threat, applied pressure on President Theodore Roosevelt to end Japanese immigration. As a result, in March 1907 Roosevelt issued an executive order that in effect prohibited further Japanese migration via Hawaii, Mexico, and Canada. Moreover, in the winter of 1907–8 a series of diplomatic notes known as the Gentlemen's Agreement was exchanged between the United States and Japan. Japan agreed to halt issuing passports to laborers, other than returning residents, seeking to emigrate to the United States. The United States, in turn, agreed not to enact overtly anti-Japanese immigration legislation. Likewise, to appease British Columbians who believed too many Asian immigrants were threatening their borders and had shown their hostility with a riot in Vancouver in 1907, Canada's Liberal government under Wilfred Laurier negotiated the Lemieux-Hayashi Gentlemen's Agreement with Japan in 1908 to allow the continued entrance of returning residents and their close relatives, but limit to four hundred annually the number of passports issued to Japanese laborers and domestic servants wishing to enter Canada.[6]

With the formerly porous West Coast borders of North America all but sealed to new sources of labor from Japan, the migrant period came to an end. It was to be replaced by the period of permanent settlement. The Gentlemen's Agreement provided for family reunification. Thus, the Japanese government continued to allow the emigration of wives, children, and parents of settled laborers into the United States. Similar loopholes existed in the Canadian agreement. More and more Japanese husbands began to send for their wives.

Unmarried men unable to afford a return to Japan to marry had family members or "go-betweens" arrange marriages for them with so-called "picture brides." Pictures and information were exchanged between the prospective bride and groom followed by a proxy marriage, a legally and socially acceptable form of marriage in Japan. Anti-Japanese exclusionists in the United States condemned the picture bride practice as a threat to the morals of U.S. society. At first, picture brides married by proxy were required to be wed again in a "Christian" ceremony on the docks before being allowed to land in the United States. Japanese wives of settlers in Canada, on the other hand, were freely admitted upon furnishing proper documentation of their marriages in Japan.

Exclusionists also perceived picture brides to be an economic threat. Because wives worked side by side with their husbands in the fields, claims rose that Japanese women were also laborers and should be barred under the Gentlemen's Agreement prohibition of Japanese laborers. The Japanese government, however, viewed the wives not as laborers, but as a necessary means to promote family reunification, "family values," and a settled family life among its emigrants. It hoped this might counter anti-Japanese accusations that Japanese were sojourners who failed to commit to life in the United States and Canada. Indeed, the immigration of picture brides ensured the permanency of Japanese settlement in both nations. Their presence resulted in an increase in the number of children born to the Japanese immigrants. Japanese community life expanded with the establishment of Japanese churches, temples, women's organizations, and Japanese language schools.

In response to exclusionists' attacks on the picture bride system, the Japanese Foreign Ministry from 1920 onward stopped issuing passports to picture brides headed for the United States. After that, single males had to incur the expense of returning to Japan for new brides. However, in 1924 the United States abrogated its Gentlemen's Agreement with passage of an immigration law prohibiting all Japanese immigration. This put pressure on the Canadian government to renegotiate its Lemieux-Hayashi Gentlemen's Agreement, which it did later in the 1920s by further reducing immigration to a quota of 150 and terminating the picture bride system altogether.[7]

Still, because immigrant males in both countries had been able to send for wives from 1908 to as late as 1928 in Canada, the Japanese communities in North America continued to grow as a new generation of American and Canadian Nisei came into being. In 1910, 57,203 Japanese Americans lived on the West Coast, including California, representing a three-fold increase over the 1900 census. By 1920 the population had increased five-fold. The population of 8,587 Japanese Canadians in 1911 was nearly double that of ten years earlier, and by 1921 it would nearly double again to 15,006.

Clearly defined generation and gender cohorts developed as a result of the discriminatory immigration laws. For example, most Nisei were born between 1915 and 1935, and most Sansei were born between 1945 and 1965. As the Nisei generation grew in numbers and absorbed American and Canadian culture in the schools and on the streets, intergenerational conflict arose; the Nisei could not communicate well with their elders. The Issei therefore established Japanese language schools for their children in an attempt to promote intergenerational communication and cultural understanding and to enable the Nisei to find jobs in the Japanese community or, if necessary, in Japan.

The increase in the size of the Japanese population, the growing success of farming enterprises in such areas as the Yakima Valley in the United States and the Fraser Valley in Canada, and the outward appearances of children being indoctrinated into Japanese language and culture infuriated exclusionists who sought to further restrict the Nikkei. The Japanese immigrants, having brought innovative farming methods with them from Japan, became successful truck farmers in the United States and competed head to head with white farmers who were cultivating much larger tracts of land to achieve similar yields. In British Columbia the Japanese gained a significant share of the berry and poultry markets.

Alien land laws in the United States designed to prevent land ownership and to limit the lengths of leases were imposed on Japanese immigrant farmers, starting with Washington State and spreading throughout the western states.[8] In British Columbia, thanks in part to pressure from London to enforce the 1902 Anglo-Japanese Alliance between Great Britain and Japan, which was renewed in 1911, the Issei were permitted to own land regardless of their status as British subjects. Although British Columbia exclusionists pressured lawmakers to emulate the U.S. alien land laws, the Canadian government instead tightened its immigration laws.[9] In so doing, limitations were imposed both by the provincial government and some professional associations on Japanese Canadian employment.

In Canada no law prevented Japanese immigrants from naturalizing to become British subjects, which was then the equivalent of Canadian citizenship. Indeed, many did so in order to secure commercial fishing licenses or the right to cut Crown timber. In the United States, however, Japanese nationals were barred from becoming citizens. United States naturalization laws allowed only "free white persons" and persons of African nativity or descent to become naturalized citizens. Because the Supreme Court in 1922 ruled that Japanese were racially "Mongolian" and therefore fell outside the established criteria, the Issei were denied naturalization and condemned to being forever foreigners in the United States. Although the Immigration Act of 1924 did not specifically prohibit Japanese by name, it did bar entry to "aliens ineligible to citizenship." Yet, the Fourteenth Amendment to the U.S. Constitution established birthright citizenship, which led to a growing number of U.S.-born Nisei who could vote and own land.

In British Columbia, however, Japanese Canadian citizens by birth or naturalization had been denied the right to vote since 1895, a civil right they would not enjoy again for another half century. That restriction also denied them access to such professions as law and pharmacy, whose professional organizations only admitted members who were qualified to vote.

Despite these discriminatory conditions, on the eve of World War II culturally vibrant and stable Nikkei communities were well rooted in the Pacific Northwest on both sides of the border. All this changed on December 7, 1941, when the United States and Canada plunged into war against Japan. The U.S. government, suspicious of Japanese immigrants since Japan's incursion into Manchuria in 1931, had been quietly building dossiers on Issei community leaders, and the FBI began arresting them before the evening of the seventh. Most were sent to INS immigration stations or locked up in local jails. Detainees not released were soon sent off to Justice Department detention camps.[10] The effect was to decapitate the Japanese communities; most Nisei had not yet come of age, and few were available to fill the leadership void.

Japanese immigrants, all of them denied the right of naturalization, suddenly became enemy aliens. They and their citizen children were first subjected to an escalating series of restrictions that was stepped up after the signing of Executive Order 9066 on February 19, 1942. At the end of March the forced exile of more than 110,000 Japanese Americans by the army began. Most were first sent to nearby assembly centers and eventually to relocation centers in isolated areas in California, Idaho, Wyoming, Utah, Colorado, Arizona, and Arkansas. Approximately half still remained locked up behind barbed wire fences at the end of the war. Two-thirds of those incarcerated were U.S. citizens, while the rest were resident aliens who had been in the country for at least eight years but denied the right of naturalization. The exclusionists' ultimate goal of physical removal had finally been achieved. Japanese Americans literally disappeared from the West Coast of the United States.

Japanese Canadians fared similarly. They too were banished from their residences and work places in western British Columbia, home to 95 percent of the Nikkei in Canada. Able-bodied men, both Issei and Nisei, were sent out to work projects in forests, on railroads, and highways outside the exclusion zone. Families were subsequently banished from their coastal homes to remote inland mining ghost towns and hastily built housing centers, sent to work on sugar beet farms in the prairie provinces, or permitted to go to self-supporting settlements east of the Cascade Mountains, where the government restricted their movements, only nominally oversaw their activities, and provided them with no financial assistance. Approximately eight hundred recalcitrants of both generations and a few dozen Issei whose loyalty the Canadian government suspected ended up under armed guard in an internment camp in northern Ontario. Land, buildings, and other properties were seized without compensation and sold without owners' permission and, in many cases, without their knowledge.[11]

Unlike their counterparts in the United States who began to return to the West Coast in 1945, Japanese Canadians were barred from within a hundred miles of the Pacific Coast without a police permit until 1949. After more than a half century without the franchise, Japanese Canadians, including those born in Canada, finally were permitted to vote in British Columbia in 1949.[12]

The immediate postwar period found Nikkei communities scattered throughout the North American continent, as many former coastal residents never returned to their prewar homes. In 1948 the Japanese American Claims Act, for which there was no Canadian counterpart, settled property claims for pennies on the dollar. Four years later the McCarran-Walter Act (1952) removed race as a barrier to immigration and naturalization in the United States. By the end of the 1950s, with Nikkei populations along the Pacific Coast once again on the rise, the transition of leadership from the Issei to the Nisei generation was nearing completion, and the third, or Sansei generation was entering public schools.

Beginning in the mid-1960s, some Sansei became active in civil rights, anti–Vietnam War, Third World Liberation, Asian American, women's, and gay and lesbian movements. Their subsequent outrage at the experience of

their elders in World War II became a driving force behind the redress movements in the United States and Canada, which resulted in monetary compensation and government apologies beginning in 1988.[13] Although Sansei
activism provided much of the energy needed to mount a redress campaign,
Nisei were instrumental in the ultimate success of the movement. As the
essays in this collection review, such Nikkei activism may be traced to the
beginnings of their presence in the Pacific Northwest.

These essays explore varied modes of Nikkei resistance and agency while
operating within the constraints of oppressive legalized racism and discrimination. The Nikkei deployed self-conscious strategies to achieve their
goal of permanent settlement and full participation in the United States and
Canada. Their resistance to racism and oppression, which at its extreme
sought to literally erase their presence in the United States and Canada, transformed the societies in which they lived.

In her essay, "Writing Racial Barriers into Law: Upholding B.C.'s Denial
of the Vote to Its Japanese Canadian Citizens, *Homma v. Cunningham*, 1902,"
Andrea Geiger-Adams addresses the legal challenge by Tomekichi Homma
to British Columbia's Provincial Voters Act that denied citizens of Japanese
and other Asian ancestry the right to vote in provincial elections. Although
Canadian scholars have written about the Homma case for a long time,
Geiger-Adams, a historian with a law background, is the first to take on, in
detail, the logic and substance of the 1902 decision by the Judicial Committee of the Privy Council in London, at that time the final arbiter of Canadian law, to overturn the lower courts' rulings to vacate the Provincial Voters
Act. Because being listed on the provincial voters list was a prerequisite for
voting in federal elections and for working in various occupations, such as
pharmacy, law, hand-logging, jobs on public works projects, and mining,
the Act had additional, far-reaching consequences. Not just a simple, narrow analysis of court decisions, Geiger-Adams examines the lengths to which
the Judicial Committee was willing to go in using a legal artifice to establish and maintain racial boundaries. In so doing it incorporated into Canadian law legal doctrine developed, in part, to accommodate the demands
of slave states in the United States. Moreover, she exposes the direct links
between race and gender in this decision as B.C. government officials
rationalized their position by arguing that the exclusion of white women
from the franchise entitled them to exclude any other subset of potential
voters that they chose.

Gail M. Nomura's "Becoming 'Local' Japanese: Issei Adaptive Strategies on the Yakama Indian Reservation, 1906–1923" examines the early development of the Japanese American community centering on the federally administered Yakama Indian Reservation in the state of Washington, and the strategies the Japanese used to maintain their presence in the Yakima Valley despite efforts by some to exclude them. Ignoring any serious consideration of Yakama Indian rights, exclusionist groups asserted their white privilege as "Americans" to farm reservation land while campaigning to exclude Japanese immigrants from farming on reservation lands. The larger importance of this particular anti-Japanese movement is its effort to secure federal intervention and policy to support Japanese exclusion. Framed as the Japanese "invasion" of federal land, the issue of Japanese farming on Yakama Indian Reservation land received close scrutiny by West Coast exclusionists, including Representative Albert Johnson, chair of the House Committee on Immigration and Naturalization. Japanese leaders analyzed the exclusionists' racist accusations and devised strategies to oppose them. One such long-term strategy was to naturalize themselves as "local" Japanese in the Yakima Valley community. They secured widespread support from the Yakama as well as whites by convincing both groups they had become a vital part of the community. Exclusionist pressure to restrict the Japanese American community's economic livelihood led to the building of ethnic community identity and organized efforts to protect and promote their collective ethnic interests.

Michiko Midge Ayukawa's essay on Yasutaro Yamaga and the Fraser Valley berry farmers of British Columbia reveals a similar strategy of resistance on the part of Japanese Canadian farmers by accommodating to Western traditions and practices while at the same time retaining their own sense of ethnic cultural identity. Yamaga saw assimilation as one means to survive in the region, both culturally and in business practices. In the post–World War I, stressed economy, the Japanese were viewed by white berry growers as unfair competitors, and organized attempts to rid them from the valley followed. Fluently bilingual, Yamaga dedicated himself to forming good relations with the mainstream populace while forcefully advocating for his fellow Japanese farmers. He and others established agricultural associations to unite all Japanese berry farmers in the area and to inform them of impending legislation to oust them. Steps were also taken to improve relations with the white community by acquainting themselves with Canadian and Protestant customs, learning English, and increasing participation in the public education of their children. These efforts succeeded in helping to preserve their farming status in the area until war broke out with Japan in 1941.

In her essay, "Americanization vs. Japanese Cultural Maintenance: Analyzing Seattle's *Nihongo Tokuhon*, 1920," Noriko Asato analyzes a series of textbooks published by Washington State Issei to teach their native language to their children. This was the first set of Japanese language textbooks created in the contiguous United States. They were concrete expressions of the immigrants' views of America and Japan. Previously, Japanese language schools in America used textbooks published by the Japanese Ministry of Education for use by Japanese nationals. Washington's textbooks were created in response to the Americanization movement that followed World War I and the attack on Japanese language schools by activists who wanted to stop Japanese immigration and limit the rights of Japanese Americans. Asato analyzes these textbooks to explore what aspects of Japanese heritage and American citizenship the Issei wanted to convey to their children and how they had to package their message to pass the scrutiny of exclusionists seeking to end Japanese language teaching. The Washington texts demonstrated on their surface 100 percent Americanism while preserving Japanese heritage, its roots, values, and language.

In "'The Nail That Sticks Up Gets Hit': The Architecture of Japanese American Identity in the Urban Environment, 1885–1942," architectural and urban historian Gail Lee Dubrow argues, in a vein similar to Asato, that racism played a powerful role in persuading the Issei in Seattle to abandon or mask outward signs of ethnicity in their architecture, even while interior spaces contained robust expressions of cultural identity. The Issei adopted strategic disappearances, a strategy of blending into the American cultural fabric to ward off exclusionary federal immigration policies, restrictive state land laws, and discriminatory city ordinances. Similar to the development of Seattle's *Nihongo Tokuhon*, Seattle's Japanese Language School building was erected in 1913 as exclusionist influence was on the rise. The building was designed defensively, Dubrow argues, to minimize any cultural threat to outsiders while at the same time maintaining a commitment to ground the Nisei in their cultural heritage.

Moving beyond the simple paradigm of assimilation theory that has dominated the study of ethnic cultural traditions in vernacular architecture, Dubrow's work indicates that a fuller conceptualization of racism is needed to understand the architectural history of ethnic communities of color in the United States. Furthermore, her research suggests that community responses to racial discrimination, particularly strategies of resistance, are critical to interpreting the meaning of ethnic signs in the built environment.

The bombing of Pearl Harbor unleashed a tsunami of cultural and economic destruction onto the Japanese communities of the Pacific Northwest on both sides of the border. All hard-earned trust and good will between the Japanese and whites crumbled. The Japanese Canadian communities in British Columbia were soon forced away from the Pacific Coast, while 110,000 Japanese in Washington, Oregon, California, and parts of Arizona, most of them U.S. citizens, were removed from their homes by the army and eventually sent to "relocation centers" in the arid high desert regions of the interior West and sultry Arkansas. Nikkei communities on the Pacific Coast literally disappeared overnight. The essays focusing on the World War II period address issues of loyalty and betrayal, which have occupied the collective conscience of Japanese America down to the present time.

James A. Hirabayashi, in "Four Hirabayashi Cousins: A Question of Identity," outlines the personal responses to wartime exclusion and incarceration of Japanese Americans by four Nisei Hirabayashi cousins. His essay draws attention to the complexities inherent in the concept of loyalty beyond the simplistic dichotomy of loyal versus disloyal. The cousins were forced individually to decipher what America meant under the critical circumstances they had been placed in World War II as Japanese Americans. The story of Gordon Kiyoshi Hirabayashi's principled behavior is well known. His refusal to obey a militarily imposed curfew and to comply with the army's order to evacuate from Seattle ultimately led to his conviction and imprisonment. His appeal to the U.S. Supreme Court proved unsuccessful. In 1987 his Supreme Court case was reopened on the basis of newly discovered documents, and a lower court subsequently vacated both convictions. James Hirabayshi, Gordon's younger brother, reveals the family and community backgrounds of the four cousins: Gordon Kiyoshi Hirabayashi, Grant Jiro Hirabayashi, Henry Nobuo Hirabayashi, and Robert Taro Mizukami. Each cousin narrates his individual response to the sudden wartime emergency thrust upon him. Although sharing a common background and adhering to basic American values, the four cousins took diverse actions as they individually interpreted the meaning of being an American citizen in response to challenges to their civil rights.

In January of 1944, the federal government added to the sufferings of the incarcerated Japanese Americans by conscripting young men imprisoned in the camps into the U.S. Army. In his essay "The Minidoka Draft Resisters in a Federal Kangaroo Court," Eric L. Muller relates the experience of one of the aforementioned four Hirabayashi cousins, Hank, and forty other draft resisters from the Minidoka Relocation Center in the wake of their refusal to report for active duty in order to protest their mistreatment. Appearing before a racist judge and without proper counsel, the resisters, acting out of the conviction that with incarceration their civil liberties were being trampled upon, were convicted and sent to McNeil Island Federal Penitentiary to serve out three-year prison terms. The legal system failed them, offering only sham trials by biased judges and jurors. But in a larger sense, the law itself failed them in that it did not offer a solid legal theory to capture the moral outrage in their mistreatment at the hands of the government. Moreover, subsequent pardons by President Harry Truman did little to reduce the ostracism the group endured from the Nikkei community. Only in 2000 did the Japanese American Citizens League (JACL) apologize for its public vilification of the group nearly sixty years earlier.

Historical perspective can be altered by the words chosen to describe it. Roger Daniels, in his essay "Words Do Matter: A Note on Inappropriate Terminology and the Incarceration of the Japanese Americans," points out the improper use of "internment" to describe the incarceration resulting from President Franklin Roosevelt's executive order. The legal internment of enemy aliens followed the rules set down in American and international law, but, says Daniels, the incarceration of West Coast Japanese Americans in army and War Relocation Authority concentration camps was "simply lawless." The term "internment" thus confuses the lawful and lawless actions of the government.

Daniels first traces the deliberate verbal distortions and euphemisms that the federal government used to mask its violation of the rights of Japanese Americans during World War II, and then describes and analyses the changing ways in which, over time, both the victims and their chroniclers adopted inappropriate and misleading language to describe the wartime events. This inappropriate terminology would have political consequences in the latter decades of the twentieth century as many tried, for reasons both innocent and malign, to deny the uniqueness of what was done to Japanese Americans.

Louis Fiset's "In the Matter of Iwao Matsushita: A Government's Decision to Intern a Seattle Japanese Enemy Alien in World War II" is a case study of how the U.S. government decided which enemy aliens should be interned and who should be released. Iwao Matsushita was arrested and detained on suspicions he had engaged in espionage and had served as a foreign agent, both in violation of federal law. Information gathered by intelligence groups over the period of a decade, much of it from Issei and Nisei informants, and none of it sworn testimony subject to cross examination, provided the basis for his detention and ultimate internment. Matsushita's case illustrates the government's attitude of guilt by association and its apparent policy to intern rather than parole an individual enemy alien about whom the least doubt existed as to his loyalty to the United States.

Robert C. Sims, in "The 'Free Zone' Nikkei: Japanese Americans in Idaho and Eastern Oregon in World War II," brings to light a little-known group of Japanese Americans who were not incarcerated during World War II because they lived outside the military exclusion area, or in the "free zone," and were not subject to most of the restrictions imposed on coastal Japanese Americans. Sims examines the prewar history of "free zone" Japanese Americans in Idaho and Oregon and then recounts their complex and at times troubling interactions with Japanese Americans evicted from their West Coast homes. To complicate matters more, Sims points out that Japanese Americans who were able to move inland during the "voluntary 'relocation'" period and those who left the assembly centers and incarceration camps to work in the region became "free zoners" themselves and added another layer of interaction. The army poorly prepared the citizenry of the interior states to accept them, leaving residents there to believe if Japanese Americans were a national security threat on the coast, they would a threat in their states as well. Moreover, Nikkei heading for Idaho were discouraged from entering the state both by a racist governor and the preexisting population of "free zone" Japanese Americans who felt threatened by the visibility and potential negative consequences it would bring them. At first spurned by Idaho farmers, voluntary migrants and Nikkei from the nearby Minidoka Relocation Center harvested 20 percent of the state's sugar beet crop in a labor-starved region, thus staving off financial disaster to the growers. Although their labor helped turn attitudes in their favor and led to greater acceptance by the white citizenry in the war years, Sims cautions that the lasting effects should not be overstated, since most "relocated" people did not permanently settle in Idaho. Further, Sims points out that the legacy of friction between "free zone" Nikkei and "relocated" Nikkei remains a smoldering issue.

For many Nikkei, the return to the Pacific Coast was an agony. Whereas those in the United States began returning to the Pacific Coast early in 1945, Canada did not permit its Nikkei residents to return freely until spring 1949, a story Patricia E. Roy tells in "Lessons in Citizenship, 1945–1949: The Delayed Return of the Japanese to Canada's Pacific Coast." In British Columbia, popular opposition to the return of Nikkei gradually faded so that by 1947, some major newspapers, civil libertarians, church groups, and labor unions were calling for an end to the restrictions. The atavistic ideas of federal politicians, however, kept the restrictions in force. Nevertheless, while discussing the ban on the return of the Japanese, Canadians became more conscious of their newly defined Canadian citizenship and the need for a bill of rights.

If words can alter historical perspective, Arthur A. Hansen's essay on Nisei journalist James Omura, "Peculiar Odyssey: Newsman Jimmie Omura's Removal from and Regeneration within Nikkei Society, History, and Memory," shows that an individual can be erased from history altogether. Omura stood out in his community as an individual who refused to conform to cultural norms. Like the draft resisters, he too was vilified by the JACL both during and after the war, and this ostracism cost him employment opportunities and possibly his long-term health. Powerful people in the Nikkei community opposed him, as did the U.S. government, which in 1944 charged him with conspiracy to counsel, aid, and abet Nisei draft resisters. His acquittal was virtually ignored, and he dropped out of the Nikkei community for more than thirty years.

This essay also describes how, after testifying at the 1981 Seattle hearings of the Commission on Wartime Relocation and Internment of Civilians, Omura gained community support within the contemporary Japanese American redress movement through younger Asian American activists and the National Council for Japanese American Redress. He was reborn as a crusading writer and soon achieved near iconic status within Nikkei society for his courageous wartime opposition to the U.S. government–JACL alliance, which he held responsible for the mass exclusion and incarceration of Japanese Americans as well as conscription of Nisei out of the camps.

Masumi Izumi's essay, "Reclaiming and Reinventing 'Powell Street': Reconstruction of the Japanese Canadian community in Post–World War II Vancouver," concludes this anthology as a reminder of the long-term impact World War II had on Nikkei communities on the West Coast. Izumi examines the reconstruction of the postwar Japanese Canadian community, placing special focus on the revitalization of the former center of Vancouver's Japanese community in the 1970s. Although Los Angeles and San Francisco have revitalized their Nihonmachi (Japantowns) since World War II, Seattle's International District no longer sits at the core of Japanese American culture as it did prior to the war. With the forced wartime expulsion of Vancouver's Nikkei, the Nihonmachi centering on Powell Street disappeared and never recovered its prewar vitality, even with the postwar return of a number of Issei. The nearby Chinatown was nearly destroyed altogether by the iron blade of urban renewal that scraped through the city in the 1960s, when slum clearance displaced 3,300 residents from the area. The former Nihonmachi had long ago been rezoned an industrial area, thus eliminating the possibility of any financing to upgrade the housing stock. Grassroots activism in the 1970s combined with a shift in attitude of the government toward multiculturalism infused human energy and federal money into addressing the needs of local residents in the inner city, including the impoverished Issei still living there. This led to a recovery and reconstruction of the Powell Street neighborhood as the symbolic ethnic "home" of Vancouver's Japanese Canadian community.

Today, few Nikkei reside along Powell Street, and most ethnic organizations have moved away. Nevertheless, the 1970s reclamation and reinvention of Powell Street sustained the historical memory of that vibrant Japanese Canadian community, ensuring that the "imagined" community will continue to be reinvented and reimagined in changing times. One marker of this is the ongoing physical reappearance of the community at the annual Powell Street Festival.

In all, this diverse group of essays provides a historical focus on the survival and resilience of Nikkei in the face of overwhelming forces opposing their existence in the United States and Canada that sought to make their communities literally disappear. The authors explore and question modes and possibilities of resistance and agency within the constraints of oppressive legalized racism. They examine complex and nuanced meanings of resistance and agency, cognizant of the limitations and constraints faced by the Nikkei, especially in the prewar era. Actions taken by the Nikkei were not mere responses in reaction to and conditioned by exclusionary initiatives, but were self-conscious strategies to achieve their goal of permanent settlement in the United States and Canada.

These essays also point to the significance of the Pacific Northwest for Nikkei history. We hope this regional history, the first major history collection that consciously studies a Nikkei region outside California, will serve as a springboard for further study of connections, similarities, and differences between and among regional Nikkei communities. These studies should include perspectives we were not able to directly address at this time, such as gender, religion, and art.

Further, in presenting historical essays on the Nikkei in the Pacific Northwest on both sides of the political border between the United States and Canada, we have initiated a discussion of parallels, intersections, and divergences in twentieth-century Nikkei history in these two countries. Additional studies of cross-border connections in this region are also warranted.

Nikkei history complicates and enriches our understanding of the Pacific

Northwest and challenges a dominant narrative that centers upon and privileges the experiences of white males without properly acknowledging the
presence and influence of people of color and women in shaping the
region's development. Nikkei presence is part of what defines the Pacific
Northwest. In these troubling times of the early twenty-first century,
brought on by the events of 9/11, an ongoing reflection on the Nikkei past
(dis)appearances seems even more important than ever.

Notes

1. For a history of the Vancouver Asahi, see Pat Adachi, *Asahi: A Legend in Base-
ball, A Legacy from the Japanese Canadian Baseball Team to its Heirs* (Etobicoke,
Ontario: Asahi Baseball Organization, 1992). For a discussion of Japanese Amer-
ican baseball in the Pacific Northwest, see Gail M. Nomura, "Beyond the Playing
Field: The Significance of Pre–World War II Japanese American Baseball in the
Yakima Valley," in *Bearing Dreams, Shaping Visions: Asian Pacific American Per-
spectives,* ed. Linda A. Revilla et al. (Pullman, Wash.: Washington State University
Press, 1993), and Samuel O. Regalado, "'Play Ball!' Baseball and Seattle's Japanese-
American Courier League, 1928–1941," *Pacific Northwest Quarterly* 87, no. 1 (winter
1995/96): 29–37.

2. William G. Robbins, "Complexity and Regional Narratives," in *The Great
Northwest: The Search for Regional Identity,* ed. William G. Robbins (Corvallis, Oreg.:
Oregon State University Press, 2001), 1–11.

3. Jeremy Mouat, "The Forty-Ninth Parallel: Defining Moments and Changing
Meanings," in Robbins, *The Great Northwest,* 121–44.

4. John M. Findlay, "A Fishy Proposition: Regional Identity in the Pacific
Northwest," in *Many Wests: Place, Culture, and Regional Identity,* ed. David M. Wro-
bel and Michael C. Steiner (Lawrence, Kans.: University of Kansas Press, 1997), 37–70.

5. For insight into U.S.-Canada border policies, see Erika Lee, *At America's Gates:
Chinese Immigration during the Exclusion Era, 1882–1943* (Chapel Hill: The University of North Carolina Press, 2003), 151–87.

6. W. Peter Ward, *White Canada Forever: Popular Attitudes and Public Policy
Toward Orientals in British Columbia,* 2nd ed. (Montreal: McGill-Queen's University Press, 1990), 75–76.

7. Patricia Roy, J. L. Granatstein, Masako Iino, and Hiroko Takamura, *Mutual
Hostages: Canadians and Japanese during the Second World War* (Toronto: Univer-
sity of Toronto Press, 1990), 16. See also Ken Adachi, *The Enemy That Never Was:
A History of the Japanese Canadians* (Toronto: McClelland & Stewart, 2nd ed., 1991);

and Ann G. Sunahara, *The Politics of Racism: The Uprooting of Japanese Canadians during the Second World War* (Toronto: James Lorimer & Company, 1981).

8. Washington State's 1889 constitution prohibited agricultural land ownership by aliens who did not in good faith register their intent to become citizens. First targeted at the British in Washington, the law in the early twentieth century focused primarily on Japanese and other Asian immigrants who were deemed ineligible for citizenship and thus could not register in good faith their intent to become citizens. The Washington state alien land laws were tightened in 1921 and 1923 following California's passage of alien land laws in 1913 and 1920. Other states passed similar alien land laws, including Oregon and Idaho in 1923.

9. Roy et al., *Mutual Hostages*, 12–13.

10. For general histories of the internment experience of Japanese nationals in the United States, see Tetsuden Kashima, *Judgment Without Trial: Japanese American Imprisonment during World War II* (Seattle: University of Washington Press, 2003); and Louis Fiset, *Imprisoned Apart: The World War II Correspondence of an Issei Couple* (Seattle: University of Washington Press, 1997).

11. For a comparison of treatment of Nikkei in Canada and the United States, see the following works by Roger Daniels: *Concentration Camps, North America: Japanese in the United States and Canada during World War II* (Malabar, Fla.: Kreiger, 1981; 2nd ed., updated, Krieger, 1993); "Japanese Relocation and Redress in North America: A Comparative View," *The Pacific Historian* (spring 1982); and "Chinese and Japanese in North America: The Canadian and American Experiences Compared," *Canadian Review of American Studies* 17 (1986): 173–87.

12. Roy et al., *Mutual Hostages*, 139–91.

13. For accounts of the redress movements in the United States and Canada, see Mitchell T. Maki, Harry H. L. Kitano, and S. Megan Berthold, *Achieving the Impossible Dream: How Japanese Americans Obtained Redress* (Urbana: University of Illinois Press, 1999); and Roy Miki and Cassandra Kobayashi, *Justice in Our Time: The Japanese Canadian Redress Settlement* (Vancouver: Talonbooks; Winnipeg: National Association of Japanese Canadians, 1991). For an account focusing on Seattle redress efforts, see Robert Sadamu Shimabukuro, *Born in Seattle: The Campaign for Japanese American Redress* (Seattle: University of Washington Press, 2001).

2 / WRITING RACIAL BARRIERS INTO LAW

Upholding B.C.'s Denial of the Vote to Its Japanese Canadian Citizens, *Homma v. Cunningham*, 1902

ANDREA GEIGER-ADAMS

During the last decades of the nineteenth century, the province of British Columbia was a rapidly growing, predominantly immigrant society that was increasingly fractured along racial lines.[1] Although its white citizens shared many of the same anti-Asian prejudices as their neighbors south of the U.S.-Canada border, Canada—unlike the United States—did not bar Japanese immigrants from becoming naturalized citizens. Canadian law and policy thus appeared more inclusive than U.S. law.[2] The 1902 decision in *Homma v. Cunningham*, which upheld British Columbia's denial of the franchise to naturalized Asian immigrants and their Canadian-born children, revealed, however, the equal ability of Canadian law to deny its citizens the rights of citizenship on racial grounds. Notwithstanding differences in the constitutional structure of the United States and Canada it otherwise regarded as important, the Judicial Committee of the Privy Council in London, final arbiter of the case, reached south across the Canada-U.S. border for doctrine to justify its reversal of existing case law.[3] British Columbia's pursuit of that result, and its acceptance of the Privy Council's reasoning, suggests how permeable the boundary between the United States and Canada was when it came both to racist attitudes and to justifying the expression of those attitudes in law. *Homma v. Cunningham*, which fixed B.C.'s denial of the franchise to citizens of Japanese, Chinese, Native, and East Indian ancestry in the law for the next half century, stands as an example of the tendency for citizen and subject alike to become ever more thoroughly racialized categories in early twentieth-century North America. As the debate surrounding this case reflects, the rationale advanced by British Columbia officials to justify the Province's position invoked the politics of gender as well as race.

⅃ Even before British Columbia joined Confederation in 1871, its residents sought to exclude Chinese immigrants from voting in local elections.[4] Once it became a province, B.C. legislators, focused on crafting a society that was both white and essentially British, acted quickly to fix those barriers in provincial law.[5] Invoking the same kind of anti-Asian rhetoric relied on by nativists in California and elsewhere along the Pacific coast, B.C. legislators amended British Columbia's voters' legislation in 1875 to bar Chinese and Native residents of B.C. from voting in provincial elections.[6] Because there were virtually no Japanese immigrants in B.C. at the time, they were not included in the initial proscription. In 1895, however, the B.C. legislature added Japanese immigrants to those already excluded from the franchise, even though its own records reflected that there were fewer than 130 naturalized Japanese immigrants in the province at that time.[7] The attorney general of B.C. later suggested that the legislature acted in that year in part because it was aware that growing numbers of Japanese laborers were taking advantage of opportunities to find work abroad, in the wake of the Japanese government's 1885 removal of the bar it had maintained on labor emigration.[8]

As amended, the Provincial Voters Act provided that "no Chinaman, Japanese, or Indian shall have his name placed on the Register of Voters for any Electoral District." The term "Japanese," as used in the statute, referred not just to anyone who was a "native of the Japanese Empire or its dependencies not born of British parents," but also to "any person of the Japanese race, naturalized or not."[9] Because it applied not just to Japanese immigrants, but to anyone born in B.C. who was of Japanese descent, the issue became one not just of national origin but of race. The legislature ensured that its proscription would be enforced by imposing a fifty-dollar fine and up to one month's imprisonment on any collector of voters who violated the act by adding the name of someone of Asian descent to the voters list.[10]

On October 19, 1900, Tomekichi Homma, a naturalized British subject born in Japan, applied to Thomas Cunningham, collector of voters for Vancouver, B.C., to have his name added to the voters list for that electoral district.[11] Homma's request was a deliberate challenge to the Provincial Voters Act. As Homma anticipated, Cunningham refused to place his name on the voters list for Vancouver, B.C.[12] Within a week, Homma filed a lawsuit challenging Cunningham's refusal and the 1895 amendment to the Provincial Voters Act on which he relied.[13] Homma did not act alone in mounting his challenge. His attempt to register to vote was part of a larger, coordinated effort by naturalized Japanese immigrants in British Columbia to challenge

FIG. 2.1 *Tomekichi Homma,*
Vancouver, B.C., 1909.
(Courtesy of the Homma family)

the discriminatory provisions of the Provincial Voters Act. Collector of Voters Thomas Cunningham reported that several other naturalized Japanese immigrants had applied to have their names added to the provincial voters list at the same time, and that he had also refused them.[14] The resources of the Japanese immigrant community were limited, however, and the cost of filing multiple lawsuits prohibitive. For that reason, those intent on challenging the Provincial Voters Act decided to focus the community's resources on Homma's legal action and to use it as a test case, which would serve as precedent for others in the same position.[15]

Homma was chosen as the public face of a broader challenge to the Provincial Voters Act because of the leadership role he had already assumed in B.C.'s Japanese immigrant community. Homma, who had arrived in Canada in the mid-1880s,[16] had worked to organize the Gyosha Dantai (Japanese Fishermen's Association) in 1897 and had served as its chairman until 1899.[17] In 1897, Homma also helped to establish a bimonthly newsletter called *Dai Nippon* to provide Japanese immigrants living in B.C., many of whom were not yet able to read English-language newspapers, with news of both Canada and Japan.[18] By 1900, the year in which he undertook his challenge to the Provincial Voters Act, Homma was operating a boarding house in downtown Vancouver and had joined with a partner to provide laborers

ır the Canadian Pacific Railway.[19] In the early fall of that year, he also helped
ı establish an organization dedicated to upholding the dignity and defend-
ıg the rights of Japanese living in Canada.[20] Regarded as both principled
nd resolute by his peers, Homma was considered the person best able to
_ıe the test case through.[21]

Members of the Gyosha Dantai, the fishermen's association Homma had
helped found, were the staunchest supporters of his challenge to the Provincial Voters Act, rallying behind him and working to collect funds from the
larger Japanese immigrant community to help pay the legal fees that quickly
accumulated.[22] On October 23, 1900, just four days after Homma attempted
to register to vote, the *Vancouver Daily Province* noted with some interest
a report in a local Japanese-language newspaper that a local Japanese association had concluded that the Provincial Voters Act was unconstitutional.[23]
Opinion within the Japanese immigrant community as a whole about the
wisdom of filing suit, however, was divided. Many Japanese immigrants—
a large majority of whom had only recently arrived from Japan—doubted
that any individual could win a lawsuit against a government, and feared
that aggravating provincial authorities would only make things more
difficult for Japanese immigrants already dependent on their good will.[24]
Seizaburo Shimizu, the Japanese consul in Vancouver, B.C., also distanced
himself from Homma's case, explaining to a local reporter that "once a Japanese becomes a naturalized British subject, he passes out of my jurisdiction, and I keep track of him no longer."[25]

Homma was undeterred by the criticism. His biographer, Shigeharu
Koyama, attributes Homma's determination not just to his strength of character but to a deep sense of responsibility traceable to his family's status in
Japan.[26] As the third son of a former samurai family that traced its lineage
back to retainers of the Ashikaga shoguns in the 1400s, Koyama argues,
Homma felt obliged to assume a leadership role in challenging the racist
legal barriers Japanese immigrants encountered in B.C.[27] Motivated in part
by indignation that rights available to other adult males in B.C. should be
denied to those from Japan, Homma also understood that the ability to vote
would give Japanese immigrants a voice in shaping legislation that affected
them.[28] As his decision to pursue the test case demonstrates, Homma was
a careful student of his adopted country and its processes of government.

Homma served notice of his intention to challenge the Provincial Voters Act on October 25, 1900, less than a week after Cunningham refused to
place his name on the voters list.[29] Cunningham, who released that notice
to the press, remained defiant, flatly telling a reporter that he would "put

FIG. 2.2 *Tomekichi
Homma and his wife,
Matsu, with sons Joseph
and Junkichi, Vancouver,
B.C., 1909. (Courtesy of
the Homma family)*

no Asiatic name on the voters' list." He was unconcerned that his own action might be found by the courts to be unconstitutional. "Courts or no courts, orders or no orders," Cunningham told a reporter, he would rather go to jail than add a single Chinese or Japanese name to the voters list he was responsible for preparing.[30]

Homma's case was first argued before Chief Justice McColl of the B.C. Supreme Court, sitting as a county court judge, on November 29, 1900.[31] Homma was represented in that action by local barrister R. W. Harris of the law firm Harris & Bull. Harris argued on Homma's behalf that the B.C. legislature lacked the power to exclude any subset of its male citizens from the franchise, emphasizing that section 91 of the British North America Act— Canada's constitution—stated unequivocally that naturalization was a subject over which the Dominion government had exclusive control.[32] The Naturalization Act, passed by the Dominion government pursuant to its power over naturalization, provided in turn that every naturalized alien was entitled to "all political and other rights, powers and privileges to which a natural-born British subject is entitled within Canada."[33] For that reason, Harris argued, the Province had no power to exclude naturalized citizens from the franchise. That principle was reaffirmed in 1899, he reasoned, when the Privy Council decided *Union Colliery Company v. Bryden,* in which it rejected B.C. legislation that had barred Chinese miners from working underground. In *Bryden,* the Privy Council had expressly declared that it was the Dominion government that was "invested with exclusive authority in all matters which directly concern the rights, privileges, and disabilities" of aliens resident in Canada, whether or not they were naturalized.[34] The Privy Council's declaration made it clear, Harris argued, that the Province lacked the power to deny the franchise to any subset of its naturalized male citizens. Because the legislation was *ultra vires,* it was also invalid.[35] Cunningham's lawyer, Charles Wilson, disagreed. He argued on behalf of Cunningham and the Province that the question of who could vote in provincial elections was an issue of "purely local concern" over which the Dominion government had no authority.[36]

Chief Justice McColl handed down his decision the day after he heard argument in the case. He agreed with both sides that the outcome turned on the narrow constitutional question of whether the Dominion or the provincial government had the power to determine the rights and privileges of naturalized citizens.[37] And he agreed with Harris that *Bryden* was binding. For that reason, he concluded, the only possible conclusion was that the B.C. legislature lacked the power to pass any legislation that did not "apply alike to born and naturalized subjects of Her Majesty."[38] Although Chief Justice McColl suggested he reached this result reluctantly, he was not insensitive to the broader ramifications of the legislature's action, expressing concern about B.C.'s attempt to create two separate classes of citizens. "The residence within the Province of large numbers of persons," he wrote, "British subjects in name, but doomed to perpetual exclusion from any part in the passage of legislation affecting their property and civil rights would surely not be to the advantage of Canada, and might even become a source of national danger."[39] Based on his conclusion that the 1895 amendment barring Japanese-born citizens from the franchise was invalid, Chief Justice McColl ordered that Homma's name be placed on the voters' register.[40] Civil authorities, however, were determined to ignore that order. In the words of the deputy returning officer, "All the judgment does is to express a judicial opinion that the Japanese are entitled to registration . . . I shall as returning officer see that no [Japanese] votes are polled."[41]

The provincial government also ignored the chief justice's concerns about the danger of creating two separate classes among its male citizens, and it immediately appealed his decision.[42] Both the media and the B.C. legislature followed Homma's case closely as it wound its way through the courts.[43] The *Victoria Daily Colonist* warned its readers that all naturalized "Orientals" would be entitled to vote if Chief Justice McColl's decision were upheld.[44] Echoing charges often repeated in other B.C. newspapers of the time, it declared that the ballot box had been opened "to a large number of Mongolians, who obtained their naturalization through fraud."[45] Japanese immigrants, it was often alleged, were interested in citizenship only because it was a prerequisite to obtaining a fishing license.[46] The *Vancouver Daily Province* adopted a different approach, assuring its readers that they had nothing to fear from the chief justice's decision. "Chinese and Japanese as a matter of fact care little indeed for the authority to vote," it told its readers, and "not . . . many (if indeed any) would seek to exercise the franchise."[47] Indeed, it surmised, it was safe to assume that Homma's own action in pursuing the franchise was motivated not by his own understanding of its significance, but was "taken at the suggestion or initiation of scheming white men base enough to jeopardize the liberties and interests of their fellow whites for the sake of a little brief political capital," as part of a larger effort on their parts "to control the political situation locally simply by droving the Asiatics to the polls." Chief Justice McColl's decision, the editors declared, had "fully awakened the public to the menace to their liberties which would be given existence should naturalized Chinese or Japanese be permitted to vote."[48]

On March 8, 1901, the B.C. Supreme Court heard arguments in the Province's appeal. Just one day later, that court affirmed Chief Justice McColl's decision.[49] Although the Supreme Court justices expressed some sympathy for the Province's position, they agreed that they were bound by the Privy Council's earlier decision in *Bryden*.[50] As one justice explained, the Privy Council itself had noted in *Bryden* that section 15 of Canada's Naturalization Act—passed by the Dominion government pursuant to its power over naturalization—expressly provided:

 An alien to whom a certificate of naturalization is granted shall, within Canada, be entitled to all political and other rights, powers and privileges, and be subject to all obligations to which a natural-born British subject is entitled or subject within Canada.[51]

Political rights, the justice added, should be broadly construed and encompassed "rights which belong to a nation, or to a citizen, or to an individual member of a nation, as distinguished from civil rights, namely, local rights of a citizen."[52] As such, the law was clear that "an alien, when naturalized, shall, [in] Canada, have all the ordinary and inherent rights and privileges of a Canadian, or of a natural-born British subject."[53] Another justice who wrote separately agreed, observing that "'political rights, powers and privileges' are very general terms, and import the right of exercising the franchise."[54] It followed from the language of the Naturalization Act and the Privy Council's reasoning in *Bryden,* he reasoned, that "the subject of naturalization includes the power of enacting what shall be the consequences of naturalization." The justices of the B.C. Supreme Court agreed that the only result they could reach under the law that bound them was that the Province lacked the power to withhold from its naturalized citizens any of the "political rights, powers and privileges" to which a British subject born in Canada was entitled.[55]

Buoyed, perhaps, by ongoing media support for its position, the provincial government again refused to accept the court's ruling. Although the Provincial Voters Act did not provide for a direct appeal to the Privy Council, the Province requested a waiver that would allow it to file such an appeal. The B.C. Supreme Court granted its request, assuming correctly that the Privy Council would accept it, and the Dominion government intervened on Homma's side of the dispute.[56]

In June 1901, D. M. Eberts, attorney general of British Columbia, wrote to the London barrister who was to argue the Province's case to the Privy Council, listing the various points British Columbia wished to make.[57] Eberts's argument that the guarantee of political rights in Canada's Naturalization Act did not disable the Province from denying the right to vote to its Asian citizens rested heavily on the fact that white women, though citizens, were not allowed to vote. Together, Eberts explained to the barrister, Chinese and Japanese numbered about 12,000 out of a total population of 125,000 in B.C. While that might not seem to pose a serious danger to white British Columbians' maintaining control of the electoral process, the threat, Eberts insisted, was greater than it appeared. The Chinese and Japanese population consisted "almost exclusively of adult males," he explained, and because white women and children were not allowed to vote, the Asian segment of the population would have a disproportionate impact if they voted in any election. In Eberts' view, clearly, the most effective way to silence the political voice of people of Asian ancestry in B.C. was to relegate them to the same political status as women and children.[58]

Eberts also argued that naturalized Japanese and Chinese citizens would not exercise the franchise responsibly. They had no real interest in Canada, he told the barrister, and no knowledge of its political institutions. Their votes would simply be bought, and they would "impersonate one another at the polls," since it was, in Eberts's words, impossible to "distinguish one Jap or Chinaman from another." But Eberts was also willing to accommodate his argument to the possibility that B.C.'s naturalized Japanese and Chinese citizens would exercise the franchise as responsibly as any other citizen. If that were the case, he told the barrister, he should argue that they could not be assimilated (ignoring, presumably, that voting responsibly suggested precisely the opposite). It was intolerable, Eberts insisted, that "these foreign races, which can never be assimilated with our population should in many constituencies determine who shall represent the people in the legislature."[59]

It appears to have been Eberts who first suggested that the Privy Council rely on U.S. legal principles to hold that British Columbia had the power to deny the vote to some groups among its naturalized male citizens. Ignoring that the provisions of the United States Constitution had no bearing whatsoever on questions arising in the context of the very different constitutional structure of Canada, Eberts pointed to a discussion of Article 4 of the U.S. Constitution in an American legal treatise to argue that the political rights referred to in Canada's Naturalization Act did not necessarily include the right to vote. In particular, Eberts noted, political rights in the United States were almost always withheld from women.[60] It was the guarantee of political rights in Canada's Naturalization Act, Eberts told the barrister, that the British Columbia courts had seen as the stumbling block. But in B.C., too, a large class of white British subjects—women—whose claim to citizenship was not in question, were already excluded from the franchise.[61] From that it followed, Eberts argued, that the Province was entitled to deny the vote to any other class of citizens it chose. If the people of British Columbia had realized that the Dominion government would be able to exercise any control over the scope of the provincial franchise, he declared, the people of British Columbia would never have consented to enter into Confederation.[62]

The courts' decision that the amendment to the Provincial Voters Act was *ultra vires* was also problematic, in Eberts's view, because it threatened to erode the bar against Native participation in the political process. While, on the one hand, the power to deny the franchise to people identified as "Indians" under Canada's Indian Act appeared clear, he told the barrister, an anomalous situation might arise where Indians born in B.C. could be

excluded from the franchise, while Asian immigrants could not.[63] The bar
B.C. had erected to exclude B.C. citizens of Asian ancestry from political
participation, Eberts seemed to suggest, served not only to ensure that they
did not vote, but also to reinforce barriers against Native participation
in the political process. There was, he reminded the barrister, no provision
in the British North America Act comparable to the Fifteenth Amendment
of the U.S. Constitution which forbade "denying citizens the right to vote
on account of race, color, or previous condition of servitude."[64]

On December 17, 1901, the Privy Council reversed the B.C. courts' decisions, upholding the discriminatory legislation that the courts below had
ruled invalid. It began by carefully disclaiming the racially discriminatory
consequences of its ruling. The wisdom of excluding a particular race from
the franchise, the Privy Council declared, was not a topic it was entitled
to consider. The only question before it—as the parties had argued—was
whether the provincial or the Dominion government had the power to
determine the rights and privileges of naturalized Canadian citizens.[65] The
Privy Council rejected Homma's argument that section 91 of the British
North America Act gave the Dominion government exclusive authority over
naturalization and the privileges and obligations that pertained to it, holding instead that the Province did have the power to exclude certain categories of its citizens from the franchise.

The Privy Council's decision is remarkable both in its lack of clarity and
in the poverty of its reasoning. Although the Privy Council reviewed the
parties' arguments regarding the question whether it was the Dominion or
the provincial government that had the power to determine the voting rights
of naturalized citizens, and noted that Canada's Naturalization Act provided
that "a naturalized alien shall within Canada be entitled to all political and
other rights, powers and privileges to which a natural-born British subject
is entitled in Canada," it avoided any substantive discussion of section 91
of the British North America Act.[66] It need not consider section 91, the Privy
Council suggested, because more than just the rights of naturalized citizens
were at stake, since the Provincial Voters Act also applied to anyone of Asian
ancestry born in B.C.[67] The Privy Council went on to observe that the "extent
to which naturalization will confer privileges has varied both in England
and elsewhere."[68]

Apparently unable to find any precedent in Canada or any other
British Commonwealth country for its conclusion that political rights did
not necessarily include the right to vote, the Privy Council turned instead
to a source of law it normally would not have considered binding or even

persuasive[69]—an outdated 1863 edition of a U.S. legal treatise called "Lawrence's Wheaton,"[70] published during the American Civil War. Brushing aside the fundamental differences in the histories and constitutional structures of Canada and the United States, as Eberts had, the Privy Council quoted from "Lawrence's Wheaton," using the language it extracted as the only direct precedent cited for its conclusion. "Lawrence's Wheaton," the Privy Council said, noted that although

> (in the United States) the power of naturalization be nominally exclusive in the Federal Government, its operation in the most important particulars, especially as to the right of suffrage, is made to depend on the local constitution and laws.[71]

Without any explanation as to why Canadian law would follow U.S. law in this regard—even assuming this was an accurate summary of U.S. law— the Privy Council declared that it followed from this observation about U.S. law in "Lawrence's Wheaton" that the reference to political rights in Canada's Naturalization Act did not necessarily entitle naturalized citizens to vote in any given Canadian province.[72]

Not only did the Privy Council fail to acknowledge that U.S. constitutional law necessarily had no application in Canada, but it also ignored that the doctrine it invoked had its origin in the history of the formation of the United States, and particularly the need to accommodate the concerns of slave states that local control over the attributes of citizenship be preserved in order to maintain racial boundaries.[73] The Privy Council also ignored the broader point Lawrence made regarding the principle it invoked. While individual states retained the practical power to define voter qualifications in each state, Lawrence explained, any such qualifications "must apply equally to all classes of citizens in the State, whether native or naturalized."[74] If it were possible for "individual States to disfranchise naturalized citizens," he reasoned, "the federal power over naturalization becomes a nullity."[75] The Privy Council, in short, did not just borrow—but distorted and expanded— the doctrine it grafted onto Canadian law.

The Privy Council distinguished its own decision in *Bryden*. Even though it had declared in that case, seemingly unequivocally, that the Dominion government's power over naturalization included the power to determine "the consequences of naturalization" and the rights and privileges of naturalized citizens in Canada, it now—in what one legal scholar has called "one of the most interesting constitutional somersaults in Canadian history"—

disclaimed its prior pronouncement.[76] *Bryden,* the Privy Council summarily announced in *Homma,* was an entirely different case. In the prior case, it insisted, it had merely invalidated a law intended to keep Chinese immigrants from being able to earn a living in B.C.[77] It was obvious, it declared, that this question was in no way related to the question of whether a naturalized citizen was entitled to vote in the province in which he resided.[78] In fact, because being listed on the provincial voters list was a prerequisite to obtaining various kinds of occupational licenses, the Privy Council's decision did deny Canadian citizens of Asian ancestry the ability to earn a living in various employment areas. Occupations that remained closed to B.C. citizens of Japanese and Chinese ancestry as a result of the Privy Council's decision included pharmacy, law, hand-logging, jobs on public works projects and, ironically, in light of the Privy Council's rationale for *Bryden,* mining.[79] Naturalized citizens of Asian descent, moreover, were barred from voting not just in provincial elections but also in federal elections, since the ability to vote in federal elections depended on being listed on the provincial voters list. They were also not allowed to hold public office or to serve on juries.[80]

The B.C. press celebrated the Privy Council's decision. "No Japanese Need Apply to be Voters," the *Vancouver Daily Province* proclaimed after news arrived from London that the Privy Council had reversed the lower courts' decisions. B.C. did indeed have the power to "refuse the franchise to Orientals." The decision was "of great importance," it opined, "as settling once and for all the question of Japanese power at the polls."[81] The *Victoria Daily Colonist,* in turn, declared:

> We are relieved from the possibility of having polling booths swamped by a horde of Orientals who are totally unfitted either by custom or education to exercise the ballot, and whose voting would completely demoralize politics. . . . We have a right to deprive Chinese and Japanese and Indians of the franchise, and we do so without hesitation because they have not the remotest idea of what a democratic and representative government is, and are quite incapable of taking part in it.[82]

Other English-language newspapers in B.C. echoed these sentiments. Absent, in any English-language paper, was any criticism of the Privy Council's decision.

When the Dominion government revisited the issue in 1904, urging B.C. to reconsider its 1895 amendment excluding citizens of Japanese ancestry from the franchise for diplomatic reasons arising out of the Anglo-Japanese Alliance of 1902,[83] the *Victoria Daily Colonist* indignantly defended British Columbia's continued refusal to do so. Echoing the sentiments expressed by the Japanese consul at the time Homma filed his lawsuit, the editors insisted that excluding persons of Japanese ancestry from the franchise in no way infringed on the rights of any subject of the Japanese Empire, since immigrants to whom that legislation applied were no longer Japanese subjects.[84] "The exclusion of certain racial elements from the voters' list," they declared, was "the only constitutional right left to the Province whereby it can protect itself against being governed by foreigners."[85] Ignoring that the vast majority of B.C.'s residents at the time were themselves immigrants, the editors declared that B.C. was justified in denying the franchise to Japanese immigrants because its geographical "contiguity with Japan" made it more vulnerable to the effects of unchecked immigration than any other Canadian province.[86]

During the decades that followed the Privy Council's decision, Homma largely withdrew from the leadership roles he had previously assumed within the Japanese immigrant community, moving onto the grounds of the Great Northern Cannery in West Vancouver in 1909.[87] There he walked down to the beach on many mornings to gather firewood and visited with family and friends.[88] Financial support from the larger Japanese community had dwindled even before the case was completed, and it was his own family, including his wife Matsu, on whom the financial burden fell.[89] Homma continued to write and helped with the compilation of two histories of Japanese immigrants in Canada in the 1920s, but rarely spoke about his role in challenging the Provincial Voters Act.[90] Members of the Japanese immigrant community who had criticized Homma for proceeding with the case felt justified in their concern, and some blamed him for the Privy Council's decision.[91] In 1942, soon after the start of the Pacific War, Tomekichi Homma was forced to move to a relocation camp in the B.C. interior along with other Japanese Canadians. There he was confined to a single room by a stroke that had left him partially paralyzed. The room was almost bare, his son Keay Homma recalls, adorned only by a single portrait of the king and queen of England hung on one wall—ongoing, if mute, testimony to his status as a British subject.[92]

Not until March 1949, under pressure from the federal government of Canada, which had itself only recently restored the federal franchise to its Japanese-Canadian citizens, did the B.C. legislature introduce legislation to permit citizens of Japanese ancestry to vote.[93] Homma, who died on October 28, 1945, did not live to see that day.[94] His son Seiji, however, who continued his father's fight for the franchise, was present in the public gallery on the day the legislation was introduced.[95]

Homma's challenge to the Provincial Voters Act makes clear that he understood the power inherent in legal process to effect political change in Western societies. The fact that both the lower courts that considered Homma's case were convinced that they had no alternative, under the law as it existed at the time, but to overturn the discriminatory provisions of the act, demonstrates the strength of Homma's argument that the legislation was invalid. Homma failed in his effort to overturn the exclusionary amendment to the Provincial Voters Act only because the Privy Council adopted an artifice that was both legally and logically unsound. Notwithstanding Canada's insistence on its own identity as distinct from that of the United States, it was to distorted U.S. legal principle that the Privy Council turned to reinforce race-based barriers in Canadian law. By extracting a phrase from a discussion of U.S. constitutional law in an outdated American treatise, and using that as the only direct precedent for its conclusion regarding the scope of political rights in Canada, the Privy Council at once expanded and grafted onto Canadian law doctrine developed in significant part to accommodate the demands of slave states in the pre–Civil War United States. The Privy Council's decision was readily tolerated in Canada because the idea that citizenship did not necessarily confer a right to vote was already deeply imbedded in North American law—in Canada as well as in the United States—not just along racial lines, but along gender lines as well. Notwithstanding the substantial differences in the histories and constitutional structures of the two countries, racist attitudes common to both allowed the Privy Council—and those who relied on its decision to justify the exclusion of Canadian citizens of Asian ancestry from the franchise for the next half century—to overlook distinctions between Canada and the United States they would otherwise have regarded as important in order to establish and maintain similar kinds of racial barriers.

Notes

I am grateful to the Homma family and to the staff of the Japanese Canadian National Museum, as well as to all who have commented on a draft of this essay since its first presentation as a conference paper at the University of Victoria in 1998.

   1. See, for example, Cole Harris, "Making an Immigrant Society," in *The Reset-*

tlement of British Columbia: Essays on Colonialism and Geographical Change (Vancouver: UBC Press, 1998), 250–75; Patricia E. Roy, *A White Man's Province: British Columbia Politicians and Chinese and Japanese Immigrants, 1858–1914* (Vancouver: UBC Press, 1989), xiv.

2. For an analysis of some of the many ways in which law has been used to create and maintain racial barriers in the United States, see Ian F. Haney Lopez, *White by Law: The Legal Construction of Race* (New York: New York University Press, 1996).

3. *Cunningham v Homma,* [1903] A.C. 151 (P.C.). The Judicial Committee of the Privy Council ("the Privy Council") was created in 1833. It was the final court of appeal for decisions arising out of the courts in Britain's overseas dependencies for most of the next hundred years. J. P. Kenyon, *A Dictionary of British History* (New York: Stein & Day, 1983). The Privy Council stopped hearing appeals from Canadian court decisions in 1949. S. H. Steinberg and I. H. Evans, eds., *Steinberg's Dictionary of British History,* 2nd ed. (New York: St. Martin's Press, 1970). For a general discussion of the Privy Council and its role in the appellate process, and of the differences between the legal and political systems of Canada and the United States, see Herbert Arthur Smith, *Federalism in North America: A Comparative Study of Institutions in the United States and Canada* (Boston: The Chipman Law Publishing Company, 1923). Because Canada was created as a Dominion of Great Britain under the British North America Act, 1867, and remained subordinate to the United Kingdom, Canada's citizens, including those who were naturalized, were also British subjects. See, for example, Charles Arnold-Baker, *The Companion to British History,* 2nd ed. (London and New York: Routledge, 1996). To avoid confusion, I have chosen to use the term "citizen" rather than "British subject" in most instances.

4. W. Peter Ward, *White Canada Forever: Popular Attitudes and Public Policy Toward Orientals in British Columbia* (Montreal: McGill-Queen's University Press, 1978), 30–31.

5. W. Peter Ward and Patricia E. Roy both explore in detail the processes through which "whiteness" emerged as an essential criterion for defining citizenship in British Columbia. Ward, *White Canada Forever;* Roy, *A White Man's Province.*

6. *An Act relating to an Act to make better provision for the Qualification and Registration of Voters,* 38 Vic. 1875, no. 2, s.1 (B.C.).

7. *An Act to amend the "Provincial Voters' Act,"* S.B.C. 1895, c. 20; *Vancouver Daily Province,* 1 December 1900 (citing numbers provided by Thomas Cunningham, Collector of Voters for Vancouver, B.C.).

8. D. M. Eberts, B.C. Attorney General, to Christopher Robinson, Esq., K.C., London, 29 June 1901, published in the *Victoria Daily Colonist,* 3 January 1903. Eberts states that "it was after 1888 that the Japanese began to come to this province in large numbers" and attributes the 1895 amendment to the Provincial Voters Act to that

"fact." What constitutes a large number is, of course, a matter of interpretation. The 1902 Royal Commission on Chinese and Japanese Immigration found that a majority of the 4,578 Japanese immigrants in B.C. at that time (out of a total population of 177,272) arrived after July 1, 1899, some four years after the 1895 amendment was passed. *Report of the Royal Commission on Chinese and Japanese Immigration, 1902 Session,* 2 Edward VII, Sessional Paper No. 54, A. 1902, 329, 389.

9. *Provincial Elections Act,* S.B.C. 1897, c.67, s.3. "Chinese" was similarly defined to include children of Chinese ancestry born in B.C.

10. Ibid.

11. *Vancouver Daily Province,* 1 December 1900.

12. *Victoria Daily Colonist,* 28 October 1900.

13. *Vancouver Daily Province,* 27 October 1900.

14. Ibid.

15. Ibid. See also Shigeharu Koyama, *Nikkei Kanada imin no chichi: Homma Tomekichi oo no shogai* (The father of Japanese immigrants in Canada: the life of Tomekichi Homma) (Tokyo: n.p., 1996), 61–62.

16. Homma was born in Chiba Prefecture on June 6, 1865. There is some question as to the date on which he arrived in Canada. Some sources give his date of arrival as 1884 and others as 1887, while his family register in Chiba, Japan, states that he left for Canada in 1883. Koyama, *Nikkei Kanada imin no chichi,* 9. Homma himself, writing in 1921, says he arrived in Canada thirty-three years earlier, which would have been about 1888. Jinshiro Nakayama, ed., *Kanada doho hatten taikan* (Vancouver, B.C.: n.p., 1922), appendices, 151–60. The article that Homma contributed to this volume, which carefully documents the development of the Japanese immigrant community in B.C., was translated into English and published in 1977 with the assistance of the Japanese Canadian Citizens Association in *The New Canadian* 41, no. 58 (9 August 1977).

17. Jinshiro Nakayama, *Kanada no hoko* (Tokyo: n.p., 1921), 646.

18. Ibid., 1450, 1589. See also Roy Ito, *Stories of My People: A Japanese Canadian Journal* (Hamilton, Ont.: S-20 and Nisei Veterans Association, 1994).

19. *Vancouver Daily Province,* 27 October 1900; Nakayama, *Kanada doho hatten taikan,* appendices, 151–60 (article by Tomekichi Homma).

20. Nakayama, *Kanada no hoko,* 1450.

21. Nakayama, *Kanada doho hatten taikan,* 111.

22. Koyama, *Nikkei Kanada imin no chichi,* 61–62. Koyama reports that Homma's supporters were able to raise just over $1,500—a fairly substantial sum at that time—over a two-year period based on donations by members of the Japanese immigrant community of $1.50 at a time.

23. *Vancouver Daily Province,* 23 and 27 October 1900. The Japanese newspaper,

which the *Province* referred to as *"The Vancouver Weekly,"* was probably the *Bankuba shuho* (Vancouver Weekly Report), to which Homma also contributed. The *Province* examined the issue it had obtained in some detail with the aid of an interpreter, describing it as "essentially an up-to-date newspaper [that] contains most interesting articles on all the questions of public interest of the day." Unfortunately, no copies of *Dai Nippon* or the *Bankuba shuho* (later renamed the *Kanada shimpo*) are known to exist today.

24. Koyama, *Nikkei Kanada imin no chichi*, 66.

25. *Vancouver Daily Province*, 1 December 1900. The consul conceded, however, that he did take an interest in anything that affected "the Japanese as a race," and he sought to ensure that they received any rights to which they were legally entitled. He later lodged several protests on behalf of the Japanese government against legislation directed at Japanese immigrants in B.C. *Victoria Daily Colonist*, 3 January 1903.

26. Koyama, *Nikkei Kanada imin no chichi*, 8. A tribute to Tomekichi Homma published in 1922 described him as a man of great courage, who was both strong-minded and generous of spirit. Nakayama, *Kanada doho hatten taikan*, 111.

27. Koyama, *Nikkei Kanada imin no chichi*, 8; Homma Family Genealogy, Homma Collection, File 94/88, Japanese Canadian National Museum, Burnaby, B.C. Keay Homma, Tomekichi Homma's youngest son, reports that his father never told his children of their family's samurai heritage. All would become clear, he told them, when they read his diaries after his death. Unfortunately, all but one of the diaries were later destroyed in a fire. As a result, much that might have been known about Homma's thoughts about this and other matters can no longer be discerned. Conversation with Keay Homma in Surrey, B.C., January 19, 1998.

28. Koyama, *Nikkei Kanada imin no chichi*, 60.

29. *Vancouver Daily Province*, 27 October 1900.

30. Ibid.

31. *Victoria Daily Colonist*, 30 November 1900.

32. The *Constitution Act, 1867 (British North America Act)*, ss. 91 and 92, provides in pertinent part:

S.91. It shall be lawful for the Queen, by and with the Advice and Consent of the Senate and the House of Commons, to make Laws for the Peace, Order, and good Government of Canada, *in relation to all Matters not coming within the Classes of Subjects by this Act assigned exclusively to the Legislatures of the Provinces;* and for greater Certainty, but not so as to restrict the Generality of the foregoing Terms of this Section, it is hereby declared that (notwithstanding anything in this Act) *the exclusive Legislative Authority of the Par-*

*liament of Canada extends to all Matters coming within the Classes of Subjects
next herein-after enumerated; that is to say;*

. . . .

25. *Naturalization and Aliens.*

. . . .

S.92. In each Province the Legislature may exclusively make Laws in relation
to Matters coming within the Classes of Subject next hereinafter enumerated; that is to say, —

. . . .

13. *Property and Civil Rights in the Province.*

. . . .

16. *Generally all Matters of a merely local or private Nature in the Province.*
[Emphasis added.]
The quintessential question in Canadian constitutional law prior to the adoption of the Constitution Act, 1982, was whether a matter "in pith and substance"
came within section 91 or 92, it being assumed that all matters came within one or
the other. Smith, *Federalism in North America,* 108–9.

33. *Naturalization Act,* R.S.C. c. 113, s. 15.

34. *Union Colliery Company of British Columbia, Limited v Bryden* [1899], A.C.
580, 587 (P.C.).

35. *In Re the Provincial Elections Act and In Re Tomey Homma, a Japanese,* (1900)
7 B.C.R. 368, 369 (Co. Ct.) (setting out the arguments of counsel). *Ultra vires* literally means "outside the powers or capabilities of." Henry Campbell Black, *Black's
Law Dictionary* (St. Paul, Minn.: West Publishing Co., 1951) 1692, 1742.

36. *In Re the Provincial Elections Act and In Re Tomey Homma, a Japanese,* 371–72
(Co. Ct.). Wilson's argument was based on the language in section 92 of the British
North America Act which gave the provincial legislature exclusive jurisdiction with
regard to "the amendment from time to time, notwithstanding anything in the Act,
of the constitution of the Province, except in respect of the office of Lieutenant-
Governor." Ibid., 371.

37. Curiously, although the County Court was clearly satisfied that Homma "was
naturalized in Canada more than six months prior to October 19th, 1900" and the
Record of Proceedings gives April 4, 1893, as the date on which Homma was naturalized, an RCMP investigator in 1932 reported that Homma's naturalization papers
were dated January 28, 1902. Letter from RCMP Corporal J. R. O'Reilly to Com-
manding Officer, "E" Division, RCMP, 12 March 1932. National Archives of Canada,
Record Group 76. Because it is unlikely that the courts would have proceeded with
the case had they not ascertained that Homma was a naturalized citizen, it appears

that the corporal's letter is in error. *Kanada no hoko,* to which Homma contributed, also lists April 4, 1893, as the date on which he was naturalized. Nakayama, *Kanada no hoko,* 1450.

38. *In Re the Provincial Elections Act and In Re Tomey Homma, a Japanese,* 372 (Co. Ct.); *Victoria Daily Colonist,* 30 November 1900. Chief Justice McColl's conclusion that the Province lacked the power to pass legislation that did not "apply alike" to all subjects of the Queen was based on the language of the Naturalization Act itself. In the British North America Act, which was then Canada's constitution, there was no equivalent to the Equal Protection Clause of the U.S. Constitution. Canada incorporated a Charter of Rights into its Constitution in 1982, after the British Parliament granted it the power to amend its own Constitution. Arnold-Baker, *Companion to British History,* 189. The Charter of Rights includes a provision guaranteeing all citizens the right to vote.

39. *In Re the Provincial Elections Act and In Re Tomey Homma, a Japanese,* 372 (Co. Ct.).

40. Ibid., (1901) 8 B.C.R. 76, 77 (S.C.).

41. *Vancouver Daily Province,* 1 December 1900.

42. On January 23, 1901, just as the Province was in the process of appealing Chief Justice McColl's decision to the full B.C. Supreme Court, the *Vancouver Daily Province* chose to reprint an article entitled "Uncle Tom's Cabin is Now Designated a Criminal Mistake" from a recent edition of the *New York Herald.* The article reported the opinion of a Mr. Smith, a Southerner living in New York, that it was that book's "distorted view" of conditions in the antebellum South that "made compromise between the north and the south impossible" during the U.S. Civil War. Former slaves, the article quoted Mr. Smith as saying, were "far happier under slavery" than they were after the war. The excerpt concluded abruptly with the observation that "Mr. Smith is a firm believer that the enfranchising of the negro was a tremendous blunder."

43. British Columbia, Legislative Assembly, *Sessional Papers* (1901), 611–15; British Columbia, Legislative Assembly, *Sessional Papers* (1903), J7–J8.

44. *Victoria Daily Colonist,* 1 December 1900.

45. Ibid.

46. See, for example, *Vancouver Daily Province,* 1 December 1900; *Victoria Daily Colonist,* 27 July 1900 ("Fraudulent Naturalization").

47. *Vancouver Daily Province,* 1 December 1900.

48. Ibid.

49. *The Daily Columbian,* 9 March 1901.

50. *In Re the Provincial Elections Act and In Re Tomey Homma, a Japanese,* 76, 80 (S.C.).

51. *Naturalization Act,* R.S.C., c. 113, quoted in ibid., 79 (S.C.).

52. *In Re the Provincial Elections Act and In Re Tomey Homma, a Japanese,* 79 (S.C.) (quoting "Ency. Dict.").

53. Ibid.

54. Ibid., 82.

55. Ibid., 80, 83. There was some uncertainty as to whether the lower court decisions also applied to naturalized citizens of Chinese ancestry (*Vancouver Daily Province,* 1 December 1900). For that reason, a Chinese Canadian, Alexander Won Cumyow, born to Chinese immigrant parents in B.C. in 1861, filed a separate case challenging the exclusion of B.C. citizens of Chinese ancestry from the franchise after Thomas Cunningham also refused to add his name to the provincial voters list. *Vancouver Daily Province,* 22 December 1902; *New Citizen,* 24 March 1951. The fact that Cumyow was born in B.C. potentially allowed him to raise legal issues regarding the application of the Provincial Voters Act to citizens born in B.C., that Homma, as a naturalized citizen, could not directly raise.

56. Ibid., 83–84.

57. Eberts to Robinson, 29 June 1901, published in the *Victoria Daily Colonist,* 3 January 1903. An extravagant tribute published by the *Vancouver Daily Province* on 4 May 1901 described the Hon. David McEwen Eberts as "the ablest man in British Columbia's government." Few, according to the *Province,* would "deny the brilliancy of intellect by which he is enabled to grasp even the most abstruse public question almost at a glance." Eberts, it said, was "a man's man every inch of him, charming companion and prince of gentlemanly good fellows, a sportsman true at heart in every game of wits or field, a man born to command and to be popular, a warhorse in the strife of politics when once he discards the mantle of his indolence, [and] a keen and accurate reader of men and motives."

58. Ibid. One Member of Parliament in Canada invoked a similar comparison in 1885 during a debate in Parliament concerning the question as to whether Native Canadians should be enfranchised: "[T]o give the franchise to women would interfere with their proper position, . . . it would be a burden instead of a benefit to them. This, I believe, to be exactly the case as regards the Indians." Mr. Fairbanks, House of Commons Debates, 2 May 1885, p. 1532. Quoted in R. H. Bartlett, "Citizens Minus: Indians and the Right to Vote," *Saskatchewan Law Review* 44 (1980): 173 n. 39.

59. Eberts to Robinson, 29 June 1901, published in the *Victoria Daily Colonist,* 3 January 1903.

60. Ibid. Eberts wrote:

It is provided by Article IV of the Constitution of the United States that citizens of each state shall be entitled to all privileges and immunities of citizens in the several states. In discussing this provision, Von Holst, in his work on the Constitutional Law of the United States, at page 249, says:

"Political rights, such as the franchise, the right to hold office, etc., are never an unconditional result of citizenship. This is evident from the fact that they are always withheld from minors, and almost without exception from women."

The work being quoted by Eberts is *The Constitutional Law of the United States of America,* originally written in German by Dr. H. von Holst, a professor at the University of Freiburg. An English edition, translated by Alfred Bishop Mason, was published in 1887 by Callaghan & Company in Chicago, Illinois.

61. Local newspaper editors also frequently invoked this idea. See, for example, *Victoria Daily Colonist,* 25 April 1905, which justified the exclusion of people of Asian ancestry from the franchise on the ground that "not even all British subjects were entitled to vote" and cited the fact that women were not allowed to vote as a telling example.

62. Ibid. As noted above, British Columbia became a Canadian province only in 1871.

63. Ibid. Why Eberts was so certain that the Province had the power to deny the franchise to B.C.'s Native population is not clear from his remarks. For a general discussion of the law in this regard, see Bartlett, "Citizens Minus," 163. The issue was more complicated in Canada than in the United States, Eberts said, because Indians were not citizens in the United States, whereas in Canada Indians were British subjects (quoting *Gibb v White,* 5 Ont. Practice Reports, 315, affirmed in *Johnson v Jones,* 26 Ontario Reports 109).

64. Ibid. While the Fourteenth and Fifteenth Amendments guaranteed both citizenship and the right to vote to children born in the United States, first-generation Asian immigrants were denied citizenship in the United States. For that reason, the focus in the United States was on the denial of citizenship in the first instance. See, for example, *Ozawa v United States,* 260 U.S. 178 (1922). Although the Fourteenth and Fifteenth Amendments were passed soon after the end of the U.S. Civil War, U.S. courts acted quickly to limit their scope. Kenneth L. Karst, *Belonging to America: Equal Citizenship and the Constitution* (New Haven: Yale University Press, 1989), 56–61.

65. *Cunningham v Homma, supra,* 155–56.

66. Ibid.

67. Ibid., 156.

68. Ibid. The Privy Council noted, without reference to any particular source, that in England, "from the time of William III down to Queen Victoria," naturalized aliens were not permitted to sit in Parliament or on the Privy Council, but failed to explain why this was relevant to the question before it, which involved the interpretation of the *British North America Act* as it applied to Canada.

69. In the context of Canadian aboriginal law cases, Canadian courts have sometimes turned to decisions of U.S. courts for precedent, based on the rationale that federal Indian law doctrine in both Canada and the United States has its origins in pre–Revolutionary War, British colonial Indian policy. No similar rationale exists, however, for invoking U.S. law in this context, since the language in question arises out of a discussion of an article of the U.S. Constitution, which, by definition, has no application in Canada.

70. Henry Wheaton, *Elements of International Law,* 2nd annotated edition, edited by William Beach Lawrence in 1863 and published in 1864 ("Lawrence's Wheaton") (London, 1864).

71. *Cunningham v Homma, supra,* 156, quoting "Lawrence's Wheaton," 903. The phrase "in the United States" is in the original. Thus, there can be no question that the Privy Council was aware that the phrase it extracted occurred within the context of a discussion of U.S. law and policy.

72. *Cunningham v Homma, supra,* 156. The Privy Council also made the general observation that the franchise had sometimes been withheld from British subjects in England "conspicuously upon grounds of religious faith," suggesting that the fact that British law had historically tolerated the denial of civil rights on religious grounds somehow justified the denial of civil rights on race-based grounds. It again failed to explain, however, how this justified its conclusion as to the scope of political rights in Canada.

73. See, for example, "Lawrence's Wheaton," 904; Von Holst, 18–19. For a detailed discussion of the historical debates regarding the scope of the franchise in the United States, see Alexander Keyssar, *The Right to Vote: The Contested History of Democracy in the United States* (New York: Basic Books, 2000).

74. "Lawrence's Wheaton," 909. The Privy Council also avoided any acknowledgement that, even assuming the clause it extracted was good law in 1863, it was no longer good law even in the United States at the time the Privy Council made its decision in 1902. The flaw in (or perhaps even the reason for) its choice of the 1863 edition of "Lawrence's Wheaton" instead of a more current summary of the law becomes quickly apparent when one examines later editions of the treatise. Not just the language quoted by the Privy Council to support its decision, but the entire chapter of which it was a part, was completely cut from all post-1864 editions.

75. "Lawrence's Wheaton," 910.

76. *Bryden,* [1899] A.C. 586; Ross Lambertson, "After *Union Colliery [Bryden]*: Law, Race, and Class in the Coalmines of British Columbia," in *Essays in the History of Canadian Law,* vol. 6, ed. Hamar Foster and John McLaren (British Columbia and the Yukon) (Toronto: Osgoode Society, 1995), 396. Other legal scholars have used the word "bizarre" to describe the Privy Council's reasoning in *Homma v Cun-*

ningham. Anthony Lester and Geoffrey Bindman, *Race and Law in Great Britain* (Cambridge: Harvard University Press, 1972), 37.

77. Lambertson characterizes this description of *Bryden* as "a distortion of the facts" of that case. Lambertson, "After *Union Colliery,*" 397.

78. *Cunningham v Homma, supra,* 157. While most other Canadian provinces did not exclude naturalized Japanese citizens from the franchise, this was of little practical consequence, since 95 percent of all Japanese immigrants in Canada lived in British Columbia.

79. Kunio Hidaka, *Legal Status of the Japanese in Canada,* c. 1940. Unpublished paper in the possession of the University of British Columbia Special Collections and University Archives Division, Japanese Canadian Collection.

80. Ibid.

81. *Vancouver Daily Province,* 17 December 1902.

82. *Victoria Daily Colonist,* 18 December 1902.

83. Roy, *A White Man's Province,* 275 n. 20. Roy explains that the Japanese government repeatedly complained that anti-Japanese legislation in B.C. violated the terms of the Anglo-Japanese Alliance, concluded between Great Britain and Japan in 1902. Ibid., 124, 127–28.

84. *Victoria Daily Colonist,* 25 April 1905. This sentiment was also shared by the Japanese consulate in London which, Koyama reports, refused to do anything to help Homma when his case was before the Privy Council because it regarded those who became naturalized British subjects as people who had abandoned their own country. Koyama, *Nikkei Kanada imin no chichi,* 72–73. Naturalized Japanese immigrants in British Columbia, as this suggests, were arguably the most vulnerable of all groups of Japanese immigrants in North America: not only were they denied any political voice as Canadian citizens, but they were also denied the diplomatic protections to which they might have had access as Japanese subjects. See Hidaka, *Legal Status of Japanese in Canada.*

85. *Victoria Daily Colonist,* 25 April 1905.

86. Ibid.

87. Conversation with Keay Homma, Surrey, B.C., January 19, 1998.

88. Tomekichi Homma, *Diary,* 1933 (in the possession of the Homma family).

89. Conversation with Keay Homma, Surrey, B.C., June 7, 2002; Yoshimaru Abe, "Tomekichi Homma," *Nikkei Images* 8, no. 1 (spring 2003): 6–8 (text of speech by Tomekichi Homma's son-in-law).

90. Homma contributed to the research and compilation of both *Kanada no hoko* and *Kanada doho hatten taikan* in the early 1920s. Abe, *Nikkei Images,* 7. Keay Homma learned of his father's role in challenging the exclusion of Japanese-born

citizens of Canada from the franchise only at his father's funeral. Conversation with Keay Homma, Surrey, B.C., June 7, 2002.

91. Conversation with Keay Homma, Surrey, B.C., June 7, 2002. See also *Nikkei no koe* (Nikkei Voice), vol. 13, no. 10 (December 1999/January 2000), which notes that Homma was very likely exposed to public censure within the Japanese immigrant community for his role in the case. Nakayama likewise suggests that Homma was ostracized for much of his life by some members of the community. Nakayama, *Kanada no hoko,* 111.

92. Conversation with Keay Homma, Surrey, B.C., January 19, 1998.

93. *The New Canadian,* March 12, 1949. The legislation was introduced in March 1949, just three weeks before the federal government's restoration of the franchise was to take effect on March 31, 1949. B.C. had already acted to restore the franchise to Chinese, East Indians, and Natives living off reserves (ibid.). The federal franchise allows citizens of Canada to vote for members of Parliament, as opposed to voting in provincial elections for members of the legislative assembly.

94. Japanese Canadian National Museum, Burnaby, B.C., File 94/88. The case of Cumyow filed on behalf of citizens of Chinese ancestry in B.C. was dismissed in the wake of the Privy Council's decision in *Homma v. Cunningham,* but Cumyow lived long enough to see the franchise restored to citizens of Chinese ancestry. "Franchise Returned to Alex Cumyow After 51 Year Wait," *The New Citizen,* 5 July 1949.

95. *The New Canadian,* 12 March 1949; 19 February 1964.

3 / BECOMING "LOCAL" JAPANESE

Issei Adaptive Strategies
on the Yakama Indian Reservation, 1906–1923

GAIL M. NOMURA

I n 1932, in the midst of the Great Depression, the Yakima Valley Japanese
American community in the state of Washington planted seventy-four
flowering cherry trees in the Japanese section of Tahoma Cemetery, a public cemetery administered by the city of Yakima. The establishment of a Japanese public cemetery had been the first collective ethnic activity for Yakima
Valley Japanese immigrants, the Issei (first generation). In 1903 they had
bought three blocks of land in the Yakima city-administered Tahoma
Cemetery to establish this Japanese public cemetery. By 1904 eight of their
compatriots were buried there. The Japanese graves marked the permanent
presence of Japanese in the Yakima Valley and the commitment of those
who immigrated to remain in the valley until their death.[1] The flowering of
the cherry trees at the cemetery each spring symbolized the stunning
"appearance" of the Yakima Valley Japanese American ethnic community.
In their community history written in 1935, the Issei declared, "Year after
year, when spring comes to Tahoma Cemetery, cherry blossoms, the symbol of the Japanese spirit, bloom in profusion and glory covering the tomb-
stones of our deceased compatriots. It is at such times that our hardworking
compatriots in the Yakima Valley are reminded anew of their great mission, impressed by the importance of their responsibilities, and inspired with
hundredfold courage to strive for the prosperity of the people."[2]

This essay examines the adaptive strategies and political mobilization of
this Japanese American community centering on the Yakama[3] Indian Reservation in central Washington in the period from when the first leases were
issued in 1906 to Japanese immigrants to 1923, when the Department of the
Interior more stringently restricted their leasing rights. Racialized discrimination and exclusionist pressures to restrict Japanese immigrant economic

livelihood led to the formation of ethnic identity and organized action to protect and promote their collective interests. I analyze the rhetoric of white exclusionists who, in ignoring the Native Yakama rights to control their own land, asserted their white privileges as "Americans" to farm Yakama reservation land. They campaigned to exclude Japanese immigrants from farming on these same reservation lands on the basis that the Issei could never become "American" and posed a threat to the nation as colonists who represented the vanguard of Japanese imperialist expansion to U.S. soil. This study argues that the Issei were not merely passive victims of this widespread West Coast anti-Japanese exclusion movement, but rather were proactive in asserting their rights and perspectives. Issei leaders analyzed the exclusionists' racist accusations and devised strategies and measures to counter these allegations while deploying their own discourse for inclusion into "America" and, in this study, the Yakima Valley. Barred from legal naturalization, the Japanese "naturalized" themselves into the Yakima Valley community as "local" Japanese, cultivating an ultimately tenuous but widespread community support for their continued presence in the Yakima Valley.

Settlement on the Yakama Indian Reservation

The Yakima Valley was created by the flow of a river through the million acres of land in what is now central Washington State. Despite the rich lakebed soil, the Yakima Valley's six to nine inches of annual rainfall is inadequate for agriculture. However, by the closing of the nineteenth century, large-scale irrigation projects helped to realize the rich agricultural potential of the fertile but rain-poor land.[4] The irrigated Yakima Valley became the "fruit bowl" of Washington, producing apples, peaches, pears, cherries, and grapes, as well as potatoes, onions, hay, hops, sugar beets, and asparagus.

One of the major croplands in the Yakima Valley lay within the borders of the Yakama Indian Reservation. Established by the Yakama Treaty of 1855 between the confederated tribes and bands of the Yakama Nation and the United States, the Yakama Reservation encompassed 1,200,000 acres of land. In 1920 there were almost three thousand Yakama living on the reservation. In the early twentieth century, the federal government encouraged the leasing of reservation lands at low cost in exchange for improvements to the land which would revert back to the Yakama allottee. In addition, federal land was exempted from county taxes, and Yakama Indian allotments were guaranteed a certain amount of water. The superintendent of the Yakama Indian Agency handled the leasing of most of the Yakama allotments, and a few Yakama, approved by the agency to be "competent" to manage their own affairs, were allowed to farm or lease their own lands. The U.S. Department of Interior's Office of Indian Affairs issued regulations and approved leases.[5]

Besides the Yakama Indians and whites, Japanese farmed on the reservation. As the Yakima Valley Issei written community history declared, "Rich land, irrigation, and climate; with these three excellent conditions why would the diligent perseverant Japanese farmers leave the Valley uncultivated?"[6] The first Issei are reported to have arrived in the Yakima Valley in 1891.[7] Increasing numbers of Japanese settled there after 1900, becoming an integral part of the regional development of the agriculturally rich area. Issei farmers in the Yakima Valley figured importantly in the state's vegetable and melon production, for with irrigation the sandy loam desert soil produced some of the best yields of tomatoes, melons, onions, potatoes, peas, beans, cucumbers, sweet corn, and squash. By 1915 there were some five hundred Japanese in the Yakima Valley, mainly living around the reservation town of Wapato, and by 1920 the population had nearly doubled.

Most Japanese in the valley settled on leased land on the federally administered Yakama Indian Reservation. Issei farmers obtained their first leases on the reservation in 1906, when new irrigation projects were expanding areas of cultivation. There were numerous reasons for the high concentration of Japanese on the reservation. Primary was the exclusion of Japanese from the ownership of land in Washington. In 1889 Washington's constitution prohibited land ownership "by aliens other than those who in good faith have declared their intention to become citizens of the United States, except where acquired by inheritance, under mortgage or in good faith in the ordinary course of justice in the collection of debts. . . ." The race of an alien was key to his ability to "in good faith" declare his intention to become a citizen. U.S. naturalization laws restricted naturalization to an alien who was a "free white person" or aliens of African nativity or descent. It was generally held that Japanese were neither white nor African. Therefore, Japanese immigrants as aliens ineligible for citizenship could not own land in Washington because they could not "in good faith" declare their intent to become naturalized citizens.[8] Excluded from ownership of land the Issei turned instead to leasing or renting farmland.

The Issei found it easier to acquire larger acreage of leased land for agriculture on the Yakama Indian Reservation than in any other area in Wash-

ington. This was because the Yakima Valley was still developing agriculturally, and vast expanses of uncultivated land were available, especially on
the reservation. The lease fee for unimproved lands on the Yakama Indian
Reservation was fifty cents to one dollar an acre during the first decade of
the twentieth century. In addition to the low lease fee, large acreage from
eighty to four hundred acres or more could be leased due to the great area
that needed improvement and the shortage of farmers requesting leases on
the reservation. Japanese farmers could thus acquire far greater acreage on
the reservation lands than they could in the more populated and settled Puget
Sound region. Moreover, with a sympathetic or at least non-hostile agency
superintendent in charge of leasing reservation land, it was easier to acquire
leases there than in more developed areas of Washington, where the Japanese had to negotiate with individual, often racist landowners.

It took hard work to clear the sagebrush, level the land for irrigation and
cultivation, and make the other improvements required by the federal government. Fusakichi Konishi stated, "Together Yoshioka and I challenged the
uncultivated land. In summertime it got as hot as 115 degrees Fahrenheit.
Wiping off the sweat, we threw ourselves into the job of clearing."[9] Leases
for unimproved land required lessees to "clear, level and cultivate all the
arable land; build house, enclose allotment with regulation fence . . . dig well,
keep all improvements in good repair." All improvements, of course,
reverted to the Yakama allottee after termination of the lease even though
many leases were renewed.[10]

But the sweat and toil often paid off since, with virtually no capital, one
could potentially make huge profits. Sakitaro Takei explained, "Empty-
handed we began clearing the land, having borrowed for everything. Bro-
kers advanced the money against the coming harvest—a kind of contract
farming—$20 for one acre of cantaloupes, or $200 for ten acres, for example. As for food, the stores issued a $50 coupon book. Therefore without
having a cent of capital, a person could struggle with the sagebrush desert."[11]

Physically taming the sagebrush desert of the Yakima Valley was difficult
enough, but with profitable crops at last planted the Japanese were faced
with an even greater challenge: further political oppression through tightened legal restrictions that threatened their economic opportunities. A growing anti-Japanese movement that was sweeping through the West Coast states
culminated in the passage of alien land laws targeting Japanese farmers in
California in 1913 and 1920.[12] In the Yakima Valley, white exclusionists now
claimed that Japanese were monopolizing the most fertile parcels of agricultural land from white farmers, and such fertile land should be in the hands

of "Americans." They ignored the facts that these were the same lands white farmers did not want to lease and crops that white farmers did not desire to grow. Moreover, on the reservation lands, white farmers were not being dispossessed of farmland, since thousands of acres of reservation land went unleased.

Rise of the Anti-Japanese Movement

Washington had a long history of anti-Asian exclusion.[13] The treatment of Chinese immigrants set the pattern for discrimination against later Asian immigrants. Chinese were constantly subjected to regulations and prohibitions that sought to exclude them from Washington.[14] Japanese immigrants inherited this legacy of anti-Asian sentiment in Washington. Moreover, xenophobes feared that the Issei posed a threat to national security since they came from a rising non-Western world power.

Japanese were a visible and growing community in the Yakima Valley. In the boom days surrounding the U.S. declaration of war against Germany in 1917, the increasing success of Issei farmers stirred resentment and cries of unfair competition from white farmers in the area. Japanese potato growers in the Yakima Valley, who had speculated on rising prices by storing their crop to sell in winter when prices were high rather than in the fall when there was a glut of potatoes, were especially successful in marketing their potatoes during the winter of 1917.[15] But this successful business strategy was attacked as unfair. In testimony before the 1920 House Committee of Immigration and Naturalization hearings on Japanese immigration, Edwin S. Gill, an attorney and credit manager testifying as a representative of the Retail Grocers' Association in Seattle, accused Japanese of raising prices after unfairly securing control of the market.[16]

The fast-growing sugar beet industry in the Yakima Valley that employed increasing numbers of Japanese laborers and sugar beet growers further stirred anti-Japanese sentiment in the valley. On February 13, 1917, the Toppenish Commercial Club requested that Japanese laborers not be used for sugar beet fieldwork on the reservation. The local field agent for the Utah-Idaho Sugar Company reported to the club at a meeting later that month that more than 50 percent of the farmers contracting with the sugar company had expressed a preference for "Oriental" labor. The agent attributed this preference as "due to the willingness of the Japanese to load the beets on wagons at only $2 an acre more than other labor demands for merely topping and stacking the beets in the field."[17]

The *Toppenish Tribune* reported that at a McKinley district meeting of reservation farmers held on February 22, 1917, "an organization was formed to carry on an active campaign against further encroachment of Orientals."[18] A similar meeting had been held several weeks earlier at Harrah and another would be held at Wapato. These meetings were followed by a general meeting of reservation farmers in Toppenish.[19]

As anti-Japanese sentiment was building with the increase in Japanese recruited by the Utah-Idaho Sugar Company, Japanese sought to counter the rising animosity. In early March 1917, Frank Fukui, a Japanese who had been farming on the reservation for some six years, approached the *Toppenish Tribune* to subscribe to the newspaper, but then proceeded to raise the issue of Japanese and sugar beet farming with the editor. Fukui declared "There is little danger of Japanese invasion on the Reservation." He said that the Japanese were "all making good money, and not looking for hard work like sugar beets," and the sugar company would find it difficult to secure much Japanese labor. Responding to the charge that Japanese overbid for leases so white farmers could not get leases, Fukui answered, "We only pay what land is worth." Fukui declared that "Some white farmers bid $10 for land not worth $5. Then they lose money. Say 'Hell with the Japs.' When they make money, Japs, all right."

Fukui laid out the perspective of the "local" Japanese. "There are now about 100 Japanese families on Reservation. We do not want any more Japs here. We don't want trouble with white farmers. If white farmers and Commercial Club go to sugar company and say they don't want Japs in sugar beets, we will be glad. If more Japs come, white men get mad and make trouble for us already here." He concluded "we don't want trouble. Keep other Japs out. We help. No trouble. That's all."[20] For the local Japanese— the "us already here"—nativist trouble would follow the influx of "more Japs," so they were agreeable to keeping "other Japs out." It was not uncommon for other immigrant group leaders to similarly respond to nativist pressure.

German immigrant Presbyterian minister and farmer Hans Benz mobilized the growing anti-Japanese feeling among the white farmers into organized action. In March 1917, at a mass meeting of white reservation farmers held at Wapato by the Citizen-Farmers' Protective League, Hans Benz chaired the event by stating that the object of the meeting was to formulate plans to check what he termed Japanese "immigration" to the reservation. Benz claimed Japanese farmers were crowding out the white farmers especially on the reservation. He stated that the establishment of a sugar beet factory at Yakima further stimulated sugar beet growing, which employed large numbers of Japanese. Benz introduced a Mr. Eagle, who was a grower of sugar beets in Colorado and Montana. He was now growing sugar beets on a reservation-leased tract west of Toppenish. Eagle declared, "I have grown beets eleven years, and I want to say flatly that they can be grown success-fully without Japs."[21] He went on to describe how white beet growers in Mon-tana had "cut out" the Japanese five years ago by organizing against the use of Japanese labor and refusing to lease to them. Eagle described how he had employed immigrant Germans from Russia and, for a time, Belgian immi-grants. Eagle claimed that not only were these "classes" good at growing sugar beets, but "Better than that, they make good citizens and good general farm-ers, which the Japs do not. The Russians and the Belgians are strictly hon-est and industrious. They live like white people."[22]

Benz racialized the issue of free enterprise and competition. Benz accused Japanese immigrants of unfair competition due to their supposed low stan-dard of living and paying what he claimed to be exorbitant rent for the leased land. He denied the argument that Japanese farmers were able to bid more for leases on the reservation because they were more efficient farm-ers, stating that "It is not a question of efficient farming methods, but of lower standards of living. The Jap will live in a tent where the white man requires a house, or a shack, at least. The Jap will subsist on a ration that will not be accepted by the white man. He will wear poorer clothes, be satisfied to get along without little comforts and luxuries that are necessary in the white home, and will sacrifice amusements and recreations that go with civilized living. The real issue is whether the white farmer is to be reduced to the Oriental standard of living, or be driven out of the country by the Orientals."[23]

One of the speakers at the meeting suggested that the solution to the Japa-nese problem was to restrict the leasing of reservation lands only to citizens or persons who had declared their intention to become citizens. The point was made that the government in the "threatened war crisis" was mobiliz-ing its industrial forces and appealing to farmers to be patriotic by producing needed crops and livestock as much as possible. The speaker said that "It would seem entirely logical that means of preparedness should include plac-ing the nation's lands in the hands of its citizens and intending citizens, instead of in the hands of those who owe no allegiance whatever to the United States, and who may at any moment be called upon by their mother coun-try to take up arms against America."[24] Of course, the speaker failed to note that U.S. naturalization law prohibited Japanese immigrants from becoming U.S. citizens and that Japan had entered the war in 1914 on the side of the Allied powers at the request of the British in accordance with the Anglo-Japanese Alliance.

The irony of a German resident alien, in this time of "threatened war crisis" with Germany, leading a nativist exclusion movement was not lost on the Japanese immigrants. Benz's attack has the appearance of being part of what has been termed the "German propaganda machine" in the United States, which functioned along with the Hearst press to promote anti-Japanese propaganda. Between 1915 and the declaration of war by the United States, dozens of "yellow peril" pamphlets were published, one pamphlet reportedly with a distribution of 300,000. Another yellow peril pamphlet, *Preparedness for the Pacific Coast,* was published in Seattle in 1916 by the German Newspapers Association. This pamphlet urged Americans to prepare for war against Japan rather than Germany and claimed that Japan "wants a foothold on the Pacific Coast."[25]

Countermeasures

While the rhetoric of exclusion focused on painting the Japanese as "inferior," the Yakima Issei attributed the exclusion movement to the racism and envy of whites towards the success of Japanese in agriculture. They wrote, "The notion behind the oppression toward the Japanese is basically the same as that toward other colored races, such as blacks and Chinese."[26] The Yakima Issei decided to take advantage of the "enemy's power" to "tighten the unity of their own community."[27]

On April 3, 1917, the Japanese held a special meeting regarding the anti-Japanese movement launched by Benz. Issei leaders analyzed the exclusionist accusations and devised measures to counter these charges and assert their interests. On April 8 they agreed on a plan and elected an executive committee to carry out the decided countermeasures, which were deployed in the following months. The Japanese were accused of paying too much for lease rents and thus driving up local land prices. The Yakima Japanese Association, an Issei representative organization that had its origins in 1906 as the North Yakima Cooperative Association, took charge of the leasing process by making Japanese immigrants report their planned rent and term of lease to the association in order to coordinate lease rents and selection of lease tracts with white farmers' organizations, which would prevent leasing rivalry. To counter the charge that the Japanese were not involved or concerned with the prosperity of the local community, the Yakima Japanese Association urged Japanese farmers to increase patronage of white businesses by buying as much food as possible from local white grocery stores and by making white grocers sell Japanese commodities. The local media were utilized in their campaign. The Japanese association informed local newspapers that the Japanese were going to do business with local shop owners as much as possible. With regard to moral issues raised, the association demanded that the labor contractor supplying Japanese laborers for the Utah-Idaho Sugar Company "pay extra attention to the morality of Japanese in each camp to avoid undesirable affairs which come from gambling and drinking." The labor contractor agreed to the association's demands. The association also encouraged an "enlightenment" campaign for general residents, which included distributing notices to local Japanese residents.[28]

As part of their public relations media plan, K. Sakai reported to the *Wapato Independent* what had been discussed at the Yakima Japanese Association meeting, and on April 19, 1917, the newspaper published an article that extensively quoted Sakai in what took the form of an open letter to the community. The newspaper described Sakai as "an intelligent Japanese farmer" who had been "a resident of the reservation for several years, during which time he has been a successful farmer." Sakai said that the Japanese farmers had decided to meet with white farmers to "arrange a schedule of prices for reservation land." The Japanese farmers believed "a schedule of prices could be agreed upon that would be equitable and just to the Indian" and would allow the farmer "to at least make a living return for his labor." Sakai declared that the local Japanese desired "to do only that which will be conducive to the best interests of the entire farming community" and the "best interests" could "only be ascertained by all getting together and having a liberal discussion of matters which are of general concern." Sakai went on to state that the Japanese had also discussed "the question of rendering assistance to the United States, our adopted country, during the war crisis." He said that they had expressed a desire "to assist in any manner possible" and would cooperate with Red Cross auxiliary work. He declared, "We are in the United States to make our permanent home. We are doing better here than we could possibly do in Japan, hence we wish to remain. And we feel that it is up to us to do all possible for the country which gives us better opportunities, when that country is in trouble." Sakai concluded that the local Japanese were ready to meet to discuss "matters of general interest to farmers."[29]

In July 1917, the Yakima Japanese Association established an agriculture department in order to promote the progress of the Japanese and to improve their relations with white farmers. The department was to deal with land lease affairs, research on agriculture, labor recruiting agreements, prevention and mediation of conflict between farmers, and other relevant issues. The agriculture department worked successfully to promote farming cooperatives, crop grading regulations, and the appointment of melon inspectors. It also set up rules concerning leases. Those who wanted to lease land had to declare to the agriculture department the address, the number of acres, and ownership of the land to be leased. They would be allowed to start negotiation of the lease after it was ascertained that no one else had made a declaration for that lease. They were required to inform the agriculture department of the results within two days, unless there was a reasonable cause for the delay. The declaration of intent to lease could be cancelled at any time by the individual. Those who intended to renew their present lease had priority to do so. Individuals were required to report to the agriculture department if they abandoned their right to lease or failed to establish a renewal lease. The agriculture department kept records of lease applications, and in case there were two or more applicants, the right was offered on a first-come, first-served basis.[30]

In countering anti-Japanese sentiment against Issei sugar beet growers and laborers, the Yakima Japanese Association took its case directly to white business interests. Representatives of the association attended a meeting at the Toppenish Commercial Club concerning the establishment of the sugar beet factory in the Yakima Valley. Pointing to the economic importance of Japanese growers and labor, they got the group to cooperate in suppressing the anti-Japanese movement and to establish a beet growers' union to check weight of the beets, soil condition, and seeds and to elect officers for negotiation and general inspection.[31] The association continued to work with the Utah-Idaho Sugar Company to counter the anti-Japanese movement.

The Issei thus countered the anti-Japanese movement in the Yakima Valley by combining a measure of accommodation with resistance. They came together to strategize and implement formal, organized action to forcefully argue for and maintain their economic livelihood in the Yakima Valley.

World War I

The entry of the United States into World War I on April 6, 1917, put the anti-Japanese movement on pause. Japanese were no longer the straw man potential enemy "who may at any moment be called upon by their mother country to take up arms against America." There was now a declared enemy, Germany, and Germans had become the enemy aliens. On April 9, a day after the Yakima Japanese Association had decided on countermeasures to the anti-Japanese movement started by Benz, the Commission of Indian Affairs sent Yakama Agency Superintendent Don M. Carr a telegram stating that the "War situation makes it imperative that every tillable acre of land on Indian reservations be intensively cultivated this season to supply food demands, particularly wheat, beans, potatoes, corn and meat. Call farmers and leading Indians together immediately for organized united effort under your continuous supervision. This is of the highest importance and requires aggressive action. There must be no delay in anything necessary to insure result."[32] Rather than expelling the Japanese, the cooperation of Japanese farmers was now needed for this "united effort." The federal government in this wartime crisis marked increased agricultural production as a vital act of patriotism. The cooperation of the Japanese farmers was thus recognized as critical to wartime production and to the economic success of the Yakima Valley.

In August 1917 the Potato Growers Association of the Yakima Valley elected three Japanese, Kay Moriyama, G. Suzuki and S. Hirano, to the executive board of the association.[33] The *Wapato Independent* described the newly elected Japanese executive board members as "all influential Oriental potato growers." The newspaper wrote that the Japanese controlled two thousand acres of potatoes on the reservation in 1917 and that their "cooperation" was being sought. The president of the Potato Growers Association, F. Benz, a brother of Hans Benz, needed to gain the cooperation of the Japanese potato farmers to agree to sell their potatoes for not less than $25 a ton that fall.[34] To maintain the highest price possible for their crops, white growers had to get Japanese potato farmers to agree to not market their crops below the $25-per-ton opening price. The election of the three Japanese to the association's executive board recognized the presence and importance of Japanese farmers on the reservation.

During World War I the "local" Japanese community not only demonstrated their patriotism through economic cooperation and production, but they were also mindful of displaying their community spirit by regularly contributing patriotic floats to the Yakima City Fourth of July parades and by contributing monetarily to the war effort. The theme of their 1917 Fourth of July float was the Liberty Bell ringing liberty all around the world.

Japanese names were especially prominent in the Liberty Loan campaigns of 1917. The Liberty Loan Act was a war finance measure to issue convert-

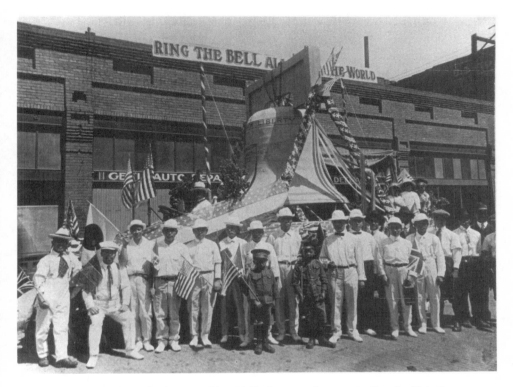

FIG. 3.1 *The theme for the 1917 Yakima Valley Japanese Community Fourth of July float was the Liberty Bell ringing liberty around the world. (Harry Honda Collection)*

ible gold bonds for public subscription. Local campaign committees were organized in the Wapato district of the reservation. The *Wapato Independent,* whose editor, William Verran, was the chairman of the advertising committee for the local Liberty Loan campaign, declared that "The patriotism of the American people will come to the front in support of the government in its effort to preserve democracy and freedom to the people of the earth."[35] The Wapato-Donald district committee raised nearly double their quota. W. K. Hirano and Shu Matsushita, who chaired the Wapato district committee's fund raising from Japanese on the reservation, collected $6,000 out of a total district contribution of $35,000. The local newspaper asserted that the generous contributions indicated that "in no section of the country are the people more patriotic."[36] The newspaper published a list of names of those who had contributed on its front page, and Japanese names were prominently present.[37]

Japanese farmers were also prominent contributors to the Red Cross fundraising drive in the Valley. Japanese names prominently appeared in the newspaper list of Red Cross fund contributors "who assisted in the generous total for Wapato District."[38] The newspaper listed contributors by "teams," with individual as well as team total contributions noted. Japanese participated in the fund drive in a multi-ethnic team and a nearly all-Japanese team. The multi-ethnic team was led by William Norbert Luby, manager of the Wapato Trading Company and stockholder in the Union State Bank, and included such prominent whites as Alexander E. McCredy, founder of the town of Wapato and president and owner of its first bank, the Wapato State Bank, and William Verran, editor of the *Wapato Independent*. K. Takahashi was a top contributor for the multi-ethnic team, which donated the largest amount of all the teams. There were about eighty-five Japanese contributors to the fund.[39] Years later, in defending the presence of Japanese on the reservation, a Japanese spokesperson argued that Japanese should be given credit for "patriotic purchase of liberty bonds and Red Cross subscriptions during the war."[40] Patriotic performances were critical to those seeking incorporation into the nation while being denied the rights and responsibilities of citizenship.

Wartime Anti-Japanese Agitation

While most scholars agree that widespread anti-Japanese agitation went into abeyance during World War I,[41] the exclusionists did not stop their efforts to oust the Japanese from the Yakama Indian Reservation. Realizing that removal of Japanese from the reservation required action by the federal government, the McKinley Grange #596 of Yakima County in April 1918 drafted a resolution containing the same arguments presented at the 1917 Wapato meeting. The resolution was sent in May to President Woodrow Wilson, Secretary of the Interior Franklin K. Lane, Indian Commissioner Cato Sells, U.S. Senators Wesley L. Jones and Miles Poindexter, U.S. Representative William LaFollette, and Yakama Agency Superintendent Don M. Carr. The McKinley Grange resolution noted that there was a critical need for "maximum food production" during the "great world war" but that "scores of Reservation farms are being leased by the Indian Department to aliens and persons incapable of American citizenship, who have no interest in permanent roads, economical government, good schools and churches, or in the education, social, political and religious life of the community; who do not assimilate with other races here, and whose standard of living is a constant menace to genuine progress."[42] Grange members called for "the timely enactment of laws and departmental rules" to prohibit "the farther leasing of United States Indian Reservation lands to persons other than citizens or intending citizens of the United States, until citizen farmers have been accommodated. . . ."[43] They argued that such a restriction would not only maximize food production but ensure that the "production, sale, and distribution of farm products, may be under control of persons whose citizenship or intending citizenship tends to a greater degree of loyalty and patriotic devotion to our country, than is apt to be true of persons who owe allegiance to another government and cannot become citizens of these United States."[44] The wording of the resolution left some room for interpretation in that in opposing the "farther" leasing of land to aliens "until citizen farmers have been accommodated," the Grange, in recognizing the national wartime imperative for agricultural production, did not specifically oppose the renewal of existing leases to local Japanese.

Faced with persistent anti-Japanese sentiment, the superintendent for the Yakama Indian Reservation, Don M. Carr, had worked out a compromise with the Yakima Japanese Association in which the Yakama Agency would consider "the renewal of leases to satisfactory Japanese tenants, with the understanding that no additional applications for leases from Japanese would be considered, nor would Japanese tenants of the renewal class be permitted to increase their acreage."[45]

Despite this agreement, the local Japanese found it difficult to regulate the influx of nonlocal Japanese hoping to profit from the wartime economic boom. Japanese farmers steadily increased their acreage and numbers of leases on the reservation.

Postwar Agitation and Alien Land Law

Anti-Japanese agitation in West Coast states grew in the post–World War I years with the resurgence of super patriotism and fear of the foreign, stimulated by the Bolshevik revolution and growth of radicalism at home and increasing uneasiness with perceived Japanese military aggression.[46] More concretely, those xenophobes inclined to oppose Japanese immigrants channeled their hostility into a defense of veterans' preferences. In California, a renewed postwar anti-Japanese movement combined the forces of politicians with the Native Sons and Native Daughters of the Golden West, the American Legion, the California State Federation of Labor, and the California State Grange to pass a referendum in 1920 to plug the loopholes in the 1913 alien land law.[47] Not fully satisfied with just state level action against the Japanese, exclusionists in California after 1920 turned to enacting a federal prohibition of Japanese immigration.[48]

In Washington State, similar alliances between politicians, the American Legion, and the Anti-Japanese League combined to push for a tightening of their alien land laws, leading the Washington State Legislature to pass in 1921 and 1923 further anti-alien land laws that prohibited not only land ownership by aliens who had not declared in good faith their intention to become U.S. citizens, but also prohibited their leasing, renting, and sharecropping of land. The laws also disqualified aliens from acting as trustee, executor, administrator, or guardian of an estate that included land. Lands held by such aliens were to be escheated to the state.[49] Japanese were thus by state law dispossessed of their land in Washington except on the Yakama Indian Reservation, where state law did not apply to federally administered land.

It was clear to exclusionists that federal intervention was necessary to completely remove Japanese from farming in Washington. The Yakama Indian Reservation was seen as pivotal in securing a federal anti-Japanese land policy, not just state law. Exclusionists stepped up their calls for formal prohibition against leasing reservation lands to Japanese. Although federal laws did indeed prohibit land ownership of federal lands by aliens, it did not prohibit the leasing of such lands by aliens. Exclusionists groups such as the Grange and the American Legion pressured the Department of the Interior, under Secretary Albert B. Fall, to make federal leasing policy governing reservation land conform to the Washington State anti-alien land laws.[50]

Representatives of the Wapato Post of the American Legion reported at a July 1920 meeting of the American Legion in Yakima that Japanese were out-competing "Americans" in the acquisition of lease land on the reservation. In a gendered argument, they asserted that "American" farmers could not compete with Japanese because the Japanese used "his women" to work in the fields with their small children strapped to their backs. Completely ignoring the vital role of women in U.S. agriculture, they declared that although some American women might be willing to labor in the fields like the Japanese women, American husbands would not even consider the idea. The American Legion agreed to work with the Wapato Post to provide information on the "Japanese situation" in the Yakima Valley to the congressional committee investigating immigration headed by Representative Albert Johnson.[51]

The state convention of the American Legion met in Spokane in December 1920 and passed a resolution against the leasing of reservation land to

Japanese. In response to a report and resolution from the Wapato Post, the Sunnyside Post No. 73 of the American Legion in the Yakima Valley sent a protest on January 25, 1921, to Secretary of the Interior John Barton Payne "against the continuance of the practice of leasing the Yakami [*sic*] Indian Reservation Lands to Japanese."[52] Copies of their protest were sent to U.S. Senators Wesley L. Jones and Miles Poindexter and to U.S. Representative John W. Summers.

The James J. Sexton Post #224 Veterans of Foreign Wars of Aberdeen, Washington, wrote to the secretary of the interior and U.S. Bureau of Indian Affairs charging that "We are rapidly approaching the following condition throughout the West: Either the Jap must leave, or the white man will have to live [*sic*]. The white man cannot live in competition with the Jap. Are you going to allow the future inhabitant of Our West to be a Mongolian, or a Hybred [*sic*]. Will you save America for the American; if so we urge you and request you to use all possible influence to put a stop to the leasing of lands to the Japanese either directly or through renegade white men."[53]

Issei farmers on the Yakama Reservation continued to build their case that as "local" Japanese they were integral, contributing members of the Yakima Valley community. They demonstrated their commitment to the Yakima Valley community through their donations. For Christmas 1921, the Issei gave $225 to the Wapato schools "in appreciation of the educational opportunities given Japanese children in the community."[54] School officials said they would use the money to purchase new reference books for the school library.

Again, utilizing the strategic display of *gaimendoka,* external assimilation, and *naimendoka,* internal assimilation, advocated by many West Coast Issei leaders and incorporated in the Pacific Coast Japanese Association Deliberative Council Americanization campaign,[55] the local Yakima Japanese Association tried to respond to the accusations of exclusionists that they could not assimilate into American society. The *Wapato Independent* reported on February 22, 1922, in a front-page article, that "Local Japanese have decided upon a plan of practical Americanization through actual contact with Americans in their homes."[56] This plan of "practical Americanization" involved having an "American" woman who was able to speak Japanese live with Japanese families for a week to "teach her American ideals of child hygiene, social customs, and home comfort."

But the anti-Japanese forces were able to persuade Secretary Fall to revise reservation leasing policies to conform to state alien land laws. After visiting the Yakama Indian Reservation and other reservations, Secretary Fall instructed the issuance of written instructions to all Indian agents on all reservations that there be no renewal of leases and no new leases made to any aliens or persons who were not citizens of the United States. Preference rights were to be given to the returned soldiers of the United States.[57] Again, it is noteworthy to see how veterans' preferences were used to legitimize racist practices.

Before the circular was approved on March 15, 1922, Yakima Valley Issei farmers sent Fall a telegram asking him to clarify the policy of the Department of the Interior with regard to leasing of land to Japanese on the Yakama Indian Reservation.[58] Fall claimed that no discrimination against the Japanese was intended, but that this policy was a general one in the interests of American citizens and, in particular, American veterans. However, it was a fact that non-Asian aliens could avoid the prohibition on leasing to aliens on federal reservations by taking out first papers for naturalization. Japanese on the Yakama Indian Reservation did not have that option, since as aliens ineligible for citizenship they could not declare their intent to become citizens by taking out first papers for naturalization.

Building Support for Maintenance of Local Japanese

After receiving Secretary Fall's letter, the Yakima Japanese Association devised a strategy to gain support for the continued leasing of reservation land by Japanese. First the association urged the Japanese to share existing leases and land with one another and avoid subleasing on the reservation. It urged the Japanese to further Americanize their lifestyle and buy as many commodities as possible from local shops. Leaders were elected to secure wider support for rescinding the order prohibiting leasing of reservation land to Japanese.

Another strategy utilized their economic leverage. The Wapato Japanese Commercial Club had previously joined the Wapato Chamber of Commerce at a cost of $500 a year. It appealed to the chamber for political support. In a key move, Issei leaders ensured the dependency of local businesses on the continued patronage and services of Japanese. For example, Issei had deposited money in key local banks, and thus local banks stood to suffer severe financial losses if their Japanese clientele had to close accounts and leave the area suddenly. Appeals were sent to churches, the Indian Council, Indian Chamber of Commerce, and English newspapers. In a bold move, the Yakima Japanese Association organized a meeting with the mayor of Wapato and twenty-eight influential whites in December 1922. The association also sent opinions from local activists to the Japanese Embassy in Washington, D.C., in hopes of the solving the problem through diplomatic channels.[59] Thus, the Yakima Japanese Association implemented a multi-faceted strategy to resist exclusion from reservation farming through ethnic cooperation, Americanization, moral pleas, media campaigns, appeals for diplomatic intervention, working with Yakama Indian organizations, and creating economic dependencies on the continued presence of local Japanese.

The campaign was successful in drawing widespread support for the Japanese farmers. Between December 1922 and January 1923, Secretary Fall's mail was inundated with letters and telegrams from Yakima Valley residents, businesses, and churches advocating the rescinding of Fall's order to extend the state anti-alien land law to reservation lands. The Ministerial Association of Yakima and Vicinity and the Seattle Council of Churches separately telegrammed Secretary Fall stating that they deplored the ruling and requested leniency for the Japanese.[60]

Letters from The First National Bank in Toppenish and the Union State Bank in Wapato attested to the industriousness and good credit of the Japanese and to the adverse financial consequences for the community if the Japanese were forced off the reservation.[61] According to the letter from Union State Bank cashier Lon Boyle, in 1921 Japanese farmers produced an early crop which "exceeded 500 cars of melons, tomatoes and the like" and that netted "a safe average of $400.00 per car." Boyle stated that "Two Hundred Thousand Dollars flowing into a community in the months of August and September is an item of such interest that one would hardly expect its elimination without some objection on the part of the business houses that benefit from it."[62] J. E. Bacon of Bacon & Prentice, a Wapato produce buyer and warehouse, declared that the Japanese reservation farmers were "above the average farmer to deal with" and were "honorable, honest and always ready to keep their word with you." Bacon asserted that the Japanese contributed to diversified farming, which was essential to the needs of the community, and that the early returns on their truck crops, which they deposited in local banks, provided "a means to the other farmers (whites) to secure some of this money in the way of loans from the banks to further carry on their work and harvesting."[63]

Wapato physician J. H. Ragsdale pointed out that "The Japanese are not an obstruction to efficient white men. The latter are learning to emulate them. . . . A certain type of white man who could not make a living on rent from land, is very outspoken against any one as thrifty as the Japanese."

Ragsdale further noted the specious arguments about unfair labor competition: "the American Legion is agitating against the Japanese but very few veterans of foreign wars are contemplating work on a farm. Most of this propaganda is due to collectors of political capital."[64]

In light of the 1917 anti-Japanese campaign of Hans Benz, it is instructive to note that an H. C. Benz, writing for Benz Brothers & Company, stated, "We believe that as a class [the Japanese] have proven themselves exceptional farmers, being unusually diligent in their work. They have thus added much to the improvement of our reservation and have placed a large acreage of heretofor [sic] waste lands under cultivation." He went on to say "Our business relations with them as a people have always been satisfactory. We have found them prompt in meeting business obligations and honest in the settlement of their transactions." Benz concluded, "If they now must go, subject to recent ruling by the Secretary of Interior, we feel our locality will loose [sic] a very worthy and particularly progressive set of business men and farmers."[65]

Letters of support repeatedly extolled the contributions of Japanese to the economic development of the reservation and Yakima Valley. F. Stanley Millichamp, a wholesale fruit and produce buyer, warehouseman, and shipper, claimed that had it not been for the "untiring work" of the Japanese in "clearing up, improving and cultivating of these arid lands," thousands of acres of land would remain in "arid condition to-day."[66] Form letters signed by scores of residents of the Yakima Valley stated similar views, and one writer concluded that "There is ample land for all and I have no objection to Japanese farmers as neighbors."[67]

A prominent Yakama Indian, Nealy N. Olney, in his capacity as secretary for the Yakima Indian Commercial Club, wrote Secretary Fall presenting the Yakama perspective and support for the continued presence of Japanese farmers on the reservation. Olney claimed that Fall's ruling ending farming of reservation lands by Japanese and "forbidding any farmer or Indian in hiring them on their farms" was "a very detrimental ruling to all classes of people on the Reservation. It may help some to monopolize the Indian lands and not help the ones intended." Based on his "more than fifteen years" of experience with Japanese farmers on the Yakama Indian Reservation, Olney "found them in all dealings honest and very industrious, and in almost every case ready and willing to carry out the provisions of the leases made with the government." He said, "When they have the money they pay their rents more promptly than the white renters and in most cases take better care of the land. They make good neighbors in every way. They are more

law abiding than most any other class of farmers on our reservation. . . ."
Olney asserted that the Japanese were "the class of farmers that has built
the reservation up to its present production and value. . . . They helped to
improve considerable of the raw lands of the Yakima Indian Reservation."[68]

Olney pointed to the role of Japanese farmers in World War I. "They were
one of the main helps in time of the great war in raising production so as
we could successfully carry on the war." He further noted, "They paid good
rents so as to enable the Indians to buy considerable Liberty bonds, with
surplus money, and which also helped in the time of need." Olney concluded
by stating, "In my belief I think they deserve better treatment than is made
under your ruling. I believe they deserve some consideration for what they
have done as above setforth [sic]. I believe they should be given a specified
time in which to arrange to close up their business in the valley and not be
forced to leave with unpaid obligations." Olney reiterated the request by
the Yakama in an earlier letter to Fall requesting that "land between the
railroad track and the Yakima River be leased to the Japanese." He further
recommended that "the leases of all poor grade or worthless farmers be cancelled and that leases be granted to people, regardless of race, if they are
good farmers and will live up to the terms of the leases. . . ."[69]

Though this campaign did not lead to the rescinding of the order, the
Japanese secured widespread community support for their continued presence in the Yakima Valley. This support would help to maintain their presence on the reservation despite Secretary Fall's ruling.

The superintendent of the Yakama Indian Reservation, Don Carr, contested the Bureau of Indian Affairs' order to stop leasing to Japanese farmers by arguing that lands would go unleased and the Yakama would suffer
loss of income. The bureau ordered Carr to not issue any more leases to
Japanese farmers. Secretary Fall threatened removal of Superintendent Carr
if he did not comply with the bureau's orders: "Of course I can understand
that the Agent is more interested in getting all he can for the Indians, and
is not at all interested in the general administrative policy. If the present
Agent is so far committed that he feels it would be embarrassing to him to
carry out this policy, it might be well to consider transferring him to some
other equally good position in the Government and using some one as Agent
at Yakima who may not be embarrassed by such commitments."[70] By the
summer of 1923, Don Carr was indeed removed as superintendent of the
Yakama Indian Agency.

As a result of the application of Washington State anti-alien land laws
to the reservation lands, many Japanese farmers left for states that had not

as yet passed alien lands laws, such as Montana or Oregon, or entered service jobs. Others chose to remain on the reservation and sublease from
Yakama Indian allottees and white farmers through labor agreements.
Before such labor agreements could be drawn up, Issei farmers still pos-
sessing unexpired leases shared their tracts with those who had lost leases.
Efforts were made by exclusionists to end any Japanese farming by seeking to prohibit even wage labor by Japanese on reservation land. But this
measure was not passed because such an extreme discriminatory prohibition restricting a legal resident's basic means of economic livelihood would
have serious civil liberties implications for all people and would reduce the
labor pool available for agriculturalists.

There had been more land available than could be leased by the other
white farmers. If these reservation allotments could not be leased, the Indian
allottee received no income from it. From the mid-1920s the Issei increasingly cultivated a direct relationship with the Yakama Indians in negotiat-
ing directly with the Yakama allottee rather than through the Yakama Indian
Agency. The issue of who controlled ownership and use of the land was now
foregrounded. The Bureau of Indian Affairs was supposed to administer
this land for the benefit of the Indians. The Yakama began to assert themselves as being "competent" to manage their own land and assert their right
to determine who could work and lease their land. Technically the Japanese
did not have the right to lease, since the alien land laws were being followed
on the federally administered reservation lands. What developed was the
utilization of labor agreements. The Yakama owner would say that he was
hiring the Japanese immigrant at a certain rate to work his land. Everyone
knew that this was a form of subleasing. But the Japanese developed a legal
labor agreement that was able to survive court scrutiny.[71] There was an
interim period between 1922 and 1930 when labor agreements were drawn
between Yakama and Japanese. The Yakima Valley Issei wrote that "the anti-
Japanese land law. . . . was not flawless. . . . However strict the laws may be
anyone who tries to ignore individual rights, the international treaty, and
the rights enjoyed by every U.S. citizen is to lose in the end."[72]

The Issei were determined to retain a place for themselves in the Yakima
Valley and struggled to survive until they were able to reestablish their right
to farm through their citizen children, the Nisei. Although the Issei were
prohibited from becoming naturalized citizens by law, the Nisei, by their
U.S. birth, could not be denied citizenship. As the Nisei reached maturity
they were able to directly lease or buy land for themselves and their parents
and other noncitizen Japanese farmers who farmed land through labor

agreements with the Nisei. By the early 1930s the Japanese community, through their Nisei children, had reached a level of economic stability. Although acreage farmed decreased from a high of 12,000 acres in 1922 to 4,000 acres in 1932, Issei farmers had switched from large-scale farming in potatoes to small-scale, labor intensive farming (tomatoes, cantaloupes, onions, corn), so gross earnings remained almost the same.[73]

"Local" Japanese

Exclusionist legislation and pressure to restrict the Japanese American community's economic livelihood led to the building of ethnic community identity and mobilization to protect and promote their ethnic interests. Presenting themselves as "local" Japanese who contributed to the economic and social development of the Yakima Valley, Japanese immigrants were able to build recognition, support, and cooperation from significant segments of the wider community through their political mobilization and adaptive strategies.[74] In a 1939 dissertation, sociologist John Rademaker wrote about the relationship of Japanese with whites in the Yakima Valley, concluding that "The Japanese farmers of this community have established cordial and close relationships with their white neighbors."[75] On the eve of World War II the "local" Japanese appeared to have naturalized themselves into the landscape of the Yakima Valley.

The Issei viewed themselves as pioneers and took great pride in their ability to economically survive in the Yakima Valley. Symbolic of their commitment to remain in the Yakima Valley and of their ethnic community identity was their contribution in 1932, in the midst of the Great Depression, of seventy-four cherry trees to Tahoma Cemetery. The cherry trees also symbolized the rooting of the Japanese American community in the Yakima Valley and the blossoming of their Nisei citizen-children. A few of the aging cherry trees planted in 1932 still bloom every spring in Tahoma Cemetery to decorate the final resting place of pioneering Issei. The cherry trees serve to remind all of the historical presence of Japanese Americans in the Yakima Valley.

Notes

I thank Eichiro Azuma, Roger Daniels, Gail Dubrow, Louis Fiset, and Sucheta Mazumdar for their helpful comments and suggestions.

1. Yakima Nihonjin-kai, *Yakima Heigen Nihonjin-shi* (History of the Japanese in the Yakima Valley) (Yakima, Wash.: Yakima Nihonjin-kai, 1935), 21. See also Masako Notoji, "From Graveyard to Baseball: The Quest for Ethnic Identity in the Prewar Japanese Immigrant Community in the Yakima Valley," *The Japanese Journal of American Studies* 3 (1989): 29–63.

2. Yakima Nihonjin-kai, *Yakima Heigen Nihonjin-shi*, 23.

3. In 1994 the Yakama Tribal Council adopted Resolution T-053–94, which restored the spelling of Yakima to Yakama "in accordance to our Treaty's original spelling of June 9, 1855." Resolution T-053–94, January 14, 1994, Yakama Nation Records Management/Archives, Wapato, Washington. Except in direct quotations, when I refer to the Yakama Indian Reservation and the Yakama people, I use this spelling, and when I refer to the city of Yakima and to the Yakima Valley, I retain the geographic spellings.

4. U.S. Department of the Interior, Bureau of Indian Affairs, Planning Support Group, Report No. 235, *Yakima Indian Reservation, Agricultural Potential* (Billings, Mont.: n.p., 1976), 43–70. For an account of the development of irrigation agriculture in the Yakima Valley, see Joyce Benjamin Kuhler, "A History of Agriculture in the Yakima Valley, Washington from 1880 to 1900" (master's thesis, University of Washington, 1940) and Richard Morgan Highsmith, Jr., "Irrigation Agriculture in the Yakima Valley" (master's thesis, University of Washington, 1946).

5. See Ernest Melvin Loudon, "A Study of the Federal Government Indian Land Politics and the Yakima Indian Confederation, 1855–1934" (master's thesis, Washington State University, 1967), 30, 89, 122–27; and Census 1920 (June 30), Yakima Indian Agency RG75 Yakima 1917–21, M595, Indian Census Rolls, 1885–1940, roll 674, National Archives and Records Administration (NARA), Pacific Alaska Region (Seattle).

6. Yakima Nihonjin-kai, *Yakima Heigen Nihonjin-shi*, 20.

7. Ibid., 16.

8. In 1922 the U.S. Supreme Court ruled in *United States v Ozawa* that white meant Caucasian, and therefore Japanese who were of the "Mongolian race" could not become naturalized U.S. citizens. For a detailed discussion of Japanese immigrants and U.S. naturalization, see Yuji Ichioka, *The Issei: The World of the First Generation Japanese Immigrants, 1885–1924* (New York: Free Press, 1988), 210–26.

9. Kazuo Ito, *Issei: A History of Japanese Immigrants in North America,* trans. Shinichiro Nakamura and Jean S. Gerard (Seattle: Executive Committee for Publication of Issei: A History of Japanese Immigrants in North America, 1973), 430.

10. See leases for Yakama Indian Reservation land in Record Group 75, NARA, Pacific Alaska Region (Seattle).

11. Ito, *Issei,* 427.

12. See Roger Daniels, *The Politics of Prejudice: The Anti-Japanese Movement in California and the Struggle for Japanese Exclusion* (Berkeley: University of California Press, 1962).

13. It should be noted that this anti-Asian exclusion movement in Washington was preceded by exclusion of Native Hawaiians. In 1849 during the territorial organization of Oregon, which included present-day Washington State, Hawaiians were denied the right to become American citizens, and in 1850 they were denied the right to claim land. Denied citizenship and the right to claim land, many Hawaiians returned to Hawaii or moved to California, where they were still valued for their seamanship. Many others intermarried with Indians and remained. See Janice K. Duncan, *Minority without a Champion: Kanakas on the Pacific Coast, 1788–1850* (Portland: Oregon Historical Society, 1972); Milton Bona, "Hawaiians Made Life 'More Bearable,'" *Fort Vancouver Historical Society* 12 (1972): 158–75; and E. Momilani Naughton, "Hawaiians in the Fur Trade: Cultural Influence on the Northwest Coast, 1811–1875" (master's thesis, Western Washington University, 1983).

14. One of the first measures adopted by the newly created Washington territorial legislature in 1853 was a law denying the Chinese voting rights. Additional laws were adopted by the territorial legislature in 1863 to bar Chinese from testifying in court cases involving whites. In 1864 a poll tax was levied on Chinese living in Washington territory, an act whose title clearly stated its racist intent, "An Act to Protect Free White Labor Against Competition with Chinese Coolie Labor and to Discourage the Immigration of Chinese in the Territory."

15. "Reservation Crops Bring Good Money," *Wapato Independent*, 8 January 1917.

16. U.S. Congress. House. Committee on Immigration and Naturalization, *Japanese Immigration Hearings*. 66th Congress, 2nd session, Part 4, Hearings at Seattle and Tacoma, Wash. (Washington, D.C.: Government Printing Office, 1921), 1106–7.

17. "Farmers Want Japs Assert Sugar Beet Men," *Toppenish Tribune*, 1 March 1917.

18. Ibid.

19. Ibid.

20. "Jap Scorns Charge His Countrymen a Menace," *Toppenish Tribune*, 9 March 1917.

21. "Jap Problem Is Discussed by Farmers," *Toppenish Tribune*, 22 March 1917.

22. Ibid.

23. Ibid.

24. Ibid.

25. Daniels, *Politics of Prejudice*, 74–75.

26. Yakima Nihonjin-kai, *Yakima Heigen Nihonjin-shi*, 154.

27. Ibid., 169.

28 Ibid., 80–82. Compare with the adaptive strategies of *gaimenteki doka* and

naimenteki doka, advocated by Japanese leaders in California. See Ichioka, *The Issei,* 176–96.

29. "Would Regulate Prices for Leases," *Wapato Independent,* 19 April 1917.

30. Yakima Nihojin-kai, *Yakima Heigen Nihonjin-shi,* 80–82.

31. Ibid., 43.

32. The telegram was reprinted in "Intensive Farming on Reservation," *Wapato Independent,* 19 April 1917.

33. "Potato Growers Plan for Future," *Toppenish Tribune,* 24 August 1917.

34. "$25 Not Too Much for Spuds—Benz," *Wapato Independent,* 23 August 1917.

35. "Liberty Loan Campaign On," *Wapato Independent,* 11 October 1917.

36. "Big Contributions for Liberty Loan," *Wapato Independent,* 25 October 1917. To this sum was added $15,000 contributed from the Donald section of the reservation for a grand total of $50,000 for the reservation.

37. "Is Your Name Among the List, Those Who Made It Possible for the Wapato-Donald District to Exceed Liberty Loan Quota," *Wapato Independent,* 8 November 1917.

38. "Contributors to Red Cross Fund," *Wapato Independent,* 5 July 1917.

39. Ibid., 5 and 12 July 1917.

40. "Itow Appears before Legions," *Wapato Independent,* 26 October 1922. For an assessment of Japanese monetary contributions to the war effort, see Michinari Fujita, "The Japanese Associations in America," *Sociology and Social Research* 13 (1929): 225–26. Fujita claims that Japanese contributions per capita were significant.

41. For example, see Daniels, *Politics of Prejudice,* 64, and Izumi Hirobe, *Japanese Pride, American Prejudice, Modifying the Exclusion Clause of the 1924 Immigration Act* (Stanford: Stanford University Press, 2001), 5.

42. Resolution of McKinley Grange, #596, 21 May 1918, RG 75, NARA, Pacific Alaska Region (Seattle).

43. Ibid.

44. Ibid.

45. Superintendent [Don M. Carr] to Kay Moryama [*sic*] , President, Japanese Association, 30 October 1920, RG 75, NARA, Pacific Alaska Region (Seattle). Carr reminded Moriyama of their verbal agreement in this letter, in which he complained that the increase in Japanese making lease applications in the fall of 1920 was violating their mutual agreement.

46. See Daniels, *Politics of Prejudice,* 65–78, for a discussion on the fear of the Yellow Peril.

47. Ibid., 79–91.

48. Ibid., 92–105.

49. For a discussion of the passage of the 1921 and 1923 alien land laws and their

impact on Japanese farmers, see John Isao Nishinoiri, "Japanese Farms in Washington" (master's thesis, University of Washington, 1926), John Adrian Rademaker, "The Ecological Position of the Japanese Farmers in the State of Washington" (Ph.D. diss., University of Washington, 1939), especially 17–112, and Douglas Roscoe Pullen, "The Administration of Washington State Governor Louis F. Hart, 1919–1925" (Ph.D. diss., University of Washington, 1974), 219–60.

50. For an excellent account of the anti-Japanese movement in the Yakima Valley based on newspaper reports of the period (especially analyzes the reporting of the *Wapato Independent*), see Thomas H. Heuterman, *The Burning Horse, Japanese-American Experience in the Yakima Valley, 1920–1942* (Cheney, Wash.: Eastern Washington University Press, 1995).

51. Information from *Yakima Morning Herald*, 29 July 1920, as reprinted in "American Legion Scores Japanese," *Wapato Independent*, 29 July 1920.

52. Sunnyside Post, No. 73, American Legion to John Barton Payne, Secretary of the Interior, 25 January 1921, RG 75, NARA, Pacific Alaska Region (Seattle).

53. Memorial of James J. Sexton Post #224, Veterans of Foreign Wars, 3 February 1921, RG 75, NARA, Pacific Alaska Region (Seattle).

54. "Japanese Present $225 To Schools for Xmas," *Wapato Independent*, 5 January 1922.

55. For a discussion of Issei views on adaptation to U.S. society, see Ichioka, *The Issei*, 176–96.

56. "Japanese Will Try Americanization," *Wapato Independent*, 2 February 1922, p. 1.

57. U.S. Department of the Interior, Circular No. 1768, February 27, 1922, RG 75, NARA, Pacific Alaska Region (Seattle).

58. Yakima Japanese Association (by W. K. Hirano) to A. B. Falls, 3 March 1922, RG 75, National Archives, Washington, D.C.

59. Yakima Nihonjinkai, *Yakima Heigen Nihonjinshi*, 90–93.

60. Telegram from W. A. Henry to Secretary of the Interior, 19 December 1922, and telegram from Russel F. Trap to Hon. Albert B. Fall, 21 December 1922, Record Group 48, National Archives, Washington, D.C. The next day the Rainier Noble Post of the American Legion in Seattle sent a telegram that condemned the Ministerial Association of Yakima and Vicinity resolution. Ewing D. Colvin to Hon Albert B. Fall, 20 December 1922, RG 48, National Archives, Washington, D.C.

61. See John G. Phlliose, The First National Bank, Toppenish, Washington, To Whom It May Concern, 21 December 1922; Lon Boyle, Cashier, Union State Bank to Mr. A. B. Fall, Secretary of the Interior, 20 December 1922; A. C. Ness, President of The Union State Bank, to Hon. Secretary Fall, 26 December 1922; RG 48, National Archives, Washington, D.C.

62. Boyle to Fall, 20 December 1922.

63. J. E. Bacon, To Whom It May Concern, 23 December 1922, RG 48, National Archives, Washington, D.C.

64. J. H. Ragsdale, M.D., To whom it concerns, 20 December 1922, RG 48, National Archives, Washington, D.C.

65. Benz Brothers & Company (by H. C. Benz, Vice President/Manager), To Whom It May Concern, 23 December 1922, RG 48, National Archives, Washington, D.C.

66. F. Stanley Millichamp to Hon. A. B. Fall, 23 December 1922, RG 48, National Archives, Washington, D.C.

67. For example, see form letters dated November 1922, signed by C. W. Patterson, S. H. Olson, N. C. Hougton, Edward Bennett, John F. Phillips, Postmaster at Harrah, Washington, W. P. Johnson, and Joe Kuhn; RG 48, National Archives, Washington, D.C.

68. Nealy N. Olney to Hon. Albert B. Fall, 22 December 1922, RG 48, National Archives, Washington, D.C.

69. Ibid.

70. Albert B. Fall to The Commissioner of Indian Affairs, 1 July 1922, RG 48, National Archives, Washington, D.C.

71. For a discussion of how these labor agreements worked, see Gail M. Nomura, "Within the Law: The Establishment of Filipino Leasing Rights on the Yakima Indian Reservation," *Amerasia Journal* 13, no. 1 (1986–87): 99–117.

72. Yakima Nihonjin-kai, *Yakima Heigen Nihonjin-shi*, 163–64.

73. Ibid., 46, 256–57.

74. A similar type of "localization" is seen in the relationship of the Yamato Colony and the white Livingston community in California. The people of the Yamato Colony were referred to as "our Japanese," while the opposed influx of new Japanese forming the Cortez Colony was called "the Japanese." See Valerie Matsumoto, *Framing the Home Place, A Japanese American Community in California, 1919–1982* (Ithaca, N.Y.: Cornell University Press, 1993), 35.

75. Rademaker, "The Ecological Position of the Japanese Farmers," 175.

4 / YASUTARO YAMAGA

Fraser Valley Berry Farmer,
Community Leader, and Strategist

MICHIKO MIDGE AYUKAWA

The Fraser Valley of British Columbia was home to more than 550 Japanese Canadian families before the uprooting that followed the bombing of Pearl Harbor in December 1941.[1] The area north and south of the Fraser River, between New Westminster and Mission City, was the heart of the berry industry, which was virtually dominated by the Japanese by the late 1930s. After April 1949, when Japanese Canadians were finally allowed to return to "the protected area," only a small number resumed farming, since the vast majority of Japanese farms had been sold to the Veteran Land Administration in 1943 after confiscation by the Custodian of Enemy Properties.[2] This is one of the most striking examples of "Nikkei (dis)appearance" in the Pacific Northwest.

The story of the rocky road these pioneers were forced to travel has been told by Yasutaro Yamaga in his book *The History of the Haney Agricultural Association* (Hene'e nokai shi).[3] Yamaga was one of the most influential community leaders in the Fraser Valley agricultural community. He was charismatic, intelligent, and daring, and he urged integration with the mainstream populace—a rather radical idea at a time when many Japanese farmers were still emotionally tied to their land of birth. He continued his community work in the postwar period, and the fruits of his contributions are still enjoyed more than thirty years after his death in 1971. In a compendium of eminent Issei, Gordon G. Nakayama, an Anglican minister, wrote: "Yasutaro Yamaga is perhaps one of the most well known among Japanese leaders— in the farming field, in adult education, in the co-operative union movement, and in social work."[4]

Through the story of Yamaga's life and his efforts on behalf of his community, we can learn much about the history of the Japanese berry farmers

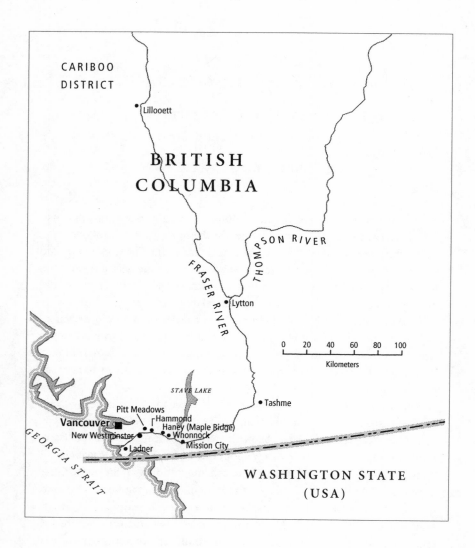

FIG. 4.1 *Map showing the Fraser River Valley berry farming area prior to World War II.*
(Map drawn by Tim DeLange Boom)

of the Fraser Valley. It is a tale of ambitious young men who emigrated with dreams of becoming landowners and settling down in a strange land. They were unlike the earlier and still more common Japanese emigrants who were *dekasegi rodo* (temporary migrant laborers). Wives later joined these venturesome farmers, and together they strove to succeed by sheer hard work. There were many obstacles they needed to contend with—the complexities of the market place, the enmity of the mainstream populace, and unfamiliar social customs. Moreover, there were the problems of rearing their children, who not only needed to be protected from feelings of inferiority but also from becoming strangers to their parents.

There is a dearth of information on the early years of Japanese settlement in Canada. I have relied mainly on two books published in 1921 by Jinshiro Nakayama.[5] Nakayama wrote laudatory short biographies of many prominent people in the community, including one of Yamaga. It is evident that as early as 1920 Yamaga had already made quite an impact on his fellow immigrants. His biography stated in part: "He has since childhood shown signs of brilliance. It is said that there was no one who could outdo him scholastically. He has robust health and is sincere. He is thoughtful and has foresight."[6]

In Yamaga's memoirs, very little information exists about his background in Japan.[7] He noted that he was born in 1886 in Toyohama village in Toyota county, Hiroshima prefecture. His village was located on a small island with a circumference of only five *ri* (one *ri* equals 2.44 miles), ten *ri* south of Kure, near Hiroshima city. It is one of many small islands in that area. While a few inhabitants on the island farmed, the majority survived by fishing.

Yamaga first went to the Seattle area and worked on the railroads. He moved to Canada in 1908 with a "dream of becoming the owner of five thousand acres of golden field in the Canadian Prairies"[8] (an assertion that is clearly overstated for effect). He did not explain how and why he had gone to Seattle first. In my research on Hiroshima emigrants to Canada, there were a number of stories of migration in both directions in the early years. It appeared as if the men (at times accompanied by their wives) simply followed job opportunities.[9] This movement between British Columbia and the U.S. Pacific Northwest flowed freely until 1907, when an executive order by President Theodore Roosevelt prohibited any alien from entering the United States if his passport had been issued for another destination.[10]

Yamaga wrote in his memoirs that while still in the United States, he had read in Canadian Japanese-language newspapers a number of articles written by Jiro Inouye, of the rural area of Haney in the Fraser Valley.[11] Inouye, a graduate of Waseda University of Tokyo, urged Japanese immigrants to go into agriculture. Presumably he invited Yamaga to join him, but Yamaga found it necessary to earn some money first by working in a shingle bolt camp. It is likely that he went to the Stave Lake area north of Haney, where many other men (and at times their wives) worked, felling tall cedar trees and sawing them into shingle bolt lengths of four feet four inches.[12] Yamaga then farmed with a partner until 1917, when he managed to buy twenty acres of land and finally became an independent farmer. He was then able to settle down, have a family, and help his fellow immigrants. He and Jiro Inouye were of like minds. They both believed "that in order to be accepted as a Canadian it was necessary to integrate."[13]

Years later, in 1962, now an elder in the community, Yamaga was urged by former Haney-area berry farmers to write *The History of the Haney Agricultural Association*. An invaluable record of the Japanese berry industry in the Haney (Maple Ridge) area of the Fraser Valley, his book details education of Japanese Canadian children, the relationship of the Japanese farmers with the mainstream populace, and the actions taken to alleviate racial tensions. Seven former executive members of the Haney cooperative, who were at that time living in various locations across Canada, corroborated the work. In a foreword, they wrote that most of the information had been gathered earlier for a publication that had been planned to commemorate Japan's 2600 year celebration (1940). We are truly fortunate that the groundwork had been laid over twenty years earlier when memories were still vivid.

In his history of Japanese agriculturalists in Haney, Yamaga writes about the *kusawake* (literally, "the ones who parted the grass"), the Japanese pioneers who farmed in various parts of the Fraser Valley. The earliest record of a Japanese farmer in the area is from 1904, when a man from Yamaguchi prefecture settled in Pitt Meadows.[14] By the early years of the second decade of the twentieth century, many individuals from various prefectures were farming in the Fraser Valley.

The relative ease of getting started and the desire for self-employment attracted many would-be farmers. It was possible to lease five acres of rough bush land with an agreement to clear the land within seven years. Although the lessee could clear small plots, plant strawberry plants, and reap a harvest within a year, it was necessary to supplement agricultural income with earnings from seasonal labor in the salmon fisheries and the lumber camps. Those who leased, cleared their land in the winter months. But this was a slow and arduous process, and seven years often passed before the land was barely half cleared. When this happened, the land was forfeited because the contract demanded that the whole property be cleared within seven years. Settlers soon realized that it was more prudent to use their summer earnings to buy land on the installment plan. Five or ten acres could be purchased at fifty dollars per acre, with a quarter down and the rest to be paid within three to four years at 6 percent interest.[15]

Individuals purchasing land were able to live rent-free because they built their own homes immediately. Yamaga wrote:

> We could not afford to buy lumber to build our houses so we helped each other by felling large cedar trees and bucking it [sic] into three feet lengths to make cedar shakes for the walls and roof of a shack. The unwritten law was for everyone to go to help their new neighbours, carrying their own tools and lunches. We cut out long and straight poles for studs and rafts [sic]. Thick shakes were laid on the ground for the floor. Bed and furniture were also made by hand; an apple box for a chair, etc. We used straw for our mattress.[16]

The only financial outlay was for windows and nails. House building and well digging were cooperative ventures that were also social events, with a great deal of eating and drinking. Yamaga further tells us:

> Money was scarce and our labour was cheap in those days. Often times we could not afford to buy stumping powder so we dug around the stumps of many feet in diameter with a mattock and shovel. In the hole dug underneath we would build a fire and burn it day after day. Some stump roots would take two weeks to burn. We planted strawberries as we cleared the land. . . .[17]

Yamaga's memoir went on to give a vivid description of early bachelor life, the drinking of *sake,* free-for-all fights, and raucous participation in the Armistice Day parade in 1918. "We sang at the top of our voices Russo-Japanese war songs which were the only songs we knew."[18] He wrote further:

> We settlers were all husky young men and seldom saw the opposite sex of our own race. We all felt the loneliness and emptiness of this life. Some found their way out of this by drinking, some by gambling.[19]

Eventually, after ten to fifteen years, a bachelor was able to build a frame house with lumber, and he was ready to send back to Japan for a wife, usually a picture bride. The picture bride system of marriage was a modification of the custom then prevalent, where marriage arrangements were made by the heads of families. In Japan the principals would have had an opportunity to meet face-to-face and presumably approve or disapprove of the selected mate. But when the husband-to-be resided overseas, decisions were often made after merely an exchange of photographs.[20] Yamaga wrote that many women found they had been misled by the photographs and were extremely distraught. Unable to return to Japan, most accepted their fate by remaining and assuming spousal duties. Some, he said, reiterated the folly of youth whenever they quarreled with their husbands.[21]

In the farming community, wives were brought in by mature men who were prepared to settle down and pursue dreams of becoming successful in their berry-growing ventures. On the other hand, sojourners entered marriages because their original dreams of returning to Japan after a few years had been thwarted by the low wages they had encountered as laborers in British Columbia and racism.

This racism can be tied back to the time of the mid-nineteenth-century gold rush in the upper Fraser River, when Chinese laborers migrated from the western United States to British Columbia. Their presence became increasingly noticeable when many more were imported from China to provide cheap labor on the railroads, and later in the mines and forests. Resentment by white laborers towards the Chinese escalated and was then directed towards Japanese immigrants as well.

The first Japanese in Canada is reputed to have been Manzo Nagano, who jumped ship at New Westminster in 1877. Others trickled in until 1891, when the first group of one hundred contract laborers arrived from Hiroshima.[22] Japanese immigrants continued to arrive gradually until 1907, when in the first ten months of that year the number rose precipitously to 8,125 in the wake of President Roosevelt's executive order.[23] White British Columbians claimed that Asian immigrants were "non-assimilable" and were undercutting the wages of white workers.

Hostility grew. The Asiatic Exclusion League, which was patterned after similar groups in Seattle, San Francisco, and other U.S. cities, organized an anti-Asian demonstration in Vancouver on September 9, 1907. It turned violent and resulted in a great deal of property damage in Chinatown and the Japanese section on Powell Street.[24] In the aftermath of the "Vancouver riot," the Lemieux-Hayashi Gentlemen's Agreement of 1908 was drawn up between Canada and Japan. The Gentlemen's Agreement not only decreased the number of male immigrants to four hundred per year, but also restricted them to domestic work or farm labor. Family members such as wives and children remained exempt, however. Hence, the immigration of women accelerated.

Yamaga placed great emphasis on the roles wives played in berry farming. He stated that not only did the wives work tirelessly alongside their husbands, but they also worked in their homes doing all the household chores. He wrote:

> The distinctive feature of labour on the Japanese berry farm is the women's share in it. The picture bride worked with pick and shovel with her husband when they cleared bush land to plant strawberries. Then hoeing and cultivating the berry patches beside her house chores. She would get up very early in the morning and go to bed at eleven at night. Upon rising in the morning, she fed the chickens and horses, then prepared breakfast, washed the dishes; after which she followed the family to the field where she may drive a horse with her husband, behind a plow or cultivator. She would come in shortly before dinner, prepare supper, and clean up then return to the field. During the berry picking season, she picked the berries or packed them, from dawn to dusk, taking very little time for the household chores. After the berry season was over some of them would work in the fruit cannery or hired [sic] out as a domestic worker.[25]

Many women took on the full responsibility for farming while their husbands worked in sawmills and lumber camps. On all these farms, rough bush land was painstakingly cleared and planted with strawberry plants and raspberry canes. Throughout the year every member of the family, including young children, worked long and hard. A local historian wrote, regarding the area around Mission: "The Japanese added an enormous amount of new acreage to the [berry] industry, because they were willing to buy unused, poor or stump-covered land and make it productive through an immense amount of hard work and frugality."[26]

The efforts of the early Japanese farmers in the Fraser Valley, however, did not meet with the unmitigated approval of their contemporaries. White farmers protested that "these industrious immigrants would soon squeeze them out of markets. The Japanese farmer bought cheap land the white man would not touch, cleared and drained it, and the following year harvested a crop equal if not superior to that of his white neighbour."[27]

The earliest farmers depended a great deal on Jiro Inouye (and later Yamaga) for help with contract negotiations with the white community and with

translation. At times as many as twenty people imposed on Inouye's hospitality during Japanese national holiday celebrations. Once a concert was
held at the Inouye home.[28] As the number of Japanese grew, it was obvious
that a club would be necessary, and in 1913, Yamaga, Inouye, and another
person negotiated purchase of an aging one-room schoolhouse that had been
built in the 1860s and was situated on a one-acre lot. Yamaga reminisced
about how the building became a vibrant meeting place. It was used for
English language night classes, a Japanese language school, a Sunday school,
and social gathering place for games of *go* and *shogi*. The women prepared
meals that sold for fifteen cents. One New Year's day, they all enjoyed a concert with singing and stage plays from 7:00 P.M. to 2:00 A.M., only to find
that they could not return home due to a heavy snowfall. Unconcerned, they
merely laid down blankets and slept on the floor.[29]

During World War I the berry market flourished. The price of strawberries soared from four cents a pound to twenty-one cents, and customers
swarmed to buy the produce. Many Japanese immigrants eagerly went into
farming at that time, often borrowing funds. Little antagonism arose from
the white farmers, since they were well aware that Japan was an ally whose
navy was protecting the west coast of Canada.[30] However, after the end of
the war, when prices plummeted and growers had to compete for a limited
market share, anti-Japanese feelings rekindled. Japanese farmers discussed
seriously whether to organize as a group, not only to cooperate among themselves but also to improve relations with other producers. Jiro Inouye, dubbed
the "Haney Village Headman" by Japanese, feared that an organization of
Japanese farmers would make them more visible and convey the impression to the white populace that the Japanese were setting up a separate society. Thus, for four years the Japanese gathered together as a "social club."
However, when anti-Asian unrest escalated, Japanese growers in the Haney
area formed the Haney Japanese Agricultural Society. On February 23, 1919,
six men, including Inouye and Yamaga, drafted plans, and on March 15 a
general meeting was held where forty-two people registered as a charitable
group with Inouye as president.

The Haney association met a number of times with their counterparts
in nearby Mission, Whonnock, and Hammond to discuss how they might
improve relations with the white community. They also shared farming hints,
such as how to combat frosts, make known the requirements and conditions for bringing in agricultural laborers from Japan, and agree on wages
for pickers. The executive board of the Haney Japanese Agricultural Association met every month. Yamaga noted that one of the most difficult chal-

lenges the board faced was how to mitigate the animosity against the Japanese farmers who worked on Sundays; that is, the white society's perception that the Japanese were breaking the Lord's Day Act, a law which prohibited commercial transactions on Sundays. Yamaga described one illustration of this feeling in detail:

> One Sunday, a certain Japanese man was working from early morning clearing land using blasting powder. A white woman dressed in her Sunday finery came by on her way to church. She said gently to the man, "Today is Sunday. You should be resting." It seems as if this man thought that only Christians needed to rest so he retorted, "Me Buddhist, you no policeman. I don't care." The lady phoned the police immediately. She must have understood his English babble. A policeman came and gave him a tongue-lashing. "Even Buddhists—everyone in Canada has to obey the Sunday law." He warned the farmer that since this was the first offence, he would be excused, but that next time he would give him a fine.[31]

This incident aroused a great deal of concern among the association leaders, who realized it was next to impossible to prevent their fellow Japanese from working on Sundays. They urged their members to work inconspicuously and quietly, away from public view.

Although the threatening policeman cited the Lord's Day Act, it appears that the toiling man had not actually broken any law. The act had been passed primarily to "regulate Sunday trading."[32] The Lord's Day Act was a criminal law, and once enacted by the federal government, it applied automatically to all the provinces. While it was possible for provinces and municipalities to opt out of certain sections, the law could not be made more extensive.[33] Contemporary newspaper articles reported debates in some municipalities in British Columbia over Sunday store closing and accusations of "prosecution of culture and music." It is doubtful that a farmer clearing his own agricultural land was prohibited under the act's Regulation Number Four:

> It is not lawful for any person on the Lord's Day, except as provided herein, or in any provincial Act or law in force on or after the first day of March 1907, to sell or offer for sale or purchase any goods, chattels, or other personal property, or any real estate, or carry on or transact any business of his ordinary calling, or in connection with such calling, or for gain to do, or employ any other person to do, on that day, any work, business or labour. R.S., c.171, s.4.[34]

Whether or not the policeman believed he was upholding the law is difficult to determine. Yet, public opinion surely believed the farmer to be breaking the Lord's Day Act. In his history of the Mission area, John Cherrington claimed the white community "viewed their [Japanese] entry into the valley as a threat to Protestant customs and beliefs. Japanese violated the Lord's Day Act by working on Sundays."[35] In a similar vein, a *Vancouver Daily Province* article on April 3, 1928, reported a complaint against "Oriental farmers":

> We have nothing against them racially, but we want them to live up to our standards. On the second Sunday of July last year I personally counted twenty-six trucks of vegetables in charge of Orientals on the Ladner ferry which was too crowded to carry white men's pleasure cars. When Orientals who ignore the Sabbath are hauled into court they avoid the penalties of the Lord's Day Act by stating that those who labour in their fields are their brothers or partners and not employees.[36]

The "Orientals" depicted in the article were most likely Chinese market gardeners, but the white public did not differentiate between the Chinese and Japanese. In the November 12, 1927, issue of the *Vancouver Daily Province,* an article confirmed that they were in fact Chinese. "At the Westminster market, three out of four vegetable sellers were Chinamen and one morning by actual count thirty-two Chinese and two Hindue [sic] vegetable trucks crammed the Ladner ferry to Vancouver."

The Haney Japanese Agricultural Association was also sensitive towards the white neighbors' disapproval of the conspicuous hard labor of Japanese farming women. The long hours these women spent clearing land, working in the berry fields, and chopping wood—often with babies strapped on their backs—had drawn much local criticism. Since warnings about this at meetings fell on deaf ears, the executives decided to hold gatherings at different sites in the Haney area in order to alert everyone in the Japanese farming community to the danger involved in continuing to fuel such criticism. It is likely that the men in the households were the ones who attended the association meetings and that they did not tell their wives about how the white neighbors felt about Japanese women working so hard. Inouye and Yamaga thus agreed to organize a series of sessions in which they spoke to small neighborly groups of women. Since the women did comply to some extent, Yamaga thought that this endeavor had good results.[37]

The association also counteracted the marketing problem of the random shipping of berries to the East on consignment by Japanese farmers. Because this practice had led to significant financial losses by many producers, the Japanese farmers formed a partnership, the Pacific Berry Growers Association, with a white wholesale outlet in 1922.[38]

The Haney association tried to improve Japanese relationships with non-Japanese agriculturalists by encouraging its members to learn English. Leaders felt it was imperative that English be taught to Japanese agricultural workers known as *yobiyose* (literally "called over" men), brought in under the agricultural worker stipulation of the Gentlemen's Agreement of 1908.[39] The association decided that it would arrange twice-weekly English language classes for these employees with their host farmers paying the tuition. It was felt that learning English would facilitate the workers' adjustment to Canadian life. The *yobiyose* were a special category of immigrants; that is, "emigrants brought in under contract by Japanese resident agricultural holders in Canada and especially required for the promotion of such agriculture; such contracts to be accompanied by the certificate of Japanese consular authority in the district where the labourers are to be employed."[40] The farmers paid the travel fares for the men involved, who were usually relatives or fellow villagers; each was given room and board and a stipend under a three-year contract.[41]

Haney Japanese Agricultural Association members also concerned themselves with a Japanese language school. Yamaga emphasized the need for Japanese farmers to adjust to the Canadian way of life, but he also believed that Japanese language instruction was a necessity for Canadian-born children. Because their parents had a poor command of English, he felt it was only through Japanese language that children could converse at home and be able to understand the viewpoints of their parents. Later, when the children matured and left home for further education or work, they would be able to keep in touch by writing letters home. This was obviously a widely shared view, as parents certainly did not begrudge expenditures of time and money for this education.

Haney schooling began when informal classes were held in a family home in 1913. By 1915 the school had moved to the Haney Japanese Community Hall. Unlike all the other Japanese schools in British Columbia, which used textbooks issued by the Ministry of Education of Japan, the Maple Ridge (Haney) Japanese language school employed books that had been developed for use by Japanese language schools in California.[42] The California texts had been adopted in 1926 because the goal of the school was not only to teach Japanese, but also to produce good Canadian citizens and avoid incul-

cating Japanese nationalism. Chokichi Ariga, who became the principal of
the school in 1933, enthusiastically followed this philosophy.[43] A Nisei who
had attended that school remembered the textbooks:

> The major difference was in the setting . . . they would be American rather
> than Japanese, street scenes, classrooms, etc. I also recall some stories of Amer-
> ican heroes, George Washington and the cherry tree, Abraham Lincoln and
> the slaves, etc. And Ariga would supplement these textbooks with articles he
> had written himself about Canadian heroes. His approach was not above crit-
> icism. In my own home, my father thought that anything not approved by
> the *Mombusho* [Japan's Ministry of Education] was faulty. My mother tended
> to be less critical.[44]

Yamaga wrote that Ariga also held discussions on the moral codes and
laws of Canada, and arranged inter-Japanese school activities, recitations,
and mothers' groups. He made a great effort to implant in the Nisei a self-
awareness of their Canadian roots.[45] Yamaga acknowledged that there were
families who did not take much interest in the education their children were
receiving in the Canadian public schools and who wanted the Japanese school
to provide moral training and proper behavior; that is, Japanese ethics and
ideas. These parents objected to the California textbooks.

In the mid-twenties a movement began in many Japanese communities
towards developing textbooks more appropriate for the Canadian Nisei.[46]
Representatives from B.C. Japanese schools met regularly. They decided that
the California texts used in Haney were not suitable for Canadian youth
and were also outdated. Amidst a great deal of disagreement, through con-
certed effort a new set of primary books for Canadian use was prepared. In
1941, Tsutae Sato, the principal of the Vancouver Alexander Street Japanese
School, went to Tokyo to arrange the printing, but he quickly returned to
Canada when war appeared imminent.

In about 1924, a discriminatory movement began to spread in B.C. to separate Japanese students from others in the public schools. Activists claimed
the Japanese children were taking a disproportionate amount of the teachers' time due to their lack of English comprehension. The Japanese Consul
and concerned Japanese community members conferred with Dr. S. S. Oster-
hout, director of Oriental Evangelization of the Methodist Church. They
decided that Japanese children should attend kindergartens so they could
learn English in preparation for school. In January 1927, a kindergarten was
started at the Haney Japanese Community Hall under the jurisdiction of

the United Church Women's Association.[47] The Haney Japanese Agricultural Association provided the classroom and equipment. In the first class were twenty-one pupils five years or older. These classes continued until 1942.[48] Such church-run kindergartens were also begun in many other Japanese communities.[49]

Yamaga was also instrumental, along with the devout Baptist William Hall, in organizing an interracial nondenominational Sunday School at the Haney Japanese Community Hall in April 1917, which later included adults. It began with about fifteen children. By 1920 eighty children and twenty adults, both Japanese and white, participated in the prayer meetings. At Easter, potluck dinners were held, with entertainment for the children. Yamaga noted that through this social intermingling a close relationship developed between the white and Japanese people in Haney.[50] These interracial Sunday services were most unusual at a time when the majority of the Japanese lived in separate communities, had difficulty understanding English, and had little contact with the whites. Other Japanese Christian congregations existed, but they all had Japanese-speaking ministers.[51]

Yamaga urged Japanese women to participate in the Parent Teachers Association at Robinson School in Haney, a public school that by 1924 had a student population that was 50 percent Japanese.[52] He often drove Japanese women to the P T A meetings and interpreted for them. He said that the children were pleased to see their mothers working alongside the white mothers at school functions. Yamaga encouraged participation in P T A activities at other schools in Maple Ridge as well. What the Japanese women who went to P T A functions thought about this experience is unfortunately unknown, and it is not known whether their P T A participation reached beyond attendance at meetings.[53]

The association also dealt with innumerable problems that arose due to parents' ignorance of school attendance regulations. For instance, parents often kept their children home from school when their labor was required on the farm. The farmers needed to be reminded that according to the 1901 amendment to the Public Schools Act, the age of compulsory schooling was seven to fourteen in cities, and that in 1912 this was extended to all municipalities. In 1921 the age requirement for compulsory schooling was extended to fifteen years. In Japan, although compulsory education existed, school attendance was not always strictly enforced. According to Ministry of Education figures, when enforcement finally became stricter in 1899, school attendance in Japan rose from a low of 45 percent in 1887 to 72.8 percent in 1899 and 88.1 percent in 1901. The figures for girls were lower—less than 30 percent attended school in 1887, 59.0 percent in 1899, and 81.8 percent in 1901.[54] By 1906, elementary school attendance figures had reached 96 percent, 98 percent for boys and 95 percent for girls. Nevertheless, "children of poor farm families were frequently kept out of school to help on the farm and at home or to take care of their baby brothers and sisters."[55]

The Japanese government's school enrollment statistics do not tell the full story of school attendance. Coming from this background, before the 1920s the Issei in Canada did not always worry about strict school attendance. Later, they obeyed the law, but they still made maximum use of their children's labor. There is no doubt that the daily labor of children contributed to the financial success of these farms. Casual conversations as well as carefully directed interviews with the children of these pioneer berry farmers in my research revealed that from early childhood they were working members of their families' enterprises. They weeded, hoed, and picked berries in the early morning before leaving for school, after school, and on weekends. They also chopped wood, hauled water, did the laundry, cooked meals, looked after younger siblings, and performed whatever chores were required that they were capable of doing.[56]

Yamaga strove to familiarize the Issei with Canadian customs and laws so that the white community would not be aroused. However, when he became aware of injustices towards the Japanese, in particular the Nisei children, he did not hesitate to speak up. An example of how forceful he could be is apparent in his handling of the "May Queen affair."[57]

Yamaga was a PTA representative of the school his children attended. Seven schools in the district celebrated May Day together.[58] Usually a queen was selected by a group of twenty women who represented the seven schools. In 1927 they asked the high school principal to recommend the May Queen. His choice was a fourteen-year-old Nisei. In attendance at the meeting when the selection was to be made were twenty women, two white men, Yamaga, and a local newspaper reporter. The women protested that "the method of selections was not right," "the children should choose," "the high school students should choose," and even that "a child who is from a voteless race is not suitable." Yamaga wrote that after an eye signal from the Chair, "a refined, cultured woman who had been raised in England," Yamaga stood up and said, "Chairman, the person being discussed is a Canadian-born British citizen. It is written in the Canadian constitution so this matter cannot be disputed. It is also written clearly that discrimination cannot be made against skin color or religion. At present you are opposing the PTA constitution and Canada's educational ideal, and are setting an irretrievable example of prejudice to an impressionable student body. I think we should reconsider seriously. Thank you." The Chair then asked for a withdrawal of the motion, or she would resign. After much more discussion, the Nisei May Queen was accepted, the matter was reported in the local paper, and Yamaga claims that discrimination in the educational field was eased.

By the mid-1920s, the growing numbers of Japanese farmers and the haphazard selling of their berries in a depressed economy began to intensify the hostility of white society.[59] Yamaga deplored the ignorance of the Japanese farmers who did not understand the complexities of the marketplace. When admonished by a fellow Japanese farmer, some Japanese farmers selfishly refused to think beyond the growing and selling of their own crop. They would reply, "I grew it myself, so it's my own business where I sell it!"[60] Moreover, due to their inability to read English, they were unaware of the growing anger directed towards them that was reflected in newspapers and agricultural magazines. For example, the August 16, 1924, issue of the *Vancouver Daily Province* stated: "The vegetable farmer and small fruit grower of this province is becoming Oriental—the strawberry patches are taking on a yellow tinge. . . . Agricultural depression favors Oriental farming because the Japan and Chinaman dispense with luxuries in living, work out all daylight, and incur no expense in eating or amusement that is above their income. . . . [They are] all smiles because living is so much better here than in Japan."

Astute farmers such as Yamaga realized that demands for legislation in British Columbia similar to the alien land law in California and other U.S. western states were on the ascent and that the situation was serious. Since the late nineteenth century, farmers of British descent had been growing strawberries in Gordon Head on the Saanich Peninsula of Vancouver Island. Since sales in Victoria and Vancouver brought them much profit, they had expanded production, and by 1925 they were sending their berries east of the Rockies by refrigerated freight cars. The gradually increasing production by Fraser Valley Japanese berry farmers who also started sending their produce eastward by railway was diminishing the incomes of Saanich growers.[61] Moreover, since the Fraser Valley season began a week or so ahead of that on Vancouver Island, Saanich berry growers missed the high prices producers could demand at the beginning of the season.[62]

By 1925 white farmers were demanding an alien land law. They also insisted that people ineligible for the voting franchise should not be allowed to own land.[63] The Anglo-Japanese Alliance, signed between Japan and Britain in 1902 and renewed in 1911, had for a number of years protected

Japanese immigrants in Canada from some of the unjust laws passed by the B.C. legislature, since Canada, as a dominion within the British Empire, had its diplomatic affairs controlled by Britain. In 1925, however, when the alliance was not renewed and the Washington Treaty, which led to closer ties between the United States and Canada, was signed, the position of Japanese immigrants became more precarious.

A *Victoria Times* item in April 1925 declared that an anti-Japanese B.C. land law was urgent. Executive members of the extremist White Canada Association were working actively towards ousting the Japanese.[64] Japanese farmers faced possible annihilation.

Their leaders decided to meet the problem head on. They consulted with the Japanese Consul, Japanese Canadian journalists, provincial government ministers, and the Canadian Japanese Association.[65] Then they traveled throughout the Fraser Valley talking to Japanese farmers, explaining the enormity of this legislation, how it had affected the U.S. Japanese farmers, and what the consequences could be. More than three hundred Canadian Japanese agreed to the formation of an organization that would include all the Japanese farmers in the Fraser Valley, the Union of Berry Producers Association (*Ichigo seisansha rengo kumiai*). Yamaga, representing the north Fraser farmers, and Jiro Kumatani, representing the south Fraser farmers, were sent to the 1925 annual meeting of the British Columbia Fruit Growers Association in Kelowna. After the committee campaigning for the adoption of an alien land law delivered a report, Yamaga addressed the association assembly. He declared that Japanese farmers realized that through ignorance of the marketplace they had caused monetary losses to themselves and to others. However, now quite aware of their past mistakes, the Japanese farmers were at this moment creating a cooperative and hoping to unite with farmers of all ethnic backgrounds in the interest of mutual aid and regulation of the market. Yamaga said that after his address, the assembly's honorary secretary, Dr. Barss, an agriculture professor at the University of British Columbia, proposed an urgent motion to immediately dissolve the "anti-Japanese resolution committee," and it was passed unanimously. To Yamaga this signaled a tremendous breakthrough in interracial relations.[66]

The Maple Ridge Berry Growers Co-operative Exchange was organized in 1927 by Yamaga, "the dominant figure in the struggle to establish amicable inter-racial relations."[67] The *Victoria Daily Colonist* reported January 18, 1928, on the British Columbia Fruit Growers Association meeting being held in Kelowna: "Tension Relaxed. There is not the same tense atmosphere and excitement which marked the convention a year ago." Obviously some concrete steps had been taken. The various Japanese growers associations amalgamated into the Consolidated Farmers Association, "and its annual meeting even attracted white growers."[68] Later, under the Natural Products Marketing Act, white and Japanese groups cooperatively regulated under a local board the marketing of small fruits and rhubarb produced in the Fraser Valley.[69] The makeup of the board, which consisted of two white farmers and one Japanese, met with Japanese objections, as Japanese farmers were responsible for over 80 percent of the products. But the protests never went beyond grumbling.[70] By 1934 the dire effect of the unregulated "buyers' market" for jam berries was also mitigated by exporting jam berries to England packed with sulphur dioxide in wooden barrels. The Maple Ridge Berry Growers Co-operative Exchange pioneered this packing process.[71]

In 1933, when the B.C. Coast Growers Association became independent of the B.C. Fruit Growers Association, Yamaga was elected its vice-chairman. The group dealt with such matters as stopping the United States from dumping its berries onto the Canadian market and reporting to the government bureaus of marketing, legislation, and research.[72] In 1934 Yamaga was reelected.[73] Yamaga was also elected managing director of the Maple Ridge Berry Growers Co-operative Exchange and served that organization for fifteen years. During this time the berry farmers gradually diversified into tree fruits, rhubarb, and hops.

Through the efforts of leaders such as Yamaga and the herculean efforts of the farming families, many berry growers of the Fraser Valley had built flourishing enterprises by 1940. Many others had laid down foundations and were nearing success. Annual production by Japanese farmers in the area reached approximately one million dollars.[74]

The bombing of Pearl Harbor by Japanese naval forces in December 1941, however, vaporized the dreams of all Japanese Canadians. The fate of the berry farmers in the Fraser Valley was devastating. All their land was confiscated by the government and sold, even that which World War I veterans had acquired through the Soldier Settlement Board.[75] In the spring of 1942, when the Japanese were being removed from the West Coast, government surveyors recorded in minute detail the layout of each farm, the crops grown, and the value of the house, outbuildings, and farming implements.[76] According to research to determine the economic losses incurred by the Japanese Canadian community after December 1941, conducted by the National Association of Japanese Canadians, the total farmland was worth $6,196,522 in 1949 dollars or $57,008,000 in 1986 dollars.[77]

Extensive studies of federal cabinet records have shown that by using wartime emergency as justification, the results of decades of back-breaking labor by these forward-looking, ambitious men and women were nullified.[78] Their children, who had spent their childhoods working on family farms, also lost their inheritances. A number moved forward and became doctors, engineers, and accountants. Few returned to farming. Yet many today still treasure personal and historical memories of the farming communities in the Fraser Valley that had gradually matured in four decades only to disappear within a period of mere months.

Epilogue

During the war, Yasutaro Yamaga and his family were sent to the relocation camp at Tashme, near Hope, British Columbia. While there, he started up a small sawmill fourteen miles from Tashme. In 1948, at the age of 62, he and a partner purchased a larger operation at 70 Mile House, in the Cariboo district. Eight years later he retired to an orchard he bought near Beamsville in the Niagara region of Ontario.

Driven by a growing concern for elderly Japanese Canadians, especially those now in Ontario without families, who no longer had the neighborly support of their pre-war Japanese communities and were now scattered and isolated, Yamaga pursued the creation of the Nipponia Home, an eighteen-bed retirement home. To pay for it, he solicited donations from the Japanese pioneers, added proceeds from the sale of his own home, and received matching funds from the Ontario government. Nipponia Home opened in Ontario in December 1958.[79] In subsequent years the retirement home underwent a number of additions and renovations. The last was in 1993, when the Yamaga Wing and a "Refit Project" was completed to convert the Nipponia Home into a long-term care facility. This final project was to fulfill the pledge of the founders "that residents would be able to spend the rest of his or her life in the Home."[80] In a booklet published for the celebration of the fortieth anniversary of the Nipponia Home, the Hon. Elizabeth Witmer, Ontario minister of health, wrote:

> The respect of the elderly so characteristic of Japanese culture, and the Nipponia Home, sets the standard for long-term care for seniors here in Ontario. . . . As our government moves forward with significant investment in long-term care, facilitated services to meet the needs of our growing, changing, and aging population, we are striving to provide what The Nipponia Home

exemplifies—the best possible long-term care services to Ontarians now and in the future.[81]

Despite these highly laudatory statements, the same ministry announced in July 1999 that Nipponia Home failed to meet current safety and quality of life standards and was no longer economically viable. Therefore it would be closed within six weeks. In futility, young Sansei activists joined Nisei colleagues in pointing out the need of the elderly for Japanese food, entertainment, their *ofuro* (Japanese bath), and being provided care in the Japanese language. Although there was a great deal of support by the mainstream and Japanese Canadian media, in the spring of 2000 the residents were scattered to larger provincial care homes, and the Nipponia Home was put up for sale. In June 2002, a non-Japanese church group purchased the property with plans to use it as a retreat.

Yasutaro Yamaga died in 1971 at the age of eighty-five. For six decades he had served his community, and his legacy has lived on for more than thirty years. His inclusion in the *koseki sha* (people of merit) list compiled in 1956 by the *New Canadian,* a Japanese Canadian newspaper, was well deserved. He was described as "community leader of Haney, founder of Nipponia Home."[82] As Gordon Nakayama wrote:

> Yasutaro Yamaga was one of the rare older Japanese Canadians, who was able to speak English well and to understand the Canadian way of life. He shared Jiro Inouye's belief that in order to be accepted as Canadian it was necessary to integrate. He worked diligently to this ideal to the end of his life.[83]

The Fraser Valley berry farmers' success was undoubtedly due to the unselfish and dedicated efforts of this extraordinary leader.

Notes

1. Toyo Takata, *Nikkei Legacy* (Toronto: NC Press Limited, 1983), 68.

2. National Association of Japanese Canadians, *Economic Losses of Japanese Canadians After 1941* (Winnipeg: National Association of Japanese Canadians, 1985), 13.

3. Yasutaro Yamaga, *Hene'e nokai shi* (The history of the Haney Agricultural Association) (Tokyo: Kasai Shuppan Insatsusha, 1963).

4. Gordon G. Nakayama, *Issei* (Toronto: NC Press Limited, 1984), 51.

5. See Jinshiro Nakayama, *Kanada doho hattentaikan* (Encyclopedia of Japanese

in Canada) and *Kanada no hoko* (Treasures of Canada) (Tokyo: n.p., 1921). Copies of these extremely scarce books were republished in 2000 along with other books into a single volume, *Kanada iminshi shiryo* (Historical materials of Japanese immigration to Canada) (Tokyo: Fuji Publishing, 2001). Originally, this volume was to have also included Yamaga's book but, inexplicably, publication permission was not given by his survivors.

6. Nakayama, *Kanada no hoko,* 345–46.

7. University of British Columbia Library, Special Collections and University Archives Division, Yamaga Yasutaro Papers, Box 1–2.

8. Ibid.

9. Michiko Midge Ayukawa, "Creating and Recreating Community: Hiroshima and Canada 1891–1941" (Ph.D. diss., University of Victoria, 1996), 89–90.

10. Yuji Ichioka, *The Issei* (New York: Free Press, 1988), 69.

11. There were two Japanese language newspapers published in Vancouver at that time, *Kanada shinpo,* which began in 1903, and *Tairiku nippo,* which began in 1907. Mitsuru Shimpo, Norio Tamura, Shigehiko Shiramizu, *Kanada no nihongo shinbun* (Japanese language newspapers in Canada) (Tokyo: PMC Shuppan kabushikigaisha, 1991), 39–41. Inouye was apparently a regular contributor.

12. In my research I came across a number of other Hiroshima emigrants who had worked in such lumber camps. "Bosses" *(bosu)* such as Mr. Ryuichi Miyake and other Hiroshma emigrant labor contractors hired fellow prefectural emigrants. See also Charles A. Miller, *Valley of the Slave* (Surrey, B.C.: Hancock House, 1981), 59. Miller wrote: "A cord [of shingle bolts] consisted of some thirty pieces, twelve inches square and fifty-two inches long."

13. Nakayama, *Issei,* 52.

14. Yamaga, *Hene'e,* 11.

15. Ibid., 12.

16. Yasutaro Yamaga, "My Footsteps in B.C.," 1958, UBC Special Collections.

17. Ibid., 2.

18. Ibid., 4.

19. Ibid., 2.

20. Michiko Midge Ayukawa, "Good Wives and Wise Mothers: Japanese Picture Brides in Early Twentieth-Century British Columbia," *BC Studies,* 105–6 (spring/summer 1995): 103–18. Also published in Veronica Strong-Boag, Mona Gleason, and Adele Perry, eds., *Rethinking Canada: The Promise of Women's History* (Don Mills, Ontario: Oxford University Press, 2002), 174–86.

21. Yamaga, *Hene'e,* 19–20.

22. Ayukawa, "Creating," chap. 3, 47–74.

23. Ken Adachi, *The Enemy That Never Was: A History of the Japanese Canadians* (Toronto: McClelland and Stewart, 1976), 70.

24. Ibid., 72–75.

25. Yamaga, "Footsteps," 5.

26. Andreas Shroeder, *Carved from Wood, Mission, B.C., 1886–1992* (Altona, Manitoba: D. W. Friessen, 1991), 109.

27. John Cherrington, *Mission on the Fraser* (Vancouver: Mitchell Press, 1974), 120.

28. Yamaga, *Hene'e*, 15.

29. Ibid., 16.

30. Ibid., 21.

31. Ibid., 24, slightly edited translation.

32. David N. Laband and Deborah Hendry Heinbuch, *Blue Laws: The History, Economics, and Politics of Sunday Closing Laws* (Lexington, Mass.: D.C. Heath and Co., 1957), 215–19.

33. Information received from Ross Lambertson.

34. Laband and Heinbuch, *Blue Laws,* 216.

35. Cherrington, *Mission,* 121.

36. *Vancouver Daily Province,* 3 April 1928.

37. Yamaga, *Hene'e,* 25.

38. Ibid., 53.

39. Following an anti-Asian riot on September 9, 1907, Japan voluntarily agreed to restrict issuing passports according to certain stipulations. One was that agricultural laborers contracted by Japanese resident agricultural holdings in Canada would be limited to ten for each hundred acres of land owned. Adachi, *Enemy,* 81.

40. Howard H. Sugimoto, *Japanese Immigration, the Vancouver Riots and Canadian Diplomacy* (New York: Arno Press, 1978), 263.

41. There were cases when men were released from their contracts when the farmers could not afford to pay the monthly stipend.

An example of the detailed documentation required is in William T. Hashizume, *Japanese Community in Mission: A Brief History, 1904–1942* (Toronto: Mission Copy Centre, 2002), 101–5.

42. Yamaga, *Hene'e,* 43. Adachi noted in *Enemy* that "only one school in the Fraser Valley town of Haney adopted the California texts" (129). Gordon Nakayama in *Issei* wrote, "The Haney Japanese Language School used texts compiled by the Department of Education in the State of California, USA" (53).

43. Yamaga, *Hene'e,* 42–43. For a short biography of Ariga, see Roy Ito, *We Went to War* (Stittsville, Ontario: Canada's Wings, Inc., 1984), 247–48.

44. Personal communication, Tony Tateishi, Ottawa, July 1995. His father's crit-

icism may be related to the fact that he had graduated from teachers' training school in Japan.

45. Yamaga, *Hene'e*, 42.

46. Tsutae Sato, *Kanada nihonkyoikukai shi* (The History of the Japanese Language School Educational Society) (Tokyo: Miwa insatsu kabushikigaisha, 1953), 149.

47. In 1925, the Methodist, Congregational, and Presbyterian churches united to form the United Church of Canada. See Roland M. Kawano, ed., *A History of the Japanese Congregations of the United Church of Canada (1892–1959)* (Scarborough, Ontario: The Japanese Canadian Christian Churches Historical Project, 1998), xiv.

48. Yamaga, *Hene'e*, 44.

49. The Buddhist church in Vancouver also hired a white teacher, Mrs. Young (personal knowledge).

50. Yamaga, *Hene'e*, 46.

51. Kawano, *History*, xiv-xv.

52. Yamaga served as provincial vice-president of the PTA. Kunio Hidaka, "Reflections on 'A Man for His Times,'" in *Nipponia Home: 21 Years of Service* (Toronto: Plowshare Press, 1979), 60.

53. I found this very interesting because as far as I can recall, when I was a student during the years 1936 to 1942 at Strathcona School, the large public school in Vancouver in which the children from the Powell Street area were enrolled, few Japanese parents attended any of the school's activities. My parents certainly did not.

54. Aso Makoto and Amano Ikuo, *Education and Japan's Modernization* (Tokyo: The Japan Times Ltd., 1983), 34–35.

55. Mikiso Hane, *Peasants, Rebels, and Outcasts: The Underside of Modern Japan* (New York: Pantheon Books, 1982), 51–52.

56. The lives of these farm children were of course not unique, as seen from a study made of childhood experiences of Anglophone families living in the Buckley Valley in British Columbia in the interwar years. These children were also working contributors to their family farms and were also at times kept out of school when their labor was required. Neil Sutherland, "'I can't recall when I didn't help': The Working Lives of Pioneering Children in Twentieth Century British Columbia," *Social History/histoire social* 24 (November 1991): 263–88.

57. Yamaga, *Hene'e*, 48–49.

58. May Day celebrations were held throughout British Columbia on Queen Victoria's birthday, May 24. The program varied from sports days to fireworks. The festivities were often presided over by a May Queen and her attendants.

59. Adachi, *Enemy*, 147–52; Yamaga, *Hene'e*, 50.

60. Yamaga, *Hene'e*, 51.

61. Ibid., 50.

62. Ibid., 51.

63. In 1895, the Japanese, along with other Asians in British Columbia, were denied the right to vote provincially. This included those born in Canada. This legislation, in effect, also prevented them from voting federally or municipally. Adachi, *Enemy*, 52.

64. Ibid., 150.

65. The CJA was an organization that claimed to represent the entire Japanese immigrant population. It was essentially oriented towards Japan and was the administrative organ of the Japanese consulate. Adachi, *Enemy*, 123–24.

66. Yamaga, *Hene'e*, 52.

67. Adachi, *Enemy*, 150.

68. Ibid.

69. Natural Products Marketing (British Columbia) Act, S.B.C. 1934, C. 38, 121–23. Section 3(1) of the act states: "For the purposes of this Act the Lieutenant-Governor in Council may constitute a Board to be known as the 'British Columbia Marketing Board,' which shall consist of not more than three members, who shall be appointed by the Lieutenant-Governor in Council, . . ." The lieutenant-governor is a nonelected officer and the representative of the British monarchy. According to information received at the University of Victoria Law Library, the Lieutenant-Governor in Council refers to the B.C. cabinet, and thus the B.C. Legislature has no jurisdiction over it and thus could not contest the choice or makeup of the board.

70. Yamaga, *Hene'e*, 52.

71. Yamaga, Yasutaro, "The History of Farming in B.C., 1906–41," March 1958, UBC Library, Special Collections, 6–15.

72. Yamaga, *Hene'e*, 58.

73. Information received from Patricia E. Roy, July 2002. See Patricia E. Roy, *The Oriental Question: Consolidating a White Man's Province, 1914–41* (Vancouver: UBC Press, 2003).

74. Yamaga, *Hene'e*, 5.

75. After the war only one farmer was able to return to his own land. Zennosuke Inouye, a veteran of World War I, had purchased eighty acres through the Soldiers Settlement Act in 1919. Through persistence and determination, and with assistance from the veteran's group (Royal Canadian Legion), the United Church, and a law firm, he was able to reclaim his property and return to it in 1949. Fortuitously, his property had been leased throughout the period and had not been sold. Copies of his extensive correspondence, received from his daughter, Beverly Inouye, are in my possession.

76. For my master's thesis I researched the wartime experience of the Imada family of Maple Ridge. I possess copies of government files containing detailed survey

notes. I have similar data regarding my in-laws' berry farm property in Mission. Michiko Midge Ayukawa, "Bearing the Unbearable: The Memoir of a Japanese Pioneer Woman" (master's thesis, University of Victoria, 1990).

77. NAJC, *Economic Losses,* 14.

78. Ann Gomer Sunahara, *The Politics of Racism: The Uprooting of Japanese Canadians during the Second World War* (Toronto: James Lorimer & Company, 1981).

79. Nakayama, *Issei,* 55.

80. Board of Directors, *Nipponia Home: 40 Years of Service 1958–1998* (Dundas, Ontario: LT Designs, 1998), 16.

81. Ibid., 3.

82. Roy Ito, *Stories of My People: A Japanese Canadian Journal* (Hamilton, Ont.: S-20 and Nisei Veterans Association, 1994), 131. Ito has reproduced the list in his book.

83. Nakayama, *Issei,* 52.

5 / AMERICANIZATION VS. JAPANESE CULTURAL MAINTENANCE

Analyzing Seattle's *Nihongo Tokuhon,* 1920

NORIKO ASATO

On April 1, 1921, the approximately 580 students in Japanese language schools in the state of Washington began the school year with a set of new Japanese language textbooks.[1] While this may not have seemed like a notable event to the Nisei, second-generation Japanese Americans who attended Japanese language school for an hour or so each afternoon, it was a historic moment in the development of Nisei identity. This is because these American textbooks replaced ones created by the Monbusho (the Japanese Ministry of Education). These indigenous textbooks were produced by the Northwest Junction of the Japanese Association in Seattle (Beikoku Seihokubu Renraku Nihonjinkai); henceforth called the Nihonjinkai.[2]

This paper explores the Japanese language school situation in Washington State that led to the creation of the first Japanese language textbook series composed in the contiguous United States to teach Japanese language to Nisei children. Although six thousand copies of the 1921 Washington *Nihongo Tokuhon,* or Japanese readers, were printed in Japan, only a handful have survived and are available for study in research libraries or personal collections.[3] This is understandable as even in normal times textbooks are rarely considered important documents to save, and in the days following Pearl Harbor, many surviving textbooks were burned or buried before the Japanese Americans or Nikkei were sent to concentration camps.

Seattle in 1920, however, was "the most peaceful place for immigrants on the Pacific Coast," claimed one of Seattle's Japanese language dailies, the *Hokubei Jiji.*[4] Indeed, compared with Hawaii or California, the Japanese language school situation in Washington was far less tension-ridden. Hawaii, the birthplace of the movement against Japanese language schools, had 160

Japanese language schools attended by more than 20,000 Japanese American pupils, and more than 40 percent of the territory's population was ethnically Japanese.[5] While the Nikkei population of California was four times greater than Washington's, the former had forty Japanese schools with 1,400 students attending, and the latter was home to twelve schools with only 585 students in 1920.[6] If Washington was so peaceful, then, why did Washington's Nihonjinkai squeeze out $6,000 to precede California in accomplishing this extravagantly costly textbook project? This must have been a heavy burden on the immigrant community, especially considering the fact that when California compiled its own textbook four years later, its $5,500 cost was divided over its much larger population.[7] This chapter attempts to reconstruct the social milieu of that time inside and outside the Nikkei community and to understand what factors brought about the Nihonjinkai's textbook compilation.

The chapter also examines the contents of the Washington textbooks in comparison with ones composed by the Monbusho. The Washington textbooks are among the earliest textbooks composed in North America to replace the Monbusho ones.[8] This first complete textbook set is among the earliest surviving documents that actually demonstrate how the Japanese immigrants or Issei applied their construct of Japanese identity to Nisei education. Furthermore, the study of this textbook set reveals where the Issei located Americanization in relation to their values of native and adopted countries and how they actually manifested their beliefs in a specific, albeit restricted form. Needless to say, the publication of these textbooks played a pioneering role for later textbooks in California and elsewhere.[9]

Historical Context

The nationalistic mood that peaked in the United States during World War I led to an anti-immigrant movement and to a movement to "Americanize" immigrants.[10] With the concomitant postwar economic recession, immigrants—especially Japanese—unjustly perceived as taking economic opportunities from whites, became victims of discriminatory laws in West Coast states. In California, the newly formed Oriental Exclusion League was desperate to establish a revised alien land law to stop Japanese agricultural development and to completely halt immigration to America. The 1913 California alien land law, prohibiting Issei from owning or leasing land for more than three years, had been bypassed by Issei land purchases in the names of their children, who were American citizens.[11] Therefore, to close one loop-hole, exclusionists set out to amend the United States Constitution in order to deny the Nisei their American citizenship. As a first step, they targeted Japanese language schools on the grounds of their claim that Japanese schools instilled Nisei loyalty to the Japanese emperor.[12]

Similarly, in Hawaii, after several attempts to pass language school con-trol bills failed in the territorial legislature, a federal survey commission was brought to Hawaii in the fall of 1919 to examine educational issues upon the request of the territorial government. The survey committee recom-mended placing Japanese language schools under the control of the terri-tory's Board of Education until they could be completely eliminated.[13] Concerned that public opinion might force Hawaii's legislature to take dras-tic measures, Issei leaders who had been waging serious resistance proposed a compromise school control bill. This bill, Act 30, immediately passed the legislature on November 24, 1920.[14] The Washington textbook series emerged in direct response to these attacks on Japanese language schools in Califor-nia and Hawaii, which seemed to foreshadow the situation in Washington.

The history of the legal battles concerning Hawaii's Japanese language schools has been well examined by Ann Halsted and Eileen Tamura within the context of the struggle over Nisei identity.[15] Yoshihide Matsubayashi's dissertation on language schools in Hawaii and California is a resourceful study, containing abundant primary documents.[16] Toyotomi Morimoto studied the compilation of Japanese textbooks in California, focusing on internal, political, and organizational decision-making.[17] Teruko Kumei compared the 1924 California textbook series and the 1929 second-edition Washington textbooks, and in a later study, she also examined the con-struction of Nisei identity in relation to Japanese language education in the United States over the four decades prior to World War II.[18] With the excep-tion of Myron Powers's 1932 sociology thesis on the Seattle Japanese lan-guage school, and a brief survey of Japanese language schools in the Pacific Northwest by Misako Sadahiro, no scholar has focused on Japanese language schools in Washington State or the first Japanese textbooks compiled by Issei teachers in the contiguous United States.[19]

The Inauguration of the Anti-Japanese Movement in Seattle

In 1919, the *Seattle Star*, a daily newspaper, concluded a ten-day campaign to manufacture an anti-Japanese mood in Seattle. It serially publicized a "civic mass meeting" organized by the Mutual Business Club and the American Legion on August 11.[20] The purpose of this meeting was to protest against the recent advancement of Japanese in business and to terminate their immigration.[21] Approximately 250 people attended, with "practically every civic organization" represented, according to the *Star,* to discuss the Japanese situation in Seattle. Although the meeting was well publicized, neither of Seattle's other major newspapers, the *Seattle Times* and the *Seattle Post-Intelligencer,* mentioned the meeting.[22]

One of the campaign's main arguments, expressed by Frank E. Kannear, Mutual Business Club secretary, was that the "Japanese cannot be assimilated," and "by allowing them to stay here we are raising a distinct class." He asserted that "we are creating a race here that will eventually gain control of the Coast and sweep eastward over the whole country." Rev. Ulysses Grant Murphy, who had been a missionary in Japan for fourteen years, defended the Nikkei, responding, "America can assimilate a large number of Japanese" and "the American-born Japanese child responds to American ideas." He declared that unrestricted immigration had ceased and that "the Gentlemen's Agreement is the best observed contract between the two nations."[23] Miller Freeman, secretary of the Veteran's Welfare Commission and a long-time anti-Japanese activist, also did his best to agitate for the meeting. Ten days before the meeting, Freeman gave a speech entitled "This is a White Man's Country" to 170 Seattle small businessmen. He created a fear of a Japanese invasion of the West Coast by inflating the rapidly increasing population of Japanese, falsely claiming that Japanese women bore children five times more than white women.[24] His argument was identical to the "Yellow Peril" campaign developed in California, which Roger Daniels examines in his *Politics of Prejudice.*[25] Japanese exclusionists argued that "Americanization" was impossible since Nisei children were being raised as Japanese subjects.[26] However, the exclusionists' real concern was not Japanese assimilability, but the economic advancement of the Japanese.

The Seattle mass meeting ended with a resolution demanding that Representative Albert Johnson (Republican, Washington), chairman of the House Committee on Immigration and Naturalization, investigate the Japanese situation in the Northwest.[27] The organizers also requested that Governor Louis F. Hart investigate "Japanese expansion" in the Northwest, and asked Washington Attorney General L. L. Thompson to report on Japanese ownership of land and property and to investigate legal means to end it.[28] In retrospect, the role of the civic mass meeting was threefold. First, it definitely established the Japanese as a political, economical, and social "problem" in Seattle. Second, it prepared the Washington public for the upcoming congressional immigration hearings by engaging activists in collecting information and spreading anti-Japanese sentiment. Finally, and most importantly, it was a publicity event staged by the Seattle Anti-Japanese League to launch its movement.[29]

Only ten days after the mass meeting was held, the Seattle Anti-Japanese League was established on August 21, 1919. John J. Sullivan, former assistant U.S. district attorney and American Legion first national vice-president, and Kannear, led the league; not surprisingly they were the primary figures who organized the meeting.[30] The league consisted of members of the Retail Grocers Association, the Seattle Laundrymen's Association, the Veterans of Foreign Wars, and the Retail Clerks Union, and supposedly other middle-class people holding a grudge against Japanese competition.[31] Although the anti-Japanese activists did not initially extend their attack to Nisei education directly, it triggered various smaller anti-Japanese movements among American public educators.

"The first steps have been taken to oust Japanese schools that are being maintained in the valley land between Seattle and Tacoma." Thus began a September 2, 1919, *Seattle Star* article praising Tacoma County School Superintendent Minnie D. Bean's inquiry to Attorney General Thompson regarding a foreign language school control law. Bean asked Thompson if "there [was] any school law that would prevent the leasing of a building of a public school district to any organization where languages other than English were taught exclusively?" More directly, she asked "What steps can I take, if any, to force the Firwood school directors to discontinue the leasing of a building of the Firwood School District to the Japanese?" Bean likely came up with the idea to ask Thompson for a legal procedure to suspend Japanese schools from publicity for the mass meeting. This letter illustrates how Japanese language schools quickly became perceived as a menace to public school educators and foreshadowed more organized action. The same article continued to arouse public fears, asserting that in Japanese schools, American-born Japanese children are "Japanized" by "Oriental teachers." It continued that while American schools are closed for summer vacation, the Japanese schools are open, and only Japanese are permitted to attend, and many are also sent to Japan to complete the "Japanization process." The article further inflated false information that these children of picture brides populate many Japanese schools, and enrollment had increased in the last few years, and that complete political control of Washington by these American-born "Japs" would be possible within ten to fifteen years.

Compiling the Washington Textbook Series

Aware of the rising Americanization movement, Japanese community leaders had already begun to question the value of maintaining Japanese language schools. Ototaka Yamaoka, a Seattle businessman and community leader, criticized the nationalistic attitude of Japanese language schools on the West Coast in a 1918 speech.[32] Yamaoka contended that the schools utilized textbooks composed by the Japanese state to teach the Nisei to be loyal to the emperor and the country and even hold a ceremony on the emperor's birthday, just as public schools did in Japan. He continued that in the eyes of the Americanization movement, simply maintaining a Japanese language school itself could be interpreted as a challenge to the American government.[33] San Francisco's Japanese Consul General Tamekichi Ota also discouraged providing Nisei with Japanese language education. He stated in an interview that it is natural for Japanese nationals abroad to obey all the laws of their host country. Following the same argument, Ota said it is very logical that the educational policy for Japanese American children living in America should be determined by the American government.[34]

There were, on the other hand, bold voices among Issei leaders against yielding to outside suppression and blindly following Americanization. An article in the August 16, 1918, *Hokubei Jiji* contended that unlike public schools in Japan, Japanese language schools in Washington provided neither nationalistic education nor undermined American public education. Furthermore, like foreigners studying Japanese, the purpose of the Japanese language school was to foster the ability to carry out ordinary conversation, and the teachers even had choices regarding to what extent the contents of the state-compiled textbooks should be used. It stressed the necessity of maintaining the language schools in order to prepare the children to enter a Japanese public school if they had a chance to go "home."[35]

Echoing these pressures both inside and outside of the Nikkei community, discussion of the compilation of new textbooks in Washington took priority at the fall 1918 Nihonjinkai meeting, although it was decided that the project would not be taken up at that time. The topic of creating new textbooks also came up at a central Nikkei organization meeting. Based on the 1918 Pacific Coast Japanese Association Deliberative Council's resolution, an education committee was established, and regional representatives met in San Francisco on November 16, 1918, to discuss unifying Japanese schools and compiling textbooks to replace the Monbusho series. From

Washington State, Heiji Okuda was sent to the first meeting. The meeting ended, however, without making any headway into the issue.[36]

Until early 1919, the *Hokubei Jiji* advocated Japanese language schools and was an opinion leader in insisting on Japanese rights to educate their children. A *Hokubei Jiji* editorial titled "Freedom of Education" criticized Japanese educators and politicians alike who were too easily co-opted by the dominant culture, arguing that the government's attempt to control individual thought is completely imperialistic, and that the Nikkei had the right to establish schools and provide an education for their children.[37] Nonetheless, the newspaper did reverse course on the Japanese language school issue, likely in response to Japanese exclusionists' attacks. After Seattle's mass meeting, the paper printed a translation of the *Star*'s article on Bean's effort to abolish Japanese language schools. An unsigned editorial claimed, "as I repeatedly warned," Japanese language schools would be attacked by Japanese exclusionists if these schools were maintained under present conditions. The paper reported that Miller Freeman and his group had brought about the movement to abolish Japanese language schools. It argued that the present language schools existed as public institutions, but they rather should be privately owned. Otherwise, the article continued, Japanese would have no defense from criticisms such as those that claimed Japanese language schools provided young American citizens with Japanese education and "Japanized" them or that Nikkei built their schools wherever they lived and imbued children with Japanese spirit.[38]

The Nihonjinkai finally launched the project of creating new textbooks on its own locally, after the 1919 Pacific Coast Japanese Association Deliberative Council, meeting in Portland, decided that each community would be responsible for compiling its own new textbooks.[39] The Nihonjinkai formed a textbook compilation committee consisting of several Issei leaders, including Torataro Takabatake, principal of the Seattle Japanese Language School, which served 250 Nisei students in 1920. The school, located at Weller Street and Sixteenth Avenue, had become established in 1902.[40] The textbook compilation committee in Washington attempted to solve several problems that had confronted the creation of Japanese language textbooks.[41] First, they planned a series of new textbooks on Japanese language that would not interfere with "Americanization." By doing so, they also hoped to counter the image propagated by anti-Japanese activists such as Valentine S. McClatchy of California, who testified to the U.S. Congress that a Nisei child "absorbs Japanese ideals and patriotism and that contempt for all other nations which is the spirit of every Japanese school textbook."[42] Second, the new textbooks should eliminate problems derived from the Monbusho textbooks, such as content unfamiliar to children living in America, many of whom had never visited Japan. They also modified the language to meet the abilities and needs of the Nisei. By 1920, the committee had completed its first drafts.[43]

One year after the rebirth of the campaigns to propagate a "Japanese problem" in Washington, the House Committee on Immigration and Naturalization came to Seattle and Tacoma from July 26 to August 3, 1920.[44] Unlike the earlier hearings in California, the Japanese language school issue did not seem to be a major focus in Washington.[45] However, one day after the six-day official hearings (August 4), the chairman of the committee, Representative Albert Johnson, and fellow committee member John E. Raker of California continued their own "personal investigation." They visited various businesses and educational and religious institutions run by the Japanese in Seattle.[46] According to Kojiro Takeuchi's history of Nikkei in Washington, they also visited the Seattle Japanese Language School and received drafts of all the volumes of the newly compiled Washington textbooks. Takeuchi described the details of this experience as follows:

> We believed that this was a good opportunity to sweep out the suspicion of the American public towards the Japanese language schools, and requested them to visit the Seattle Japanese Language School for observation (on August 3, 1920), and submitted drafts of all the volumes of the Japanese textbooks. . . . We acknowledged that they understood the facts about the Japanese language schools, which had been causing misunderstandings. Thus, the mission of the new textbooks was already accomplished before its real publication.[47]

His account would make it appear that the examination of the new textbook series by the immigration committee was requested by the Nikkei themselves. However, the hearings transcripts indicate that Representative Raker inquired about the textbooks and requested that Daihachi Matsumi, president of the Nihonjinkai, submit a full set of the old edition (Monbusho textbooks) and drafts of the new edition.[48] Regardless, as Takeuchi wrote, the Nihonjinkai's mission was partially accomplished, as the actual publication took place and the new 1921 school year started out with the new textbooks. However, the project failed in its larger mission to remove the dominant society's long-term "misunderstandings" about Japanese language schools; Japanese educators and Nihonjinkai leaders soon found out that they had been overly optimistic as they continued to face many more serious attacks.

This began with the Seattle school district's decision to segregate "foreign students" on October 4, 1920. This stemmed from an incident at Franklin High School, where children from Mercer Island were not admitted because of a lack of capacity. Irate parents "found" twenty-six Japanese students (born in Japan) in the school and accused the school of having room for "foreigners," but not for children of white taxpayers. The Nihonjinkai took this incident seriously and interpreted this specifically as a threat to exclude Japanese students. After discussing strategy, the Hokubei Nihonjinkai (Japanese Association of North America in Seattle), and Japanese schoolteachers sent a statement to the school administration. The Nikkei leaders tried to convince them that segregating Japanese Americans who were scattered around the city would be a costly change, since the school authorities would have to rescind local school boundaries in order to send all "foreign" students to a segregated school. Issei parents and teachers also questioned how the school district authorities would deal with other foreigners, such as Canadian-born students, many of whom were attending Seattle public schools. The Seattle School Board recognized that the segregation would not be realistic, and dropped its plans.[49] In the same month, however, the Washington Education Association endorsed a foreign language school control bill at its annual conference in Yakima.[50] The bill was proposed to the Washington State legislature on February 14, 1921. Bill 140 would have prohibited aliens from teaching in private or public schools in Washington without a special permit from the superintendent of public instruction. This closely resembled Hawaii's Act 30, which gave the superintendent of public instruction full control over the operation of Japanese language schools at the most basic level of who could teach.[51] The Washington State Senate approved the bill by a vote of thirty-seven to two, but the Beika Iinkai (Americanization Committee) of the Nihonjinkai waged a fight against the bill, and it was killed in the House Education Committee.[52]

Examining the Textbooks

It was within this historical context that the Nihonjinkai composed the eight volumes of the elementary school textbook series *Nihongo Tokuhon* (Japanese Reader) between 1920 and 1921.[53] Each volume was developed for one grade; volumes 1 through 8 cover grades one through eight. Although there is only one text per grade, they incorporate themes from history, geography, biology, novels, folk stories, and biographies, but primarily were designed to develop the students' Japanese reading ability. They are written in the three Japanese writing systems, *katakana* and *hiragana* for the lower levels, and *kanji* (Chinese characters) for the upper levels.

The Washington textbooks as well as the *Jinjo Shogaku Kokugo Tokuhon* (Japanese Elementary School Readers), volumes 1 through 12 (two volumes were used for each grade), published by the Monbusho, both fall into what Tomitaro Karasawa classifies as the "democratic period" of textbooks published between 1918 and 1932. They reflect the characteristics of the Taisho democracy combined with a suggestion of the nationalism that bloomed in the following period.[54] Since there is no existing record available indicating which Monbusho textbooks Washington's Japanese language schools used prior to the new series, one should be able to compare these textbooks to any Monbusho textbook from this period.

How did the Issei educators define "Americanization" in regard to teaching Japanese to the Nisei? How did the Issei envision raising their children as both the next generation of Japanese Americans and as American citizens? One striking difference between the Monbusho series and the Washington set is that illustrations in the latter project Japanese Americans with Caucasian features. This aspect is more significant in the lower levels of the textbooks. While figures in the Monbusho textbooks are dressed in traditional kimono, sit on their knees directly on the floor, and practice calligraphy with a brush on a low table, the model family in the Washington text is shown completely in Western style. They sit on chairs at a round table covered with a lace tablecloth, while one family member plays the piano. It would not have been surprising had the textbook shown an upper-class Japanese American family; however, it is surprising to see almost all of the faces are illustrated using Caucasian features, even though these characters were referred to by Japanese names. For example, in one illustration, a girl called Ohana shows a drawing to her teacher (see fig. 5.1).[55]

Both are illustrated with blond curly hair and Caucasian features, which are drawn differently from the features of the few Asian/Asian American figures seen in the Washington series. Almost all of the faces that are large and clear enough to examine are illustrated with Caucasian features. Since these illustrations were consistent in style and matched the texts, they had to have been specifically created for the Washington textbooks. It is highly unlikely that the illustrations were simply copied from an American textbook and translated into Japanese, as some of these stories came directly

FIG. 5.1 *The young pupil, Ohana, has a Japanese name but is portrayed as white in this illustration from Washington's* Nihongo Tokuhon *(vol. 1, 1920).*

from the Monbusho textbooks. The Washington texts contain, however, figures with Japanese features in historical stories. In these cases, both the illustrations and the stories were adopted from the Monbusho editions.

When the stories in both the Monbusho and Washington texts are examined, the Westernization or "Americanization" of their lifestyle can hardly be missed. In one Washington textbook, a character named Jiro is described as coming from a family of cattle farmers who raise cows, horses, and sheep on a large ranch. Their workers get up at four o'clock to start working, and the whole family shares various tasks, including Jiro's chore of feeding chickens.[56] A family running a ranch cannot represent a typical family in Japan. In contrast, various lessons in the Monbusho textbooks show houses with straw roofs, *shoji* (wooden-framed, paper-sliding partitions), *engawa* (Japanese-style veranda), and backgrounds of rice fields.[57] In another story in the Washington textbook, a figure eats a meal with knife and fork instead of chopsticks in the right hand and a rice bowl in the left, as in the original Monbusho version of the story, "Right and Left."[58] In another story in the Washington set, a sick child is lying in bed, and her mother, dressed in Western clothing, is tending her while another mother sits on a chair, nursing her baby with a milk bottle. In the Monbusho version of the story, a traditionally attired mother sits on the floor breastfeeding her baby (see fig. 5.2).[59]

Again, these illustrations and descriptions might merely demonstrate how the upper-class minority of Japanese Americans lived in the United States at that time. However, what they suggest is that the Japanese language was taught in a format that is stripped from its native culture and superimposed on a totally alien one.[60]

Did the Issei educators want Nisei pupils to be "100 percent American" and possess no knowledge of their parents' culture? Were they concerned that the Nisei would become so Americanized that they would lose the traditional values the Issei acquired through their traditional Japanese education, namely a moral education? In reading the text, one can see that they wanted the Nisei to inherit Japanese virtues and morals. They carefully chose the means to achieve this, however, and taught only concepts they thought appropriate for Japanese Americans.

According to Karasawa, there are several types of Japanese moral education, including "personal," "family," "social" and "national" categories, among others.[61] Although the degree of emphasis differs among these categories of ethics, the Washington textbooks include nearly all aspects of moral education, as did the Monbusho series. However, *gunkoku,* the ethic of national militarism, seen in several stories in the Monbusho editions, is completely absent from the lower level Washington volumes.[62] This is understandable, as deep-rooted anti-Asian racism and stories of the Japanese government's influence over Japanese immigrants' lives in America were fueled by Japan's increasing power and imperialistic ambitions. It was intolerable for many of these Americanization activists to accept the Japanese language schools, as some chose to believe they were centers for indoctrinating imperialism and raising the Nisei, many of whom possessed dual citizenship, as Japanese subjects. Furthermore, the Washington series transposed the national ethics or patriotism from Japan to the United States. This is seen in a story of army soldiers in volume 1 of the Washington text, where "Soldiers are lined up and going on a march. All won in battle."[63] This reading material consists of just two lines accompanied by an illustration of marching soldiers in American army uniforms, shouldering rifles, and led by a doughboy hoisting the Stars and Stripes. This illustration could be interpreted as demonstrating Nikkei determination to live as Americans and serve their adopted nation. This reading is identifiable as a modified version of a

FIG. 5.2 *Miyo-chan is held by a mother in Western dress sitting on a chair in this illustration from* Washington's Nihongo Tokuhon *(vol. 2, 1920).*

FIG. 5.3 *The mother is wearing a kimono and breastfeeding Miyo-chan in Monbusho's* Nihongo Tokuhon *(vol. 2, 1928).*

Japanese soldiers' story contained in the Monbusho's Japanese reader.[64] The adaptation of patriotism was also found in the story of the national flag: "The flag. There is the flag," referring to an illustration of the Stars and Stripes proudly flying in the sky.[65]

The trait of "personal ethics" was most emphasized. This stemmed from Japanese traditional values of filial piety, respect, and modesty, to virtues more acceptable to Americans, such as cooperation, diligence, honesty, and benevolence. These were delivered mainly through Western stories, such as Aesop's fables and biographies of famous Americans. In 1932, Myron E. Powers was told that "Stories for the younger children have been chosen from English books and translated into Japanese."[66]

Although some traditional Japanese stories, such as "Urashima Taro" (the Japanese version of Rip Van Winkle), which illustrated benevolence, and "Momotaro" (The Peach Boy), which illustrated bravery, are found, Japanese historical figures and stories were kept to a minimum.[67] It is quite interesting to note, however, that Washington's volume 4 includes the stories of Amaterasu Omikami, the mythical story of the goddess-creator of Japan, and Emperor Jinmu, the first emperor of the country, with illustrations directly from the Monbusho text. According to Karasawa, the ethic of these stories is *kokutai,* or national polity.[68] There are two important implications of this. The Issei parents and teachers *did* want to teach about the history of the country their ancestors came from and make their offspring feel proud of who they are. The other implication is that anti-Japanese sentiment as well as actual Japanese exclusion efforts in Washington were not yet as severe as they would become later.[69]

Besides moral education, students of the Japanese schools needed to learn appropriate manners, such as "How to Answer the Door," "How to Treat a Guest," and "How to Make a Request" in Japanese.[70] The basic language skills for everyday life in Japan were a component of the texts as well as learning everyday expressions and writing letters for various occasions.

The upper levels, especially volumes 7 and 8, of the Washington texts display different characteristics from the lower levels. Powers's thesis echoes this observation, explaining that the curriculum puts considerable emphasis on the problem of citizenship towards the latter part of the eighth year, since the majority of students, after finishing the eighth grade, did not continue studying Japanese.[71] Volumes 7 and 8 are full of proverbs, sermons, allegories, maxims, and biographical stories to encourage and prepare the Nisei to go out into the real world. The story "Rodo" (Work), for example, describes the attitudes and psychological preparations for work, such as "A man should determine to live on his own. . . . You eat by the sweat of your brow."[72] Another story teaches what traits will be looked for in a good worker: being modest, clean, considerate, courteous, unpretentious, attentive, and calm.[73] Another lesson stresses the importance of responsibility and the demand of willingness to be a part of a group. The textbooks also include stories on Columbus, Lincoln, and "the Nightingale" to encourage Nisei to be ambitious, inventive, diligent, devoting, persevering, and to contribute to society. Health was another concern: eating right, maintaining hygiene, exercising, sleeping well, breathing fresh air, and bathing in sunlight. The textbooks contain all kinds of knowledge related to life, work, and wisdom that the Issei acquired through their experiences and learned from earlier generations.

While these textbooks highlight Japanese traditional values and traits, they still try to bridge Japan and the United States. Aspects of Japanese geography and national holidays are introduced as being parallel to American ones. For example, Memorial Day and the Japanese "equivalent" of Obon were treated together as special days to remember and honor the deceased, and the old Japanese custom of Yabuiri is explained as a parallel to the history of Mother's Day.[74]

The very last lesson of chapter 40 in the final volume carries a clear message from the Issei to the Nisei pupils. It indirectly explains why the Monbusho textbooks were not sufficient, and why they had to create their own textbooks to raise the next generation of Japanese Americans:

> You were born in America and are being educated in American schools and are to become future American citizens. You future American citizens must do your utmost to become good citizens. This is what your parents and your parents' country hope for.

> Among the American citizens there are those who have English, French, German, Russian, Italian, Greek and other ancestors. Besides the white race there are Chinese, negroes, and miscellaneous other races all living peacefully under the stars and stripes just as you all study in school in a friendly manner with children of different nations.

> Just as [you wish your school] to strive for excellence over other schools, so must you make it your primary purpose, as a future American citizen, to raise the name of the Japanese race among the different races; therefore, do not forget the spirit of American Independence. Do not be discouraged by race prejudice. Always cultivate your personality; strive for virtue and arouse yourself and forge ahead in order that you may become a good American citizen.

> The history of Japan reveals the excellent characteristics of the Japanese race. You who learned numerous beautiful historical facts and know of the modern development of Japan should make it a point not to lose the sense of pride as descendents of the excellent Japanese race. Preserve the good points and the beautiful virtues of the Japanese so that you will cause all races to respect you as a worthy Japanese-American citizen in competition with other races.

This, indeed, is the best way to do your duty to America and at the same time repay your parents' country.

You! You future American citizens! Do not disgrace the names of your parents by self degredation [*sic*] and self humiliation. Do not disgrace the name of your parents' country.[75]

Conclusion

The Issei of Washington came originally as sojourning railroad contract workers around the 1890s. Many gradually became owners of small businesses, such as farms, laundries, barbershops, groceries, hotels, and restaurants.[76] This resulted in competition with white businessmen, and after the war, with returning war veterans looking for jobs and farmland.[77] In 1919, an organized anti-Japanese movement was reborn in Washington out of a mass meeting to fabricate a "Japanese problem" and grew into the Seattle Anti-Japanese League. Some Washington newspapers repeatedly brought the news of Japanese exclusion movements from Hawaii and California to fan the racial fire in Washington and to disseminate anti-Japanese sentiment. Perceiving this external pressure, the Nikkei community in Washington was stirred by disputes over the very existence of the Japanese language schools. The project to compile a new textbook series was launched in the midst of this controversy to answer the critical questions of how the Japanese language could be taught without confronting Americanizers, how the new textbooks could remove public suspicion of the Japanese language schools and the Nisei's loyalty, and how they could teach Japanese origins and make the Nisei feel proud while also nurturing faith in the promise of an American dream.

The Washington textbooks answered these questions by demonstrating that on the surface, such cultural aspects as clothing, lifestyle, and environment are displayed as "100 percent American"—in other words, as white. Their determination on this aspect can be seen in the use of Caucasian faces to represent Japanese Americans in the lower levels of the textbooks. The Washington textbooks also promoted American patriotism, not loyalty to the parents' mother country, and introduced the history, geography and historical figures of the United States with the hope that the Nisei would advance like Lincoln and other prominent Americans. However, the textbooks also project the Issei's desperate yearning and challenge to preserve a fundamental level of their heritage, such as Japanese roots and values, and most of all, the Japanese language. These aspects were communicated by stories of the emperor, ancient gods, and Japanese historical figures. One of the stories in volume 8 even teaches of the Japanese navy's victories during the Russo-Japanese War.[78] This should not, in my opinion, be construed primarily as instilling Japanese loyalty in the Nisei, but should be read as their plea to the Nisei to feel proud of being part of the Japanese people.[79] This last lesson of the eighth-grade text could be seen as one reading of the Issei's collective will. It summarizes the very reason why the Issei perceived the Monbusho textbooks as inappropriate for the next generation of Japanese Americans, just as much as they felt it was inappropriate because it generated so much antagonism from the dominant community. Statistics from 1920 show, however, that only eleven students made it to the eighth grade in all of the Japanese language schools in Washington State.[80] This makes one wonder how many of the Nisei over the years reached this advanced level and actually were able to discern this message.

The Washington textbook compilation also reflects the liberal, intellectual, and political atmospheres that the Nikkei community in Seattle held at that time, unique from much of what we know of other Issei communities, such as California or Hawaii. For example, many Issei from Seattle later became prominent figures in politics in Japan. Political debate was lively in the community's many newspapers and magazines, and political forums filled Seattle's Japanese Hall.[81]

The Washington textbook series and the Issei's perceptions of their children's education were later challenged by another critical incident in the history of Japanese language education in America. In 1927, the United States Supreme Court ruled that the laws of the Territory of Hawaii controlling Japanese language schools were unconstitutional. According to Tsutae Sato, principal of the Vancouver Japanese Joint Language School, this incident helped Issei educators regain their confidence in Japanese education and "rebound" towards Japanese nationalism.[82] With this background and the coming golden age of Japanese language schools, the Nihonjinkai took up the project of revising the first textbook series under the supervision of a scholar from Tokyo, which was published as a second edition in 1929.[83]

Respected Japanese historian Teruko Kumei examined this second edition in comparison to the 1924 California readers, *Beikoku Kashu Kyoiku-Kyoku Kentei, Nihongo Tokuhon*. Her findings support Sato's observation that the California version displays more "American" characteristics than the Washington version, which had "rebounded" to more Japanese content than its 1921 first edition. Kumei points out that some of these Americanized elements in the California readers are illustrations of features and word choices. Kumei describes girls in the California series as being depicted with "large eyes and curly hair" while girls in the 1929 counterpart have "almond shaped eyes and black straight hair." According to Kumei, the selection of words, either American or Japanese, differ between the two readers. For example, the California readers introduce *buraun* and *isuto* to refer to "brown" and "east," although Japanese has equivalents, *chairo,* and *nishi,* respectively. The Washington readers, however, utilize English words only when Japanese does not offer equivalents. Kumei insightfully analyzes: "In adopting the mixed language spoken among Japanese immigrants, the California readers can be regarded as Americanized Japanese-language textbooks."[84]

These attributes of the Americanized California textbooks could partially be explainable by historical context. The project to compile California's readers was under strict scrutiny by state authorities as well as the public, since State Senator James M. Inman (Republican, Sacramento) introduced another foreign language school law on January 12, 1923, to eventually abolish Japanese language schools. Therefore, California Japanese language schoolteachers had to submit the newly complied textbooks to the State Board of Education for approval in August 1923. Furthermore, before authorizing the textbooks, the Board of Education sent them to the American Legion, a core anti-Japanese organization that had lobbied for the school control law for its imprimatur.[85]

It was the mission of the Washington Issei to produce textbooks for their children in order to transmit their unfulfilled ambitions. Considering this, it is ironic that both Washington's and California's textbooks suffered countless criticisms within the ethnic community. They were accused of being full of misprints, too difficult, and worse than Monbusho textbooks. Both textbook series, however, continued to be published and used until 1941, when Japanese language schools were closed.[86]

These surviving Washington textbooks show us Issei parents' aspirations of cultural resistance and permanence. They are important documents in returning Issei agency into Japanese American history and in broadening our understanding of how the Issei community viewed its role in America.

Notes

I would like to thank Ellen Hale, John Litz, Sam Taniguchi, and Sadie Yamazaki at the Seattle Betsuin Archives. Scott Edward Harrison of the University of Washington and Kuniko Yamada of Harvard University helped locate important documents

AMERICANIZATION VS. JAPANESE CULTURAL MAINTENANCE 113

regarding Japanese language schools. I also appreciate the Nisei Heritage Research Project, University of Nebraska-Lincoln, for funding my attendance at the Nikkei Experience in the Pacific Northwest conference. Finally, I would like to thank Gail Nomura and Louis Fiset of the University of Washington for their challenging and perceptive questions.

1. U.S. Congress. House. Committee on Immigration and Naturalization, *Japanese Immigration Hearings*. 66th Cong., 2nd sess. (1921; reprint, New York: Arno Press, 1978), 1177–78. Many Japanese language schools in the United States began the school year in April, following Japanese tradition.

2. The Beikoku Seihokubu Renraku Nihonjinkai was originally called the Hokubei Renraku Nihonjinkai until October 1, 1920. Kazuo Ito, *Issei: A History of Japanese Immigrants in North America*, trans. Shinichiro Nakamura and Jean S. Gerard (Seattle: Japanese Community Service, 1973), 202. This was one of the six representative Japanese associations located under the jurisdiction of six Japanese consulates in the United States, which included several local Japanese associations. The Beikoku Seihokubu Renraku Nihonjinkai, located in Seattle, consisted of fifteen local Japanese associations, including the Hokubei Nihonjin Kai in Seattle. Beikoku Seihokubu Renraku Nihonjinkai, *Beikoku Seihokubu Zairyu Nihonjin Hatten Ryakushi* (An overview of the historical development of Japanese in northwest America) (Seattle: Beikoku Seihokubu Renraku Nihonjinkai, 1923), 149–50.

3. One thousand copies of volumes 1 through 4 were produced for each grade, and five hundred copies were produced of volumes 5 through 8. Kojiro Takeuchi, *Beikoku Seihokubu Nippon Iminshi* (History of Japanese immigration in northwest America) (Seattle: Taihoku Nippo, 1929; reprint Tokyo: Yushodo, 1994), 430–31; Katherine J. Lentz, "Japanese-American Relations in Seattle" (master's thesis, University of Washington, 1924), 11.

4. *Hokubei Jiji*, 3 August 1920.

5. U.S. Congress. House. Committee on Immigration and Naturalization, 418, for Japanese language schools in Hawaii, and pages 1177–78 for Washington. See Department of the Interior, Bureau of Education, *A Survey of Education in Hawaii* (Washington D.C.: GPO, 1920), p. 12, for the Japanese population in Hawaii.

6. For the number of Nikkei in California and Washington, see Roger Daniels, *Asian America: Chinese and Japanese in the United States since 1850* (Seattle: University of Washington Press, 1988), 153. The number of the Japanese language schools and the Japanese students attending the schools in California in 1920 are from Shinichi Kato, *Beikoku Nikkeijin Hyakunen Shi* (A history of one hundred years of the Japanese and Japanese Americans in the United States) (Tokyo: Shin Nichibei Shinbun Sha, 1961), 119. Figures for Washington in 1920 are from U.S. Congress, House Committee on Immigration and Naturalization, 1178.

7. Toyotomi Morimoto, *Japanese Americans and Cultural Continuity: Maintaining Language and Heritage* (New York: Garland, 1997), 45. $3,300 was assigned to Northern California and $2,200 to Southern California to underwrite compiling the textbooks.

8. Only five textbooks had been complied by 1918 to replace the Monbusho ones. Yuji Ichioka, *The Issei: The World of the First Generation Japanese Immigrants, 1885–1924* (New York: Free Press, 1988), 205. Ichioka does not mention the details of these early textbooks.

9. *Rafu Shimpo*, 2, 12 July 1921. For more on the Nisei generation, see David K. Yoo, *Growing Up Nisei: Race, Generation, and Culture among Japanese Americans of California, 1924–49* (Urbana: University of Illinois Press, 2000).

10. John Higham, *Strangers in the Land: Patterns of American Nativism 1860–1925* (New York: Atheneum, 1955).

11. Roger Daniels, *The Politics of Prejudice: The Anti-Japanese Movement in California and the Struggle for Japanese Exclusion* (Berkeley: University of California Press, 1962), 63. For the impact of the law, see Ichioka, *Issei*, 214–16.

12. The first target of the movement was to proscribe instruction of the German language in private and public schools. See Frederick C. Luebke, "Legal Restrictions on Foreign Languages in the Great Plains States," in *Languages in Conflict: Linguistic Acculturation on the Great Plains,* ed. Paul Schach (Lincoln: University of Nebraska Press, 1980), 1–19.

13. See Noriko Asato, "Mandating Americanization: Japanese Language Schools and the Federal Survey of Education in Hawaii, 1916–1920," *History of Education Quarterly* 43, no. 1 (summer 2003): 10–38, for the development of the federal Survey of Education in Hawaii.

14. Ann Halsted, "Sharpened Tongues: The Controversy Over the 'Americanization' of Japanese Language Schools in Hawaii, 1919–1927" (Ph.D. diss., Stanford University, 1989), 95–96.

15. Ibid.; Eileen H. Tamura, *Americanization, Acculturation, and Ethnic Identity: The Nisei Generation in Hawaii* (Urbana: University of Illinois Press, 1994).

16. Yoshihide Matsubayashi, "The Japanese Language Schools in Hawaii and California from 1892 to 1941" (Ph.D. diss., University of San Francisco, 1984).

17. Morimoto, *Japanese Americans and Cultural Continuity.*

18. Teruko I. Kumei, "Making 'A Bridge over the Pacific': Japanese Language Schools in the United States, 1900–1941," *American Studies in Scandinavia* 32 (2000): 65–86; Teruko I. Kumei, "'The Twain Shall Meet' in the Nisei? Japanese Language Education and U.S.-Japan Relations, 1900–1940," in *New Worlds, New Lives: Globalization and People of Japanese Descent in the Americas and from Latin America in*

Japan, ed. Lane Ryo Hirabayashi, Akemi Kikumura-Yano, and James A. Hirabayashi (Stanford: Stanford University Press, 2002), 108–25.

19. Myron E. Powers, "Telic Attempts of Two Racial Groups to Retain Their Social Inheritance" (master's thesis, University of Washington, 1932); Misako Sadahiro, "How Education before and during World War II Shaped Nisei Identity," in *The Japanese American Experience,* ed. Jennifer Jopp (Salem, Oreg.: Willamette University, 2000), 27–35. While editing this, I discovered another exception. Mitsuhiro Sakaguchi added background information on the Seattle Japanese Language School in his *Nihonjin Amerika Iminshi* (A history of Japanese immigration to America) (Tokyo: Fuji Shuppan, 2001).

20. *Seattle Star,* 12 August 1919.

21. Just days earlier, U.S. Representative Albert Johnson of Washington announced he was planning to come to Seattle with Immigration and Naturalization Committee members to investigate alleged smuggling of Japanese organized by the Japanese Association. Ibid., 1 August 1919.

22. Ibid., 1, 4, 5, 9, 11 August 1919.

23. Ibid, 1 August 1919.

24. *Tacoma Times,* 30, 31 July 1919, cited in Ronald E. Magden, *Furusato: Tacoma-Pierce County Japanese 1888–1988* (Tacoma, Wash.: Nikkeijinkai, 1998), 57.

25. Daniels, *Politics of Prejudice,* 68.

26. *Seattle Star,* 1 August 1919.

27. Ibid., 12 August 1919; *Tacoma News Tribune,* 12 August 1919.

28. *Seattle Star,* 1, 4, 5, 9, 11 August 1919.

29. As evidence, see articles promoting membership in ibid., 22 August and 3 September 1919.

30. Shortly after the league was formed, Sullivan resigned on September 9, 1919, after being designated as the primary investigator on the Japanese situation by the American Legion. U.S. Congress. House. Committee on Immigration and Naturalization, 1405; Thomas H. Heuterman, *The Burning Horse: Japanese-American Experience in the Yakima Valley, 1920–1942* (Cheney, Wash.: Eastern Washington University Press, 1995), 20. By the time the immigration hearings came to Seattle, Miller Freeman was president of the Anti-Japanese League.

31. *Seattle Star,* 22 August 1919; Douglas R. Pullen, "The Administration of Washington State Governor Louis F. Hart, 1919–1925" (Ph.D. diss., University of Washington, 1974), 234.

32. Ototaka Yamaoka was the second president of the Japanese Association of Washington State. Ito, *Issei,* 136.

33. *Hokubei Jiji,* 27, 31 August and 2, 3 September 1918.

34. Ibid., 13, 14 February 1919. In 1923, Seattle Consul General Chuichi Ohashi also advocated the complete abolishment of Japanese language schools. Shuichi Fukui, *Tacoma Oyobi Chiho Nihonjin Shi* (A history of Japanese Tacoma and vicinity), (Tacoma, Wash.: Tacoma Shuho Sha), 38.

35. *Hokubei Jiji*, 16, 17 August 1918.

36. Takeuchi, *Beikoku Seihokubu Nippon Iminshi*, 427.

37. *Hokubei Jiji*, 12 March 1919.

38. Ibid., 3 September 1919. The paper does not report more details of Freeman's campaign, which is a part of my larger study, *Teaching Mikadoism: The Attack on Japanese Language Schools in Hawaii, California, and Washington, 1919–1927* (Honolulu: University of Hawai'i Press, 2005).

39. Takeuchi, *Beikoku Seihokubu Nippon Iminshi*, 428.

40. Ito, *Issei*, 592.

41. Takeuchi, *Beikoku Seihokubu Nippon Iminshi*, 431.

42. U.S. Congress. House. Committee on Immigration and Naturalization, 383.

43. Takeuchi, *Beikoku Seihokubu Nippon Iminshi*, 432.

44. The hearings came to Washington after San Francisco, Sacramento, Stockton, Angel Island, Fresno, Livingston, Turlock, Auburn, and Los Angeles, between July 12 and 21. The hearings were held in Washington from July 26 to 29, and August 2 to 3, 1920.

45. The president of the Washington Nihonjinkai Daihachi Matsumi submitted a statement regarding the Japanese situation in Washington, in which he included Japanese language schools. U.S. Congress. House. Committee on Immigration and Naturalization, 1205.

46. *Seattle Star*, 5 August 1920.

47. Takeuchi, *Beikoku Seihokubu Nippon Iminshi*, 432. Translation by the author. Apparently, the date that Johnson and Raker visited the Seattle Japanese Language School does not match the one reported in *Seattle Star* and Takeuchi's description.

48. U.S. Congress. House. Committee on Immigration and Naturalization, 1192.

49. Takeuchi, *Beikoku Seihokubu Nippon Iminshi*, 180–81.

50. Ibid., 429.

51. Senate Bill 140 in State of Washington, *Printed Bills of the Legislature, 17th sess. Senate*, (1921), n.p.

52. Takeuchi, *Beikoku Seihokubu Nippon Iminshi*, 429; Magden, *Furusato*, 61. The establishment of Beika Iinkai was reported in the November 5, 1919 *Hokubei Jiji*.

53. The Seattle Japanese Language School offered grades one to eight and, above that, two years of advanced levels. Yoriaki Nakagawa, *Akiko* (Seattle: self-published, 1934), 234; Powers, "Telic Attempts," 29. Seattle Japanese Language School Principal Nakagawa wrote that first through eighth graders used the textbooks compiled

in Seattle, but after that, the advanced levels used ones compiled by a professor in Tokyo. From this, it is assumed that each volume was made for a respective grade. Some of the textbooks indicate different publication years. For example, copies of volumes 2 and 5, examined by the author, were printed in 1926. Japanese textbooks, however, indicate the year of printing. I am thus assuming that they are essentially the same edition of textbooks published between 1920 and 1921.

54. Tomitaro Karasawa, *Kyokasho no Rekishi* (History of textbooks) (Tokyo: Gyosei, 1989), 399. According to Karasawa's categorization of Japanese national textbooks, the Japanese textbooks used in this study were categorized as Period II. Period I textbooks (1910–1917) emphasized nationalistic and imperialistic factors, such as the importance of family and ancestors. These were taught in parallel to the relationship between Japanese subjects and the emperor. If the present study compared Period I national textbooks and Washington textbooks, the difference between them would have been much more significant.

55. Beikoku Seihokubu Renraku Nihonjinkai, *Nihongo Tokuhon* (Japanese language reader), vol. 1 (Tokyo: Jiyu Kappansho, 1920), 81.

56. Beikoku Seihokubu Renraku Nihonjinkai, *Nihongo Tokuhon* (Japanese language reader), vol. 5 (Tokyo: Jiyu Kappansho, 1926), 27–31.

57. An illustration of a Japanese house with a straw roof, *engawa* and *shoji,* can be seen on volume 1 of the Monbusho textbook. Monbusho, *Jinjo Shogaku Kokugo Tokuhon* (Elementary school reader), vol. 1 (Tokyo: Nihon Shoseki, 1918), 38.

58. The Washington version of the story "Right and Left" is contained in volume 2 of *Nihongo Tokuhon,* 1926, and the same story of the Monbusho version is also in volume 2 of *Jinjo Shogaku Kokugo Tokuhon,* 1928.

59. The story "Miyo-chan" is found in the second volume of both the Monbusho and Washington sets.

60. Because the language was taught in a culturally alien environment, some words were invented as direct translations of English words, such as *hataraki-nin* for "workers" (vol. 2, p. 28) and *uma-zukai* for "a servant who takes care of horses"(vol. 5, p. 151).

61. Karasawa, *Kyokasho no Rekishi,* 282.

62. One of the stories to inspire nationalism and militarism in volume 5 of the Monbusho textbook is the story of "Suihei no Haha" (Sailor's mother). The theme of the story is to praise the self-sacrifice of a mother who wrote a letter to her son on the battleship *Takachiho.* In the story, an officer sees a soldier crying while reading a letter and accuses him of remembering his beloved wife and children and rather than giving up his life for the country. However, the soldier shows the letter to the officer, which expresses his mother's disappointment that her son had not been able to serve the emperor by giving his own life in battle. She prays for her son to

serve the country by dying in battle. The officer is impressed by the letter and encourages the soldier to tell his mother that they will die for the emperor and for the honor of the battleship. Karasawa, *Kyokasho no Rekishi,* 54.

63. Beikoku Seihokubu Renraku Nihonjinkai, *Nihongo Tokuhon,* vol. 1, 25.

64. Monbusho, *Jinjo Shogaku Tokuhon* (Elementary school Japanese language reader), *vol. 1,* (Tokyo: Nihon Shoseki, 1918), 32.

65. Beikoku Seihokubu Renraku Nihonjinkai, *Nihongo Tokuhon,* vol. 1, 16.

66. Powers, "Telic Attempts," 36–37.

67. The stories of "Urashima Taro" and "Momotaro" are found in volume 2 of the Washington textbook. The author used Karasawa's categorization regarding what kind of an ethical aspect each story was supposed to teach. However, more than one moral aspect could be included in one story.

68. Karasawa, *Kyokasho no Rekishi,* 49.

69. When California's 1921 Foreign Language School Law was enacted, California's textbook compilation project was still in process. Therefore, Japanese educators in California submitted the Monbusho textbooks along with a translation to the State Board of Education for permission to use them until the new readers could be completed. The state permitted them to be used after eliminating several stories, including the one on Emperor Jinmu. Morimoto, *Japanese Americans and Cultural Continuity,* 45.

70. Volume 2 contains the subject of "How to Treat a Guest" and volume 3 contains "How to Answer the Door" and "How to Make a Request." To teach the proper way to make a request, a mother teaches her boy to say *dozo* (please). While this is considered to be good manners in English, it is awkward in Japanese.

71. Powers, "Telic Attempts," 37.

72. Beikoku Seihokubu Renraku Nihonjinkai, *Nihongo Tokuhon* (Japanese language reader), vol. 8 (Tokyo: Jiyu Kappansho, 1921).

73. Beikoku Seihokubu Renraku Nihonjinkai, *Nihongo Tokuhon* (Japanese language reader), vol. 7 (Tokyo: Jiyu Kappansho, 1921).

74. Beikoku Seihokubu Renraku Nihonjinkai, *Nihongo Tokuhon* (Japanese language reader), vol. 6 (Tokyo: Jiyu Kappansho, 1921).

75. Powers, "Telic Attempts," 37–38.

76. Beikoku Seihokubu Renraku Nihonjinkai, *Beikoku Seihokubu Zairyu Nihonjin Hatten Ryakushi* (An overview of the historical development of Japanese in northwest America) (Seattle: Beikoku Seihokubu Renraku Nihonjinkai, 1921), 3–4, 50.

77. Although the 1919 legislature passed a land settlement grant bill for veterans, the legionnaires maliciously claimed that the Japanese farmers' occupancy of the best land on the Yakima Indian Reservation prevented veterans from farming. Pullen, "The Administration of Washington State Governor Louis F. Hart," 234.

78. Beikoku Seihokubu Renraku Nihojinkai, *Nihongo Tokuhon* (Japanese language reader), vol. 8 (Tokyo: Jiyu Kappansho, 1921), 88–92.

79. The Issei themselves showed their patriotism to both Japan and the United States. For example, when two Japanese warships came to Tacoma in 1929, the Japanese community welcomed them by waving flags and playing both Japanese and American music. Magden, *Furusato,* 94.

80. U.S. Congress. House. Committee on Immigration and Naturalization, 1178.

81. Ito, *Issei,* 137–38. See Shotaro Frank Miyamoto, *Social Solidarity among the Japanese in Seattle* (Seattle: University of Washington Press, 1939), for the characteristics of the Japanese community in Seattle during the 1920s and 1930s.

82. Tsutae Sato, *Beika ni Okeru Dai Nisei no Kyoiku* (Education of the second generation in the United States and Canada) (Vancouver: Jikyo-Do, 1932), 29–30. Sato categorizes this period as the "Rebound Period."

83. Kato, *Beikoku Nikkeijin Hyakunen Shi,* 1008.

84. Kumei, "Making 'A Bridge over the Pacific,'" 73–74.

85. Kato, *Beikoku Nikkeijin Hyakunen Shi,* 120.

86. Morimoto, *Japanese Americans and Cultural Continuity,* 46–47; Kato, *Beikoku Nikkeijin Hyakunen Shi,* 120.

6 / "THE NAIL THAT STICKS UP GETS HIT"

The Architecture of Japanese American Identity in the Urban Environment, 1885–1942

GAIL LEE DUBROW

Scholars of American ethnic studies and architectural history rarely have been in dialogue, yet both groups share overlapping concerns that would benefit from the conversation. While literature, film, and the fine arts frequently have been studied as expressions of ethnic identity, the meanings of architecture remain largely unexplored by scholars of American ethnic studies. Meanwhile, scholarship by architectural historians on the expression of ethnic cultural traditions in the built environment has not always benefited from recent conceptual advances in American ethnic studies. As a result, architectural historians often have overlooked or misinterpreted signs of ethnicity in the built environment. The study of Japanese American architecture in Seattle's Nihonmachi, or Japantown, however, suggests the value of bringing scholars of these two fields into dialogue, which would result in a more complex interpretation of the meaning of ethnic signs in the urban landscape.

Whether examining the adaptation of Rhenish barn-building traditions in Pennsylvania or the sole surviving joss house in a rural California Chinatown, most studies of vernacular architecture have taken the presence of ethnic signs to indicate the robustness of cultural traditions and their dynamic adaptation in a new land, while their disappearance generally has been taken as evidence of cultural assimilation. While the conventional wisdom suggests that Japanese immigrants quickly "lost" ethnic traditions and rapidly conformed to American architectural practices, findings from this study suggest that racism played a powerful role in persuading Japanese immigrants to abandon or mask outward signs of ethnicity in the architecture of one western Washington Japantown, even while the interior spaces contained robust expressions of cultural identity. Japanese immigrants adopted a strategy of blending into the American cultural fabric in an effort to ward off racist hostility from exclusionary federal immigration policies, restrictive state land laws, and discriminatory city ordinances. Unfortunately, these efforts to minimize cultural differences proved unsuccessful in the face of a wave of anti-Japanese sentiment that swept the western states in the early decades of the twentieth century.

Moving beyond the simple paradigm of assimilation theory that has dominated the study of ethnic cultural traditions in vernacular architecture, this paper suggests that a fuller conceptualization of racism is needed to understand the architectural history of ethnic communities of color in the United States. Furthermore, it suggests that community responses to racial discrimination, particularly strategies of resistance, are critical to interpreting the meaning of ethnic signs in the built environment.

In western cities with a population of Japanese immigrants large enough to sustain the development of Nihonmachi, the design and construction of key community institutions were occasions when collective decisions had to be made about how much to stand out as Japanese immigrants or blend in as potential Americans. Seattle's Japanese community adopted a strategy of blending into the American cultural fabric in the design of its secular institutions, such as the language school and community hall, hoping their Americanization efforts would counter racist perceptions of them as inassimilable aliens and ward off exclusionary policy initiatives. In defense, the community pursued a strategy of architectural assimilation, a kind of "strategic invisibility." The architectural metaphor of a popular Japanese proverb, "Deru kugi wa utareru," captures the thought perfectly. Translated into English, it reads: "The nail that sticks up gets hit." If building facades by and large were exercises in "passing" safely in a hostile environment, their interiors—into which few Caucasians passed—more openly expressed the Issei's deep commitment to ensuring continuity in cultural practices.

One likely factor shaping the choice of western rather than Japanese forms for the civic institutions established by Seattle's Nikkei community was the adoption of European and American building practices in the design of public buildings in Japan during the Meiji era. Beginning in 1861, Western-style buildings were erected in Japan as part of the Meiji government's efforts to adjust treaties with England and the United States on more favorable terms.[1] Foreign architects were commissioned to design the most important new public buildings of the period.[2] Western styles became normative for new construction in the public sphere, even while Japanese architectural styles persisted in the private realm of domestic architecture.[3]

Far-reaching reforms of Japan's educational system during the Meiji era, emphasizing universal education, meant that primary schools were a focus of new Western-style construction.[4] The Issei responsible for establishing cultural institutions such as the Seattle's Japanese Language School and the Nippon Kan or Japanese community hall were Meiji men who accepted the notion of employing western conventions in the design of public buildings, even as the spaces they created were dedicated to transmitting traditional cultural practices to the next generation, born in America.

The language school that Seattle's Japanese community erected in 1913 (with later additions) took most of its formal architectural cues from the City of Seattle's stock of wooden public school buildings. There are no known models for the design of Seattle's language school back in Japan, where brick was adopted as the preferred material in new Western-style school buildings.[5]

The school began operation in 1902, but formal plans for a purpose-built structure were initiated several years later, fueled by charitable contributions by visiting Japanese dignitaries. Active fundraising to support the construction of a school building coincided with a period of heated public debate over the presence of Japanese children in San Francisco public schools, which led many Nikkei communities to question whether they should establish their own educational institutions or fight for their right to attend public schools on an integrated basis. Seattle's nascent Japanese Language School became caught up in the debate. In June 1908 the *Seattle Times* reported the headline story: "Japanese to Quit Public Schools: Seattle Orientals Will Educate Their Children Privately." The report claimed that:

> Seattle Japanese have decided to withdraw their children from the public schools because, it was alleged at a special meeting of the Japanese Association of the State of Washington, held in the Baker Building last night, the education given is not satisfactory to them. Japanese Schools and Japanese instructors will be substituted for American schools and American instructors.[6]

This would be one of the last times that Japanese language schools could openly claim an attachment to Japanese heritage, saying the students would "be instructed in loyalty to the Mikado," as the rise of the exclusion movement made it necessary to conceal or modify these aims by 1920.

Despite momentary agitation for separate Japanese schools, first among white racists and soon after by some segments of the Japanese community, the San Francisco school crisis was averted due to the intervention of President Theodore Roosevelt. Likewise, Seattle's Japanese immigrants never

FIG. 6.1 *Although Seattle's Japanese language school was intended to ground Nisei children in their cultural heritage, Japanese architectural traditions were rejected for the building design; instead, it was modeled on Western public school buildings. (North American Times Yearbook, 1936)*

actually withdrew their children from the city's public schools. By the end of the first decade of the twentieth century, Issei debate over the education of the Nisei clearly had shifted from the former emphasis on "'pure' Japanese schools" to replace American public schools toward "supplementary education in Japanese ethics, history, geography and language." According to Ichioka, "by 1910 it can be said that the Issei recognized the primacy of American public school education."[7] Thus Seattle's Japanese Language School ultimately was designed to be an after-school facility.

The pervasive development of Japanese language schools wherever Japanese immigrants settled in the American West testifies to Issei anxiety over their status as aliens ineligible for citizenship as well as concerns over the likely assimilation of their American-born children.[8] For these reasons, most families believed that training their children in Japanese language, history, and culture would provide an insurance policy should they be expelled from the United States or choose to return to Japan. The schools might also help to bridge emerging generational differences by teaching the Nisei to appreciate their Japanese heritage. At the very least, it would prepare them for work in Nihonmachi enterprises should their wider ambitions be frustrated by racial discrimination.

If Meiji-era public buildings were designed to aggressively persuade Western powers that Japan was a civilized nation worthy of superior treatment on the world stage, Seattle's Japanese Language School (which was completed one year after the death of the Meiji emperor, Mutsuhito, and in the first year of the Taisho era) was designed more defensively: minimizing the perceived threat by exclusionists while maintaining a commitment to ground the Nisei in their cultural heritage. Reducing the threat was critical because Japanese language schools were "ever the center of anti-Japanese agitation" in California and other western states.[9] Valentine S. McClatchy, one of the most vocal exclusionists, testified before Congress that Japanese children were "educated in separate Japanese schools . . . where they are taught to be loyal and ideal Japanese citizens."[10] To fend off the exclusionists, who charged both Buddhist churches and Japanese language schools with "indoctrinating the children with Emperor worship," Japanese associations attempted to distance secular language schools from those operated by Buddhist churches, whose public displays of Japanese customs were more difficult to recast in a form likely to pacify their common enemy.

The 1920 hearings of the House Committee on Immigration and Naturalization offer clear evidence that leaders of the Nikkei community employed this strategy of disassociation in an effort to protect the language schools from repressive state regulation and fight the looming threat of exclusion. D. Matsumi of Seattle, who served as a manager with the Furuya Company and as president of the United North American Japanese Associations, explicitly distanced the Seattle language school from Buddhism when he testified that "in California the Buddhist Church maintains its own language school, but in this part of the country they do not."[11] Meanwhile, Karl Kiyoshi Kawakami, who was regarded as "an unofficial publicist for the Japanese foreign ministry throughout much of his career,"[12] suggested in his 1921 book, *The Real Japanese Question,* that no more than ten of fifty-four California language schools were maintained by the Buddhist church. The clear implication was that the majority of language schools could be redeemed by a program of Americanization, which he advocated.

Presumably the public image of tradition-bound Buddhists could not

FIG. 6.2 *California agricultural communities whose Japanese populations were predominantly Buddhist hired Issei carpenters to build language schools with traditional Japanese construction details, such as this school in Castroville, California. (Photo by Gail Lee Dubrow)*

be rehabilitated, besides which they enjoyed constitutional protections of religious freedom that did not extend to other aspects of Japanese American community life. Since Buddhist temples and language schools both were charged with "Mikadoism,"[13] one bureaucratic strategy for protecting language schools may have involved establishing them as independent entities. Certainly this was the case in cities such as Seattle, with a sufficiently large population to support both a language school run by the Seattle Buddhist Temple and an independent language school.[14] A second strategy for protecting the language school and distancing it from Buddhists' traditionalism may have been iconographic, namely: to abstain from the use of Japanese architectural conventions often featured in the design of Buddhist temples. Thus the choice of Western-style wooden clapboard architecture for Seattle's Japanese Language School, with a roof that was as conspicuously flat as the roofs of Buddhist temples were steeply pitched, broadcast the message that Seattle's Japanese Language School was a secular institution with no formal ties to Buddhism. This despite the very real relationship between the two institutions: after all, the Seattle Buddhist Church had housed the language school in the years immediately preceding the 1913 opening of the Weller Street building. However, in the politically charged climate of anti-Japanese agitation, appearances literally mattered. While this interpretation remains conjecture in the absence of direct evidence, such as minutes of the building committee or other records of decision making,

support for this interpretation can be found in the fact that California agricultural communities such as Castroville and Concord, whose Japanese populations were almost exclusively Buddhist, hired Issei carpenters who built
language schools with *irimoya* roofs and other Japanese construction details.[15]

Nevertheless, despite the Seattle Japanese Language School's public display of assimilation projected in the Western-style wood-frame construction and American public school house type, the formal etiquette required
of students once they entered the building clearly marked language schools
as ethnic cultural space. Surviving remnants of interior decoration, which
mirror conventional classrooms, suggest that architectural features were not
particularly important in the process of defining the language school as Japanese. Rather, its power derived from the fact that Issei parents invested the
principal of the language school with substantial authority to enforce rituals of normative behavior in this space on a daily basis—in sharp contrast
with the behavioral norms the Nisei absorbed though their immersion in
American culture. In her memoir of attending Seattle's Japanese Language
School, Monica Sone explained that

> As time went on, I began to suspect that there was much more to Nihon Gakko
> than learning the Japanese language. There was a driving spirit of strict dis-
> cipline behind it all which reached and weighed heavily upon each pupil's
> consciousness.[16]

Nisei who attended Seattle's Japanese Language School as children in the
1930s echo Sone's impatience with Issei proscriptions, particularly the
emphasis on *shushin* (ethics). One former language school student interviewed in the 1990s prodded her peers to remember the formal occasions
when Japanese dignitaries came to call at the school, recalling that

> they used our gym and we all had to file in and we stood there and they told
> us to bow and we'd bow and then nobody would listen to what ever it was
> and then we'd all have to march back to school.[17]

The sternness and solemnity of Issei men proved alienating to the American-
born children of Japanese immigrants, whose critical perspective on traditional cultural practices was magnified from the vantage point of the freedom they briefly enjoyed during the daily walk between the American and
Japanese school buildings.

Architectural historians are well aware that the proscribed and actual uses of space aren't necessarily identical, and psychologists recognize that public behavior doesn't always correspond to internal feelings. Both of these insights are useful for understanding the tensions between Issei and Nisei perceptions of their cultural identity that were negotiated in the contested space of the language school. Perhaps the most telling aspect of the Seattle Japanese Language School's floor plan was the location of the principal's office immediately inside the front entry, where the students' behavioral shift was expected to take place. The notion that the language school was all about learning how to behave properly across the divide of Japanese and American cultural spaces is reinforced by the fact that the principal of Seattle's language school, Yoriaki Nakagawa, was also the author of *The Common Sense of Japanese and American Etiquette,* published in 1937.[18] His motive for writing the book was

> that I felt keenly the over-riding importance of etiquette for us who lived in a foreign land. Since the old days we had been the race of courtesy, and I wanted people to demonstrate this national characteristic as international citizens in America. I used this as a teaching material for the study of both language and etiquette.[19]

Perhaps not surprisingly, the most significant interior decorations in Seattle's Japanese Language School hung from the walls in the form of framed calligraphic souvenirs from visiting dignitaries, posters dictating proper behavior, and other reminders of a distinctively Japanese etiquette under which most American-born children of Japanese immigrants chafed.

While Principal Nakagawa reportedly ran the school "with an iron fist" (as one student put it: "he was the boss and there was no escape"), even the principal was bemused by the level of resistance he sometimes encountered from students, as former teacher Tamaki Nagai recollected:

> There were some students who were beyond the teachers' control. For example, after school one of the woman teachers asked Principal Nakagawa to discipline a certain student. I was there at the time and heard the student. When he was scolded, he called the Principal, "ojisan" (old man). I reproached him, saying, "The Principal is not ojisan! Call him sensei!" (teacher). But the student repeatedly said "ojisan, ojisan." In the end, Mr. Nakagawa sighed and said with a grin on his face, "Boy, he's audacious."[20]

While few former students retained much of the language, for better or for worse many remembered the moral lessons that were enacted in the distinctively Japanese cultural spaces that they occupied for a part of each day. As Tama Tokuda recalled,

> They tried to instill in us all kinds of Japanese customs—like *Toban*—that means little chores like erasing the board, helping sweep the floors. . . . So that was a carry over from Japan. We all stood up and bowed before the class started.[21]

Because attending language school was a common experience, and by all appearances it was aimed at inducing conformity, Nisei gave it the nickname "Typs School." According to Bill Hosokawa, it stood for "typical Jap." Some former students remembered calling it "Gyp School," grousing about their janitorial chores under the Toban system as well as feeling shortchanged on playtime compared with *hakujin* kids.

Perhaps because they enjoyed less access to or control over other public recreational spaces, girls seem to have enjoyed going to language school to a greater degree than boys. Boys especially were resentful, since it closed off the possibility of heading for the basketball court or baseball diamond with their *hakujin* classmates in after-school activities. Tama Tokuda remembered that the boys "just went wild when they went to Japanese Language School," which left her feeling sorry for the female teachers, who "had tears in their eyes because they had such a hard time disciplining the boys." One of the boys, Sam Shoji, who avowedly spent a significant part of his language school education sitting in the principal's office, recalled that

> the teachers were interested in . . . teaching us the language, but also a lot of the culture discipline, history and typical things that were taught in school in Japan.
>
> Well, speaking for myself, I wasn't too interested in it. I was tired and I wanted to play. . . . My reputation was that I just wouldn't mind anybody— pulling pranks, finding ways to distract the class, walking in late, eating in class. They never kicked you out of class, but they sent you down to the principal's office.

The emphasis on etiquette also may have seemed unmanly. Even in Meiji Japan, where both sexes enjoyed access to education, special spaces in the Japanese style were set aside in high schools for girls to learn the traditional arts that made for good wives and mothers. As late as 1933, an official guide to Japan issued by the Japanese Government Railways noted that a

> feature of the girls' High Schools is the course in etiquette, including the tea ceremony and the arrangement of flowers. For this purpose every girls' High School has a special building in Japanese style, with a room which may be called "a laboratory of manners."[22]

Perhaps not surprisingly, girls alone illustrated proper behavior in Principal Nakagawa's etiquette book. But by all accounts, Sam Shoji's resistance to accepting the authority his parents had invested in the language school was not unique or limited by gender. Even the most devoted female students resented the way language school interfered with their ability to participate in after-school activities, including organized sports, as they became rebellious American teenagers. As a result of the tension between Issei expectations and Nisei desires, language schools became critical sites of intergenerational conflict and negotiation, as many Nisei youth resisted efforts to bolster the Japanese part of their hyphenated identity.

Like the language school, the relatively austere facade of Seattle's Nippon Kan or Japanese community hall concealed a vibrant array of ethnic performances that took place inside.[23] Construction of Seattle's Nippon Kan hall started in 1907 and was completed several years later. Early plans to house a language school within the community building were abandoned in favor of a combination hotel and clubhouse, which initially was intended to accommodate an influx of Japanese tourists in conjunction with the 1909 Alaska-Yukon-Pacific Exposition. However, it was not built in time to profit from the event.[24]

Seattle newspapers, reporting on early plans for the Nippon Kan, identified the model for this building "as an American club house, though not as expensive as the more pretentious homes of the Seattle clubs."[25] In a sense this was accurate, since the building was intended to serve as an umbrella for many community organizations. As built, it constituted a hybrid type that served not only as a workingmen's hotel, but also as a theatre and community hall for Seattle's Japanese immigrants and their children.[26] The three-and-a-half-story brick building, overlooking Seattle's Nihonmachi, lacked any distinctively Japanese architectural features, other than the mix of residential, commercial, and civic uses typical of buildings in urban Nihonmachi. Budd Fukei's description of the Nippon Kan's entry suggests that it was designed to blend into the urban fabric rather than call attention to itself:

FIG. 6.3 *The relatively austere brick façade of Nippon Kan Hall concealed a vibrant array of ethnic performances inside. (Courtesy of Puget Sound Regional Archives)*

FIG. 6.4 *A group of performers at the Nippon Kan Hall welcomes the Japanese Navy to Seattle. (Courtesy of the Archives Committee, Seattle Buddhist Temple)*

Nippon Kan was located in a hotel building, its unpretentious doorway was between the hotel entrance and the door to a grocery store. Inside, the Nippon Kan was equally informal.[27]

The fact that the construction of the Nippon Kan was contemporaneous with the Japanese Building at the Alaska-Yukon-Pacific Exposition as well as the Seattle Buddhist Church suggests that more expressive models of ethnic and national identity were available as architectural alternatives but actively rejected as models for the design of this community building. Then again, the relatively neutral facade may have helped to mark the Nippon Kan as a civic space with the potential to transcend many of the lines of cleavage that organized the Japanese immigrant community and had the potential to divide it by class, religion, and prefectural origin, among other factors.

There are some indications that theaters in Japan also were not particularly expressive in façade treatments, though they conformed to Japanese vernacular forms. Terry's *Guide to the Japanese Empire* (1927) suggested that theater structures "often occupy mean sites in side streets and with few exceptions are devoid of architectural charm." Yet their interiors clearly were designed to support dramatic traditions that were distinctively Japanese in character:

> The peculiar lateral aisles which project from the side of the stage *(butai)* are called *hanamichi* ("flowery way"), and are used by the actors *(yakusha)* and actresses *(onnayakusha)* in approaching or leaving it. The stage usually rests upon rollers, like a railway turntable, and when a new scene is wanted it is turned round with the scenery and actors in position. The latter sometimes speak their parts (often in strained and hoarse, apoplectic voices); at other times they posture and make pantomimic gestures which are interpreted by the chorus accompanied by samisen.[28]

If the façade of the Nippon Kan building was relatively unadorned with ethnic symbols and signs, crossing the threshold took Japanese immigrants into a vibrant cultural space inside. Its construction literally made space for the community to gather when it was otherwise in short supply. As Miyoshi Yorita recalled, "the only entertainment facilities in Japanese town were movie theaters," such as the Atlas, "and Japanese Hall." Nippon Kan supported a wide range of community meetings and ethnic performances whose ephemeral decorations left no permanent imprint on the building. The tran-

sitory and flexible nature of the space, designed especially for performances, could accommodate a full range of expressions of ethnic identity,
from powerful displays of nationalist sentiment among the Issei to the Nisei's
preoccupation with distinctively American entertainment forms such as har-
monica players and big band music.

But the theater fundamentally was an Issei institution, and as such, it was
designed with at least one traditional architectural element required for Japanese drama. The stage was built with a small extension called a *hanamichi*
or runway that was an essential element in Kabuki performances. So too,
the enactment of traditional dramatic practices in the theater transformed
the Nippon Kan into a distinctively Japanese space, at least for the duration
of the performance, as Tama Tokuda vividly recalled:

> When the Nippon Kan was in use, they used to use a hand-pulled curtain,
> which is the way it's done in Japan. A man pulls it from side to side. And while
> he opens it, they always have a man that uses wooden clackers—it's a little
> stick about 8 or 10 inches—you clack the two together and it makes this very
> clear sound. As the curtain is pulled, the tempo gets faster and faster. Every
> performance was ushered in with that sound. It still thrills me when I hear
> that sound.

The Issei took great pleasure in the Nippon Kan's performances of ancient
Japanese plays, *shamisen* and *shakuhachi* (bamboo flute) players, and the
classical odori, which provided the Nikkei with opportunities for engaging
in traditional cultural activities as performers as well as spectators. Traditional values such as filial piety often were reinforced as dramatic themes,
reflecting the Issei's hope that at least their children would absorb some Japanese values.

> Dance, drama and other entertainments were performed at Japanese Hall.
> Besides Sesshu [Sessue] Hayakawa and Sojin Kamiyama, then movie actors
> in Hollywood, well known singers like Tamaki Miura, Toshiko Sekiya and
> Yoshie Fujiwara came from Japan to perform. And even local talents gave
> shows such as rokyoku. So people could forget that they were living so far
> from home.[29]

Yet for the Nisei, home was only a few blocks away.

Recounting her experiences attending events at Nippon Kan hall, Monica Sone ably paints a portrait of the conflicts that could arise when Issei

and Nisei occupied the space together in light of the generational differences that shaped their cultural orientation and identity. On the occasion of viewing her first classical dance recital, she was horrified by the degree of restraint required by the art. What her parents viewed as graceful movement, she interpreted as female powerlessness and confinement:

> I saw a small girl standing as motionless as a statue in the center of the stage, her back turned to the audience. Her wide sash of glittering old brocade was tied into an elaborate butterfly bow. Suddenly, a chorus of women's voices, which sounded as if it were being strained through a sieve, drifted out from offstage, accompanied by the plucking of samisens, banjolike instruments. The singing sounded alarmingly like growling, moans and strangulation. Then the girl turned slowly around. Her face was masked in deathly white rice powder, with jet black eyes and eyebrows, and a tiny red dot of a mouth. On her head, she wore a huge, black pompadour wig, decorated with bright, glittering hair ornaments. Her rich purple kimono was patterned with gorgeous golden chrysanthemums. I waited for her to start dancing . . . that is, to leap and whirl and get going, but all I saw were undulating, butter-soft hands, a slight tremor of the head, and a delicate foot stamp which could hardly have hurt an ant. During the entire performance, the dancer did not cover more than a few square inches. And she never smiled.[30]

Similarly, the annual celebration of the reigning emperor's birthday required a level of patriotic feeling mostly lost on the Nisei, who felt trapped by Issei rituals that meant little to them:

> Once a year when spring rolled around, sensei made the announcement: "Tomorrow there'll be no school because it's Tenchosetsu. We'll meet at Nippon Kan Hall at 2 p.m. I'll be taking roll call there." I groaned. I thought it was wasteful to spend a beautiful spring afternoon crowded into a dingy, crumbling hall and sit numbly through a ritual that never varied one word or gesture from year to year. But I knew there was no escape.[31]

Japanese and Western etiquette tended to come into conflict in just these sorts of high-stakes public events. The fact that they were largely closed to outsiders may have made it possible to display tensions within the Japanese American community that would have been suppressed in the presence of *hakujin*. In Sone's account, the high school girls' efforts to come to the event dressed in their best spring bonnets deeply offend the principal of the language school, who considers it "an insult to the Emperor that you should keep your hats on."[32] The evidence suggests that the Nippon Kan accommodated rituals of ethnic solidarity and at the same time served as a powerful backdrop for the drama of emerging differences in the meaning of cultural identity across generations in the Japanese American community.

In contrast with these secular buildings, many Buddhist temples and churches established during the opening decades of the twentieth century boldly embraced traditional forms and methods of construction drawn from Japanese architecture. Documented examples of buildings associated with the Buddhist churches of America range from clumsy interpretations of Japanese style by the Seattle firm of Saunders & Lawton, which designed the Seattle Buddhist Temple that stood at 1020 Main Street from 1908 to 1939,[33] to finely crafted examples of temple architecture by Japanese carpenters in the California communities of San Jose and Watsonville.[34] Some additions to Buddhist temples planned during the 1920s and built during the 1930s, as well as adjustments over time in American Buddhist religious practices, might be regarded as evidence of assimilation. Gymnasia, for example, were added to attract Nisei youth, and the growing use of the term "church" as opposed to "temple" reflected a conciliatory impulse. In the case of Seattle,

> The need to become related to American society was begun to be felt in the early 1920's and, finally, in 1926, the official title of the Temple became "the Seattle Buddhist Church."[35]

As a result, by the 1930s Buddhists were perceived to be:

> making definite efforts to be American in the architecture of their buildings and in the development of preaching and Sunday schools. A Buddhist church with an altar bearing its lotus flowers, candles and figure of Amida Buddha, just as one might see in Japan, combined with an auditorium containing pews, hymn books and an organ, is symbolical of what is happening to Buddhism in America.[36]

However, up until the eve of World War II internment, Buddhists retained even the most public of rituals associated with traditional religious practices (such as Bon Odori) and temple construction (from *muneage* ceremonies celebrating the erection of the building framework to processionals conveying the sacred Shrine of Amida from old to new buildings). As a result, Buddhists remained the target of a great deal of criticism—even from

FIG. 6.5 *Documented examples of buildings associated with the Buddhist Churches of America included clumsy interpretations of Japanese style, such as that found in the Seattle Buddhist Temple designed by the Seattle firm Saunders & Lawton. The building stood at 1020 Main Street from 1908 to 1939. (Courtesy of the Archives Committee, Seattle Buddhist Temple)*

FIG. 6.6 *This surviving Buddhist temple in San Jose, California, is an example of finely crafted temple architecture by Issei carpenters. (Photo by Gail Lee Dubrow)*

within the Japanese community—by those who feared that their practices contributed to the popular perception of Japanese immigrants as aliens incapable of assimilating, hence unsuited for basic rights of immigration or citizenship.

While the Western style adopted for the facades of civic buildings gave the appearance of assimilation, their interiors' continuing accommodation of traditional cultural practices suggests that the Japanese community made strategic decisions about the architectural expression of cultural differences. The example of Seattle, at least, suggests that in their civic architecture, Japanese American communities practiced extraordinary restraint in the public expression of their ethnic heritage during their greatest period of community building. This phenomenon can be attributed to the force of racial oppression and a well-developed strategy of invisibility, or at least evasive action that should not be narrowly equated with assimilation.

Japanese immigrants' efforts to deflect hostility paralleled the diplomatic strategies employed by the Japanese government, whose philosophy of voluntary restraint reached its zenith with the 1907 Gentlemen's Agreement, when it enacted its own emigration controls to ward off a wholesale lockout by American exclusionists. The social and architectural implications of this principle of voluntary restraint were well articulated in 1913 by two distinguished Japanese visitors who investigated the conditions that had led to the passage of California's alien land law:

> Those who are already in the States must strive more and more for assimilation with the people and observance of the laws and customs of the land. They must work strenuously to remedy their faults and do nothing to startle and irritate the people with whom they are living. Nothing must be done which would furnish material for attack. . . . Noisy Buddhist rituals, playing of *samisens,* keeping of tea-houses, which arouse opposition and afford room for criticism, might better be avoided. Studying the language, customs, and manners of the Americans . . . will go far towards bringing about a better understanding. . . . Every effort must be made to cast off the old undesirable customs and to adapt themselves to the new environment, so far as it is required by decency and courtesy.[37]

Self-appointed white defenders of Japanese immigrants, such as Sydney Gulick and Herbert Johnson, were serving up graphic examples of immigrants' capacity to adapt to American styles of living in an effort to fight the exclusionists, pointing out that they "dress in American style, live in American homes, use American furniture, and very largely adopt our food and methods of serving it."[38] The Issei, however, understood their own actions in rather different terms. For one thing, beyond simple courtesy the Japanese regarded the ability to negotiate international differences as a sign of cultural superiority as well as a matter of Japanese national pride. Brian Hayashi has argued (with particular reference to Japanese American Protestants) that:

> On the surface their faith appeared to function as a strong mechanism for assimilation, yet their support for cultural assimilation was associated with their identification with Japan—as proof that the Japanese were not inferior to whites.[39]

Stephen Fugita and David O'Brien have argued that much of the desire on the part of Japanese immigrants to be "good Americans" was rooted in the high value Japanese culture placed on maintaining harmonious group relations. That is to say, "to be a 'good Japanese' is to 'fit in' and 'not to make trouble.'"[40] Ironically, abandoning certain cultural practices allowed Japanese immigrants to preserve core cultural values. The traditional value that the Japanese placed on subordinating personal needs to the welfare of the group as a whole also led them to minimize signs of cultural differences, which was critical for protecting all Nikkei, whose rights to immigrate and earn a livelihood in the United States were threatened by discriminatory immigration, property, and licensing laws. If it is indeed true, as Fugita and O'Brien as well as many other scholars have maintained, that group survival is the "supreme ethical standard"[41] in Japanese culture, then the evidence presented in this paper supports and extends that claim by suggesting that decisions were made by Japanese immigrants to express and suppress signs of ethnic identity under political duress.

The hallmark of assimilation is a permanent transformation in cultural identity. Yet Issei displays of Americanism had more of a performative quality, since they clearly differentiated between public expressions of conformity directed to sooth the ruffled feathers of hostile *hakujin* and vibrant expressions of ethnic identity enacted among their own people: in the home, among extended family, and in community-controlled spaces.[42] In contrast to the common wisdom that Japanese immigrants "quickly shed their cultural traditions, conforming to Anglo-American ways,"[43] the evidence suggests that they used superficial manifestations of cultural conformity to pursue strategic objectives, particularly advancing the self-interest of the Nikkei community.

Expressions of ethnicity were suppressed in particular venues, namely at the interstices between *hakujin* and *nihonjin* spaces, where one's behavior potentially reflected on the whole community. Banzo Okada's recollection sums it up well: "whenever we saw a sign of the whites we were instinctively on guard." Hiding chopsticks from the eyes of curious onlookers during picnics at public parks was one approach to deflecting the negative attention that accompanied intolerance of cultural differences. Obscuring ethnicity in architecture was another facet of "showing a 'good face' to the *hakujin*,"[44] or to use another metaphor, a way of creating a demilitarized zone that might reduce the odds of drawing enemy fire. But neither action implied a full turn away from Japanese traditions or values. That development awaited the rise of the Nisei, as one young man raised in the Sacramento Delta vividly illustrated in a 1944 interview conducted while he was still imprisoned in an internment camp:

> It was embarrassing when I met my Japanese teacher at a time that a hakujin playmate was with me. They would razz me about it so that I began to think that this bowing business was a lot of baloney. I didn't like to speak Japanese when I was with my hakujin friends either.[45]

If Japan indeed was as strict a place as the language school has made it seem, all things Japanese seemed unattractive. Besides, constant ridicule from white playmates intolerant of cultural differences led the Nisei to associate their cultural heritage with a sense of shame, which was better avoided by turning their backs on practices associated with their greenhorn parents. Not to mention the obvious but unspoken fact that their Japanese heritage landed the Nisei, who were American citizens, in internment camps along with their noncitizen parents. All these factors combined with a thorough immersion in American culture to produce genuine movement toward assimilation in the second generation.

Still, some apparent gestures toward assimilation among the Issei merit an explanation. Rising anti-Japanese feeling immediately after World War I led some segments of the Issei community to press forward with their own Americanization campaign. When the Japanese Liaison Association started an Americanization committee in Seattle in 1919, according to committee member Kikuzo Ueminami, it set about eliminating potentially dangerous expressions of Japanese identity in the built environment. One of the committee's first projects was to remove from Main Street the signboards printed in Japanese. I myself took down the sign which said in Japanese "Ee-Bii-Keian." (A-B Employment Agency) The electric sign in front of Maneki Neko (The Beckoning Cat) restaurant, well known to the Japanese community, was darkened. At that time I heard the proprietress, Mrs. Umida, wept. She was a popular lady in Japanese town, masterful and yet not beautiful, and when children on Jackson Street begin to cry, their mothers sometimes said, "Hey, here comes Grandma from The Beckoning Cat!" Even this lady wept over the disappearing Japanese signboards. We sadly resigned ourselves to the Americanization program.[46]

According to Kazuo Ito, among many Japanese restaurants in Seattle, Maneki "was the only one which duplicated purely traditional Japan from the building to the furnishings."[47] As such, it constituted an interesting and important sacrifice, since it symbolically represented the allegedly unassimilable nature of the Japanese. The Americanization program was designed to broadcast the message, "Hey, look, you've got it wrong. We ARE willing to remove the obvious signs of difference that are making you uncomfortable."

But the removal of Japanese signs was only the most visible initiative of the Americanization committee, one specifically designed to capture and tame the *hakujin* gaze. An examination of the work of Seattle's American Cultural Committee lends support to the argument that Japanese immigrants strategically suppressed aspects of their ethnic identity as part of a broader political effort to resist exclusion.

Anti-immigrant sentiment at the end of World War I fueled a renewed attack on Japanese immigrants in the west. At the federal level, exclusionists focused on immigration restrictions. At the state level, the most aggressive push was to pass alien land laws, though efforts to regulate language schools also were pursued in state legislatures. In Seattle, exclusionists used the city's authority to issue licenses as a means to discriminate against the Issei. When the Seattle City Council passed a 1921 law that prohibited issuing licenses to noncitizens, the council specifically intended to shut down Issei businesses that catered to Japanese laborers, such as employment agencies, pawnshops, dance halls, and billiard parlors.[48] It was in this context that the American Cultural Committee organized both to take down the Japanese signs on their businesses and to fight the city's discriminatory licensing policies in the legal arena.

FIG. 6.7 *Japanese language signs, such as that seen behind the two men at lower left, were removed in 1919 by Seattle's Japanese Liaison Association, which hoped to persuade exclusionists that Japanese immigrants were not inassimilable aliens.* (Ken No Hitobito: Soritsu Nijunen Kinen, *Tokyo, 1919*)

FIG. 6.8 *Despite the conciliatory gesture of darkening Japanese language electric signs, Japanese immigrants aggressively fought discriminatory laws in the courts.* (*Courtesy of Puget Sound Regional Archives*)

Issei throughout the Pacific Northwest provided financial support for the American Cultural Committee to pursue their political and economic interests in the face of a growing exclusion movement. While the highly visible publicity campaign that surrounded sign removal suggested that the Japanese were willing to assimilate, it was only the tip of the iceberg in terms of their strategy. In actuality, the American Cultural Committee vigorously defended the Issei's rights through direct court challenges to the discrimination they encountered, as well as by searching for loopholes that would allow them to survive despite their unequal standing before the law. Kikuzo Ueminami, who had taken down the Japanese sign from his own business, the A-B Employment Agency, joined with a second Nihonmachi employment agency, Togo, to sue the City of Seattle's licensing department. All of the expenses for their successful case were covered by the American Cultural Committee. This case strongly suggests that the Issei did not lose their culture and adopt American ways; rather, they strategically suppressed signs of ethnic identity, both literally and figuratively, to serve political objectives.

While the American Cultural Committee was relatively successful in fending off hostile local initiatives, it failed to prevent the passage of Washington's alien land laws in 1921 and 1923, or the federal ban on immigration in 1924. Where direct challenges failed, the committee pursued alternative strategies for protecting Nikkei interests. The local strategy had emphasized removing signs of Japanese identity as a goodwill gesture while suing the municipality. Once legal challenges failed at the state level, the strategy was to mask or hide Japanese interests behind a faceless corporate identity, or behind a majority of sympathetic white shareholders if necessary. Because state land laws proved more difficult to overturn, the American Cultural Committee established the Lake Washington Investment Company as a corporation in the state of Ohio, which had no alien land law. It served as a safe haven for Issei property until their American-born children were old enough to take title.[49]

Unfortunately, Nikkei efforts to minimize signs of cultural difference in personal behavior and the built environment did not win Japanese immigrants the acceptance they deserved and steadfastly desired. Anti-Japanese sentiment that swept the western states in the early decades of the twentieth century and during the Second World War repeatedly positioned Japanese immigrants and their American-born children as aliens who embodied differences that could not be overcome.

The racist hysteria that followed the Japanese bombing of Pearl Harbor and pending internment persuaded even the most tradition-conscious

Buddhists that they no longer could afford to retain the reverse swastika as a religious emblem in their architecture, despite its long tradition as an Indian symbol for Buddhism and its extensive use in American Buddhist temples. Public perceptions of its meaning immediately were transformed with the advent of war. The reverse swastika was misinterpreted as a sign of loyalty to the Axis powers, providing tangible "evidence" to confirm existing prejudices about the suspect status of people of Japanese descent in America. So Buddhists reluctantly removed these signs from their architecture and related material culture in the closing days before internment. In the postwar period they substituted more benign symbols, such as lotuses and eight-spoked wheels, in architectural ornamentation.[50]

While conventional wisdom suggests that Japanese immigrants quickly "lost" ethnic traditions and rapidly conformed to American architectural practices, findings from my research in the Pacific Northwest suggest that racism played a powerful role in persuading Japanese immigrants to abandon or mask outward signs of ethnicity in the architecture of Western Washington Japantowns and rural communities even while the interiors of buildings central to Japanese American settlements contained robust expressions of cultural identity. Japanese immigrants adopted a strategy of blending into the American cultural fabric in an effort to ward off racist hostility in the form of exclusionary federal immigration policies, restrictive state land laws, and discriminatory city ordinances.

Moving beyond the simple paradigm of assimilation theory that has dominated the study of ethnic cultural traditions in vernacular architecture, this research project suggests that a fuller conceptualization of the relationship between racism and resistance is needed to understand the architectural history of ethnic communities of color in the United States. Furthermore, it suggests that a built environment can be a powerful lens for understanding the ways in which ethnic identity is negotiated. Whereas in past times scholars of American architectural history and ethnic studies had little to say to one another, this work suggests the potential for a rapprochement that will enrich both fields immeasurably.

Notes

For a related analysis of the rural environment, see Gail Lee Dubrow, "'Deru Kugi Wa Utareru' or the Nail that Sticks Up Gets Hit. The Architecture of Japanese American Identity, 1885–1942. The Rural Environment," *Journal of Architectural and Planning Research* 19, no. 4 (winter 2002): 319–33.

1. Shibusawa Keizo, *Japanese Life and Culture in the Meiji Era* (Tokyo: Obunsha, 1958), 105. (Translated and adapted by Charles S. Terry.)

2. Ibid., 108.

3. Ibid., 109.

4. Ibid., 295.

5. See Botond Bognar, *The Japan Guide* (New York: Princeton Architectural Press, 1995), and Dallas Finn, *Meiji Revisited: The Sites of Victorian Japan* (New York: Weatherhill, 1995).

6. *Seattle Times,* 30 June 1908.

7. Yuji Ichioka, *The Issei: The World of the First Generation Japanese Immigrants, 1885–1924* (New York: Free Press, 1988), 198–99.

8. See Toyotomi Morimoto, *Language and Heritage Maintenance of Immigrant Japanese Language Schools in California, 1903–41* (Ph.D. diss., University of California, Los Angeles, 1989).

9. Testimony of Kiichi Kanzaki, General Secretary of the Japanese Association of America, October 1920. U.S. Congress. House. Committee on Immigration and Naturalization, *Japanese Immigration Hearings before the Committee on Immigration and Naturalization,* 66th Cong., 2nd. sess. (Washington, D.C.: GPO, 1921), 696.

10. V. S. McClatchy, testifying in U.S. Congress. Senate. *Hearings Before the Committee on Immigration,* 68th Cong. (March 11, 12, 13, and 15, 1924), 9.

11. U.S. Congress. House. *Japanese Immigration Hearings before the Committee on Immigration and Naturalization,* 1193.

12. K. K. Kawakami, *The Real Japanese Question* (New York: Macmillan, 1921), 151, 193.

13. Ichioka, *Issei,* 205.

14. Among Seattle's Japanese who were formally affiliated with a Japanese church or temple in 1936, Christians predominated (1,200), followed by Shinshu Buddhist (250 actual members, 650 adherents), Nichiren Buddhist (150), Shinto (120), and Tenrikyo (60). Shotaro Frank Miyamoto, *Social Solidarity among the Japanese in Seattle* (1939; reprint, with a new introduction by S. Frank Miyamoto, Seattle: University of Washington Press, 1981), 45, table 7.

15. Concord's language school is documented in *Five Views: An Ethnic Historic Site Survey for California* (Sacramento: California Department of Parks and Recreation, Office of Historic Preservation, 1988). The Castroville property has been inventoried by the California Office of Historic Preservation and photographed by the author. Thanks to Eugene Itagawa for directing me to the Castroville property.

16. Monica Sone, *Nisei Daughter* (Boston: Little, Brown, 1953; 2nd ed., Seattle: University of Washington Press, 1991), 24–25 (page citation is to the 1991 edition).

17. Oral histories with former students of Seattle's Japanese Language School were conducted by the author in conjunction with research for Gail Dubrow with Donna Graves, *Sento at Sixth and Main: Preserving Landmarks of Japanese American Heritage* (Seattle: Seattle Arts Commission, 2002). Unless otherwise cited, all quotations in this chapter are from these interviews.

18. Yoriaki Nakagawa, *Nichi-Bei Saho No Joshik* [The common sense of Japanese and American etiquette] (Tokyo: Uedaya Shoten, 1937).

19. Yoriaki Nakagawa, posthumous manuscript, quoted in Ito, *Issei*, 595.

20. Ito, *Issei*, 597.

21. Even today, Toban is a way of engaging Japanese children in the work of maintaining their schools. Buddhist temples also use the Toban system to cut janitorial and gardening costs by having volunteers clean, mop, and do yard work.

22. *An Official Guide to Japan* (Tokyo: Japanese Government Railways, 1933), 4–83.

23. Edward Burke and Elizabeth Burke, "Nippon Kan/Astor Hotel: National Register Inventory-Nomination Form" (Olympia, Wash.: Office of Archaeology and Historic Preservation, 1977).

24. David A. Rash, "The Asian American Presence in Seattle" (unpublished manuscript, 1998), 17. Rash has documented the design and construction of many of Seattle's Nihonmachi buildings. He generously shared his unpublished paper with me, which jump-started my research on the Japanese Language School and Nippon Kan hall.

25. *Seattle Times*, 24 September 1905, 8.

26. Rash, "The Asian American Presence in Seattle," 17.

27. Budd Fukei, *The Japanese American Story* (Minneapolis: Dillon Press, 1976), 122.

28. T. Philip Terry, *Terry's Guide to the Japanese Empire* (Boston: Houghton Mifflin, 1927), 116.

29. Miyoshi Yorita of Seattle, quoted in Ito, *Issei*, 801.

30. Sone, *Nisei Daughter*, 46.

31. Ibid., 66.

32. Ibid., 70.

33. The Seattle Buddhist Temple moved from 1020 to 1427 Main Street in 1941. The dedication ceremony for the newly constructed building was held on October 4, 1941.

34. *Buddhist Churches of America: 75 Year History, 1899–1974, vol. 1* (Chicago: Nobart, Inc., 1974), 173, 222. The 1908 structure in Watsonville "was a typical Japanese Buddhist temple built by Japanese carpenters" (223). The 1907 and 1939

churches erected by the San Jose Buddhist community were built by the Nishiura brothers. The 1937 structure reportedly is "one of the best examples of traditional Buddhist architecture in the United States" (175).

35. *Buddhist Churches of America*, 167.

36. Albert W. Palmer, *Orientals in American Life* (New York: Friendship Press, 1934), 62–63.

37. J. Soyeda and T. Kamiya, *A Survey of the Japanese Question in California* (San Francisco: n.p., 1913), 12–13.

38. Herbert Buell Johnson, *Discrimination Against the Japanese in California: A Review of the Real Situation* (Berkeley: Courier Pub. Co., 1907), 27. See also Sydney Lewis Gulick, *The American Japanese Problem: A Study of the Racial Relations of the East and the West* (New York: Scribner's Sons, 1914), and Herbert Buell Johnson, *America's Japanese Problem* (Berkeley: H.B. Johnson, 1920).

39. Brian Masaru Hayashi, *"For the Sake of Our Japanese Brethren:" Assimilation, Nationalism, and Protestantism Among the Japanese of Los Angeles, 1895–1942* (Stanford: Stanford University Press, 1995), 149.

40. Stephen S. Fugita and David J. O'Brien, *Japanese American Ethnicity: The Persistence of Community* (Seattle: University of Washington Press, 1991), 41.

41. David J. O'Brien and Stephen S. Fugita, *The Japanese American Experience* (Bloomington and Indianapolis: Indiana University Press, 1991), 8.

42. Ibid., 9.

43. See Hayashi, *"For the Sake of Our Japanese Brethren,"* 1.

44. Akemi Kikumura, *Through Harsh Winters: The Life of a Japanese Immigrant Woman* (Novato, California: Chander & Sharp, 1981), 125, citing Harry Kitano, *Japanese Americans, The Evolution of a Subculture* (Englewood Cliffs, N.J.: Prentice Hall, 1976), 103.

45. Dorothy Thomas, *The Salvage: Japanese American Evacuation and Resettlement* (Berkeley: University of California Press, 1952), 182.

46. Ito, *Issei*, 148.

47. Ibid., 874.

48. Ito, *Issei*, 153.

49. Ibid., *Issei*, 154.

50. Tetsuden Kashima, *Buddhism in America* (Westport, Conn.: Greenwood Press, 1977), 115.

7 / FOUR HIRABAYASHI COUSINS

A Question of Identity

JAMES A. HIRABAYASHI

The sudden onset of World War II on December 7, 1941, thrust the issue of identity to the forefront for all Japanese Americans. On February 19, 1942, President Franklin D. Roosevelt signed Executive Order 9066 authorizing the War Department to prescribe military areas from which any or all persons might be excluded. This order served as the basis for Lt. Gen. John L. DeWitt to issue the curfew and exclusion orders. Public Proclamation No. 3 established a curfew from 8:00 P.M. to 6:00 A.M. for Japanese Americans in Military Area No. 1, which covered the western portions of Washington, Oregon, and California, and the southern portion of Arizona. The curfew required them to stay within a five-mile radius of their homes. The implementation of the exclusion order began on March 24, 1942, and by October 1942, all Japanese Americans were removed from the West Coast and incarcerated in hastily constructed concentration camps, also known as relocation centers.[1]

Early in 1943, the War Department and the War Relocation Authority devised a questionnaire to test the loyalty of persons aged seventeen years and older in all camps. The purpose was to sort out the "loyals" from the "disloyals." The questionnaire included two critical questions, numbers 27 and 28, which asked: "Are you willing to serve in the armed forces of the United States on combat duty, wherever ordered?" and "Will you swear unqualified allegiance to the United States of America and . . . forswear any form of allegiance or obedience to the Japanese emperor. . . ?"[2] Answering "yes" to these questions was mandatory for those applying for resettlement out of camp to areas of the United States outside of the West Coast exclusion zones. It also made male Nisei of draft age eligible for conscription into the armed services. Beginning in February 1943, the army scheduled visits to the camps to register all male Nisei of draft age.[3]

The exclusion of all Japanese Americans from the West Coast and the conscription of Japanese Americans into the United States Army led to diverse reactions on the part of four Nisei cousins who were raised in Japanese American communities in and around Seattle, Washington.[4] The cousins are Grant Jiro Hirabayashi, Gordon Kiyoshi Hirabayashi, Robert Taro Mizukami, and Henry Nobuo Hirabayashi. They are the sons of Issei immigrants from an extended family neighborhood of eleven Hirabayashi households in the township of Hotaka, Nagano prefecture, Japan. Toshiharu Hirabayashi, father of Grant; Shungo Hirabayashi, father of Gordon; Isami (nèe Hirabayashi) Mizukami, mother of Robert; and Hamao Hirabayashi, father of Henry, were the relatives who emigrated to America.

The primary theme of this essay is Japanese American identity formation. It examines the nature of Nisei identities as Japanese Americans and Americans and how these issues impacted the decisions they made as Americans. It concludes with a discussion of ethnic identity formation in America and implications for America as a democratic and a multicultural society. This essay considers the Hirabayashi cousins' family and community backgrounds, presents vignettes of their lives prior to the war, and describes their reactions and decision-making during the critical wartime period. With a common background, the four Nisei cousins identified as Japanese Americans, but they took different trajectories in response to the exigencies they faced during World War II. Each cousin, operating in terms of his own understanding of American citizenship, made independent decisions in response to challenges to his citizenship rights.

Immigrant families seeking security in an often-hostile land formed ethnic communities. In his classic study on the Japanese in the Seattle area, Frank Miyamoto points to a tightly knit social organization as being the key feature of the community: "almost every Japanese minority member seemed in some way linked to an elaborate social network in the Japanese community."[5]

Collective responsibility led to social solidarity. Miyamoto refers to the initial years of Issei immigration as the "frontier period": "the population was composed largely of laboring-class males, almost all of whom were 'birds of passage' eager to make quick money and return to Japan. Families were few, and only the bare framework of the institutional organization necessary to the wants of a normal community was existent." After the signing of the Gentlemen's Agreement in 1907, the community entered what Miyamoto termed the "settling period": "Families were emphasized. . . . New institutions were necessitated to bridge the gap for the settling Japanese immigrants between their native heritage and the American environment."[6] It was a setting, however, characterized by racism: "prejudice and discrimination were much more manifest than they are today . . . it was caste-like."

Nestled in the foothills of the Japan Alps in Nagano prefecture is the township of Hotaka. In a semi-rural setting at the edge of town was a cluster of eleven Hirabayashi households. In 1907, several young Issei from this extended kin group emigrated to the Seattle area, where they maintained close relationships with each other. "There had been an adventurous man in Azumi who had come to America, made a fortune in five years, and returned home . . . advertised America's wealth and opportunities, and under his influence, these four young men made their decision to cross the ocean."[7]

In preparation for their overseas sojourn, several Issei cousins attended a private academy, Kensei Gijuku, in order to learn English. While there they converted to Christianity. The founder and principal of the school, Iguchi Kigenji, was a disciple of Uchimura Kanzo, the founder of Mukyokai (Non-church Christian movement) in Japan.[8] The Mukyokai movement repudiated institutionalized church structures and sectarian animosities. It instead advocated the equality of believers and established fellowships (Kyoyu Kai) devoted to living a Christian life, nurturing faith and morals, engaging in the study of the scriptures, and looking after the welfare of fellow members.[9]

Upon arrival in America the Issei cousins worked on railroad crews. They subsequently moved to Seattle and found work in hotels, restaurants, and stores. Some became small entrepreneurs, and others turned to farming. Several cousins, along with friends from Nagano prefecture, began a vegetable garden that later became the site of the Sand Point Naval Air Station, just a few miles east of the University of Washington campus in Seattle. They peddled their vegetables at the Pike Place Market above the Seattle waterfront, hauling their produce by horse and wagon. After a few years the Issei cousins sent for their Japanese brides, and they began families. They formed an extended family group and saw to each other's social and economic needs.

Together with fellow immigrants from Hotaka township in Nagano, the Issei cousins established a Hotaka Club in Seattle. They kept in close contact with each other and met regularly throughout the year on holidays and other special occasions. They even invited Caucasian acquaintances from the neighborhood to picnic gatherings. In addition to the Hotaka Club, the

Issei cousins belonged to the Nagano Prefectural Association, a social and mutual aid association. They also belonged to the Japanese Association of North America, a social and political organization established to look out for the interests of all immigrant Japanese in the Seattle area.

In 1919, four Issei from Nagano prefecture, including two of the Hirabayashi cousins, moved their families to Thomas, Washington, a rural community twenty miles south of Seattle. They purchased forty acres of land in the name of the eldest Nisei child in the group and began to develop their property. In the early 1920s, John Isao Nishinoiri, a graduate student from Japan, was engaged in field research on Japanese farms for his M.A. degree in sociology at the University of Washington. He wrote:

> About five miles south of Kent on the west road leading to Auburn stand four neatly painted houses . . . this is the White River Gardens . . . [they] came from the same district in Japan, Azumi in Nagano prefecture . . . Although four different families live there, they plant, crop, buy and sell together. Machinery, tools, barns, horses and all equipment are owned and used in common. Cooperation is not a theory with them; it is a daily practice. . . . This occupational cooperation finds its source in their spiritual cooperation . . . acquired in Japan under the influence of a non-denominational evangelist [which] binds them together closely. . . . They maintain their simple Christian faith in its puritanical form. . . . They do not work on Sunday even in the busiest seasons, and never fail to meet for the purpose of worshipping God. They have no minister, so each of them speaks in turn of his thoughts and experiences. Their simple service is opened and closed with hymns and prayer, and when I attended I felt as if I were sitting with the Puritans of the colonial period.[10]

The Mukyokai Issei established relationships with local Christians. They joined with their Christian neighbors, both Japanese and Caucasian, to start the Union Sunday School in Thomas. The grade school annex was rented, and over fifty people attended each week: "Occasional pastor was Rev. Ulysses Grant Murphy from Seattle, a former missionary to Japan. [He] came up from Seattle once a month to preach to the group; in the evening he spoke in Japanese [to] the Thomas *Kyoyukai*—Friends of Jesus Society."[11]

The White River Gardens families cleared their land, began raising crops, and in successive years built houses for each of the families. In 1922, Malcolm Douglas, prosecuting attorney for King County, claimed the land was in control of alien Japanese and in violation of the Alien Land Act of 1921, which prevented noncitizens from owning land. He filed suit, claiming:

"Wherefore, the plaintiff prays that this court enter a decree herein declaring that said land is forfeited and escheated to the State of Washington, and that the defendants have no right, title or interest therein."[12] Although the land title was held by a Nisei, the government contended the Issei were really in charge. The Washington Supreme Court ruled against the families, who were then forced to lease the houses and land they had built and improved from the State of Washington. "They continue their humble life and hard work and quiet prayer in spite of the uncertainty of their position."[13]

In spite of these hardships, they settled down, raised their children, and joined with others in community affairs primarily through the local Japanese Association. They wrote essays about their American lives in a journal titled *Shin Kokyo* (New Homeland), reflecting their attitudes towards their new homes and the transformation of their collective identities from being Japanese to being American.[14]

From these intimate contacts, the Nisei learned about Issei conceptions of social relationships. The Nisei were in direct contact with mainstream society in their daily activities, but particularly with educational institutions. The aim of the public schools was to socialize all students into becoming good citizens of the Republic.

The social context of the 1920s and 1930s was a complex setting for the Issei. The period included racism, economic hardships of the Depression era, and mounting political tensions resulting from Japan's move to increase its hegemony in Asia. As the Nisei matured, they established their own communities, building on the influences of both the Issei and the mainstream society. A distinctive Nisei lifestyle appeared during this period that was characterized by "the Nisei's assimilation of the Japanese interpersonal style, modified to fit the American scene, and the resulting emergence of a Nisei culture and associative patterns with which the Nisei felt themselves especially comfortable."[15]

The education of the Nisei cousins included not only their Issei parents' Mukyokai teachings but also exposure to mainstream Christianity through the Union Sunday School and the summer Vacation Bible School, which was located in Auburn, a town to the south of White River Gardens. As they grew older, the cousins also attended periodic meetings of the regional Japanese American Christian Association. This was a general pattern for the Christians in the Japanese American community. The church "established interpersonal ties of unusually enduring quality and also laid relational networks which spanned regional communities."[16]

There was a strong advocacy of education within the Issei community:

"Every Japanese community feels a strong duty about educating its young, and this projects itself down into a deep concern on the part of the parents over the training of their children."[17] It was primarily through the formal educational system that the Nisei were exposed to and learned about American life. Here they had daily social interaction with their Caucasian peers. Their teachers introduced them to the basic precepts of the American society: "Some general characteristics of Americanization included a staunch support for democracy, representative government, law and order, capitalism, general health (diet, hygiene, and sanitation), and command of the English language."[18]

A tightly knit ethnic community based within the general context of American society provided the setting within which the Nisei were approaching adulthood just before the onset of World War II. It was within this societal milieu that the four Nisei cousins negotiated issues of identity and nationality. Out of the family came training in ethics and morals, and in the public schools they were drilled on the democratic principles and ideals of American life. With this nurturing in the family and community and exposure to American cultural norms in the school system, identity as Japanese American and American merged into an integrated whole.

Over the centuries, ten Hirabayashi branch *(bunke)* households segmented from a single main *(honke)* household. These households operated as a kind of a corporate entity *(dozoku)*.[19] It was out of some of these related Hirabayashi households that these Issei "cousins" originated. When Issei immigrants arrived in the United States, those who had any kind of kin relationship often formed "new" kin groups. A redefinition and a reformulation would occur, resulting in a transformation of selected relatives into new, closely knit kin groups.[20] The Hirabayashi Issei "cousins" formed a new kin group, while the Nisei "cousins" extended this relationship into their generation, even though the only first cousins in the genealogical sense are Gordon Hirabayashi and Bob Mizukami. Gordon's father and Bob's mother were siblings. The new kinship formation was yet another example of social solidarity among this evolving immigrant community.

Grant Jiro Hirabayashi

Grant Jiro Hirabayashi was born in November 1919. He was named after the Rev. Ulysses Grant Murphy, a Methodist minister and former missionary to Japan who befriended the Mukyokai group. Grant's father, Toshiharu, was considered the most knowledgeable among the Mukyokai fellowship, since he had attended academy in Hotaka longer than any of the others. Grant's early religious exposure came from his family setting: "My parents made sure we went to church. I had at least three Bibles for perfect attendance so there was something passed on; the twelve years I spent here left a strong impression."[21]

Grant's desire to visit Japan was sparked by two of his boyhood friends. They had gone to Japan during summer vacation, making Grant envious of their experience and knowledge: "I heard Kenji and Tom talking about their visit to Japan. My gosh, I'd better learn more about Japan, in order to stay with the crowd." Grant's father told him that since he was one of eight children, he couldn't afford to send him just for a vacation. But if he would stay and study for two years, he would send him: "I had to make that commitment, which I readily accepted." In 1932, at the age of thirteen, Grant was sent to live with his father's eldest brother.

In school, the teachers were sympathetic, allowing him to wear Western clothing and keep his hair long. After a year, however, in order to conform, he switched to wearing *zori* (sandals) and had his hair styled in a crew cut. His peers generally accepted him. Being fast on his feet, he made the track team, and with his ability to help fellow students with their English, he was able to gain some popularity among his peers. His teachers appointed him "moral officer" of the class.[22]

During these school years he took mandatory military training classes: "For some reason the officer favored me, so I was one of the commanders of the school." After three years, Grant was ready to return home, but was told by his father to finish high school. He remained in Japan for a total of eight years, not returning home until 1940.

Although Grant tried to conform to the ways of his peers, he realized that he was somewhat different and never thought of himself as a Japanese: "Noooo, I considered myself an American." This distinction was reinforced at times, such as when all of the moral officers were sent to Tokyo to represent the school and he was not selected to accompany them. "And then I said to myself, oh I'm not a citizen. I knew I was different and, of course, I always felt like an American for some reason." They wanted to recommend him for officer's training school, but he declined: "I said thank you but no thank you because I am an American." In spite of eight years of Japanese education, Grant's self-identity did not change:

> I'm sure I was influenced and brainwashed to some extent, but still I identified myself as American. I know what my friends in Japan are being exposed to

and I know how they think, I have strong feelings for them, but as far as my experiences, at no time did I hesitate as far as my loyalties were concerned. I think, twelve years however short, for some reason—my parents and Christianity, the upbringing was such that I always associated myself here.

Although he was exposed to various religious beliefs in Japan, Grant had no inner conflicts because of it. "To me, I didn't see anything wrong with Buddhism, Shintoism, Confucianism—I like Confucianism—and Christianity and the ten commandments. I think they all share—have things in common." And while he was in Japan "there was no one telling me that you can't believe in Christianity." He still considers himself a practicing Christian.

After Grant was in Japan for eight years, his brother Martin, who had a scholarship to study the Japanese language at Kyoto University after graduating from the University of Washington, "told me to go home because the political situation—the international relations between the two countries was deteriorating." Returning home in 1940, "I was told at Kent High School, you can get credit for work done in Japan, so I finished high school in one year." He found work in a local garage operated by an Issei. But that lasted only a few months: "I enlisted in the Army Air Corps after being inducted into the army. My thinking then was that war was inevitable and that if I am going to serve in the army, I wanted to pick up a trade, and what I had in mind was to become an airplane mechanic." He was sent to Fort Lewis, Washington.

Within a few days the war began, and Grant was immediately sent to Jefferson Barracks in Missouri. "All of the Nisei were placed into 'protected custody' and confined to barracks for forty days. During that period we were marched to the mess hall, marched to the PX, no recreation. There were about thirty of us Nisei." After basic training in June 1942, all assignments for Japanese Americans serving the Army Air Corps stationed at Jefferson Barracks were terminated, and they were reassigned. Grant was sent to Fort Leavenworth to work in a hospital during the summer of 1942.

Soon Grant received a letter from Col. Kai Rasmussen "asking me for my history and experience, and before I knew it, I received orders to report to the Military Intelligence Service Language School, Camp Savage, Minnesota." He trained to become a translator and interrogator.[23]

While at Camp Savage, Grant obtained leave and traveled by train to the Tule Lake camp to visit his parents, who had been incarcerated there since late summer 1942. He was surprised and shocked by the conditions he saw:

When I got to the desert, and finally arrived at Tule Lake, a desolated area with barbed wire, watch dogs, and guards that were facing not out, facing inside, I'm sure that they [parents] were quite depressed, yeah, but they were happy to see me. After a brief visit I left, and that was quite depressing. I got on the train and was totally devastated.

The army relocated the Military Intelligence Service Language School to Fort Snelling, Minnesota, in 1944. While awaiting assignment, a call went out for volunteers for a "dangerous" mission. Two hundred volunteers stepped forward, and Grant was among the fourteen selected. They were sent to India, where his unit received jungle training. Subsequently the unit was designated as 5307 Provisional Unit, with Brig. Gen. Frank D. Merrill as commander. They later became well known as "Merrill's Marauders."

During their first encounter in Burma with soldiers of the Japanese Army in early September 1944, they came upon scattered food supplies. Among them was a torn miso bag labeled "Shinshu Miso," produced in the region where Grant had lived: "I didn't want to meet any of my classmates, but fortunately the unit we fought was from Kyushu in southern Japan."

Among his duties was interrogating POWs. He developed a standard procedure for interrogating them:

I asked him if he was wounded, sick, or if he needed medical attention. And then I said, where you from? Your parents, have you heard from them lately? And while conversing with him, I smoked a cigarette with him and of course, his attitude changed and actually a tear came down and taken by surprise, he said: 'You aren't going to shoot me?' Ah no, I won't shoot. And so he became very cooperative.

Once, however, an officer who was taken prisoner challenged him: " 'You're a traitor.' I said I'm an American. He called me a traitor and refused to answer my questions. I was quite disappointed when he called me a traitor. Subsequently, however, he became cooperative."

After the war Grant served with the occupying forces in Japan from 1947 to 1951. He worked there for the supreme commander for the Allied Powers (SCAP) as an interpreter, translator, and interrogator during the war crimes trials. Whether he was serving the prosecution or the defense, he wanted to be truthful and fair: "I always wanted to help as much as possible. As a matter of fact, I had many lawyers from the defense coming to me because they felt I was more understanding." And, after all his years in Japan, he did strongly empathize with the Japanese: "Well, I just go by the facts, whether one is on the defense or prosecution. I could feel for the Japanese. I know how they felt." In his mind, however, his loyalties were never in question:

> Although there were many things which I didn't like about America because of discrimination, at no time did I hesitate as far as my loyalties were concerned. I knew I was an American and couldn't be anything else.

After his work with the war crimes trials, Grant returned to the United States and went to college on the G.I. bill. He attended the University of Southern California, where he received his bachelor's and master's degrees in International Relations. He subsequently worked for the Department of State, the Library of Congress, and the Department of Defense. He is now retired and as of 2002 lives in Silver Spring, Maryland.

Gordon Kiyoshi Hirabayashi

Gordon Kiyoshi Hirabayashi's father, Shungo, together with Grant's father, Toshiharu, formed the core of the Thomas Mukyokai fellowship. Gordon was born in 1918 in Seattle, but his earliest memories are of living on the farm in Thomas, Washington, next door to his cousin Grant. The family moved to Seattle one winter to escape from the hard farm life, but returned to try farming again at the urging of the Mukyokai group. Gordon's mother, Mitsu, was concerned over disciplinary problems because young Gordon was picking up bad habits on the streets of Seattle near the Skid Road area. Because she also attended the Kensei Gijuku academy in Hotaka before emigrating, she was a strong promoter of Mukyokai practices. Training in ethics came through example:

> A good portion of the influence of the parents didn't come from their lecturing to me and disciplining me. It was the way they lived. People in the community trusted Dad; their teaching came by their actions, so I got that training one way or another.

Gordon and Grant grew up on neighboring farms. On Sundays, Gordon and his cousins attended the local Union Sunday School:

> It was Foursquare-type fundamentalist, Pentecostal. They ran the Bible stuff, contest for kids. I got a new testament for memorizing all the books of the

Bible. It took me until high school to kick them out of my life, the fundamentalists. I threw out all the literal things of the fundamentalists, but I didn't
throw religion out.

Gordon did well in public school. He took a state exam while in seventh
grade, and: "I skipped a grade and went on to junior high school by the age
of thirteen." His mother had high aspirations for him: "Ahh, these guys going
to University of Washington—a farm school. You're going to a school like
Yale or Harvard." He also attended a Japanese language school sponsored
by the local Japanese Association.

In his youth Gordon belonged to a mixture of Japanese American and
mainstream groups, which included the local Boy Scout Troop 53, the Hi-Y
(High School YMCA), and the Auburn Christian Fellowship (a Japanese
American interdenominational group). He participated in sports at the public schools. He also organized a Nisei basketball team and played in the
regional Nikkei league. Later, while at the University of Washington, he had
a room at the University YMCA near campus. He received a scholarship to
attend the YMCA President's School, a leadership training program offered
at Columbia University. He also joined the American Society of Friends
(Quakers) while attending the University of Washington.

When Gordon saw the first exclusion orders posted on telephone poles
in the early spring of 1942, during his senior year, he was confronted with
a dilemma:

Do I stay out of trouble and succumb to the status of a second-class citizen,
or do I continue to live like other Americans, and thus disobey the order? I
was not accustomed to disobeying the government. At the same time I was
not sure I could abandon my values, goals and self-respect, and still be useful to my family, community and country.[24]

At the University YMCA Gordon had numerous discussions with Bill
Makino, a Nisei honor student several years his junior. Recalling these discussions, Gordon commented: "At one point I said, this is all wrong. If I go
I am giving tacit approval of what's going on, so I can't go." Bill agreed, "I
can't go either." When Bill informed his parents of this, however, they were
shocked: "They gave me the works." Since he was the only child of an elderly Issei couple, his duty and obligations to his parents weighed heavily
upon him. Gordon was pressured by his mother, as well: "We don't know
where we are going and what the government is doing, but one thing we

could do is to try to keep together." Gordon, comparing his situation with Bill's, felt that in his case the family was in good hands, since his brother Ed, who was just graduating from high school, and his next brother, Jim, who was just finishing his sophomore year, would both be with the family. "My parents found it difficult to cope with me and my decisions, but they came around and supported me."

Gordon dropped out of the university in March 1942, after completing the winter term. He then volunteered for the American Friends Service Committee to help the Seattle Nikkei community prepare for evacuation. Then, on May 16, 1942, Gordon walked into the Seattle FBI office and challenged the "exclusion order" with a four-page typewritten statement he titled "Why I Refused to Register For Evacuation."

> Even though the exclusionary orders bore the imprimatur of the Western Defense Command on behalf of the United States government, I knew I must refuse what I considered to be a gross violation of the Constitution. I must maintain my Christian principles [and] the democratic standards for which this nation lives.[25]

Gordon was arrested. The army, however, hoping to avoid such confrontations, was willing to drop all charges provided he leave for the temporary detention center at Puyallup, Washington. He refused and thus remained in jail.

Subsequently, the charge was amended to include violation of the curfew orders. At his trial on October 28, 1942, with Judge Lloyd D. Black presiding, Gordon's attorney, Frank Walters, argued that his client's Fifth Amendment right of due process was violated by the exclusion order. The judge dismissed the argument: "We have been engaged in a total war with enemies unbelievably treacherous and wholly ruthless. [The due process argument] should not be permitted to endanger all of the constitutional rights of the whole citizenry."[26] Judge Black instructed the jury to find Hirabayashi guilty on both counts, which it did. He was sentenced to a year in prison.

On appeal, the United States Supreme Court considered only the curfew verdict, and on June 21, 1943, Chief Justice Harlan Fiske Stone, upholding the conviction, wrote: "The danger of espionage and sabotage to our military resources was imminent, and the curfew order was an appropriate measure to meet it."[27] Throughout, Gordon remained convinced that he had taken the correct stand: "I fully expected that as a citizen the constitution would protect me. Surprisingly, even though I lost, I did not abandon my beliefs and values."

After serving out his initial sentence in a federal prison for violation of the curfew and exclusion orders, Gordon went to work for the American Friends Service Committee in Spokane. There he was required to respond to the same special "loyalty questionnaire" administered to all Japanese Americans in camp. On February 22, 1944, he sent it back to the draft board:

> This questionnaire, which I am returning to you unfilled, is an outright violation of both the Christian and American principles of justice and democracy. The form, entitled, "The Statement of United States Citizen of Japanese Ancestry," is a form based purely on the grounds of ancestry. . . . If I were to fill in this form I would be cooperating with a policy of race discrimination. I cannot conscientiously do so.[28]

Moreover, as a Quaker and a pacifist, Gordon declined to further participate with the selective service process. The FBI thereby arrested him for draft evasion, and in the subsequent court trial he was sentenced to a prison term at McNeil Island Federal Penitentiary. Ironically, he was there at the same time as his cousin Hank.

After the war, Gordon completed his graduate studies at the University of Washington. He conducted field research among the Doukhobors of British Columbia and received his Ph.D. degree in Sociology. He taught for three years at American University in Beirut, Lebanon, and for three years at American University in Cairo, Egypt. In 1959 he joined the Department of Sociology at the University of Alberta, at Edmonton, where he stayed for the remainder of his academic career.

Gordon is retired and presently living in Edmonton with his wife, Susan. He is a member of the National Board of the Religious Society of Friends.

Robert (Bob) Taro Mizukami

Bob Taro Mizukami was born in 1922 in Star Lake in the hills above Kent, Washington. His mother, Isami, was the younger sister of Gordon's father, Shungo, and attended the academy Kensei Gijuku, before emigrating to America. Gordon's mother, Mitsu, served as an informal "go-between" in his parents' betrothal. Raised during the Depression, it seemed to Bob that the family was moving almost once a year. The Mizukamis lived and farmed in Thomas right next to cousin Gordon's farm before moving back to Renton. He and

FIGS. 7.1–7.4 (Top left) *Grant Jiro Hirabayashi, undated photo from World War II;* (center left) *Gordon Kiyoshi Hirabayashi, ca. 1941;* (bottom left) *Robert Taro Mizukami (right) on leave in France with a fellow member of the 442nd RCT, 1945;* (right) *Henry Nobuo Hirabayashi at the Minidoka Relocation Center, ca. 1942*

Gordon's younger brother, Ed, were best friends and together attended the Union Sunday School, festivals in the nearby urban centers of Kent and Auburn, as well as family picnics at Redondo Beach, Washington.

After returning to Renton, Bob attended a church where a Baptist preacher came from Seattle to give sermons. Even though his father was Buddhist, "he believed that all of his kids should have some kind of religious training. So we went to Sunday School and daily Vacation Bible School during the summer." Bob was baptized in a Baptist Church in Seattle. Today, he attends the Methodist Church just a block down the street from the Buddhist Church in his hometown of Fife, Washington.

The Mizukami family moved from Renton to Fife in 1937. Bob was a sophomore in high school and soon became a part of the high school crowd, attending classes and participating in extracurricular activities. He was interested in sports but was "too small for football, too short for basketball, and even too light to make the ninety-pound weight class in wrestling." So he got involved in athletics by assisting the coaches as a student manager and earned his varsity letter three years running. He graduated from high school in 1940.

After graduation Bob worked in the family greenhouse business: "Didn't have much choice in those days." When the army issued its exclusion orders in the spring of 1942, being the eldest son, he suddenly incurred the responsibility of registering the family with the authorities and preparing the household for the move to camp. May was the height of the bedding season, one of the biggest months in the greenhouse business. "We left everything intact when we left. The War Relocation Authority eventually sold the property [so] we didn't have any place to come back to after the war."

On May 15, 1942, the Mizukami family moved to the nearby temporary detention center in Puyallup on army orders. "We had our truck and put all our stuff on it, drove down to Puyallup and unloaded." In September, they were transferred to the Minidoka camp in southern Idaho. Soon after arriving there Bob signed up for a work furlough and went to harvest potatoes and sugar beets in Aberdeen, Idaho.[29] He returned to camp in time for Christmas, 1942, and found a job working in internal security.

Bob answered "yes, yes" to the critical questions, numbers twenty-seven and twenty-eight, on the so-called "loyalty questionnaire." "I don't recall when we filled out the questionnaire, during the time of recruitment or when, but we all had to fill it out. It was an individual thing. It seemed only natural that I answer 'yes—yes.' There were 'no—no' people, but I was not aware of them at that time." During early spring 1943, an army team arrived at Minidoka

camp to recruit volunteers for the segregated all-Nisei unit, the 442nd Regimental Combat Team (RCT).[30] "Some of us might have talked about signing up, one way of getting out of camp and getting something done. So I
went down and signed up. There wasn't a big debate, should I or shouldn't
I, it just seemed like a natural thing to do when your country is at war." He
didn't ask his parents for advice: "One thing about my dad, he was a pretty
learned person. And so when I told him what I was going to do, he didn't
argue." Regarding his induction into the army, Bob reiterated his views:
"When you take an oath to swear into the service and things like that—those
things come home to roost, you know, from the upbringing that you had
in the past—like I say, it seems like the natural thing to do."

Before leaving Minidoka, Bob had told his younger brother Bill, "You
stay and take care of the family, I'm going into the service." Much to his
surprise, while training at Camp Shelby, Mississippi, a couple of months
later, "Here comes Bill. I said, 'I thought I told you to stay home!'" There
were about two hundred men in a company, which was divided into four
platoons. Bill was in the Third Platoon while Bob was in the Headquarters
Platoon. They didn't see much of each other during the day, but spent time
together during off hours: "He always seemed to have money and I didn't,
so I used to borrow money from him all of the time."

After training in a heavy weapons company, "I ended up in the kitchen.
I don't know what decided me, but they were looking for volunteers to go
into the kitchen." Bob became a mess sergeant. The brothers shipped out
together and were involved in the Rome-Arno Campaign in 1944. In early
July, they crossed Cecina River and were a little south of Arno River, advancing to a place called Hill 140 ("Little Casino"):

> The Germans were using the Leaning Tower of Pisa as a field artillery obser-
> vation post and they had us pinned down for awhile. I saw Bill one night, we
> were hauling hot meals up to the line. I was talking to him, and he was telling
> me some of those shells are getting awfully close. So I was kidding him, what
> do you want me to tell them when I get home. Man, I can still remember say-
> ing that, what a smart-ass thing to say. I keep thinking about that all of the
> time. He was caught in a mortar barrage, killed in his own foxhole.

Bob stayed with the 442nd RCT throughout the European campaign. Some
of the more memorable battles he participated in were the liberation of Bruyeres, the Lost Battalion battle, where the 442nd RCT lost more men than the
Texans they saved, and the critical breaking of the Gothic Line.[31] It was dur-

ing the liberation of Bruyeres that Bob earned a purple heart: "A couple of mortar shells came over . . . hit about 10 feet away . . . got shell fragments and drew blood."

After eighteen months in Europe, Bob returned to the United States and was discharged at Fort Lewis, Washington, in December 1945. Meanwhile, his family had left Minidoka camp on a work furlough program and were then working in a nursery in Spokane. During the summer of 1946, the family went back to Fife on a vacation and visited the old homestead. "We made a deal to buy the place back; paid twice as much as when we bought it before the war." Together with his parents and younger siblings, they resumed the family business. Bob got married, raised a family, and ran a successful greenhouse business.

In 1956, a rumor floated around that the city of Tacoma wanted to annex Fife. Some of the locals wished to maintain their autonomy, and Bob became a member of the original incorporating committee. After incorporation he was elected to the original city council. In 1980, when the incumbent mayor was elected the county commissioner, the city council elected Bob as mayor pro tem. Subsequently, he was elected to serve an additional four-year term. "I had a total of seven years. At the end of 1987, I was sixty-five at that time, I decided that's enough. During that period, there was no other Nisei elected to a political office in the State of Washington."

Bob served thirty years in local politics. He is retired and lives in Fife with his wife, Lily. His son Greg now runs the family business.

Henry (Hank) Nobuo Hirabayashi

Hank Nobuo Hirabayashi was born in Seattle on April 29, 1923. His father, Hamao, appears in many early photographs taken during the first decade of the 1900s with his bachelor cousins and friends. He was one of the earliest to emigrate and urged his cousins to join him. The families were to maintain close relationships throughout the pre-war years. Beginning in a day job in a hotel in Tacoma, Hamao saved his money and eventually opened the Belltown Grocery in Seattle:

> We were about a half-mile directly north of the Pike Place Market on First Avenue. We lived in the back of the store and had a nice view of Elliott Bay and West Seattle. At that time, Belltown was known as part of Skid Row, so it was not the best place to grow up. In our block alone there were three tav-

erns and three houses of ill repute and on weekends there were many
fistfights in the street.

Hank's mother, Sanae, arrived to America from Okayama prefecture with
her parents when she was fourteen. In Seattle she attended a local grade
school: "She spoke English fairly well for an Issei." Her parents, the Numo-
tos, also ran a grocery store nearby. "I had grandparents, one of the few
Nisei to have grandparents in this country."

Contact with his cousins in Thomas came through informal family gatherings, particularly on holidays. His mother had converted to Christianity
and encouraged Hank to go to church. He was therefore raised as a Christian. Before attending elementary school he was sent by bus to the Japanese
Baptist Church preschool. During his high schools days, he went to Blaine
Methodist Church in Seattle, a Japanese American congregation known
today as Blaine Memorial United Methodist Church.

Few Japanese families resided in Hank's neighborhood, and only three
or four Nisei attended his grade school. At Queen Anne High School, most
of his schoolmates were white. Aside from attending regular classes, his extracurricular activities were concentrated in sports. Prior to the war, an important activity among his classmates involved participating in the National
Guard. Twice a week they went to train at the armory, located not far from
his family's grocery store: "I tried to get in, and they rejected me because
I'm Japanese. That left quite an impression on me."

Hank graduated from Queen Anne High School in 1941. That summer,
he visited a friend on the Olympic Peninsula: "It was an isolated place where
you could fish and hunt, and I wanted to buy some land and settle out there.
There was logging, fishing, oysters, a lot of things to do to get by on." But
he returned to Seattle, and just before December 7, he was hired on at a fish
processing plant on the waterfront through an Issei contact in the neighborhood. The next day, Hank's father, president of the Seattle Japanese Grocer's Association and a prominent member of the community, was arrested
by the FBI and detained at the federal immigration station on Airport Way.
Hank tried to visit him:

> There was somebody waving through the bars, so I was waving, and right away
> the guards came, took me into the building and threatened to put me behind
> bars. Finally they let me go, but they wouldn't let me see him. It was a trau-
> matic experience.

Being the eldest son, Hank had to shoulder all of the family responsibilities: closing the store, selling the inventory and equipment, arranging for the family possessions, and preparing for their impending incarceration. In May 1942 they boarded a bus that took them to the temporary detention center in Puyallup. Later that summer they were sent by train to the Minidoka camp in Idaho.

Initially, Hank worked at the camp canteen. During the fall of 1942 he left on a temporary work furlough to harvest sugar beets and potatoes. When harvest ended he returned to camp. Soon the Army came to camp looking for volunteers for the 442nd RCT: "Mike Masaoka came to recruit, and for some reason I missed him. But I heard that a lot of people were impressed with his presentation because he was a dynamic speaker." Referring to the loyalty questionnaire, Hank said: "I was willing to serve, so I signed 'yes, yes.'"

During the fall of 1943, Hank signed on with the National Youth Administration (NYA) to attend a vocational school program in Weiser, Idaho. He acquired skills in auto mechanics. He then moved to Salt Lake City, where he served tables at a University of Utah sorority house. He then tried to enlist in the Army Air Force, but was rejected: "I had an enemy alien status." He wanted to become a mechanic and subsequently attempted to enter the aeronautical mechanics program at Weber State College: "I couldn't get into that either." He returned to camp.

On February 6, 1943, the army scheduled visits to the ten camps administered by the War Relocation Authority to register all male Nisei of draft age. Recalling events surrounding his refusal to comply with the draft, Hank said: "I guess it was when the draft actually came. Up until then, I guess it was a slow process of starting to think about what was happening." He thought about his rejection by the National Guard, his father's sudden disappearance and detention, the Army Air Force rejection, and his inability to enter the aeronautical mechanics program at Weber State College.

> I was always told by my parents that if anything ever happened between Japan and the United States, it was my duty to go to the army. As a citizen that's my obligation. I started to reflect on it; it just didn't make sense to me—to be in camp and have to be drafted without having a choice. It just wasn't right.

Hank decided to refuse induction. He learned there were other dissidents in camp who decided to resist the draft because of the loss of civil rights.[32] The day they were to be inducted, U.S. marshals arrested several of them, including Hank, and they spent the first night in the Twin Falls jail. They were then taken to the Emmet County jail where they sat for two months. Hank's trial was subsequently held in Boise, Idaho.

> When my draft call came, I sent an appeal by a registered letter. The plea was not guilty on the basis that my citizenship rights were denied. My court-appointed lawyer told me there is no way out of this, you violated the draft order. Your only out is the registered letter. I had the receipt but the head of the selective service from Seattle swore he never got it.

Some of the dissidents changed their plea to guilty, and the judge gave them lighter sentences of two years. Hank did not change his stand: "I remained with the non-guilty plea and got three years and three months."

Hank was sent directly to McNeil Island Federal Penitentiary. Initially, he and the other Minidoka resisters were confined in the main prison. Later they were transferred to the penitentiary farm. They were assigned various jobs: "I happened to work on the newspaper." There were classes: "I caught up on my education with math, calculus, and vocational training." With time off for good behavior, Hank was incarcerated for less than three years.

On Christmas Eve, 1947, Hank and the other convicted draft resisters received a pardon from President Harry Truman.[33]

After his release from prison Hank returned to Seattle and stayed with his parents. For a year he worked as a gardener. But then he decided to tour the country. "Went by bus, no idea where to go." He performed odd jobs along the way and got married in Los Angeles. After a brief venture in the Los Angeles grocery business, he returned to Seattle and established himself as a successful grocer in the University District. A health problem ultimately forced him into retirement. As of 2002 he lives with his wife across Lake Washington in a community east of Seattle.

A Question of Identity

As the four Nisei cousins negotiated issues of race, identity, and nationality in the context of life in the Pacific Northwest, their life histories represent individual trajectories. They should not be viewed as mere casualties of the times, but as proactive participants in decision-making concerning their lives during a critical period. They were socialized in a nurturing Issei community as they and their Nisei cohorts created their own communities. The Nikkei community evolved within the context of American society, harmonized with the fundamental precepts of American life, the basic tenets being embedded in the Constitution.

Religious training played a significant role in the socialization of the Nisei cousins. On Sunday mornings the cousins and their siblings would jump onto the back of a flatbed truck for a three-mile drive to the Union Sunday School. They looked forward to Sunday evenings when the Mukyokai fellowship met in each other's homes, where potluck dinners meant there would be lots of "goodies" to eat, important particularly during the Depression years. Learning proper behavior was a daily affair and, as Gordon said, it came mainly through examples:

> What's good, truth—it's not unique to Japanese or English teaching. A good portion of the influence of the parents didn't come from their lecturing to me and disciplining me; their teaching came by their doing it. The one basic principle of truth—if it's valid on Sunday its valid on Monday too; one principle for all people.

Grant was exposed to alternative religious thought during his school years in Japan. He observed the religious philosophies of Buddhism, Shintoism, and Confucianism and saw them as congruent with his Christian beliefs. Christianity was linked to his identity as an American, albeit in a Japanese environment: "I think I kept it separate as long as it didn't invade my privacy, because there was no one telling me that I can't believe in Christianity."

Henry's relationship to Mukyokai influences was the most peripheral of the experiences of the four Nisei cousins. He lived in Seattle some twenty-five miles from his Nisei cousins and saw them only on special occasions. At home, religious influences came from his mother, his Baptist preschool, and the Blaine Methodist Church with its Japanese American congregation.

The cousins were socially entrenched in the local Nikkei communities. Their families belonged to various Issei regional associations as well as to the local Japanese Association. Henry's father, additionally, was the president of the Seattle Japanese Grocer's Association. The cousins' exposure to mainstream American life was largely through the educational system. They were not taught by the Issei to become nationals of Japan. They grew up within the Japanese American and American communities and never questioned their identities as Japanese Americans and Americans.

Henry's exposure to mainstream society was the strongest among the cousins. Most of his high school friends were Caucasians. Grant was extensively exposed to Japanese life with his eight years of education in Japan.

His early years in the United States, however, set the foundations of his identity as an American. Additionally, due to the ethnocentrism of the Japanese, regardless of Grant's attempts to conform to the behavior of his Japanese peers, "I knew I was different."[34]

The actions of the U.S. government forced each Hirabayashi cousin to reexamine the basic principles underlying his citizenship and make commitments in terms of his understanding of the meaning of citizenship. Grant, although educated in Japan for eight years, never doubted his self-identification as an American: "I knew I was different and, of course, I always felt like an American for some reason." In spite of the impending hostilities between the United States and Japan, he joined the army prior to the U.S. entry into the war. He served in the Military Intelligence Service Language School with distinction, using the advantage of the education he had acquired in Japan to fulfill his military duties. Gordon, the idealist, adhering to Christian and constitutional ideals, rejected any action on the part of the government making him less than any other citizen in the nation. He refused to respond to the loyalty questionnaire: "I must refuse what I considered to be a gross violation of the Constitution. I must maintain my Christian principles [and] the democratic standards for which this nation lives."

Bob, in spite of the exclusion orders and his incarceration at Minidoka, never wavered from his interpretation of what he needed to do as an American. He responded positively to the loyalty questionnaire and subsequently joined the army: "Like I say, it seems like the natural thing to do." Hank also responded positively to the loyalty questionnaire. But when confronted with the draft, he considered earlier rejections by the National Guard and the Army Air Force and challenged the government's abridgement of his citizenship rights: "It just wasn't right."

The totality of the socialization experience, both in the Nikkei community and in mainstream American society, resulted in the cousins' identifying as Japanese Americans and Americans. They internalized basic American principles, and they acted on the basis of their understanding of these principles. Interestingly, they did not consult each other, nor were they aware of each other's decisions. Loyalty for them was not defined within simple, dichotomous wartime issues. For them, the real question was what being Japanese American, qua American, meant under these historical, political, and situational circumstances.[35] They negotiated the complexities of identity formation, moving between spheres of influence, assessing their own situations, and ultimately acting out their own histories. How does a Japanese American, qua American identity become significant and operational in the context of this critical setting?[36] In their responses, each cousin was asserting his rights and duties as he individually interpreted the meaning of being an American citizen.

With their diverse actions the cousins exemplified yet another basic American value: the long-cherished value of individualism. Adherence to basic American principles need not result in behavioral conformism. Diversity exists within the Japanese American community, belying the oft-repeated stereotypic assessments of homogeneity that "they are all alike." Pluralism and diversity are found throughout America within each of its ethnic groups. Indeed, the various ways of implementing our democratic principles attest to the expression: "In America, there is strength in diversity." America must redefine itself so that ethnic communities ultimately achieve acceptance as legitimate and integral parts of American society.

Notes

I would like to thank Ako Wooley for her translations of Issei writings; Louis Fiset, Gail Nomura, and Lane Hirabayashi for insightful feedback; and the four cousins, Grant, Gordon, Bob, and Hank, for sharing their lives with the community. The author is a member of the Hirabayashi kin group and the younger brother of Gordon Hirabayashi.

1. For a discussion on the extensive literature on concentration camp experience, see Brian Niiya, ed., *Encyclopedia of Japanese American History: An A-to-Z Reference from 1868 to the Present* (Los Angeles: Japanese American National Museum, 2001), 142.

2. U.S. Government Printing Office, DDS Form 804A, January 23, 1943.

3. Niiya, *Encyclopedia of Japanese American History*, 260.

4. Issei, the first generation, are the immigrants from Japan. Nisei, the second generation, are the children of the Issei.

5. Shotaro Frank Miyamoto, *Social Solidarity among the Japanese in Seattle* (Seattle: University of Washington Press, 1984), vi.

6. Ibid., 11, ix.

7. Azumi is the traditional name of this district in Nagano Ken. John Isao Nishinoiri, "Japanese Farms in Washington" (master's thesis, University of Washington, 1926), 47.

8. Hiroshi Miura, *The Life and Thought of Kanzo Uchimura: 1861–1930* (Grand Rapids, Mich.: Wm. B. Eerdmans Publishing Company, 1996).

9. William H. H. Norman, "Kanzo Uchimura: Founder of the Non-church Movement," *Contemporary Religions in Japan* 5:1 (March 1963): 37.

10. Nishinoiri, "Japanese Farms in Washington," 50.

11. Stan Flewelling, *Farmlands: The Story of Thomas, A Small Agricultural Community in King County, Washington* (Auburn, Wash.: Erick Sanders Historical Society, n.d.), 95.

12. State of Washington Superior Court of the State of Washington. Film File C751, June 14, 1922. All Asians were prevented from becoming naturalized citizens. The U.S. Congress in 1790 limited the rights of naturalization to the free and white. Congress amended this law after the Civil War to include Africans as among those eligible.

13. Nishinoiri, "Japanese Farms in Washington," 51.

14. *Shin Kokyo* (New Homeland). Issues of this journal are in the collection of the Kensei Gijuku Museum in Hotaka, Nagano Prefecture, Japan.

15. Miyamoto, *Social Solidarity among the Japanese in Seattle*, xx.

16. Ibid., xvii.

17. Ibid., 51.

18. David K. Yoo, *Growing Up Nisei: Race, Generation, and Culture among Japanese Americans of California, 1924–49* (Urbana: University of Illinois Press, 2000), 22.

19. For a detailed discussion of the *dozoku* structure in rural Japan, see Chie Nakane, *Kinship and Economic Organization in Rural Japan* (New York: Humanities Press, 1967).

20. Sylvia Junko Yanagisako, *Transforming the Past: Tradition and Kinship among Japanese Americans* (Stanford: Stanford University Press, 1985).

21. The following vignettes on the cousins are based on interviews conducted by the author in 1996. When quoting from these interviews, the interviewee's name will always precede the quotes, and citations will not be made after the quotes.

22. *Kofukai yakunin*, a person in charge of upholding the school traditions or morals, the esprit de corps of the class.

23. For the role of Japanese Americans in American military intelligence, see Joseph D. Harrington, *Yankee Samurai: The Secret Role of Nisei in America's Pacific Victory* (Detroit: Pettigrew Enterprises, 1979), and Tad Ichinokuchi, ed., *John Aiso and the M.I.S.: Japanese American Soldiers in the Military Intelligence Service, World War II* (Los Angeles: Military Intelligence Service Club of Southern California, 1988).

24. Gordon Hirabayashi, *Good Times, Bad Times: Idealism is Realism* (Argenta, B.C.: Canadian Quaker pamphlet, no. 22, 1985), 3.

25. Personal collection, Gordon Hirabayashi.

26. Peter Irons, *The Courage of Their Convictions* (New York: Free Press, 1988), 42.

27. Ibid., 43–45.

28. Letter sent to Local Board 4, Seattle, Washington, on February 22, 1944. War Department files, ASW 014.311 WDC Exclusion Orders, 9 March 1944.

29. Louis Fiset, "Thinning, Topping, and Loading: Japanese Americans and Beet Sugar in World War II," *Pacific Northwest Quarterly* 90, no. 3 (summer 1999), 123–39.

30. For information on the 442nd RCT, see Thelma Chang, *I Can Never Forget: Men of the 100th/442nd* (Honolulu: University of Hawaii Press, 1992) and Masayo Duus, *Unlikely Liberators: The Men of the 100th and the 442nd* (Honolulu: University of Hawaii Press, 1987).

31. For a description of these battles, see Chester Tanaka, *Go for Broke: A Pictorial History of the Japanese American 100th Infantry Battalion and the 442nd Regimental Combat Team* (Richmond, Calif.: Go For Broke, Inc., 1982).

32. See Niiya, *Encyclopedia of Japanese American History*, 152–54. For an account of draft resistance in Heart Mountain camp, see Frank Emi, "Draft Resistance at the Heart Mountain Concentration Camp and the Fair Play Committee," in *Frontiers of Asian American Studies: Writing, Research, Commentary*, ed. Gail M. Nomura, Russell Endo, Stephen H. Sumida, and Russell Leong (Pullman: Washington State University Press, 1989), 41–69.

33. See Niiya, *Encyclopedia of Japanese American History*, 153.

34. The Japanese sense of uniqueness contributed to Grant's isolation from his classmates in Japan. According to historians Edwin Reischauer and Marius Jansen, the Japanese held a perception of themselves "as being so distinct from the rest of humanity as to be unique." This perception was extended to Nisei even though they had ancestral connections to Japan. Edwin O. Reischauer and Marius B. Jansen, *The Japanese Today: Change and Continuity* (Cambridge: Harvard University Press, 1995), 395.

35. For a discussion on the meaning of loyalty during wartime, see Yuji Ichioka, "The Meaning of Loyalty: The Case of Kazumaro Buddy Uno," *Amerasia Journal* 23 (winter 1997/1998): 45 ff.

36. For a discussion on issues of perspective and meaning for ethnic Americans, see Dorrine Kondo, book review of *Turning Leaves: The Photograph Collections of Two Japanese American Families* by Richard Chalfen, *Visual Anthropology Review* 8, no. 2 (fall 1992): 101.

8 / THE MINIDOKA DRAFT RESISTERS IN A FEDERAL KANGAROO COURT

ERIC L. MULLER

O n the last day of spring 1944, the United States Army staged an induction ceremony for sixty-six new Idaho draftees. It was a rather unusual ceremony in that the army welcoming the new draftees was simultaneously guarding them and their families at gunpoint. The ceremony was taking place behind the barbed-wire fence of the Minidoka Relocation Center near Hunt, Idaho, one of the ten camps the federal War Relocation Authority (WRA) set up in 1942 to house the approximately 110,000 people of Japanese descent the army had earlier forcefully removed from the West Coast out of fear that some might attempt subversion. Most Minidoka residents had been uprooted from their homes in Seattle and Portland in the spring of 1942. The draftees were, of course, all Nisei, young Japanese American men, most in their twenties and younger, who somehow found the spirit to answer the call to arms of the country that had incarcerated them.

Military service was being promoted to the Nisei as a precious opportunity to prove the loyalty and patriotism of all Japanese Americans—qualities that the Japanese attack on Pearl Harbor had sharply, if unfairly, called into question. And Nisei loyalty was what the induction ceremony at Minidoka was designed to emphasize and celebrate. But when Lt. B. M. Harrington of the Traveling Examining and Induction Board from Fort Douglas, Utah, rose to administer the military oath, things quickly went awry.

> We in the American armed forces are happy to welcome you Japanese among our ranks, even though your country, Japan, is at war with the United States. The fact that you young Japanese are willing to fight against your country proves that there [are] a few Japanese who [are] good Americans.

He concluded his remarks by congratulating "you Japanese" for "making a splendid record in our Army where you are welcomed and given all of the rights and privileges of any other citizen who is brought into [the] service."

Harrington's comments immediately sapped the crowd of its enthusiasm. "Doesn't he know we were born here and are citizens of the United States, not Japan?" muttered one young man. "Why doesn't that guy get next to himself and discover to what country we belong?" said another. "We are no Japs."

A Minidoka administrator took Harrington aside after his speech and pointed out the lieutenant's errors: the Nisei draftees were Americans, not Japanese; they were leaving the camp to fight *for* their country, not *against* it; and the U.S. Army was as much theirs as it was Lieutenant Harrington's. Harrington accepted the suggestions, but the damage was done. One of the sixty-six young men turned and walked away just before the oath was administered, joining in defiance a tiny handful of others from Minidoka who by now had decided to resist the draft.[1]

In time, that tiny handful of resisters would grow to forty. By late summer, more than three dozen Minidokans were in county jails in and around Boise, Idaho, awaiting federal court trials for draft evasion, a felony carrying a maximum term of five years in prison. However, any hopes these young Americans harbored for fair trials were misplaced. The federal courts, so often thought to be the last and best protector of American freedoms, failed the Minidoka resisters miserably, offering them only sham trials by biased decision-makers. What follows is the story of the Nisei draft resisters of the Minidoka Relocation Center and their unhappy experiences in a federal kangaroo court.

It was not only the court that failed these young men. So did the law. No clear principle of constitutional law on the books in 1944 would have permitted a young man to refuse military service because of an egregious violation of his civil rights. Indeed, no principle of constitutional law on the books *today* establishes that proposition. This may be the most disturbing lesson of the Minidoka resisters' experience—that it was not merely the court system that would countenance the immoral treatment of American citizens, but the law itself.

After January 20, 1944, when the federal government announced it was reopening the draft to the Nisei after incarcerating them and their Issei elders for nearly two years, the reaction at Minidoka was muted. At other camps, however, Nisei began resisting the draft almost immediately; at Heart

Mountain in Wyoming, a noisy and public draft resistance movement was quickly born.[2] With a small group of articulate and motivated older Nisei at its helm, the Heart Mountain group took a public and principled stand: We will gladly serve in the army if our and our families' civil rights are first restored. But through the month of April, as the numbers of draft resisters at Heart Mountain and other camps climbed into the dozens, Minidoka's rate of compliance with the selective service laws was one hundred percent.

General tensions at Minidoka, however, had been building even before the reopening of the draft. In the fall of 1943 a comparatively vocal and disaffected group had been transferred from the Tule Lake Relocation Center and soon began to agitate among the Minidokans. Late in 1943 the camp's boilermakers went on strike during a period of labor unrest. Even though the strike was resolved, labor relations with the administrators at Minidoka remained tense. In this atmosphere, resentment over the draft finally began to flare up in late April 1944. Thus, on Thursday, April 26, when fifty-seven Nisei were called for induction, six of the young did not respond.

One of the six was Gene Akutsu, the younger son of a Seattle Issei couple, Kiyonosuke and Nao Akutsu.[3] By this point in the war, the eighteen-year-old had reached the limits of his endurance. He had been uprooted from his home and his school and incarcerated for almost two years. He had seen his father taken from the family the day after the bombing of Pearl Harbor, interned for two years as an enemy alien in a Justice Department camp for enemy aliens, and then sent "home" to a concentration camp barrack at Minidoka as an emaciated, graying, and defeated old man. So disillusioned had Gene grown with the land of his birth that on February 10, 1944, weeks after the reopening of the draft, Akutsu filed a petition for "repatriation" to Japan. "Repatriation" was a somewhat odd request for a young American citizen who had never "patriated" Japan in the first place. Many other frustrated Nisei in Akutsu's position—including nearly all of those who would resist the draft—filed petitions for "expatriation" to Japan, which, as a matter of semantics, made more sense. But Akutsu denominated his petition as a request for "repatriation" for a specific reason: his treatment at the hands of his government had demonstrated to him that he was really Japanese, and no longer an American citizen.[4] Thus, when Gene Akutsu received his draft notice in April 1944, he decided that the government "had been kicking us around a lot" and he was just "not going to stand for that" any longer. When "the day finally came for [me] to go for induction," Akutsu says, "I just didn't go."

When Akutsu informed his parents of his decision, his mother became deeply distressed. She had just been reunited with her husband after two years, and now she faced the loss of her youngest son. She worried aloud that "we don't know what is going to happen to you, . . . [or] whether we'll ever see you again." With great sadness she asked Gene to give her a clipping of his hair and his fingernails, so that "if anything should happen that we should never see you again, at least we'll have something to have at your funeral."

Just after lunch on April 29, 1944, a deputy U.S. marshal appeared at the door of the Akutsu family barrack with a warrant for Gene's arrest on the charge of failing to report for induction into the armed services of the United States, in violation of section 311 of Title 50 of the United States Code. Gene surrendered peacefully, as there was "no use trying to run around," and got into the deputy marshal's car for the three-hour drive to Boise. As he climbed in, he was surprised to see another Nisei sitting in the back seat. Akutsu had no idea anyone else at Minidoka had decided to resist the draft. (Unlike the well-organized resisters at Heart Mountain, those at Minidoka acted individually.) Once in Boise, the deputy marshal took them to city hall, where the local U.S. commissioner set bail for each at $1,000.[5] This was, of course, a sum neither of the young Nisei had any hope of producing. The deputy marshal therefore packed them back in the car and drove them to the Ada County Jail, where they would sit for more than four months awaiting their September trial date.

The next month, on the day of Lieutenant Harrington's ill-advised speech at the flagpole welcoming "you Japanese" into "our army," eleven out of 108 inductees—again, just over 10 percent—refused to appear for induction, one of them dropping out moments before the oath was administered.[6] On other occasions throughout the summer of 1944, more Nisei, including Gene Akutsu's older brother, Jim, joined the ranks of those refusing to appear for induction, always at a rate of at least 10 percent of the total number of inductees called.[7] By the end of the summer, a total of thirty-eight Minidokans had opted for resistance and were in county jails awaiting trial. This was the third-highest number among the ten WRA centers; only Poston, with one hundred resisters, and Heart Mountain, with 88, exceeded the number from Minidoka.

Minidoka administrators knew their camp was faring poorly in the overall effort to produce draftees, and took steps—unavailing ones, as it turned out—to contain the apparent virus of noncompliance that was infecting the camp. One strategy was to lobby the local selective service board to call suspected "anti-draft agitators" for induction as quickly as possible so that they could be arrested, removed from camp, and thereby silenced. Jim Akutsu came into possession of a copy of a letter that was embarrassing to the administration, written in May by Minidoka's project location officer to the local draft board. The letter had been slipped under his door by a friend working in the administration office. The letter asked that Jim Akutsu be called for induction at once, noting appreciatively that the local draft board had "accommodated" the WRA in the past by calling "troublesome" internees for early induction.[8] As requested, Jim Akutsu was called immediately, charged, and arrested when he failed to report for induction in July. He was then whisked away to join his brother in the county jail in Boise. A mere six months after Nao and her husband, Kiyonosuke, were reunited, the Issei couple found themselves childless.

Another strategy for fighting the spread of resistance was to structure more expensive bail arrangements for each successive group of resisters so as to deter others still in camp from refusing to report. The U.S. commissioner fixed bail for the first two resisters at $1,000. Two weeks later, he increased the bail amount to $1,500 for the next resister who came before him, and predicted that the amount would rise to $2,000 for the next group "and later $2,500, if the 'hold-outs' continue."[9] Of course, even a minimal amount of bail was unnecessary in these cases. The purpose of bail is to guarantee that the defendant will not flee jurisdiction while awaiting trial. The Minidoka draft resisters—incarcerated behind barbed wire in a WRA internment camp—were certainly going nowhere. Still, as unnecessary as bail was in any amount, the commissioner clearly abused the bail process by ratcheting up the amount for each wave of Nisei who defied the law. Bail is not a tool for strong-arming people into obeying the law. Yet that is how the government deployed it against the Minidoka draft resisters.

A final strategy that the administrators urged for stemming the tide of resistance was to improperly accelerate the pace of the young men's arrests. A federal criminal case is typically initiated by the filing of a complaint, consisting of a sworn document alleging the commission of a crime. If the alleged crime is a felony (as draft evasion is), the Fifth Amendment to the U.S. Constitution requires the prosecutor to follow up the complaint with a formal indictment from a grand jury. It was the prevailing practice in 1944 to arrest a criminal defendant after the grand jury indicted him rather than when the complaint was filed, unless the authorities were worried that the defendant might flee the jurisdiction before the grand jury could complete its work.

In the late spring and summer complaints were filed against those who failed to appear for induction at Minidoka. The grand jury, however, was not scheduled to meet until early September, which meant those who resisted were left free to go about their business in camp. This posed a problem for Minidoka's administrators. They were trying to ensure maximum compliance with the draft laws and were unwilling to permit resisters to circulate among the general population, which might suggest to others that draft resistance had few consequences. In July, Frank Barrett, Minidoka project attorney, complained in a letter to the WRA's home office that he was "concerned over the leaving of the 'evaders' free to go about the Center" and wanted "to prevent possible bad influence of these men upon others."[10] He therefore urged that the resisters be arrested and detained when their complaints were filed, rather than when their indictments would issue in September. This was a needless distortion of policy, of course, because it is hard to imagine a criminal defendant who posed less a risk of flight than a Japanese American inmate living under armed guard and behind barbed wire in a concentration camp. Still, the camp management had its way; as a result, the Minidoka draft resisters spent much of the summer of 1944 in county jail cells rather than with their families.

These jails were a change of scenery for the resisters, but they were certainly no vacation. During his first night in jail, Gene Akutsu saw what he thought were watermelon seeds on his thin mattress. In the morning when he awoke, he was covered with bites. He lifted the mattress and saw the underside was covered with bed bugs. Killing the bugs, he recalls, took "weeks and weeks." Akutsu's sleep was disturbed by the barred windows left open day and night; daytime was pleasantly warm, but the nights got colder than the single thin blanket he was issued could handle. And the food, Akutsu remembers, was dreadful: "mush and toast, pork and beans," served two times a day.

The resisters' lives droned on throughout the summer of 1944 as they awaited the September session of the grand jury. The wait was excruciating. They grew weak, tired, and depressed from lack of exercise and stimulation. Finally, on September 6, 1944, they were walked under armed guard through the streets of Boise to the United States District Court for the District of Idaho, where they were to be arraigned on draft evasion indictments that the grand jury returned that morning.

The judge waiting to arraign them, the Honorable Chase A. Clark, had been appointed a federal district judge less than two years earlier, after losing his bid for a second term as governor of Idaho. Although new to the bench, he was not at all new to the issue of the incarceration of Japanese

Americans at the Minidoka Relocation Center. Indeed, it is not an exaggeration to say that Judge Clark was partly *responsible* for the barbed wire fences that encircled the Minidoka inmates. Two and a half years earlier, in April of 1942, when Clark was still governor of Idaho, he and the governors of the other western states were invited to Salt Lake City to meet with the men in the federal government who were trying to figure out where to move the Nikkei from the West Coast states. Milton S. Eisenhower, first director of the War Relocation Authority (and the future president's brother), was hoping the western states would agree to welcome the Nikkei at loosely structured reception centers, where they would have an opportunity to harness their fabled Japanese industriousness in the service of the state, the region, the nation, and the war effort. Although he assured the governors the forced migrants could leave the reception centers only on furloughs to work in local farming and industry, he certainly did not envision the centers as concentration camps.[11]

Clark was among the most outspoken opponents of the plan at the Salt Lake City meeting. He began his comments with an admission that he was "so prejudiced that [his] reasoning might be a little off." "I don't trust any of them," he said, referring to the Nikkei. "I don't know which ones to trust and so therefore I don't trust any of them." He then explained that he "would hate it, . . . after I am dead, to have the people of Idaho hold me responsible . . . for having led Idaho full of Japanese during my administration." Nothing in this diatribe was surprising from a public official who had openly referred to the Japanese in America as people who "act like rats" and who had argued for solving what he called the "Jap problem" by "send[ing] them all back to Japan, then sink[ing] the island."[12]

Governor Clark made clear to Eisenhower that the West Coast states' Japanese population would be permitted into Idaho only under the strictest conditions. First, they must arrive and be transported under military supervision. Second, he insisted, they should be forbidden from buying land in Idaho and forced to return to the West Coast at war's end. Finally, and most pointedly, Clark urged that any "Japanese who may be sent [to Idaho] be placed under guard and confined in concentration camps for the safety of our people, our State, and the Japanese themselves."

Clark and his fellow western governors prevailed in demanding incarceration for Japanese Americans.[13] Faced with their intransigence, Milton Eisenhower had little choice but to accede to barbed wire and guard towers, and his New Deal agency soon became the overseer of a network of American-style concentration camps.

It was former governor Clark, the man who had sought the greatest possible curtailment of Nikkei liberties, who became responsible for safeguarding the Minidoka resisters' rights. The resisters may have hoped that in donning the black robes of federal justice, Clark had found a new commitment to tolerance and fairness. A fair trial was not inconceivable; after all, just six weeks earlier, Louis E. Goodman, a federal judge in California, had angrily thrown out the draft evasion charges pending against twenty-six Nisei resisters from the Tule Lake Segregation Center, calling the prosecution "shocking to [his] conscience."[14] Judge Goodman's decision had made big news at Minidoka, raising the hopes of some that the center's Nisei might also prevail.[15] Judge Clark, however, proved to be no Judge Goodman.

As Judge Clark took the bench at the resisters' arraignment on September 6, all defendants stood before him without counsel. Naturally, they could not afford to hire their own lawyers; they and their families had lost nearly everything when they were uprooted from their homes in the Northwest two and a half years before. Judge Clark's first job was therefore to appoint lawyers to represent the several dozen young men whose cases he would be trying. This was no easy task in a city as small as Boise. To solve the problem, Judge Clark did something unprecedented: he ordered every available Boise attorney to appear in court that morning. When they got there, he broke the news to them that they were each being appointed to represent one or two of the Nisei resisters, and that, under prevailing federal court practice at the time, they would not be paid for their service.

Needless to say, the Boise bar was upset with this plan. The problem, however, was not lack of compensation. The problem was that many of the attorneys wanted no part in representing the Japanese American defendants whose cases they were being asked—or, more accurately, ordered—to handle. Gene Akutsu, for example, was appointed a lawyer named R. R. Breshears. After Akutsu entered his plea of "not guilty," Judge Clark gave Akutsu the opportunity to meet with his attorney to discuss his defense. Breshears told his client in no uncertain terms that he was a "damn fool," and then said, "I'll be damned if I'm going to help you." From that point on, the eighteen-year-old Nisei was essentially on his own. Breshears attended later hearings, Akutsu recalls, but the lawyer said and did almost nothing. Moreover, this lawyer's performance proved typical among his peers; the local newspaper reported that another attorney assigned to represent one of the resisters told Judge Clark that he did not want even to sit at the same table with his client, whom he called a "traitor to his country" in open court.[16]

On September 13, 1944, one week after the arraignments, Judge Clark heard the first cases. The first order of business was a motion by Jim Akutsu's attorney to dismiss the indictment.[17] At the core of the elder Akutsu brother's claim was the raw fact of his incarceration behind barbed wire. That fact, he argued, placed him under coercion and duress, and thereby made the government's efforts at drafting him a violation of both the Constitution's Due Process Clause and the Selective Service Act.[18]

This motion should have presented a judicial crisis for Judge Clark. On Clark's insistence that the Nikkei be incarcerated, Milton Eisenhower abandoned hopes for open relocation communities in the interior, and resigned himself to establishing concentration camps. Now, just over two years later, and wearing the robes of a federal district judge, Clark was presented with an attack on the constitutionality of the very circumstances of confinement that he himself had demanded. Federal law at the time required disqualification of any judge who had a "'personal bias or prejudice,' by reason of which the judge [was] unable to impartially exercise his functions in the particular case."[19] Jim Akutsu's attorney did not move for Clark's recusal, but sound judicial practice ought to have prompted Judge Clark to take the initiative to remove himself from the case. How, after all, could he possibly adjudicate the constitutionality of what he himself had demanded? Yet Judge Clark did not recuse himself. He heard the motion and denied it without recorded opinion.

Having rejected the constitutional attack on the proceedings, Judge Clark set in motion what can only be described as an assembly line of federal criminal justice. Over the next eleven days, he opened and concluded thirty-three separate jury trials, sometimes hearing as many as four trials in a single day. Needless to say, the trials were hardly elaborate. In each case, the government called a witness or two to establish that the defendant was classified 1-A for the draft, was duly and properly called to report for a preinduction physical examination and in some cases for induction, and that he failed to report as ordered. In some cases, an FBI agent offered in evidence a statement the defendant gave upon his arrest, usually expressing anger at the forced removal and incarceration of the West Coast Nikkei and a desire to renounce American citizenship and expatriate to Japan. At that, the government rested.

The typical defense case was also spare. The extant judicial records suggest that in each trial, defense counsel called the defendant as the lone defense witness. The recollections of surviving resisters themselves tend to show even this minimal involvement by counsel was an exaggeration. Gene Akutsu, for example, remembers struggling to mount his own defense while his attorney stood idly by in the back of the courtroom. Another of the Minidoka resisters, Frank Yamasaki, remembers a five-minute consultation with his attorney in the holding cell just before trial, and no further contact.[20] Alone and uncounseled, the young Nisei struggled to communicate their reasons for resisting the draft. While no court transcript exists to capture their exact words, most may have uttered something like what one had written to his local draft board:

> If I were treated like an American I would be more than glad to serve in the armed forces but seeing how things are especially since now that I'm put behind barbed wires for no reasons, except that I was born of Japanese parents, I must be a Jap, like the rest of the aliens. In that case I'll stick to Japan and you can have my U.S. citizenship papers, its [*sic*] never done me any good.[21]

Gene Akutsu and Frank Yamasaki both remember that their efforts to explain their reasons for resisting were in vain; Judge Clark instructed the jury to disregard as irrelevant any testimony about poor treatment by the government or why its conduct had prompted them to resist. The only issue, Clark instructed the jurors, was whether or not the defendant had willfully failed to report for induction.

Akutsu and Yamasaki both retain vivid memories of jury deliberations. "Deliberations" might be too grand a word for the work of these juries, none of which caucused for more than "a few minutes after each case."[22] When Gene Akutsu rose as his jury filed out of the courtroom to deliberate, he barely had the chance to sit down before they returned with his guilty verdict. The jurors, Akutsu recalls, went into the jury room "long enough . . . [to] circle around the table and come back out again." Frank Yamasaki remembers that by the time of his trial—his was the twenty-third—the jury was no longer bothering to deliberate. He watched the jurors walk out into the hallway for a few brief moments, long enough for a few drags on a cigarette, say nothing to one another, and then return with their guilty verdict.

Are these just the embittered memories of those whom the jury condemned, distorted by the passage of more than a half century? Or were the juries in these cases really so cavalier? Good reason exists to believe the latter. Judge Clark was not the only arbiter in the courtroom who was open to a charge of prejudgment and bias. So too were the jurors. For the thirty-three trials that Clark ran between September 13 and September 26, 1944, he called a total of thirty-four Idaho citizens to serve as jurors.[23] For each trial, he seated a new and slightly different configuration of twelve of these thirty-four people. This meant that by the time all of the trials were completed, virtually all jurors had served on at least ten separate juries. One had the distinction of hearing fifteen separate trials of Minidoka draft resisters, eight of those at a rate of two per day. Another juror who participated in a total of fourteen trials sat for two separate trials on five different days. The situation grew so absurd that on September 20, the seventh day of the trials, a lawyer for one of the defendants challenged the entire panel of prospective jurors from which he was expected to pick a jury. He protested that members of the jury panel had all sat on juries trying other Nisei on the same charges and thus might not be free of prejudice.[24] Clark said he would give the matter some thought, but resumed jury selection from the same pool of jurors the next morning.

Thus, when Frank Yamasaki recalls that his jurors "deliberated" while standing in the hallway for a silent smoke, he may well be remembering correctly. Each of his twelve jurors had already heard at least five trials of Yamasaki's fellow resisters; most had heard eight. For two "seasoned" jurors, Yamasaki's trial was their *eleventh* draft evasion trial in eight days. At that point, what was left to talk about?

Whatever its flaws, this production line of jury trials was unquestionably efficient. In the space of thirteen days, pausing only on Sundays, the juries convicted thirty-three Nisei of draft evasion at an average pace of three per day. Throughout the trial period several others entered guilty pleas and thereby avoided trials. One young man fared better: he was able to demonstrate that he had never actually received his induction notice in the mail, and on this technicality was acquitted.[25] But even this victory was short-lived; as soon as he returned to Minidoka he was properly served with an induction notice. Upon his refusal to report, he was arrested, tried, and subsequently convicted of draft evasion at a later term of court. In all, forty Minidokans were ultimately charged with and convicted of draft evasion.[26]

In late September and early October 1944, the convicted draft resisters appeared before Judge Clark for sentencing. Those who had entered guilty pleas and spared the court the minor inconvenience of a trial received eighteen-month sentences. The others were sentenced to terms of three years and three months in prison and a $200 fine.[27]

In early October 1944, the new convicts were sent to McNeil Island, Washington, to serve out their sentences. McNeil Island Federal Penitentiary was an old fortress of a prison that sat on a small piece of land in Puget Sound fifty miles southwest of Seattle. As the prison launch carried Gene Akutsu and his fellow resisters toward the penitentiary, the young man noted the irony that two and a half years earlier the government had forced them from their homes in the Puget Sound region as possible threats to national security. Now it was forcing them back as convicted felons.

The young convicts served out uneventful terms at McNeil Island. They shared several large cells in the place they called the "Big House"—a cavernous and depressing vault of a building with rows of cells stacked upon one another like so many cages.[28] At first the Nisei kept to themselves, looking after one another and mixing little with the general population of swindlers, murderers, and other federal felons. Later, the former Minidokans formed a baseball team and won the prison championship. On the diamond they came to know many of their fellow inmates and garnered respect and sympathy. "You're just a political ping-pong ball that is being bounced around," inmates would often tell the resisters.

Prison time passed slowly. On December 18, 1944, the Supreme Court held that the War Relocation Authority "ha[d] no authority to subject citizens who [were] concededly loyal" to detention,[29] yet still the Minidoka resisters sat in the Big House. On January 2, 1945, the army formally reopened the West Coast to loyal Nikkei, and still the resisters sat in the Big House. As the nation celebrated victory over Japan on September 2, 1945, the resisters still sat in the Big House. On October 28, 1945, Minidoka closed its gates permanently;[30] still its draft resisters sat in the Big House.

The closing of Minidoka did have one minor consequence for the McNeil Island convicts: their families returned to the Pacific Northwest, allowing some to visit their incarcerated sons. Nao Akutsu, for example, traveled every other Sunday, without fail, to visit her two sons, Jim and Gene. (Visits were permitted on alternate Sundays.) To reach them she had to take a series of buses from Seattle through Tacoma to the small town of Steilacoom, just across the water from McNeil Island. From there, at the appointed time, she boarded the prison ferry and finally made her way to the visiting room in the basement of the prison's administration building, where she would await one of her two sons. Eventually Jim or Gene—whichever son she had not seen the previous time—would make an appearance behind a thick mesh screen, and mother and son would talk through the screen under the watchful eyes and ears of prison guards. After a much too brief visit, during which time she was blocked from the slightest caress from her child, she would make the long return trip to Seattle, knowing she had to endure two more weeks of separation.

The Minidoka resisters remained in the Big House until April 30, 1946, when the prison transferred them to an adjacent minimum-security prison camp on the island known as "the Farm." There conditions improved somewhat. The resisters lived in dormitories rather than cells, enjoyed more freedom of movement, and had the chance to perform farm work in the open air. But it was not until April 1947, after having served well more than two-thirds of their sentences, that the Minidoka resisters were released on parole.[31] Most rejoined their families, who themselves had recently been released from captivity.

Once back with their families, the former resisters attempted to join the rest of the Nikkei community in the arduous task of trying to piece their lives and communities back together. Yet the group shouldered a unique burden in this task: unlike their fellow Nisei, they were convicted felons, for whom employment and acceptance were even harder to come by. Late in 1947, President Harry Truman removed that burden, at least as a formal matter, by granting pardons to the Nisei resisters from all of the wra's camps, including Minidoka. He did so on the recommendation of a specially appointed review board charged with the responsibility of considering pardons for thousands of convicted war resisters. It had reviewed the cases of the Nisei and concluded that they had been loyal citizens before the war who had been understandably angered by their wartime "classification as undesirables."[32] The board further concluded, and President Truman apparently agreed, that the Nisei resisters would "justify our confidence in their loyalty." With this, the political and civil rights of the Minidoka resisters were restored.

What the pardons could not restore was their good names in the Japanese American community. Sadly, some in the community mislabeled the group "No No Boys," a nickname they have not fully shaken to this day. The phrase "No No" referred to their supposed answers to the two key questions—one gauging willingness to serve in the U.S. armed forces, and the other gauging their willingness to "forswear allegiance" to the Japanese emperor—that had appeared on a questionnaire the government had made all inmates fill out in February 1943. Those who actually answered in the negative to both of these two questions—that is, those who said, "no, no,"— were branded as disloyal and shipped off for indefinite confinement at the Tule Lake Segregation Center in northern California. The Minidoka draft resisters, however, had *not* answered "no, no" to the two questions. Gene Akutsu, for example, had answered the questions "no, yes": no, he was not willing to serve in the armed forces wherever and whenever ordered, but yes, he was certainly willing to forswear allegiance to the emperor of Japan, an allegiance he had never sworn in the first place. Gene Akutsu and his fellow resisters were therefore not properly grouped with those Nikkei—primarily Issei and Kibei—whose attachments to Japan or resentments toward the United States had landed them in segregation at Tule Lake. Yet to this day they have lived with the label of "No No Boys" and the insinuation of active disloyalty that goes along with it.

In May 2002, the Japanese American Citizens League (the most prominent national Japanese American organization) ended years of often rancorous internal debate by formally apologizing to the resisters for not recognizing the legitimacy of their wartime position. This apology, however, nearly tore the organization apart, because some members of the community, most notably certain war veterans, could not stomach the idea of apologizing to the resisters for anything.

To be sure, the Minidoka resisters took a different and rather more desperate tack than the resisters from some of the other camps. The best-known group of resisters, those from Heart Mountain Relocation Center, maintained from the start that they would comply with the draft so long as the government first recognized and restored to them their civil rights. This well-organized group of Nisei managed to channel their anger at their mistreatment into a strategy—sadly, a failed one—for law reform. Virtually all of the Minidoka resisters, by contrast, chose to vent their anger through hastily filed petitions written without legal counsel for repatriation or expatriation to Japan, petitions that some saw as desperate efforts to avoid military service at any cost.

It would be a mistake, however, to characterize the Heart Mountain resisters as loyal and the Minidoka resisters as disloyal. In the first place, some among the Heart Mountain cohort may not have shared the group's stated willingness to serve in the army if their constitutional rights were restored. Many tried to avoid conviction on a technicality rather than on a judicial declaration that their conscription was unconstitutional. And once convicted, some favored quietly and safely serving out their sentences rather than appealing the constitutional issue to a higher court.[33] More importantly, some Minidoka resisters were not acting out of desire to save their own necks or avoid taking up arms against their parents' homeland. Frank Yamasaki, for example, prior to receiving his draft notice, had long lived with tuberculosis, much of it in sanitaria. Had his goal been to avoid military service he could have done so by appearing for his preinduction physical exam. Yet Yamasaki refused to report for his physical rather than taking and failing it. This was neither an act of cowardice nor an act of disloyalty. It may be seen as an act of loyal protest.

The trial, conviction, and imprisonment of the Minidoka resisters made their earlier pain of exclusion and incarceration excruciating. The pain was more than some individuals could ultimately bear. When Gene and Jim Akutsu returned to Seattle in April 1947, they found their parents living in a makeshift hostel. Their father, Kiyonosuke, was scrambling to set up a new shoe repair business around the corner from his thriving prewar shop location. Their mother, Nao, was a ruined soul. Throughout the war she had waited with determination to see her family reunited. Once back in Seattle she made the bi-weekly lonely trip to McNeil Island to spend mere moments with one or the other of her sons in the prison's visiting room. Despite her family's ultimate reunion, the personal trauma of her wartime experiences finally caught up with her and consumed the last of her emotional resources. She fell into a deep depression, plagued by the constant feeling that "there was a train" going through her head. Alas, six months after her boys came home, she died, not living to enjoy the minor solace of seeing them pardoned by the president.

Most of the resisters and their families, of course, found the means to survive their ordeal and went on to live productive blue-collar lives. But many feel the sting of their pain even today. One resister who refused my request for an interview stated that he had spent his whole life trying to forget these events and was not about to start remembering them now. Another angrily charged that this story could do nothing but hurt people and was therefore best left untold. Gene Akutsu, however, has a different view. "I don't want to be remembered as a draft evader, chicken, yellow, or whatever you want to call it," he says. "I had my reasons for doing it and I'm proud of what I did." Would he make the same decision today? "If I was treated as I was then, under the same circumstances," he says, "yes, I would probably take the same steps."

If he did take the same steps today, one might hope that the law would treat him differently. Certainly the federal courts are a bolder and more assertive force on matters of race discrimination today than they were sixty years ago. *Korematsu v. United States*,[34] the Supreme Court's 1944 decision validating the mass exclusion of Japanese Americans from the West Coast, has been tossed into the trashcan of history, where it belongs. Juries are more racially diverse than they were in 1944, and the nation's experiences with the war in Viet Nam have given a different context to military service and the draft.

Yet all of these changes might not help Gene Akutsu today. While constitutional law has matured to the point of condemning an outrage like the mass incarceration of a racial or ethnic group, it has not matured in a way that would condemn the outrage of drafting those incarcerated. As I explain in greater detail in my book *Free to Die for Their Country: The Story of the Japanese American Draft Resisters in World War II*,[35] courts have little say about who should and should not be eligible for conscription; this is a political, not a judicial, judgment. And however brutally and illegally the government may have treated a citizen by incarcerating him on account of his race, it is no more settled now than it was in 1944 that this mistreatment ought to exempt the wronged citizen from the obligation of military service. To recognize in the Constitution's vague and open-ended due process clauses a constitutional right to refuse military service would be at least as vexing and controversial an act of interpretation as to recognize in those clauses a substantive right to get a physician's assistance in committing suicide.

Sixty years have passed since Judge Clark threw the book at the Minidoka resisters, but the law itself is no closer to fairness today than it was then. And this may be the most difficult lesson of the Minidoka resisters' experience in Judge Clark's kangaroo court. It is common to assume that what is unjust must also be illegal. The cases of the Nisei draft resisters show with unusual poignancy how the law can deviate from justice.

Notes

My thanks go to Gene Akutsu, Frank and Sadie Yamasaki, and Tom Ikeda and Sara Yamasaki for their friendship and support, and to Roger Daniels, Louis Fiset, and Gail Nomura for their helpful comments. This essay is a modified version of portions of chapters 1, 3, 5, and 6 of *Free to Die for Their Country: The Story of the Japanese American Draft Resisters in World War II* (Chicago: University of Chicago Press, 2001).

1. My account of the Minidoka induction ceremony comes from War Relocation Authority, Minidoka Relocation Center Community Analysis Section, Field Report No. 303, National Archives, RG 210 (National Archives microfilm M1342,

Reel 24), and from a letter from Minidoka Project Attorney Frank S. Barrett to WRA Solicitor Philip M. Glick, 27 June 1944, National Archives, RG 210, Entry 16, Box 262, File 37.109 #10, March to July 1944.

2. For a comprehensive examination of the Nisei draft resistance movement at Heart Mountain and elsewhere, see Eric L. Muller, *Free to Die for their Country: The Story of the Japanese American Draft Resisters in World War II* (Chicago: University of Chicago Press, 2001).

3. All information about the Akutsu family comes from interviews I conducted with Gene Akutsu at his home in Seattle, Washington, on February 20, 1998, and by telephone from my office in Chapel Hill, North Carolina, on March 3, 2000.

4. This impression of Gene Akutsu's is reported in a letter that his brother Jim wrote on his behalf to President Roosevelt. See Jimmie H. Akutsu to the President of the United States, 2 May 1944, National Archives, RG 210, Entry 16, Box 262. The government never acted on Gene Akutsu's petition, except to announce generally that it would treat all such petitions filed after January 20, 1944, the day of the reopening of the draft, as illegitimate efforts to avoid the draft. See John J. McCloy to Cordell Hull, 11 May 1944, National Archives, RG 210, Entry 16, Box 262.

5. "Two Youths Held on Draft Charge," *Minidoka Irrigator*, 6 May 1944.

6. See Frank S. Barrett to Philip M. Glick, 20 and 27 June 1944, National Archives, RG 210, Entry 16, Box 262.

7. See Frank S. Barrett to Philip M. Glick, 25 August 1944, National Archives, RG 210, Entry 16, Box 262.

8. See Frank S. Barrett to Philip M. Glick, 27 June 1944. In this letter, Barrett expressed doubt about the authenticity of this letter and ordered an investigation. But in subsequent missives to the WRA home office in Washington, he never reported that the letter was a fake, and even suggested that a request of this sort from the camp to the draft board would not have been unexpected.

9. See Frank S. Barrett to Philip M. Glick, 10 June 1944, National Archives, RG 210, Entry 16, Box 262.

10. See Frank S. Barrett to Philip M. Glick, 4 July 1944, National Archives, RG 210, Entry 16, Box 262.

11. All information about the Salt Lake City conference is taken from the notes of the Conference on Evacuation of Enemy Aliens, Salt Lake City, Utah, April 7, 1942, University of California at Berkeley, Bancroft Library, Japanese Evacuation and Resettlement Study, C1.03, 67/14C, File 1 of 3.

12. *Idaho Statesman*, 26 May 1942.

13. Only one western governor—Ralph Carr of Colorado—refused to line up against the West Coast's Nikkei. For an account of Carr's courageous stance, see

Eric L. Muller, "Apologies or Apologists? Remembering the Japanese American Internment in Wyoming," *Wyoming Law Review* 1 (2001): 473–95.

14. See *United States v Kuwabara*, 56 F. Supp. 716, 718 (N.D. Cal. 1944); see also Eric L. Muller, "All the Themes But One," *University of Chicago Law Review* 66 (1999): 1425–32, and Muller, *Free to Die for Their Country*, 131–60. Two years later, a federal judge in Arizona would signal his disapproval of the government's charges against the resisters from the Poston Relocation Center by convicting them and imposing on each of them a fine of one cent. This action, however, lacked the courage of Judge Goodman's outright dismissal for two reasons. First, the judgment was a conviction, not an acquittal or a dismissal of the charges. Second, the Arizona judge reached his decision in the comparative tranquility of 1946, with the benefit of hindsight, after both the war and the internment of Japanese Americans were over.

15. See "Draft Charge of 26 Tuleans Dismissed," *Minidoka Irrigator*, 29 July 1944; see also Frank S. Barrett to Philip M. Glick, 1 August 1944, National Archives, RG 210, Entry 16, Box 262.

16. "Japanese Face Trial," *Idaho Daily Statesman*, 7 September 1944.

17. Jim Akutsu had one of the few attorneys who actually involved himself in his client's case. This involvement was, however, slight: the motion the lawyer filed was really nothing more than a redrafting of Judge Goodman's opinion dismissing the charges in the case of the Tule Lake draft resisters.

18. "Motion to Quash Indictment and to Dismiss Action," *United States v Jim Hajime Akutsu*, United States District Court for the District of Idaho—Southern Division, National Archives Branch Depository, Seattle, Wash., RG 21, Box 90, File 2984. The Due Process Clause of the Fifth Amendment guarantees fundamental fairness in the ways the federal government goes about depriving people of their lives, their liberties, and their property.

19. *Ex Parte American Steel Barrel Co.*, 230 U.S. 35, 43 (1913).

20. Frank Yamasaki, interview with the author, Seattle, Washington, February 19, 1998.

21. George K. Kodama to Seattle Draft Board, 12 June 1944, *United States v George Kodama*, United States District Court for the District of Idaho—Southern Division, National Archives Branch Depository, Seattle, Wash., RG 21, Box 90, File 2984.

22. Frank S. Barrett to Philip M. Glick, 20 September 1944, National Archives, RG 210, Entry 16, Box 262.

23. See "Lawyer Says Jurors May Be Prejudiced," *Minidoka Irrigator*, 23 September 23, 1944.

24. Ibid.; see also Frank S. Barrett to Philip M. Glick, 27 September 1944, National Archives, RG 210, Entry 16, Box 262.

25. Ibid.

26. See United States Department of the Interior, *The Evacuated People: A Quantitative Description* (Washington D.C: Government Printing Office, 1946), 128, table 30.

27. See "Federal Court Hands Nisei Jail Sentence," *Idaho Daily Statesman*, 26 September 1944.

28. For a description of the federal prison at McNeil Island, see Paul W. Keve, *The McNeil Century* (Chicago: Nelson-Hall, 1984).

29. See *Ex Parte Endo*, 323 U.S. 283 (1944).

30. See Roger Daniels, "The Exile and Return of Seattle's Japanese," *Pacific Northwest Quarterly* 88 (1998): 166.

31. This was the longest term they could have served under the law. Under federal law at the time, they were eligible for consideration for release on parole after serving one-third of their prison term. They were also entitled to ten days of "good time" credit off the end of their sentence for each month of good behavior. On a sentence of three years and three months, and with a full credit for good behavior, the Minidoka resisters would have been entitled to release after no later than two years and two months. This is exactly when they were in fact released.

32. U.S. President's Amnesty Board, *Report Granting Pardon to Certain Persons Convicted of Violating the Selective Training & Service Act of 1940 as Amended* (Washington, D.C.: n.p., 1947).

33. Yosh Kuromiya, interview with the author, Alhambra, California, October 12, 1998.

34. See *Ex Parte Endo*, 323 U.S. 283 (1944).

35. See Muller, *Free to Die for Their Country*, 145–55, 195–96.

9 / WORDS DO MATTER

A Note on Inappropriate Terminology
and the Incarceration of the Japanese Americans

ROGER DANIELS

On or about August 2, 1979, I received a telephone call from Senator Daniel K. Inouye's Washington office.[1] One of his administrative assistants read me a draft of what became Senate Bill 1647 calling for the establishment of a "Commission on Wartime Relocation and Internment of Civilians (CWRIC)." The call came because I had been advising the staff of the Japanese American Citizens League and others about the campaign for redress. After hearing the draft I commented that it sounded good to me except that the word "internment" was inappropriate and that "incarceration" was a more accurate term.[2] She asked what the difference was, and I explained that "internment" was an ordinary aspect of declared wars and referred to a legal process, described in United States statutes, to be applied to nationals of a country with which the United States was at war. I pointed out that perhaps eight thousand Japanese nationals had been formally interned by the government during World War II, beginning as early as the night of December 7–8, 1941, and that, although a great deal of injustice accompanied this wartime internment, it was conducted legally, and those interned got a semblance of due process.[3] What happened to most of the West Coast Japanese Americans in 1942, I continued, should not be described with a word describing a legal process, even though the phrase "internment" was widely used not only in the literature but by many Japanese Americans. After some discussion she said that the difference was clear to her and that the bill's text would be changed. In a second phone call, the next day, she told me that, unfortunately, the senator had not waited for my vetting and had secured the agreement of a number of other senators to co-sponsor the bill and that he would not countenance any changes.

Thus, not for the first time, inappropriate, euphemistic language was employed, officially, to describe what happened to West Coast Japanese Americans in the aftermath of Pearl Harbor. Although, over time, the consciousness of Japanese and other Americans has been raised, most notably by the successful redress movement which resulted in the passage of the Civil Liberties Act of 1988, which eventually produced both an apology and a payment of $20,000 to more than eighty thousand survivors, most of the literature about the wartime events still uses language created during and immediately after World War II. In this essay I will first outline, briefly, the history of statutory internment in American history, and then trace and analyze some of the inappropriate language that has been used and try to show why it is important to call things by their right names and how the use of such language helped to mask the true nature of an American war crime.

Internment has long been recognized in both American and international law. By World War II it was regulated by a system of rules—the Geneva Convention—which governed the treatment of prisoners of war and was sometimes extended to civilian enemy nationals, including diplomats, resident in or captured by a belligerent nation. Although the first statute to use the term "alien enemy" was passed during John Adams's administration, there was no formally declared war, and no internment occurred.[4] The first actual internment by the United States government occurred during the war of 1812 when some resident British, mostly merchants, were ordered to remove themselves fifty miles inland. British merchants in New York City, for example, were interned, but left at liberty up the Hudson at Newburgh.

The United States next resorted to the process during World War I. At that time there were about half a million unnaturalized resident aliens of German birth in the United States who were proclaimed "alien enemies" as soon as the United States declared war in April 1917. Some eight thousand enemy aliens—the vast majority of them Germans and almost all the rest subjects of Austria-Hungary—were arrested under presidential warrants, but nearly three-quarters of them were released within a short time. Only about 2,300 enemy nationals resident in the United States were actually interned, 90 percent of them German and all but a few of them male.[5]

During World War II, internment of Germans and Italians began more than two years before the United States formally entered the war in December 1941. A few seamen from German vessels stranded in U.S. ports were interned shortly after the outbreak of war in September 1939, as were, after June 1940, perhaps a thousand Italians, seamen and a group of food workers from the Italian exhibition at the New York World's Fair of 1939–40.[6] All of these were persons without permanent resident status; no resident aliens were interned in the period before the United States went to war.

Shortly after the fall of France, Congress passed the Alien Registration Act of 1940,[7] which required, for the first time in American history, that all resident aliens register annually at post offices and keep the government apprised of any change of address. Among the several million registrants were 695,363 Italians, 314,715 Germans, and 91,858 Japanese, so that, after the United States went to war, there were about a million unnaturalized natives of the Axis powers resident in the United States, all of whom were, according to both American and international law, potential internees.

When war came President Franklin D. Roosevelt signed three similar public proclamations on December 7 and 8, 1941, which, under the authority of sections 21–24 of Title 50 of the United States Code, declared that Japan, Germany, and Italy were at war with the United States and that, accordingly, in the language of the law, "all natives, citizens, denizens, or subjects of [those countries], being of the age of fourteen years and upward, who shall be in the United States and not actually naturalized,[8] shall be liable to be apprehended, restrained, secured, and removed as alien enemies."[9] Austrian and Korean resident aliens, who had German and Japanese nationality respectively, were not declared enemy aliens.[10]

The Roosevelt administration never intended to intern any sizable percentage of those million alien enemies. Attorney General Francis Biddle, a civil libertarian of sorts, and his staff in the Department of Justice wanted a minimal program and were aware of the gross injustices suffered by German and Italian resident aliens in Winston Churchill's Great Britain.[11] In preparation for war, various federal security agencies, military and civilian, had prepared Custodial Detention Lists, better known as the "ABC Lists," master indexes of persons who were, allegedly, potentially dangerous subversives.[12] The "A" list consisted of persons identified as "known dangerous" aliens; the "B" list contained individuals who were "potentially dangerous"; and the "C" list was composed of people who merited surveillance due to pro-Axis sympathies or propaganda activities. As is common for internal security lists, they were largely based not on investigations of individuals, but on "guilt by association," as most of the names came from membership and subscription lists of organizations and publications deemed subversive.

It is not yet possible—and may never be—to give precise figures for either the total number of persons interned or how many there were of each nationality. Several civilian agencies, chiefly the Federal Bureau of Investigation (FBI) and the Immigration and Naturalization Service (INS), and the military authorities made arrests, and the surviving records are incomplete. Until spring 1943, civilian internees were largely under military custody; most were then transferred to the INS, which had held some civilians since early in the war. At various times the INS reported, with what seems like studied vagueness, on the number of persons it held, but its reports do not always make clear what categories of persons were being counted. In late 1944 J. Edgar Hoover reported that 14,807 enemy aliens had been taken into custody by the FBI, of whom nearly two-fifths had "been ordered interned by the Attorney General and the military authorities."[13]

Hoover's seemingly precise figures leave room for doubt: early in the war many individuals were arrested by various local authorities and held under military auspices in places like Camp Forrest, Tennessee,[14] and they probably were not included in his totals. Given the current state of our knowledge, the best "guesstimate" of the total number of persons actually interned is something under 11,000, broken down as follows: Japanese, perhaps 8,000; Germans, perhaps 2,300 (coincidentally about the same number as in World War I), and only a few hundred Italians. Many more had been arrested and held in custody for days and even weeks without being officially interned. In addition, the United States government brought more than 2,264 Japanese (chiefly from Peru), 4,058 Germans, and 288 Italians into the United States from a total of fifteen Latin American countries, and interned them.[15] And finally, more than 3,100 Japanese, initially incarcerated by the War Relocation Authority (WRA), were later turned over to the INS for internment.

When the internment program started in 1939 there were no existing internment camps. Many of the first, pre–Pearl Harbor German and Italian internees were housed for a time at Ellis Island, Angel Island, and aboard their own ships; others were sent to INS camps set up in existing permanent army barracks and other federal buildings, where conditions were often more comfortable than in the later purpose-built or converted camps. Most of the prewar Italians, for example, were sent to Fort Missoula, Montana, where they lived in brick barracks with steam heat. Eventually most internees wound up in INS internment camps, primarily in Louisiana, Texas, and New Mexico.[16] The facilities and living conditions in all of these camps for enemy aliens were superior to those in the concentration camps in which Japanese American United States citizens were held, partly because the U.S. State Department insisted that Geneva Convention conditions be maintained in them in the hope that the Axis powers, or some of them, would reciprocate.[17]

Once war actually came, the often-competing American security agencies, civilian and military, constantly raised the number of persons to be interned. J. Edgar Hoover's FBI, for example, had a pre–Pearl Harbor list of 770 Japanese aliens who would require detention in case of war.[18] Yet, a little over two months after Pearl Harbor, it had managed to find almost three times that many —2,192 Japanese—to intern.[19] And so it went. Almost certainly very few of those interned were really threats to American national security. To be sure, many if not most of them were rooting for their native lands, but the same could be said for many of the million plus uninterned alien enemies. Many others were simply torn by conflicting loyalties, such as the Italian immigrant who had written President Roosevelt shortly before Pearl Harbor that "since Italy is my mother and the United States is my father . . . I don't want to see my parents fighting," and got interned for his pains.[20]

Often, especially early in the war, alien enemies were arrested in their homes in the dead of night, told to pack a bag, and hauled off to the nearest custodial facility, usually a local jail. Sometimes their families did not hear from them for days or even weeks. But many of those arrested were released relatively quickly, and, as the numbers cited earlier indicate, only a minority of those taken into custody was actually interned. Many, perhaps most, internments fragmented families, as in many cases the interned man—and all but a minuscule percentage of resident American internees was male—was the only breadwinner in the household. In a number of such cases, wives and minor children, some of them United States citizens, voluntarily joined the family held in internment. One INS camp, in Seagoville, Texas, was chiefly for women and children, and eventually another at Crystal City, Texas, was set up for families.[21]

In the case of the Japanese Americans, so many male leaders were seized that not just families but entire ethnic communities were decapitated. In addition, since many Japanese Americans kept their money in American branches of Japanese banks, their liquid assets were frozen as the Treasury Department seized and closed all enemy-owned banks.[22] Eventually families were allowed to draw up to $100 a month of their own money.

Those who were actually interned had some recourse. Enemy Alien Hearing Boards, composed of three or more citizen volunteers, were established in every federal judicial district. Each internee had the right to have his or her case reviewed by such a board, which could recommend parole or internment—but the attorney general was not obligated to accept board recommendations. The internee could have a relative, friend, or agent attend the hearing, but was not allowed to have legal counsel. Evidence of loyalty, testimonial letters, etc., could be presented to the board, but the internee was not entitled to know the nature of any charges against him or her or, in cases resulting from denunciations, the name of the accuser or even the existence of an accusation. Except for anecdotal evidence (see below), we know next to nothing about such boards, the persons who staffed them, how they operated, the number of cases they reviewed, the results of such reviews, or how their recommendations were treated by the Department of Justice. The review boards helped to ameliorate the internment process, as large numbers of their hearings eventually resulted in release. And, even if the review board hearing did not result in release—the internee was not informed of its recommendation—internees could forward appeals with supporting documents to the attorney general. However, some interned aliens did not want to be released, but instead signed documents indicating that they wished to be returned to their native lands as quickly as possible, which usually meant after the war.

As noted, Geneva Convention conditions generally applied. Diplomatic officials from the various "protecting powers" who looked after the interests of enemy nations within the United States inspected the internment camps regularly and made note of internee complaints. In addition to food, housing, and recreation, internees were entitled to free mail services within the United States and access to mail and parcels from their mother countries, supervised by the International Red Cross but subject to censorship.[23]

Thus internees had a very different kind of existence from that of most Japanese Americans. While the decision to intern an individual may not have been just, internment in the United States generally followed the rules set down in American and international law. What happened to those West Coast Japanese Americans who were incarcerated in army and WRA concentration camps was simply lawless.

In discussing language, perhaps the best place to start is with the three- and four-letter epithets that were all but universally used to describe persons of Japanese birth or descent. While it was common until very recently for most Americans to use ugly words to describe persons of color and others deemed to be "lesser breeds without the law"—nigger, kike, wop, spic, chink, greaser, etc.—none was more universally used than Jap or Japs. One cannot imagine, for example, a respectable politician using any of the other terms in the title of a magazine article, but Franklin Delano Roosevelt could propose to call a 1923 essay—actually intended to minimize trans-Pacific antagonisms—"The Japs—A Habit of Mind."[24] Even a casual perusal of pre–World War II American newspapers and magazines shows that in both headline and text the word was often used to describe: 1) the Japanese government; 2) the people of Japan; and, more rarely except on the Pacific Coast, 3) Japanese Americans. One does not have to be a student of semiotics to understand the dehumanizing effect of such continuous and casual usage. And, of course, once the United States and Japan were at war the usage multiplied. The language and visual contexts of World War II movies made in the 1940s and 1950s—and which still pollute our TV channels—make it quite clear that while the actions of Germany and of most Germans were evil, a distinction was often made between "good" and "bad" Germans. The actions of the Imperial Japanese Government and the actions of not only its people but of persons of Japanese ethnicity anywhere were treated as the deeds of an evil race. Perhaps the most notorious example of the casual demonization of Japanese persons were the mid-December 1941 companion pieces in the two Luce news magazines, *Time* and *Life*, which purported to tell Americans "How to Tell the Japs from the Chinese" or "How to Tell Your Friends from the Japs."[25] The *Life* article was illustrated by Milton Caniff, creator of the widely syndicated comic strip "Terry and the Pirates." Almost two months later, on February 13, 1942, just six days before FDR signed Executive Order 9066, another popular cartoonist, Theodor Seuss Geisel (1904–1991), a.k.a. Dr. Seuss, drew a particularly vicious editorial cartoon for the left-wing New York City newspaper *PM* showing an endless stream of identical, grinning Japanese men coming from the Pacific Northwest to a building on the California coast labeled "Honorable 5th Column" to receive packages marked "TNT," while atop the headquarters another of what we would now call the clones looks out to sea through a telescope. The cartoon is captioned "Waiting for the Signal From Home . . ." Popular culture had so infused the complex image of the "Jap" into the American mind that no further explication was necessary.[26] It is possible to pile up similar examples ad infinitum.[27] Government officials were well aware of this. Geisel, for example, was later commissioned as a captain in the Signal Corps and sent to Hollywood to help film director Frank Capra make propaganda films and cartoons to indoctrinate American servicemen and women.[28] This well-established mind-set made it easy for government officials to use carefully chosen words to blind Americans to the fact that their government was systematically stripping some American citizens of their most basic rights by fiat.

Before examining that process in some detail, it might be well to remind ourselves of the conclusion of the CWRIC :[29]

> The promulgation of Executive Order 9066 was not justified by military necessity, and the decisions which followed from it—detention, ending detention and ending exclusion—were not driven by analysis of military conditions. The broad historical causes which shaped these decisions were race prejudice, war hysteria and a failure of political leadership. Widespread ignorance of Japanese Americans contributed to a policy conceived in haste and executed in an atmosphere of fear and anger at Japan. A grave injustice was done to American citizens and resident nationals of Japanese ancestry who, without individual review or any probative evidence against them, were excluded, removed and detained by the United States during World War II.

The stripping of rights began long before President Roosevelt signed Executive Order 9066 on February 19, 1942. Within hours of the attack on Pearl Harbor, U.S. Attorney General Francis Biddle, in addition to arranging for and enforcing the statutory proclamations affecting "alien enemies" as set forth in sections 21–24 of the United States Code, also ordered that the borders be closed to alien enemies and "all persons of Japanese ancestry."[30] Biddle, although he regarded himself as a protector of the rights of Japanese Americans and, at the eleventh hour protested ineffectively against mass incarceration, in practice allowed the rights of citizens of Japanese ancestry to be violated with impunity. Under pressure from the War Department and, according to his memoir, somewhat overawed by the elder cabinet colleague who headed it, Henry L. Stimson, the attorney general agreed, in memoranda exchanged between the departments on January 6, 1942, that, in effect, the Fourth Amendment rights of American citizens of Japanese ancestry living on the West Coast to "be secure . . . against unreasonable searches and seizures" were null and void. The memoranda agreed that Department of Justice agents would make warrantless searches merely on verbal requests from military authorities. One short paragraph began by stating that "The term 'mass raid' will not be employed by the Attorney General" but ended with the statement "all of the alien enemy premises in a given area can be searched at the same moment." A prior paragraph recognized that there were "mixed occupancy dwellings" inhabited by native-born citizens and their alien parents or other relatives and treated these as "alien enemy's premises."[31] Although Biddle and his deputy, Assistant Attorney General James J. Rowe, who signed the memorandum, would never say—as Assistant Secretary of War John J. McCloy did—that the Constitution was "just a scrap of paper," what they agreed to, despite their protestations, effectively nullified it.[32]

Executive Order 9066, drafted in the War Department sometime after February 11 when Roosevelt gave Stimson "carte blanche," and signed in the White House on February 19, is a wonderful example of Aesopian language. It has neither ethnic nor geographic specificity, and were it to be discovered in the year 3001 without other documents giving its context, the future historian might reasonably conclude that it was a relief measure. Its official title, almost never used, is "AUTHORIZING THE SECRETARY OF WAR TO PRESCRIBE MILITARY AREAS." After authorizing the Secretary of War and "Military Commanders" he might designate to create "military areas . . . from which any or all persons may be excluded," it further authorized the secretary "to provide for residents . . . such transportation, food, shelter, and other accommodations as may be necessary . . . until other arrangements are made."

We now know the whole chain of events which this order set off. A second executive order, 9106, established the War Relocation Authority on March 18, 1942, and ordered its director to "formulate and effectuate a program for the removal . . . of the persons or classes of persons [designated under Executive Order 9066] and for their relocation, maintenance, and supervision." He was further ordered to "provide for the relocation of such persons in appropriate places, . . . provide for their needs [and] for the employment of such persons at useful work in industry, commerce, agriculture, or public projects. . . ."

Other parts of Executive Order 9106 authorized the use of the United States Employment Service and established a War Relocation Work Corps in which persons would be "enlisted." The work corps proved to be a phantom that was never activated.[33] These words misled the first director of the War Relocation Authority, Milton S. Eisenhower, into believing, until he met with western governors at Salt Lake City on April 7, that the "relocation centers"[34] could evolve into something more like the New Deal's subsistence homesteads and less like the concentration camps that they became. (It must be remembered that the mass expulsion and incarceration started only at the end of March.)

Even as the mass round-up of West Coast Nikkei began, with an isolated group on Bainbridge Island, a short ferry ride from Seattle, the government's wordsmiths were inventing new language. A "Civilian Exclusion Order" dated March 24, 1942, signed by Gen. John L. DeWitt and ominously numbered "No. 1," directed all "Japanese persons, both alien and nonalien" to report to the ferryboat landing on March 30 for "temporary residence in a reception center elsewhere," bringing with them only what they could carry, including "blankets and linens . . . toilet articles . . . clothing . . . knives, forks, spoons, plates, bowls, and cups for each member of the family."[35] Unlike most later orders, which moved persons first to neighboring, temporary enclosures called "Assembly Centers," the 257 Bainbridge Islanders were sent by train to Manzanar in southern California, as no camp in the Pacific Northwest was ready for occupancy.[36]

Thus began the wartime incarceration of the West Coast Japanese Americans, an incarceration that would last, for some, almost four years. Begun under military auspices and subject to some military control throughout its existence, the incarcerated people whom I have called prisoners without trial were, during the course of the spring and summer of 1942, turned over to the civilian War Relocation Authority. The WRA was staffed at the top and in most of its middle management by persons who would not have instituted the kind of repressive program that they were called upon to execute. Its second and last director, Dillon S. Myer, who was less liberal than many of his staffers, wrote in his memoir that:

> I believed, and still believe, that a selective evacuation of people of Japanese descent from the West Coast military area may have been justified and feasible in early 1943 [*sic*—he surely meant 1942], but I do not believe that a mass evacuation was ever justified; furthermore I believe that there was no valid argument for the continuation of the exclusion orders beyond the spring of 1943, as indicated by our letter to Secretary Stimson in March of 1943.[37]

The WRA accepted the army's nomenclature and generally tried to put the best possible face on what it did. The captive Japanese had been "evacuated," a word associated with rescue. The people who were in "relocation centers" were "residents," not inmates. Like other government agencies, it conducted a public relations campaign that tried to emphasize the positive aspects of what it did. Its photographs show "happy campers"; its press releases hailed military volunteers and ignored, as much as possible, the protesters and especially the draft resisters. So relatively successful was this wartime government propaganda that, as late as 1969, two liberal authors thoroughly opposed to the incarceration and exile could identify Heart

Mountain, where the draft resistance began, as a "happy camp."[38] The WRA and its administrators particularly resisted the notion that they were in charge of "concentration camps."

The first WRA director, Milton Eisenhower, in his 1974 memoir, is explicit about this. A specialist in "information"—his next assignment would be to the Office of War Information—he wrote:

> We called the relocation centers "evacuation centers." Never did we refer to them as concentration camps.[39]

Similarly, his successor, Dillon S. Myer, like Eisenhower, also from the Department of Agriculture, wrote in his 1971 memoir that:

> Relocation centers were called "concentration camps" by many writers and commentators, but they were very different from the normal concept of what a concentration camp is like.[40]

Lower down in the WRA hierarchy the same kinds of postwar views existed. One of the most determined literary attacks on the notion that Japanese Americans were placed in concentration camps came from Harold S. Jacoby, a member of the sociology faculty at the College of the Pacific who, in March 1942, concerned by what he saw as unjust treatment of Japanese Americans, sought and achieved employment with the WRA, first at Tule Lake and then in Chicago as assistant supervisor of resettlement there. He was clearly one of what psychiatrist Alexander Leighton called approvingly the "people-minded" WRA administrators.[41] In his 1996 memoir he attacked vigorously the notion that the WRA establishments were concentration camps. Part of his argument was that the concentration camps of the Nazis and the Soviets were much worse places. Another is that only the books published after 1967 called them concentration camps. And, finally, he argued that inmates were sometimes allowed to leave for work.[42] (He might have added that others were allowed to leave the camps to go shopping in nearby towns, etc.)

Language usage was not just a postwar concern of WRA leaders. Thomas Bodine, a Quaker activist who was an important and effective staff member of the National Japanese American Student Relocation Council, remembered in May 2000 that during the war "we couldn't use the [term concentration camps] during the work we did or the Government might have cut off granting leaves to the students we were helping."[43]

But higher up in the government hierarchy there were people who were willing to call a spade a bloody shovel. Franklin Roosevelt himself called the camps for Japanese concentration camps on more than one public occasion,[44] and Associate Justice Owen J. Roberts, dissenting in the Korematsu case, which, in effect, said the incarceration of American citizens was constitutional, insisted that:

> This is not a case of keeping people off the streets at night as was *Hirabaya-shi.* . . . It is a case of convicting a citizen . . . for not submitting to imprisonment in a concentration camp solely because of his ancestry. . . .[45]

More prosaically, an anonymous cataloguer at the Library of Congress established the subject heading "Concentration Camps—United States of America" which, so far, contains only items about the wartime incarceration of the Japanese Americans and its sequelae.[46]

But the general practice, especially after the liberation of the Nazi death camps, was to avoid the blunt term. Before the spring of 1945 the term concentration camp was not synonymous with death camp. The term was first applied to camps set up for noncombatants—as opposed to prisoners of war—by the British during the Boer War of 1899–1902.[47] The reason that Eisenhower, Myer, Jacoby, and others associated with administering the camps reacted so strongly against using the term concentration camps is that such usage made them, by extension, concentration camp keepers and seemed to put them in the same category as notorious Nazis and Japanese, and, eventually, Adolf Eichmann.[48]

Incarcerated people themselves sometimes used the term concentration camp while they were in confinement, especially while protesting against aspects of government policy. For example, in a meeting at Heart Mountain in February 1943 during the "registration crisis," one speaker said:

> Although we have yellow skins, we too are Americans. We have an American upbringing, therefore we believe in fair play. Our firm conviction is that we would be useless Americans if we did not assert our constitutional rights now; for, unless our status as citizens is cleared and we are really fighting for the perpetuation of democracy, especially when our fathers, mothers, and families are in concentration camps, even though they are not charged with any crimes.[49]

I suspect that the term was not commonly used, but since the major sources for contemporary inmate perceptions, the camp newspapers, were published under the watchful eyes of WRA staffers, its nonuse there is not significant. I have read a large number of letters written from the camps. My distinct impression is that the term was not much used in them, but since the question of nomenclature had not yet become significant to me when I was reading them in various archives, I did not keep track of its occurrence.

What is clear is that once the war was over and for decades afterwards the prevailing term among the mainland Nisei was "camp," although "evacuation," "relocation," and, to a lesser degree, "internment" were all used more or less interchangeably. When two Nisei met for the first time, an all but inevitable question was "What camp were you in?" When the past was discussed, two parameters were constant: "before the war" and "after camp." The ambiguity of the word "camp" makes it possible to argue that it was short for "concentration camp," but I am certain, but cannot demonstrate, that in the vast majority of cases it was short for "relocation camp" or "evacuation camp." In nearly a thousand interviews and conversations with Nikkei before the redress campaign began, I can remember only a few instances in which the term "concentration camp" was used by a community member. On the other hand the only Nikkei I can remember complaining about my use of the term was Mike Masaoka in 1971 or 1972. On several occasions Caucasian Holocaust survivors similarly complained. This ambiguity, plus the notorious reluctance of the Nisei to talk about their wartime experiences with their children and grandchildren, led more than one Sansei to believe that "camp" stood for some kind of summer vacation that their parents used to go on.[50]

When one examines the postwar printed record, whether memoirs by former inmates and officials or accounts by scholars and others, the result is pretty much the same. The terminology used by the government—evacuation and relocation—prevails, plus, for almost all the Nikkei authors and some scholars, the ambiguous "camp." Nothing better exemplifies the difference between expressed Nikkei attitudes just after the war and three to four decades later than successive editions of two outstanding Nisei memoirs.

The first, Miné Okubo's pioneering 1946 illustrated text, *Citizen 13660*, dealt only with wartime and told of evacuation from Berkeley and confinement at Tanforan—in a horse stall—and at Topaz. The soon-to-be ubiquitous "camp" was the most common term, but otherwise standard government terminology—including relocation and evacuation—was used. Identical words punctuate the preface to the first reprint edition, dated May

1, 1978, but by the time of the second reprint edition just five years later, Okubo had testified before the CWRIC, and her preface speaks of "Americans and Alaskan Aleuts who had been forcibly removed from their homes and incarcerated in concentration camps" (xi), but in the rest of the new text reverts to the old standard language. In addition, the word "internment" and the phrase "internment camp" have been added to her vocabulary in describing what she endured, whereas in the original such language had been reserved for the process undergone by many Issei, as in "Father had been whisked away to an internment camp" (11).[51]

A similar pattern may be discerned in the two editions of Monica Sone's 1953 memoir, *Nisei Daughter,* which deals with a Seattle girlhood and devotes its final two-fifths to uprooting from Seattle, life in the Puyallup Assembly Center and the Minidoka Relocation Center, and resettlement in Chicago and at an Indiana college. Its text uses only terminology that the WRA would have approved. But in her preface to the 1979 edition, the second, one-sentence paragraph shows clearly that consciousness-raising had taken place:

> The ten concentration camps, which received 120,000 of us in 1942, were finally closed in 1946. (xv)[52]

Since I have reviewed the first three decades of scholarly literature about the wartime incarceration elsewhere, it will not be repeated here.[53] By that time (1975) the broad outlines of what can be called a "master narrative" had emerged. Most scholars had generally agreed that the wartime incarceration was needless and would have endorsed the 1982 CWRIC conclusion cited above. Even earlier, in 1967, when Harry Kitano and I organized the first academic conference devoted to the wartime experience of the Nikkei, held at UCLA, we found it impossible to find *anyone* willing to defend the actions of 1942.

But that early scholarly consensus that the incarceration of the Japanese Americans had been wrong did not mean that historians paid much attention to it. In what was perhaps the outstanding American history textbook of the immediate postwar decades—and certainly the most liberal—Richard Hofstadter, William Miller, and Daniel Aaron in a text of 758 pages could say only this in their section on "Civilian Mobilization" in what was not yet the "Good War":

> Since almost no one doubted the necessity for the war, there was much less intolerance than there had been in World War I, although large numbers of

Japanese-Americans were put into internment camps under circumstances
that many Americans were later to judge unfair or worse.[54]

Note that the term "internment camp" has somehow, as they say, crept into
the language, where it has remained.

This down-playing of the negative aspects of the wartime experience was
a corollary of what can be called American secular triumphalism, which
affected people on the left as well as those who liked Ike and were wild about
Harry. Even today, the topic of conscientious objection, for example, is little discussed.[55] It is not an accident that the first scholarly critique of the
rationale for the incarceration, the courageous essays by Eugene V. Rostow,
wrote off the event as a "mistake" rather than as a logical outgrowth of
centuries of racism.[56] And, as late as the mid-1970s, I could lecture about
the wartime incarceration at an elite college, such as Hobart and William
Smith, and have students ask me afterwards if that "really happened."

By that time, two books about the incarceration had appeared that used
the term concentration camps in their titles.[57] These works gave an increased
credibility to the use of the term, a credibility, as we have seen, that was
challenged not only by persons like McCloy, Eisenhower, and Myer, who
had been accessories to the incarceration, either before or after the fact, but
also by three other categories of persons:

(1) A whole spectrum of conservatives and self-styled patriots who were
simply appalled that such a dreadful term could be applied to their country.
The reactions of this group ranged from mild annoyance to absolute frenzy
on the part of a few zealots, such as the incarceration denier Lillian Baker.[58]

(2) A sizable number of Holocaust survivors and their supporters who
resented deeply the term being used for anything as "mild" as the American
incarceration. Some clearly felt that the term belonged to them. The most
celebrated instance of this occurred in 1998, when a protest by some Jews
against the use of the term "concentration camp" in the title of an exhibition from the Japanese American National Museum, scheduled to open on
Ellis Island, caused such a controversy that the National Park Service superintendent in charge cancelled the exhibition until her superiors intervened.[59]

(3) And finally, there are those, such as historian Alice Yang Murray, who,
while fully understanding the arguments for using the term, nevertheless
feel that:

> while I agree that places like Manzanar and Tule Lake fulfill the dictionary
> definition of a "concentration camp," I personally can't accept the designa-

tion. The term "concentration camp" may once have been a euphemism for a Nazi "extermination camp," but I think that over time the two kinds of camps have become inextricably linked in the popular imagination. In other words, I believe the meaning of the term "concentration camp" has changed over time. During World War II, officials and commentators could say Japanese Americans were confined in concentration camps without evoking images of Nazi atrocities. I don't think that this is true today.[60]

Given this widespread resistance, it is clearly unrealistic to expect everyone to agree to use the contested term concentration camp, even though I believe that it is the most appropriate term.

But it seems equally clear to me that it is not unreasonable to expect scholars to cease using both the incorrect prevalent term "internment camp" and the stock phrase "the internment of the Japanese Americans." There are two very good reasons to suggest this.

In the first place, while there were surely injustices involved in the internment process, as there always are when compulsion is involved, it did follow the forms of law and was a recognized legal procedure dating back in American law to the War of 1812. The eleven thousand or so persons who were interned in the United States during World War II have not, until quite recently, been the subject of much historical scrutiny. What has to be remembered is that those persons were taken into custody because of their status: all were alien nationals of a nation against which the United States was at war, each was seized for reasons supposedly based on his or her behavior, and each was entitled to an individual hearing before a board. No one who reads the fine study by Louis Fiset of the internment process as it affected Iwao Matsushita can conflate his circumstances with those of Japanese Americans incarcerated under authority of Executive Order 9066.[61]

In the second place, the conflation of the two processes has allowed some authors to write as if what happened to a tiny minority of unnaturalized Italian and German residents was somehow equivalent to the mass incarceration of some eighty-thousand American citizens of Japanese ancestry and some forty-thousand Japanese nationals who were barred from naturalization by race.[62]

As I have tried to show, there has been a long history of using euphemistic language about the wartime atrocity that was wreaked upon the Japanese Americans of the West Coast during and after World War II. Begun with malice aforethought by government officials, politicians, and journalists, it has been continued, largely in thoughtless innocence, by scholars. As we are in the seventh decade after the promulgation of Executive Order 9066, it is high time that scholars begin to call things by their right names. Let us hear no more about the "internment of the Japanese Americans."[63]

Notes

I wish to thank the editors, the anonymous reader for the press, and, above all, Max Paul Friedman for thoughtful and intelligent suggestions which have, I think, improved this essay.

1. Unfortunately, I have no contemporary record of that call. I have dated it by referring to Mitchell T. Maki, Harry H. L. Kitano, and S. Megan Berthold, *Achieving the Impossible Dream: How Japanese Americans Obtained Redress* (Urbana: University of Illinois Press, 1999).

2. I also had—and have—objections to the term "relocation." "Exile" is more appropriate.

3. See Roger Daniels, "The Internment of Japanese Nationals in the United States During World War II," *Halcyon* 17 (1995): 66–75; "L'Internamento di 'Alien Enemies' negli Stati Uniti durante la seconda guerra mondiale," *Ácoma: Rivista Internazionale di Studi Nordamericani* (Rome; Estate autunno 1997): 39–49; and Kay Saunders and Roger Daniels, eds., *Alien Justice: Wartime Internment in Australia and North America* (St. Lucia, Queensland: University of Queensland Press, 2000).

4. Aliens Act of June 24, 1798 (1 *Stat.* 570). The lack of a declared war prevented any internment—or treason trials—during the Korean and Vietnam Wars or in such shorter actions as Desert Storm.

5. See Jörg Nagler, "Internment of German Enemy Aliens in the United States during the First and Second World Wars," in *Alien Justice,* ed. Saunders and Daniels, 66–79. For those who read German, his massive *Nationale Minoritäten im Krieg: "Feindliche Ausländer" und die amerikanische Heimatfront während des Ersten Weltkriegs* (Hamburg: Hamburger Edition, 2000) is a must for an understanding of the roots of the modern internment of alien enemies by the United States. Two scholarly publications about American World War I internment camps are Raymond K. Cunningham, Jr., *Prisoners at Fort Douglas: War Prison Barracks Three and the Enemy Aliens, 1917–1920* (Salt Lake City: Fort Douglas Military Museum, 1983) and William B. Glidden, "Casualties of Caution: Alien Enemies in America, 1917–1919" (Ph.D. diss., University of Illinois at Urbana-Champaign, 1970).

6. John Joel Culley, "A Troublesome Presence: World War II Internment of Ger-

man Sailors in New Mexico," *Prologue* 28 (winter 1996): 279–95, and Carol Van Valkenburg, *An Alien Place: The Fort Missoula, Montana Detention Camp, 1941–1944* (Missoula, Mont.: Pictorial Histories Publishing Company, 1995).

7. The act, also known as the Smith Act, was 54 *Stat.* 670. It had three titles, the first of which dealt with "interference with the military or naval forces of the United States," the second with "additional deportable classes of aliens," and only the third with the "registration and fingerprinting" of aliens. Title I was used in the Cold War era to convict many leaders of the American Communist Party. For an illuminating discussion of Titles II and III, see Richard W. Steele, "The War on Intolerance: The Reformulation of American Nationalism, 1939–1943," *Journal of American Ethnic History* 9 (fall 1989): 9–35. The registration provisions, unenforced for decades, were applied selectively after 9/11 by the Department of Justice to deport a variety of immigrants, mostly Muslims.

8. Except for a handful of World War I veterans, Japanese were not eligible for naturalization until the law was changed in 1952. Anyone, regardless of race or ethnicity, born in the United States is a citizen thanks to the 14th Amendment to the Constitution, adopted in 1868.

9. Proclamation No. 2525, December 7, 1941, and Proclamations No. 2526 and No. 2527, December 8, 1941. Similar control over Hungarian, Bulgarian, and Rumanian aliens was covered by Proclamation No. 2563 of July 17, 1942; the handful of aliens interned under the last are ignored in the remainder of this essay.

10. For some of the uses to which Koreans were put during the war, see Hyung-Ju Ahn, *Between Two Adversaries: Korean Interpreters at Japanese Alien Enemy Detention Centers during World War II* (Fullerton: Oral History Program, California State University,2002).

11. One of Biddle's wartime speeches, for example, was titled "Identification of Enemy Aliens: Let Us Not Persecute These People." *Vital Speeches of the Day* 8 (February 15, 1942): 279–80. For Britain in World War II, see Peter and Leni Gillman, *Collar the Lot!: How Britain Interned and Expelled Its Wartime Refugees* (London & New York: Quartet Books, 1980), and A. W. Brian Simpson, *In the Highest Degree Odious: Detention without Trial in Wartime Britain* (Oxford: Clarendon Press, 1992). For a historical survey, see Colin Holmes, *A Tolerant Country? Immigrants, Refugees and Minorities in Britain* (London: Faber, 1991).

12. The organizations creating the lists were primarily the Federal Bureau of Investigation (FBI), the Special Defense Unit of the Department of Justice, the Office of Naval Intelligence (ONI), and the Intelligence Branch (G-2) of the army. Obviously, the lists were only as good as the persons compiling them. They were filled with errors of omission and commission, particularly with regard to Japanese aliens,

as, to the best of my knowledge, only one American naval intelligence official, Lt. Comdr. Kenneth D. Ringle, could read Japanese. For his activities, see my *Asian America: Chinese and Japanese in the United States since 1850* (Seattle: University of Washington Press, 1989), 183, 210–13. The controversial Ellis Mark Zacharias, who was fluent in Japanese, was out of favor and not involved in intelligence work at the outbreak of war. The best single work dealing with any part of the U.S. intelligence apparatus before and during the war is Jeffrey M. Dorwart, *Conflict of Duty: The U.S. Navy's Intelligence Dilemma, 1919–1945* (Annapolis: Naval Institute Press, 1983). See also Marc Gallicchio, "Zacharias, Ellis Mark," *American National Biography Online,* February 2000, at http://www.anb.org/articles/07/07–00340.html.

13. J. Edgar Hoover, "Alien Enemy Control," *Iowa Law Review* 29 (1941): 396–408, at 403. Other commonly cited figures are: "by February 16, 1942, the Justice Department had interned 2,192 Japanese, 1,393 Germans, and 264 Italians," from a Justice Department press release cited in Commission on Wartime Relocation and Internment of Civilians (CWRIC), *Personal Justice Denied: Report of the Commission on Wartime Relocation and Internment of Civilians* (Washington, D.C.: GPO, 1983), 284; and "the total number [taken into custody] has not exceeded fifteen thousand. . . . fewer than ten thousand 'alien enemies' have been in custody at any one time, . . ." from Earl G. Harrison, "Civilian Internment—American Way," *Survey Graphic* 33 (May 1944): 229–33, 270 at 229–30. Harrison was commissioner general of the Immigration and Naturalization Service (INS). A government history of the INS reports 9,920 enemy aliens in custody in mid-1943 and 7,364 in mid-1945. Congressional Research Service, *History of the Immigration and Naturalization Service* (Washington, D.C.: GPO, 1980), 49–50.

14. In Tennessee, for example, "some 'civilian aliens,' mostly Japanese immigrants, were interned at Camp Forrest until May 1943, when they were transferred to North Dakota." James A. Crutchfield. *Tennesseeans at War: Volunteers and Patriots in Defense of Liberty* (Nashville: Rutledge Hill Press, 1987), 145. See also Ann Toplovich, "The Tennesseean's War: Life on the Home Front," *Tennessee Historical Quarterly* 51 (1992): 19–50, at 48 n. 30.

15. C. Harvey Gardiner, "The Latin American Japanese and World War II," in *Japanese Americans: From Relocation to Redress,* ed. Roger Daniels, Sandra C. Taylor, and Harry H. L. Kitano (Seattle: University of Washington Press, 1991), 142–45; and Gardiner, *Pawns in a Triangle of Hate: The Peruvian Japanese and the United States* (Seattle: University of Washington Press, 1981). See also Thomas Connell, *America's Japanese Hostages: The World War II Plan for a Japanese Free Latin America* (Westport, Conn.: Praeger, 2002). An important book, Max Paul Friedman's *Nazis and Good Neighbors: The United States Campaign against the Germans of Latin America in World War II* (New York: Cambridge University Press, 2003), is the source for

the precise numbers. Seiichi Higashide's *Adios to Tears: The Memoirs of a Japanese Peruvian Internee in U.S. Concentration Camps,* 2nd ed. (Seattle: University of Washington Press, 2000), is the best personal account available in English.

16. The best published accounts of wartime internment camps generally are in essays by John Joel Culley: "World War II and a Western Town: The Internment of Japanese Railroad Workers in Clovis, New Mexico," *Western Historical Quarterly* 13 (1982): 42–63; "Trouble at the Lordsburg Internment Camp," *New Mexico Historical Review* 60 (1985): 225–48; "The Santa Fe Internment Camp and the Justice Department Program for Enemy Aliens," in *Japanese Americans: From Relocation to Redress,* ed. Daniels et al., 51–71; and "Enemy Alien Control in the United States during World War II: A Survey," in *Alien Justice,* ed. Saunders and Daniels, 138–51. The essay on Lordsburg describes homicides committed by guards. Culley is engaged on a major work provisionally titled "Interned for the Duration: Alien Enemy Internment and the Japanese during World War II."

17. For the State Department's concern for Americans in enemy countries, see P. Scott Corbett, *Quiet Passages: The Exchange of Civilians between the United States and Japan during the Second World War* (Kent, Ohio: Kent State University Press, 1987).

18. Richard Gid Powers, *Secrecy and Power: The Life of J. Edgar Hoover* (New York: Free Press, 1987), 239.

19. Press release cited in CWRIC, *Personal Justice Denied,* 284.

20. Jerre Mangione, *An Ethnic at Large: A Memoir of America in the Thirties and Forties* (New York: Putnam, 1978), 344–45.

21. Many of those brought by the government from Latin America were in family units. Karen L. Riley, *Schools Behind Barbed Wire: The Untold Story of Wartime Internment and the Children of Arrested Enemy Aliens* (Lanham, Md.: Rowman & Littlefield, 2002), describes the INS family camp at Crystal City, Texas. Roger Daniels, "Educating Youth in American's Wartime Detention Camps," *History of Education Quarterly* 41 (spring 2003): 92–103, reviews the literature on education in WRA and INS camps.

22. Incarcerated Japanese Americans had no such recourse as they were incarcerated not for suspected subversion or memberships, but because of their ethnicity. There were, however, government programs that enabled many Japanese Americans to leave the camps for work, military service, and education.

23. Louis Fiset, "Wartime Communication: Red Cross Key to U.S.-Japan Mails," *American Philatelist* 104 (1990): 228–34; Fiset, "Censored!: U.S. Censors and Internment Camp Mail in World War II," in *Guilt by Association: Essays on Japanese Settlement, Internment, and Relocation in the Rocky Mountain West,* ed. Mike Mackey (Powell, Wyo.: Western History Publications, 2001), 69–100; and Fiset, "Return to Sender: U.S. Censorship of Enemy Alien Mail in World War II," *Prologue* 33 (spring 2001): 21–35.

24. William L. Neuman, "Franklin D. Roosevelt and Japan, 1913–1933," *Pacific Historical Review* 22 (1953): 143–53, at 148. FDR's essay was published as "Shall We Trust Japan?" *Asia* 23 (1923): 475–78, 526, 528, and was sanguine about future relationships.

25. The *Life* version is first. Both are dated December 22, 1941, but were on the newsstands and in the mail the previous week. Despite prompt refutation, e.g., "No Certain Way to Tell Japanese from Chinese," *Science News Letter* (December 20, 1941), this nonsense was widely believed.

26. This cartoon was, I believe, first republished in Paul Milkman, *PM: A New Deal in Journalism, 1940–1948* (New Brunswick, N.J.: Rutgers University Press, 1997). For some two hundred of Geisel's *PM* cartoons, see Richard H. Minear, *Dr. Seuss Goes to War* (New York: The New Press, 1999). Those and two hundred others may be seen on a University of California, San Diego Web site: http://orpheus.ucsd.edu/speccoll/dspolitic/Frame.htm.

UCSD has a "Dr. Seuss Collection" in its Mandeville Special Collections Library. The only book-length study of Geisel's work, Ruth K. MacDonald's *Dr. Seuss* (Boston: Twayne, 1988), mentions his *PM* career in passing, noting only "his most notable contribution being his anti-Nazi cartoons ridiculing Hitler" (8).

27. See, for example, Dennis Ogawa, *From Japs to Japanese: The Evolution of Japanese American Stereotypes* (Berkeley, Calif.: McCutchan, 1971).

28. Charles W. Carey, Jr., "Geisel, Theodor Seuss," *American National Biography Online,* February 2000 (published by Oxford University Press), at: http://www.anb.org/articles/16/16–03303.html.

29. CWRIC, *Personal Justice Denied,* 18. A 1997 University of Washington Press reprint is definitive as it contains important materials, including specific recommendations for redress, that were issued by the commission in 1983 and thus not included in the original. CWRIC, *Personal Justice Denied: Report of the Commission on Wartime Relocation and Internment of Civilians* (Seattle: University of Washington Press and the Civil Liberties Public Education Fund, 1997).

30. Proclamations 2525, 2526, 2527. They may be conveniently consulted in Roger Daniels, ed., *American Concentration Camps,* vol. 1 (New York: Garland, 1989). Biddle's comments on the internment process are in his autobiographical *In Brief Authority* (New York: Doubleday & Company, 1962), 207–9. Although he distinguishes between the selective internment and the program under E.O. 9066, he calls the latter "mass internment." His statistical data are erroneous.

31. The memoranda may be found conveniently in United States. War Department. *Japanese Evacuation from the West Coast, 1942* (Washington, D.C.: GPO, 1943), 4–6.

32. For McCloy, see Roger Daniels, *Concentration Camps, USA: Japanese Americans and World War II* (New York: Holt, Rinehart and Winston, 1971), 55–56.

33. Both executive orders are reprinted in Daniels, *American Concentration Camps,* vol. 1.

34. It is not clear who dreamed up that innocuous term or its predecessor, assembly center, but the most likely suspects are Col. Karl Robin Bendetsen, the army lawyer who managed the expulsion of the Nikkei from the West Coast, and/or a Census Bureau bureaucrat, Dr. Calvert L. Dedrick. For the latter, see Roger Daniels, "The Bureau of the Census and the Relocation of the Japanese Americans: A Note and a Document," *Amerasia Journal* 9 (#1 1982): 101–5. Work in progress by demographer William Seltzer and Margo Anderson, the leading historical authority on the census, will throw more light on Dedrick. See William Seltzer and Margo Anderson, "After Pearl Harbor: The Proper Role of Population Data Systems in Time of War" (paper presented at the Annual Meeting of the Population Association of America, Los Angeles, March 2000), and Seltzer and Anderson, "The Dark Side of Numbers: The Role of Population Data Systems in Human Rights Abuses," *Social Research* 68:2 (summer 2001): 481–513. The former is summarized in Steven A. Holmes, "Report Says Census Bureau Helped Relocate Japanese," *New York Times,* 17 March 2000.

35. Civilian Exclusion Order No. 1 and accompanying instructions are reprinted in Daniels, *American Concentration Camps,* vol. 1.

36. War Department. *Japanese Evacuation from the West Coast, 1942.* Table 47, 363. One additional Bainbridge Islander is reported as being sent to an unspecified relocation center.

37. Dillon S. Myer, *Uprooted Americans* (Tucson: University of Arizona Press, 1971), 285–86.

38. Audrie Girdner and Anne Loftis, *The Great Betrayal: The Evacuation of the Japanese-Americans during World War II* (New York: Macmillan, 1969), 247. For the best account of Heart Mountain, see Douglas W. Nelson, *Heart Mountain: The Story of an American Concentration Camp* (Madison: Wisconsin State Historical Society, 1976). Eric Muller's *Free to Die for Their Country: The Story of the Japanese American Draft Resisters in World War II* (Chicago: University of Chicago Press, 2001), is a fine legal history. See also the 2000 video "Conscience and the Constitution" by filmmaker Frank Abe. Its Web site is: www.resisters.com.

39. Milton S. Eisenhower, *The President Is Calling* (New York: Doubleday, 1974), 122.

40. Myer, *Uprooted Americans,* 291. The w ra photographs used in Myer's book illustrate nicely the comment about "happy campers" in the text above.

41. Alexander H. Leighton, *The Governing of Men* (Princeton: Princeton University Press, 1946), 81–88.

42. Harold S. Jacoby, *Tule Lake: From Relocation to Segregation* (Grass Valley, Calif.: Comstock Bonanza Press, 1996), xii, 9, 54–57, 60–61.

43. Thomas Bodine to Allan W. Austin, 17 May 2000. Austin shared this letter with me. A revised version of his excellent doctoral dissertation, "From Concentration Camp to Campus: A History of the National Japanese American Student Relocation Council, 1942–1946" (University of Cincinnati, 2001), is forthcoming from the University of Illinois Press.

44. See, for example, Press Conference 982, November 21, 1944, Franklin D. Roosevelt Library, Hyde Park, New York.

45. *Korematsu v U.S.*, 323 U.S. 214.

46. There is also what the Library of Congress calls a "narrower heading": "Japanese Americans Evacuation and Relocation, 1942–45."

47. Both the *Oxford English Dictionary*, 2nd edition, and the *Merriam Webster 10th Collegiate Dictionary* give 1901 as the first usage. But utilization of a digitalized database of the *New York Times* to examine all issues during 1898 produced eleven "hits" for the phrase "concentration camps." All, however, were without pejorative implication and described camps in which various U.S. Army units were concentrated before deployment overseas. One such example, on June 1 began: "The Quartermaster General's Department, in response to the complaints coming from the various concentration camps of the delay in securing supplies and equipment. . . ." For the latest scholarship on the South African concentration camps, see the essays by Shula Marks and Elizabeth van Heyningen in Greg Cuthbertson et al., *Writing a Wider War: Rethinking Gender, Race, and Identity in the South African War, 1899–1902* (Athens: Ohio University Press, 2002).

48. It may well be that Dillon Myer's negative reaction to being so characterized in Richard Drinnon's *Keeper of Concentration Camps: Dillon S. Myer and American Racism* (Berkeley: University of California Press, 1987), drove him into the arms of Lillian Baker, a vociferous opponent of any kind of amelioration for the wartime and postwar injuries that Japanese Americans endured. Too ill to appear at the CWRIC's Washington hearings, Myer authorized Baker to read a statement opposing the idea of an apology. For Baker, see her *Dishonoring America: The Falsification of World War II History* (Medford, Oreg.: Webb Research Group, 1994).

49. As quoted in Myer, *Uprooted Americans*, 73, no source given, but probably from government surveillance of the speaker (Kiyoshi Okamoto?).

50. A book by Prof. Alice Yang Murray, which is to be published soon, reveals that internal WRA memoranda warned against the use of the term "camp."

51. Miné Okubo, *Citizen 13660* (New York: Columbia University Press, 1946; 2nd ed., New York: Arno Press, 1978; 1st pbk. ed., Seattle: University of Washington Press, 1983).

52. Monica Sone, *Nisei Daughter* (Boston: Little, Brown, 1953; 2nd ed., Seattle:

University of Washington Press, 1979), xv (page citation is to the 1979 edition). (Actually, all but one of the camps, Tule Lake, had closed before 1946.)

53. Roger Daniels, "American Historians and East Asian Immigrants," in *The Asian American: The Historical Experience*, ed. Norris Hundley (Santa Barbara, Calif.: Clio Press, 1976), 1–25

54. Richard Hofstadter, William Miller, and Daniel Aaron, *The United States: The History of a Republic* (Englewood Cliffs, N.J.: Prentice-Hall, 1957), 694. There is no index reference to either Japanese Americans or internment.

55. I have commented on this general phenomenon in "Bad News from the Good War: Democracy at Home during World War II," in *The Home-Front War: World War II and American Society*, ed. K. P. O'Brien & L. H. Parsons (Westport, Conn: Greenwood, 1995), 157–71.

56. Eugene V. Rostow, "The Japanese American Cases—A Disaster," *Yale Law Journal* 54 (July 1945): 489–533, and Rostow, "Our Worst Wartime Mistake," *Harper's* 191 (August 1945): 193–201.

57. Allan R. Bosworth, *America's Concentration Camps* (New York: Norton, 1967), and Daniels, *Concentration Camps, USA*.

58. I am in the process of writing an essay about Baker and the relatively rare phenomenon of denial that any kind of punitive detention of Japanese Americans took place. I went to the Baker manuscripts at the Hoover Institute thinking that I might find links between her and the California-based group of Holocaust deniers centered around the so-called Institute for Historical Research. I found only negative connections. Baker affirmed the Holocaust, and I have mused that if there had been gas chambers at the American camps, she might have stopped complaining about what she liked to call "The Concentration Camp Conspiracy."

59. The controversy is treated in the following sources, which include an editorial and letters to the editor, all from the *New York Times:* Somini Sengupta, "What Is a Concentration Camp? Ellis Island Exhibit Prompts a Debate," 8 March 1998; "Debate on Camps Goes Back to War; Japanese Atrocities," 10 March 1998; Somini Sengupta, "Accord on Term 'Concentration Camp,'" 10 March 1998; "Words for Suffering," 10 March 1998; "Exhibition on Camps," 13 March 1998; and Clyde Haberman, "Defending Jews' Lexicon Of Anguish," 13 March 1988. For a scholarly review of the exhibit, see David K. Yoo, "Captivating Memories: Museology, Concentration Camps, and Japanese American History," *American Quarterly* 48 (1996): 680–99.

60. From a book by Alice Yang Murray which is to be published soon. Used with permission.

61. Louis Fiset, *Imprisoned Apart: The World War II Correspondence of an Issei Couple* (Seattle: University of Washington Press, 1997).

62. Examples of this unfortunate genre include: Stephen Fox, *The Unknown Internment: An Oral History of the Relocation of Italian Americans during World War II* (Boston: Twayne, 1990); Fox, *America's Invisible Gulag: A Biography of German American Internment & Exclusion in World War II* (New York: Peter Lang, 2000); Timothy J. Holian, *The German-Americans and World War II: An Ethnic Experience* (New York: Peter Lang, 1996); Arthur Jacobs, *The Prison Called Hohenasperg* (Parkland, Fla.: Universal Publishers, 1999); and Lawrence DiStasi, ed., *Una Storia Segreta: The Secret History of Italian American Evacuation during World War II* (Berkeley, Calif.: Heyday Books, 2001).

63. There seems to be a slight lessening in the use of "internment." Greg Robinson, who wrote *By Order of the President: FDR and the Internment of the Japanese Americans* (Cambridge: Harvard University Press, 2001), writes in the April 2003 *American Historical Review* of "mass incarceration without trial of American citizens of Japanese ancestry (to which the phrase 'wartime internment' is universally, if inaccurately, held to refer)." *American Historical Review* 108 (April 2003): 541.

10 / IN THE MATTER OF IWAO MATSUSHITA

A Government Decision to Intern a Seattle
Japanese Enemy Alien in World War II

LOUIS FISET

At 6:00 P.M. on December 7, 1941, hours after the Japanese attack on Pearl Harbor, two FBI agents from the Seattle field office accompanied by deputies from the office of the King County Sheriff, drove to a neighborhood one mile east of Seattle's Japantown and knocked on the door of a brick bungalow home being rented by Iwao and Hanaye Matsushita. When the man of the house appeared in the doorway, FBI agent A. W. Starratt informed him that he was under arrest and that his officers would be making a search of the premises. The Issei couple, immigrants barred from citizenship by federal statute and prohibited from owning land by both Washington state constitution and statute, were powerless to resist. They remained under watch in the parlor while the entire residence was searched for evidence that might turn up. All the couple's possessions and personal effects were examined, including an extensive bilingual library belonging to Iwao, and other effects indicating this was a household of artistic sensibility and cultural sophistication. In addition, a large volume of postage stamps revealed him to be a collecting enthusiast, and five motion and still picture cameras with considerable exposed film showed Agent Starratt they had financial means. These were no ordinary immigrants.

The arresting officers confiscated Japanese language letters, postcards, pamphlets, newspaper clippings, handbills, and miscellaneous memoranda that would subsequently be submitted to the FBI's Technical Laboratory for translation and interpretation. In addition, they impounded eight-five reels of 8 mm movie film, numerous local, state, federal, and international maps, memoranda, and two small handwritten volumes of names and telephone numbers that would help determine Iwao's associates.[1]

By 9 P.M., when quiet returned to the house, Hanaye sat alone among

FIG. 10.1 *Iwao Matsushita,*
ca. 1935

the remaining scattered possessions, fearing for the future. Iwao was on his
way to the immigration station on Airport Way, just a few miles from their
home, and both were uncertain when they would see one another again.
Although she could not have known then, in less than four months Hanaye
and seven thousand other Seattle residents of Japanese ancestry would be
forcefully removed from Seattle by the army, and she and Iwao would endure
being imprisoned apart for more than two years.[2]

Similar scenes were repeated many times at the dawn of the U.S. war in
the Pacific. Within the first twenty-four hours following the bombing of
Pearl Harbor, the FBI took into temporary custody 736 Japanese enemy
aliens; at forty-eight hours the number reached 1,291. The Seattle immigration
station jail bulged with 113 Japanese enemy aliens on December 16, with Matsushita among them.[3] These arrests followed a blanket warrant issued by the
U.S. attorney general under the authority of a presidential proclamation
and signed on December 8, 1941.[4]

That so many arrests could occur within hours after a surprise attack by

Japanese naval forces was the result of careful planning and long-time surveillance of Japanese communities throughout the country. Intelligence
organizations had been collecting information on the immigrant population since 1931, possibly earlier, following Japan's incursion into Manchuria.
By early 1941 dossiers existed on more than two thousand Issei, identifying
each of them as a potential threat to the nation's security. Individuals were
assigned to one of three classifications in prepared Custodial Detention Lists,
which later became known as the "ABC list." Group A listees were "known
dangerous" and demanded intense observation. Fishermen with presumed
knowledge of coastal waters, religious leaders, influential businessmen, farmers, and members of proscribed organizations, including Japanese chambers of commerce and the Japanese consulates, fell into this first classification.
Group B suspects included those believed dangerous but who had not been
fully investigated. Individuals on the C list were put on watch because of
their pro-Japanese proclivities and propagandist activities. Among the B
and C listees were Japanese language teachers, the Kibei Nisei (second-
generation Japanese who received part of their education in Japan), martial arts instructors, community servants, travel agents, social directors, and
newspaper editors.[5]

To be a member of a blacklisted organization was sufficient to make the
ABC list. At the outbreak of the war in 1941 more than three hundred Japanese clubs and organizations existed throughout the United States. The Office
of Naval Intelligence identified twenty-two of them to be potentially subversive.[6] Matsushita was placed on the A list because of alleged espionage
activities while employed by the trading firm Mitsui Busan Kaisha (Mitsui
and Company) and his alleged association with the proscribed Japanese
Chamber of Commerce of Tokyo. In the end it mattered little what list his
name was on because the FBI arrested most, if not all, individuals from the
three groups.

Fortunately, Department of Justice records on Matsushita survive, and
the evidence used first to detain and then intern him has been preserved.
Who then was Iwao Matsushita, and how did the government's perception
of him lead to his eventual internment?

Iwao and Hanaye Matsushita were atypical immigrants. He was born into
the family of a Methodist proselytizer, while she was raised by Christian adop-
tive parents and received much of her education in a private Christian school
in Tokyo. This religious orientation provided the couple with access to Western ideas and cultures. Following an arranged marriage in 1919, the twenty-
seven-year-old school teacher and his twenty-one-year-old bride sailed for

the United States. While many, if most, Issei came to America to acquire material wealth, which would enable a better life upon return to the homeland, Iwao's dreams centered on mastery of the English language and absorption of English literature. These intellectual achievements he planned to take back with him to Japan for use in his teaching. Hanaye viewed her future sojourn in America as an adventure. Twenty-two years after their arrival in Seattle, Iwao would tell an FBI agent that he came to America "primarily because I adored the United States—secondary to study the English literature."[7]

During the 1920s Matsushita immersed himself in the cultural life of Seattle's immigrant Japanese population. Poetry and photography suited his temperament and intellectual interests, with the Pacific Northwest outdoors serving as his muse. Hanaye was a constant companion on his outings to the mountains. He also taught a Japanese language course on the University of Washington campus, with hopes of it leading to a permanent appointment.[8]

In 1920, in order to address the couple's financial needs, Matsushita hired on as a company clerk with Mitsui and Company, a trading firm with home offices in Tokyo. His capabilities soon being recognized, his stature in the firm rose, along with his responsibilities. Frequent salary increases, even throughout the Depression years, enabled a comfortable lifestyle and made Hanaye's entry into the workplace unnecessary.

Despite the relative affluence resulting from his twenty-year association with Mitsui and Company as a low-level manager, Matsushita, on August 31, 1940, submitted his resignation to company officials. Earlier that year management had ordered his transfer to the home office in Tokyo, an offer he declined with mixed emotion. His resignation letter cited an undying desire to study English and English literature at the University of Washington, which to date had eluded him. Further, reflecting on his two decades in the Pacific Northwest, he stated, "I cannot leave Seattle when I think of the beautiful views of Mount Rainier."[9]

The price to pay for such esthetics would prove high. Walking away from Mitsui and Company meant the loss of a $530 monthly salary and a $125 per month pension scheduled to begin in six months. But the lure of the mountains was not the whole story. He disliked the nature of the work he was required to perform, especially those tasks that involved handling people. He felt tied down to his job and suppressed by having a boss over him. Only the income was satisfying, sufficient to keep him and his wife independent and comfortable. Friends in Japan wrote about how difficult it was to make ends meet and how they looked forward to their bonuses in order to pay off debts. And because of a tightening economic situation in the home islands, stiff competition existed for the higher positions for which Matsushita would be eligible.[10]

Matsushita could not stomach the thought of even one year as a "salary-man" in Japan, and Hanaye fully supported his position. Thus they surrendered financial security in exchange for continuing cultural freedom in the United States, which their accumulated savings of more than $20,000 in dollars and yen would support. He and Hanaye planned to take a trip each summer and to eventually tour the whole United States before one day returning to Japan.[11]

Despite these plans Matsushita remained unemployed for less than two months. He was soon approached by the Seattle Japanese Chamber of Commerce and offered a salary of $150 per month to run a one-man operation designed to facilitate import and export trade with Japan. His recruiter was Seizo Bitow, executive secretary of the Seattle Japanese Chamber of Commerce and the Japanese Association of North America, two organizations that shared offices in Japantown. According to testimony provided by Bitow upon his own arrest after the attack on Pearl Harbor, few rank and file Chamber members were aware of Matsushita's employment or that his salary came from gifts provided by private Japanese manufacturers who would benefit from his work.[12] The sub-rosa manner in which his employment was conducted would lead to rumors in the Japanese community of his participation in espionage activities.

Matsushita is silent on his reasons for accepting this particular employment. Perhaps attempts to seek other employment failed, such as a teaching position at the University of Washington. Few positions may have been available in the Nikkei community for this overqualified professional man. Given his experience at Mitsui and Company, Matsushita was certainly qualified for the new task before him, although the statistical reports he generated must have been dulling to his creative sensibilities.

His employment lasted only eleven months, however. Once U.S. trade relations with Japan were frozen in the summer of 1941, his salary ended abruptly on August 31. However, at the request of Japanese Consul Yuki Sato, he continued on for two months without compensation, during which time he read and interpreted freezing bulletins issued by the Commerce Department. With the outbreak of war Matsushita was now fully unemployed.

By December 7, 1941, the government had developed a well-formulated set of allegations against Matsushita based, in large part, on information supplied by informants from within the Japanese community. FBI reports indicated that as early as 1932 he was seen taking photographs of the U.S. Navy's Keyport Torpedo Station in Puget Sound while in a car registered to Mitsui and Company. The same informant, code-named SE-1, placed Matsushita in the company of Lt. Comdr. Shigeru Fujii, Japan's naval attaché in Washington, D.C., and a frequent visitor to Seattle who was later expelled for espionage activity. He was also reported seeing Kanekichi Yamamoto, a prominent espionage suspect later deported in 1938 for tax evasion.[13]

In January 1941, nearly a year before the U.S. entered World War II, Thomas Toru Ogawa, a Canadian born-Japanese employed by the trading firm Mitsubishi Shoji Kaisha, provided information to the FBI that proved damaging to Matsushita. Deported in 1932, but now in the United States legally as a merchant under a trade treaty, Ogawa (confidential informant "T-1") told FBI agents that many Japanese in the community, whose names he apparently could not produce, believed Matsushita was engaged in espionage work and that his activities were subsidized by Tokyo. The Japanese Chamber of Commerce for whom Matsushita was now working, he claimed, was affiliated with Japan's Foreign Trade Bureau and should not be confused with the Seattle Japanese Chamber of Commerce. The trade bulletins read and interpreted by Matsushita were beyond the scope of the Seattle Chamber but part of the usual work of the Foreign Trade Bureau. Although Ogawa substantiated none of his allegations, little doubt resided in his mind that Matsushita, in running the Seattle Japanese Chamber of Commerce, was secretly an employee of the Japanese government.[14]

Seattle Nisei attorney Clarence Arai (confidential informant SE-201) kept the FBI informed of Matsushita's activities, including his resignation from Mitsui and Company. On June 10, 1941, Arai provided agents with information that Matsuhita was acting as a foreign promotion trade agent for Japan, with an office in the Central Building. He alleged that Matsushita was actually working for the Japanese Chamber of Commerce of Tokyo.[15]

Additional damaging information came from two other sources. Kenji Kimura, an Issei clerk employed by the Japanese Consulate, who was himself detained after December 7, 1941, and later interned, and John Fukuyama, a Nisei coworker at the Consulate, added incriminating statements that money was transferred from Tokyo to the Japanese Consulate and then to a bank account upon which Matsushita was free to draw checks. According to FBI reports, such activities as described by the informants, if true, would constitute a violation of the 1938 Foreign Agents Registration Act and would make Matsushita subject to prosecution.[16]

Based upon this information, the allegations against Matsushita were thus twofold: that he had engaged in espionage work and that he was a foreign agent in violation of the 1938 Foreign Agents Registration Act. The FBI concluded the evidence gathered was sufficient to warrant his arrest because his activities posed a threat to national security. For these reasons Matsushita was picked up by the FBI in the first wave of arrests and detained by the INS. During his three weeks behind bars in Seattle, Matsushita was not notified of the allegations, charged with any crime, or brought before a neutral arbiter.

Why were such allegations voluntarily brought forth? The local Japanese American Citizens League had a liaison with the FBI and encouraged second-generation Nikkei to come forth with information about their elders in hopes that the Nisei would be seen as loyal Americans and not subject to incarceration like the Issei. The Canadian Issei Thomas Ogawa may have been predisposed to being an informer. His wife, Lillian, was the sister of Clarence Arai, now known to have been one of at least three FBI informants from the Seattle Japanese American Citizens League. Ogawa's status in the United States was precarious, and he may have been looking for some personal gain by informing on Matsushita and perhaps others.[17]

For motivations that may never be entirely clear, the allegations by these Nikkei against Matsushita brought grief to him and Hanaye in the ensuing two years.

On December 30, 1941, after three weeks in the immigration station jail, Matsushita and 212 other enemy aliens from Seattle and other immigration stations along the West Coast were transported by train to the Fort Missoula Detention Station, an enclosed compound near Missoula, Montana. This facility had been acquired by the INS earlier in the year to detain Italian merchant seamen whose ships had been stranded in U.S. ports when Italy entered the war in June 1940, and seized in March 1941. There the new West Coast contingent joined 364 other Japanese nationals, all of whom would undergo loyalty hearings in 1942 to determine whether they should be released or interned.[18]

In order to determine who should be released and who interned, in December 1941 the Justice Department, through its Alien Enemy Control Unit, headed by Edward J. Ennis, set up ninety-two advisory hearing boards, at least one for each of the judicial districts in which arrests were being made. In the more populated areas, where arrests were numerous, multiple boards were created to hold hearings. Civilian leaders of the community, each appointed by Francis Biddle, the U.S. attorney general, sat on these boards. Biddle required that the chairman be an attorney. These dollar-a-year men were to be joined at the hearings by representatives from the INS, the FBI, and U.S. attorney's offices. Detainees appearing before the board of the judicial district in which they were apprehended were allowed to present witnesses and documents, offer personal testimony, and to have an advisor present, all at their own expense. No one, however, was permitted representation by legal counsel.[19]

The boards operated in an advisory capacity only. Each recommendation was to be based on the evidence adduced at the individual's hearing and transmitted to the attorney general, who would review each case and make the final decision as to its disposition. The United States Attorney was responsible for enforcing the decisions in accordance with instructions sent to him by the attorney general.[20]

Matsushita's hearing took place at Fort Missoula on February 10, 1942. Presiding over the three-member board representing the Western District of Washington was Frank E. Holman. Holman, fifty-six, was a Rhodes Scholar. From 1913 to 1915 he served as dean of the Utah Law School and subsequently practiced law in Salt Lake City. After arriving in Seattle in 1924, he became senior partner in a downtown law firm and was completing a yearlong term as president of the Seattle Bar Association when the country entered World War II.[21] His fellow board members were J. Speed Smith, also a practicing Seattle attorney, and Leslie A. Stone, vice-president of the Orting State Bank, located in a small community southeast of Tacoma, Washington.

Other attendees at Matsushita's hearing, as prescribed by the guidelines, were Assistant United States Attorney G. D. Hile, FBI Special Agent R. L. Flanders, INS representative John F. Harrington, a Nisei interpreter, and a stenographer to take down every word.

The accused standing before his cross-examiners was five feet three inches tall, of medium build at about 135 pounds, with receding black and graying hair. The forty-nine-year-old enemy alien possessed a very round and full face, was neatly dressed, and possessed an alert appearance. Others would later describe Matsushita as a quiet man, nearly fluent in English and with a steady hand at both Japanese script and English handwriting. The translator's services would not be needed.[22]

In interrogating Matsushita, the board drew from the two document sources lying before them: a lengthy questionnaire completed by Matsushita on December 26, 1941, days before his transfer to Fort Missoula, and two FBI reports, dated December 18, 1941, and January 19, 1942, summarizing the allegations and outlining the evidence against him. In addition the board had in its possession five letters solicited by Matsushita in preparation for his hearing, written by Seattle-area white church leaders who attested to his loyalty and good character.

The interrogation initially focused on Matsushita's alleged activities during his association with Mitsui and Company.[23]

Q: Have you taken any pictures of the Keyport Torpedo Station?

A: No, sir.

Q: In a car belonging to Mitsui Company?

A: No.

Q: Have you taken any pictures of any of the locks, or any airfields, or Boeing?

A: I remember I take Government locks in Seattle.

Q: When?

A: I do not remember. Five or six years ago.

Q: Why?

A: Because it is interesting place.

Q: Why did you want all these maps? You had map showing radio and telegraphic communications connections between the United States and foreign countries. What did you have these maps for?

A: I do not know what maps you refer to but I had many maps at my home. Maybe it was a communication map—when I was with Mitsui, the General Department also controlled telegraph department and I thought it was very interesting. That is why I kept it.

Q: You took quite a few pictures around here?

A: Yes.

Q: You had two movie cameras and a projector and about four other cameras?

A: Yes, sir.

Q: What did you do with all those?

A: That is my hobby.

Q: What did you do with the films?

A: I have them at home.

Q: Did you give any [films] to Japanese government or give them to Mitsui Company?

A: No. You can see all negatives at my home.

Q: Did you know Shigeru Fujii?

A: I heard his name.

Q: That is not what I asked you.

A: I think I saw him two or three times when I was with Mitsui and Company.

Q: Did you go around with him?

A: No.

Q: Did you know Yamamoto?

A: Which Yamamoto?

Q: Kanekichi Yamamoto?

A: No. Not at all.

Q: Did you talk to him on the telephone?

A: No.

Q: Were you the manager of Mitsui and Company?

A: No. Just a clerk.

Q: Do they pay clerks $530 a month?

A: I got $150 when I first started. Then it raises by the year. If you go to Mitsui & Company and see the records you can see I was plain clerk. I was member of the General Department. They have many departments, lumber department, etc. I had no title at all. I saw that everything runs smooth, something like that. Just general affairs. Accounting department, freight department, lumber department, sundry department.

Q: How did you happen to leave a good job like that [with Mitsui and Company] for $125 a month?

A: This is the most important chapter in my life and if you permit I would like to tell you. I was a Methodist, in Christian family. My father was a pastor. I was brought up in American atmosphere, brought up by American missionaries. I went to high school and to school at Kobe where my brother is working now, and I was educated there by American missionaries and teachers and then I went to Tokyo College where I learned English language under Americans. I wanted to come to this country, and see this country. That is why I came to this country. And then for 20 years I worked for Mitsui and Company. In 1940 the head office of Mitsui at Tokyo ordered me to go back to Japan. That was the great crisis in my life because my attachment to this country was so great I could not sever myself from this country. If I did not go back to Japan I cannot keep my job with Mitsui. There was a pension. I thought and thought. If I worked six more months I could get a pension. I thought, and thought, and I thought, but I could not sever myself so suddenly from the United States so I sacrificed my pension and stayed in the United States. That is the story. I want to say more but—

Q: Go ahead.

A: For the last twenty-three years, that is about one-half of my life, and the best part of my life, I stayed in Seattle. I did not go to any other place and I became so Americanized and my standard of life was based on Christianity and Americanism, freedom, democracy, and humanity, and when I resigned from Mitsui that way I chose between pension and the United States, and I took the United States. At that time I thought this was my adopted country although I could not be a citizen. Someone said "You are crazy." I said "Yes, I am crazy about the United States." So I think I am like loyal American in spirit although I am not a citizen. Even at this time when my freedom is deprived, I still like this country. I believe in freedom, humanity, and justice for all. I love this country. This is my adopted country. I think that is all I want to say now.

Q: You got as much [salary] as the manager down there, didn't you?

A: When I resigned I got allowance for my wife because I was married. I think the manager gets more than that. I think my salary so large maybe that is why they wanted me to go back to Japan.

Q: Do they have a program of raising salaries each year?

A: When your salary gets larger they raise every other year.

Q: A man's salary is based upon length of service with company?

A: Yes. If you are head of department you will get more.

Q: Were you head of department?

A: Yes. I belonged to General Department. I was not head. I was plain clerk.

Q: You worked for Mitsui for a long while. They thought a lot of you?

A: I don't think so. Just get good salary. They did not make me head of department.

Q: If you asked to stay in this country wouldn't they consider that at all? Why did you insist you go back to Japan?

A: I wanted to stay in this country. That is the main point.

Q: Did you ask to be allowed to stay in this country?

A: When they order, order is order. If I cannot accept it, I must resign.

Q: Have you any contact with Japanese army or navy officers in Seattle?

A: No.

Q: Did they come to Mitsui office when you were there?

A: Yes, many times.

Q: Meet them?

A: I saw them when they came to office and manager always took care of them.

Once the board exhausted its questions concerning Matsushita's alleged subversive activities while associated with Mitsui and Company, it next turned to the second set of allegations against Matsushita, pointing to a violation of the Foreign Agents Registration Act of 1938.

Q: Why did you tell the FBI man you were unemployed after you left Mitsui & Company?

A: I did not say that. He said "Did you seek employment?" so I said "No," and he said "Why not?" I said I wanted to live on my savings.

Q: When he first asked you what you did after leaving Mitsui & Company you told him you were unemployed?

A: I was unemployed for one and one-half months. Then I was employed by Mr. Bitow.

Q: While you were acting as clerk at Seattle Association [Seattle Japanese Chamber of Commerce] did you maintain an office in the Central Building?

A: Japanese Chamber of Commerce opened office there.

Q: Did the Japanese Consul have same office?

A: Yes.

Q: Was it in the same suite of offices? Where was the Consulate office in the Central Building with reference to offices of Japanese Chamber of Commerce in the Central Building?

A: Japanese Consul's office was on the sixth floor and my office on eighth floor.

Q: After the freezing order went into effect didn't you do work in the office of the Japanese Consulate for about two months?

A: I did not work there.

Q: What were you doing there?

A: Mr. Sato asked me to do some reading. He asked me to read freezing bulletins issued by the Government.

Q: Couldn't he read English?

A: I think so.

Q: Why have you read them?

A: I don't know.

Q: Didn't he tell you?

A: He wanted to know something about regulations and I had nothing to do. I just stayed at home and did some reading so he asked me to read those bulletins.

Q: Paid for that?

A: No.

Q: Didn't you turn in accounting sheet to Consul of expenses about every month or at definite periods of time? To the Japanese Consul?

A: No. I never did.

Q: Were you as a matter of fact representing the Tokyo Chamber of Commerce over here?

A: No.

Q: Did you ever belong to the Tokyo Chamber of Commerce?

A: No, sir.

Q: Receive any compensation?

A: No.

Q: Did the Japanese government through its Consul or in any other way, compensate you in any way?

A: Not a penny.

Q: You still say no money was deposited in your account for you to check on from the government of Japan?

A: No.

Q: When you worked as clerk for the Japanese Association what was your particular function? What did you do?

A: Mr. Bitow, executive secretary, told me your duty is promoting American Japanese trade before American public so I did my best for that.

Q: What steps did you take?

A: I went to the Department of Commerce in the Federal Building almost every day and got data for merchandise which is most needed in United States, and those merchandise coming from Japan and most needed in United States. I made a study.

Q: Did you study what merchandise was needed by Japan from the United States?

A: I did. I think that was just one or two, if I remember right.

Q: How did you determine what merchandise was needed by either country?

A: Bulletins. I made a study of bulletins.

Q: Did you go to the Consul and see what—

A: I know myself. I was with Mitsui for twenty years and I know.

Q: Did you correspond with anyone in Japan about this?

A: When some fellow in United States asked me to get some information I tried to get information locally but when I could not, I wrote letter to Japan to get information for him.

Q: When someone in Japan wrote you for information—Did you have

inquiries or questions coming to you from Japan as to what could be supplied there from over here?

A: Most of my study was made for the American public and I was not
much interested in those people in Japan.

Q: As I understand it you are telling us that you were not at any time a
representative in this country of any agency in Japan, chamber of commerce,
government, or otherwise. Not at any time.

A: No, sir.

Q: That you therefore did not get any money from anyone connected with
the Consulate's office or from any person or agency except Mitsui & Company.

A: That is right.

Q: That you never submitted any sort of sheets of expenses or outlay to
the Consulate?

A: No.

Q: Did you ever make any reports of any kind of trade or furnish to the
Consulate any information at all?

A: When I made report I gave one copy to the Consulate.

Q: That is, your report to the Seattle Chamber of Commerce?

A: Yes, sir.

Q: Did the Consulate ask for a copy?

A: When I make report I make one for Mitsubishi, Mitsui, and Japanese
Consulate.

Q: You were paid $150 a month by the Association to do that type of work?

A: Yes.

Q: Do you know out of what fund the Association made that payment?

A: I do not know. Mr. Bitow knows, I guess.

Q: Were you acquainted with Tadeo Yasuda?

A: No. I saw him two or three times when I worked at Mitsui. He never
talked to me.

Q: Did you know he was an employee of the Japanese Foreign
Department?

A: That is what I heard.

Q: He was furnishing reports to Japan, industrial conditions?

A: That is what I heard. He never talked to me at all. He was kind of stuck
up man.

Q: We have been advised that this Japanese Chamber of Commerce office
in the Central Building, that you were manager of that, and that that had no
connection with the regular Seattle Japanese Chamber of Commerce. There
was another office in the Central Building on the eighth floor. We have been

advised that the office in the Central Building on the eighth floor was the office of a different organization of the Japanese Chamber of Commerce.

A: No.

Q: Who else was in that office with you?

A: Nobody.

Q: How long had you had that office?

A: Ten months.

Q: Who opened this office in the Central Building?

A: Mr. Bitow.

Q: What sign on the door?

A: Japanese Chamber of Commerce in Seattle.

Q: Did you begin work for them in this particular office in the Central Building?

A: Mr. Bitow opened this office and asked me to work there.

Q: Did anyone occupy that office with you?

A: No.

Q: Did you have a stenographer?

A: No.

Q: Do you know who paid that rent?

A: Mr. Bitow paid the rent.

Q: Did you see the check that was paid to the Central Building?

A: Yes. I had check book. Mr. Bitow issued check paying rent. The check was delivered to me. I saw it each month. The rent was $35 a month. I delivered it sometime and sometimes I sent it by mail.

As their subsequent report to the attorney general indicated, Holman and his two colleagues were impressed by Matsushita, whom they described as "a man of education and of considerable natural intelligence." They noted his frankness and willingness to answer questions intelligently. They agreed his forfeiture of a lucrative salary in order to remain in the United States demonstrated a credible loyalty to the country, and it was logical that he would have to take a salary of $150 when he began anew. In its summary finding the board put aside the statements of Thomas Ogawa, the Canadian merchant, as well as those of the earlier, anonymous informers. It pointed out the only important reason urged by the FBI for internment was based upon the authority of the two former employees of the Japanese Consulate at Seattle, who stated Matsushita was in effect an agent of a foreign principal and that he received money from some agency in Japan, governmental or otherwise. It noted these were unsworn statements and may have been made by vindictive individuals upset at a Japanese national who had made the important decision of preferring the American way of life to a life in Japan with a comfortable pension. Such charges, however serious, could only be resolved in the courtroom with live testimony made under oath and subject to cross-examination. However, should the charges be proven true, the board opined, "he should be imprisoned and not even accorded the privilege of being in an internment camp."[24]

Under mandate to decide each case only in light of the record before it, Holman, Smith, and Stone therefore concluded "said alien enemy be detained pending prosecution by the US Attorney's office at Seattle for violation of the Registration Act—but if not so prosecuted or if found not guilty upon trial, that he be released." Thus, the board found no evidence of espionage while at the same time appeared to challenge the government to proceed to trial with its unreliable witnesses on charges of Matsushita being an unregistered trade agent.

Matsushita had been permitted the final word at his hearing: "I sincerely hope that you understand my sincerity and loyalty to this country and my future is entirely in your hands, so I want you to make good recommendation."[25]

As to whose hands the forty-nine-year-old scholarly immigrant believed controlled his future, he could not have been more wrong.

Six weeks after Matsushita's hearing, sixty-four-year-old J. Charles Dennis, United States Attorney for the Western District of Washington, who oversaw the two hearing boards for his district, wrote Director Ennis of the Alien Enemy Control Unit, "We are wholly unable to agree with the conclusion of the Board in the instant case and strongly recommend that this alien be interned." Dennis saw a hotbed of espionage at Mitsui and Company and drew conclusions from the unsworn statements of informants that Matsushita, by nature of his huge salary, must have played an important managerial role and therefore was an important cog. He refuted Matsushita's testimony explaining his role with the Seattle Japanese Chamber of Commerce, and the FBI informants of Matsushita's illegal association with the Tokyo Chamber of Commerce apparently convinced him. Finally, Dennis took as fact the rumor in the Japanese community that this man was actively engaged in espionage work.[26]

Knowing that prosecuting a Foreign Agents Registration Act case would result in a time-consuming and expensive trial that might involve cross-country travel by witnesses, Dennis concluded his recommendation for internment by stating, "If during the course of his internment it develops that he should be prosecuted for failure to register as the agent of a foreign government, ample time will be had to develop a case and at the same time the subject will be in custody where he can do no harm."[27]

The Justice Department had little incentive to proceed with a Foreign Agents Registration Act case with Matsushita safely detained. Thus, he languished behind the barbed wire fences at Fort Missoula camp throughout the spring, summer, and autumn of 1942 while comrades with more clear-cut cases were paroled to their families in the recently opened assembly centers and relocation centers or sent off to internment at army installations located throughout the country. The Japanese population at Fort Missoula, having peaked at more than six hundred in mid-winter 1942, dwindled to twenty-eight in the fall.[28]

The INS, on the other hand, was anxious to dispose of its backlog of detention cases, and at the end of May 1942 began to press the attorney general's office for a resolution of Matsushita's case. Having received no response to his initial query, Director Ennis repeated his request on July 14, asking U.S. Attorney J. Charles Dennis to take the case back for reconsideration before the alien hearing board.

This follow-up brought the desired results. On August 12, 1942, the reconvened board recommended Matsushita's immediate release on the basis of Dennis having made no move to prosecute the case. This action motivated U.S. Attorney General Francis A. Biddle to seek an opinion regarding the advisability of proceeding with prosecution. On October 1, 1942, a Justice Department attorney concluded the record presented insufficient evidence to warrant going to trial. Nor would prosecution under the Foreign Agents Registration Act, he added, necessarily make the subject a dangerous person who should be interned.[29]

Prior to deciding Matsushita's case, Biddle ordered his subordinates in the Review Section to review the file. Their subsequent report indicates they found difficulty believing his association with the Seattle Japanese Chamber of Commerce was as innocuous as it appeared. That Matsushita had an appreciable sum of money in Japan, coupled with the Japanese government's apparent interest in having him return to Japan, led the primary reviewer to conclude he should be interned.[30]

Swayed by his internal reviewers' recommendations and likely influenced by U.S. Attorney Dennis's earlier statements, Attorney General Biddle, on November 16, 1942, penned his signature to an order for Matsushita's internment: "Whereas, the Alien Enemy Hearing Board has recommended that said alien enemy be released; and it appearing from the evidence before me that said alien enemy should be interned; now, therefore, it is ordered that said alien enemy be interned."[31]

Thus, after more than eleven months as a detainee, Iwao Matsushita's political status formally converted to internee of war, virtually eliminating any chance that he and Hanaye would be reunited soon. Biddle's internment order thus brought to an end a ten-year probe of an immigrant who had come to America twenty-three years earlier to seek out its intellectual riches and a culture he adored.[32]

Caution should be taken in any attempt to generalize a government policy from a single case. Matsushita was atypical because of the dual allegations against him. Moreover, he was an intellectual, a professional man who had prospered in America. During World War II the Justice Department made decisions on the loyalty of more than three thousand Japanese nationals living in the United States, including a handful of women. Each case presented unique circumstances, although most were less complicated than Matsushita's. Nevertheless, his case offers some insights.

First, the FBI and other intelligence-gathering organizations found informants in the Japanese community, including both immigrant and second-generation Japanese, willing to spy on its leaders. The "facts" of Matsushita's case suggest the government relied heavily on these individuals even though the hearing board appointed to review it questioned the integrity of their statements and they were not subjected to cross-examination. Second, the hearing boards were clearly advisory in capacity, lacking any authority to implement their recommendations. Final decisions rested in the attorney general's office, at the hands of bureaucrats who probably never attended a hearing. Nevertheless, the Justice Department relied on the boards to help weed out the open and shut cases, both for release and internment. Given decision makers' propensity to presume guilt and to err on continued confinement rather than letting a potentially dangerous enemy alien slip through the cracks, it is likely that few if any recommendations for internment were overruled by the attorney general. The ambiguities of Matsushita's case probably doomed his cause. Unlike the 673 Issei paroled to assembly centers between March 21, 1942, and October 30, 1942, Matsushita was unsuccessful in eliminating doubts in the attorney general's mind that he posed a threat to national security.[33]

Little systematic research has been published to date on the Justice Department's decision-making process to determine the level of security risk of enemy aliens whose names were placed on the ABC list before and during World War II. Most published accounts remain anecdotal.[34] A comprehensive study of the hearing boards, the men who served on them, the procedures and procedural guidelines they were required to follow, and their attitudes toward the Japanese, German, and Italian aliens who came before them is needed. The closed legal case files of detainees and internees in the Textual Reference Division at the National Archives, College Park, Maryland, should be mined for their content so they may help shed light on how one republic decided the loyalty of unnaturalized residents in a time of war.

Notes

1. Federal Bureau of Investigation File 100–1999, Seattle, Washington, December 18, 1941, Records of the Department of Justice (RG60), Closed Legal Case Files, Accession 085–53A0010, Box 697, file 146–13–2–82–322, National Archives, College Park, Maryland. (Hereafter, Matsushita Case File.) Matsushita's movie films were returned to him in 1945 while he was incarcerated at the Minidoka Relocation Center. The U.S. Marshal destroyed his other confiscated possessions in 1943.

2. Details of the lives of the Matsushita couple in Seattle may be found in Louis Fiset, *Imprisoned Apart: The World War II Correspondence of an Issei Couple* (Seattle: University of Washington Press, 1997.) The literature on the incarceration of Japanese Americans and enemy aliens during World War II is vast. See, for example, Roger Daniels, *Concentration Camps USA: Japanese Americans and World War II* (New York: Holt, Rinehart and Winston, 1971); Michi Weglyn, *Years of Infamy: The Untold Story of America's Concentration Camps* (Seattle: University of Washington Press, 1996); and Commission on the Wartime Relocation and Internment of Civilians (CWRIC), *Personal Justice Denied: Report of the Commission on Wartime Relocation and Internment of Civilians* (Seattle: University of Washington Press and the Civil Liberties Public Education Fund, 1997.)

3. Department of Justice, press releases, December 8, 13, 1942, cited in Morton Grodzins, *Americans Betrayed: Politics and the Japanese Evacuation* (Chicago: University of Chicago Press, 1949), 232; FBI memoranda, Papers of the Commission on the Wartime Relocation and Internment of Civilians, Part 1: Numerical File Archive, reel 9, 474–481. The precise number of Seattle resident enemy aliens apprehended by the FBI during World War II has not been established. The data here were extracted from contemporaneous news articles in the *Seattle Post-Intelligencer* and the *Seattle Times*. Although the FBI also arrested many German and Italian enemy aliens, this essay focuses only on Japanese nationals.

4. Roger Daniels, *The Decision to Relocate the Japanese Americans* (New York: J. B. Lippincott Company, 1975), 62–64.

5. Bob Kumamoto, "The Search for Spies: American Counter Intelligence and the Japanese American Community, 1931–1942," *Amerasia Journal* 6 (1979): 45–75.

6. Ibid.

7. Memorandum for the File, October 1, 1942, Matsushita Case File.

8. Fiset, *Imprisoned Apart*, 3–25.

9. Ibid., 24–25.

10. James Sakoda, "Journal" (April 24, 1942—October 28, 1945), March 8, 1944, file R20.81, Japanese American Evacuation and Resettlement Records 67/14c, Bancroft Library, University of California at Berkeley.

11. Ibid.

12. Lawrence K. Bailey, Department of Justice Memorandum for the File, October 1, 1942, 11–12, Matsushita Case File.

13. Federal Bureau of Investigation File 100–1999, Seattle, Washington, May 14, 1941, Matsushita Case File.

14. Federal Bureau of Investigation File 100–1999, Seattle, Washington, March 27, 1942, Matsushita Case File. To track Ogawa's presence in the U.S. beginning in 1930, see *Polk's Seattle Directory*, 1929–1941. Ogawa was subsequently interned by the INS at the Santa Fe Internment Camp, but was paroled to the Minidoka Relocation Center in September 1943. He, his wife, Lillian, and their two children left Minidoka for resettlement in New York in July 1945. "Final Accountability Roster of the Minidoka Relocation Center, October, 1945," Records of the War Relocation Authority (RG210), National Archives, Washington, D.C.

15. Federal Bureau of Investigation File 100–1999, Seattle, Washington, October 15, 1941, Matsushita Case File.

16. Bailey, Department of Justice Memorandum for the File, October 1, 1942, 16–19. This law was enacted to control Nazi and communist propaganda proliferating in the United States. Violators were subject to a $1,000 fine and two years in prison. "Dissemination of Propaganda in the United States," (PL583, 8 June 1938), 52 *United States Statutes at Large*, 631–633.

17. In addition to the informants cited in this essay, at least twenty-four officers and members of the Japanese American Citizens League were utilized as confidential informants. Seattle Nisei informants included Clarence T. Arai, Tatsue Iida, and Johnson Asato Shimizu. See Federal Bureau of Investigation, "Summary of Information: War Relocation Authority and Japanese Relocation Centers," August 1945 (67–6930–710), 77, copy in author's possession.

18. Fiset, *Imprisoned Apart*, 36–37.

19. "Instructions to Alien Enemy Hearing Boards," Supplement 1, January 7, 1942, Fort Missoula file 1016/K, Immigration and Naturalization Service Records (RG85), National Archives, Washington, D.C.

20. "Instructions to Alien Enemy Hearing Boards," December 13, 1941, Frank E. Holman papers, box 18, folder 18–8, University of Washington Libraries.

21. Holman later served as president of the Washington State Bar Association (1945) and the American Bar Association (1948–49.) For details of his life and career, see Frank E. Holman, *The Life and Career of a Western Lawyer, 1886–1961* (Baltimore: Port City Press, Inc., 1963).

22. Sakoda, "Journal," March 8, 1944.

23. Untitled transcript of Iwao Matsushita's hearing held on February 10, 1942, Matsushita Case File. Questions put by the board members did not always conform to a logical sequence. For clarity I have rearranged some of the questions/answers in this abridged text.

24. Department of Justice, Alien Enemy Hearing Board, Western District of Washington, "In re The Detention of Iwao Matsushita: Summary of Facts and Opinion," Matsushita Case File.

25. Untitled transcript of Iwao Matsushita's hearing held on February 10, 1942, Matsushita Case File.

26. J. Charles Dennis to Edward J. Ennis, 26 March 1942, Matsushita Case File. Dennis was a Tacoma, Washington, resident since 1906. He was nominated for U.S. Attorney of the Western District of Washington by Senator Homer T. Bone (R-Wash.) in 1934 and served until 1953. See *Capitol's Who's Who for Washington: The State Encyclopedia, 1949–50* (Portland, Oreg.: Capitol Publishing, 1949), 352.

27. J. Charles Dennis to Edward J. Ennis, 26 March 1942.

28. Fiset, *Imprisoned Apart,* 51.

29. Bailey, Department of Justice Memorandum for the File, October 1, 1942, 21.

30. Memorandum to Chief of Review Section, November 11, 1942, Matsushita Case File.

31. Francis Biddle, "In the Matter of Iwao Matsushita, Alien Enemy," Records of the Office of the Provost Marshal (RG389), Records of the Alien Enemy Information Bureau, Records relating to Japanese Civilian Internees during World War II, 1942–1946, box 60.

32. Matsushita was ordered paroled on January 2, 1944, and was reunited with Hanaye at the Minidoka Relocation Center on January 11. See Fiset, *Imprisoned Apart,* 81–82.

33. U.S. War Department, *Final Report: Japanese Evacuation from the West Coast, 1942* (Washington, D.C: GPO, 1943), 373, table 50.

34. See, for example, Lauren Kessler, *Stubborn Twig: Three Generations in the Life of a Japanese American Family* (New York: Random House, 1993), 115–17.

11 / THE "FREE ZONE" NIKKEI

Japanese Americans in Idaho
and Eastern Oregon in World War II

ROBERT C. SIMS

I n August 1942, during the period when Nikkei[1] from the Puyallup Assembly Center were moved by train to Minidoka, their route took them through Nampa, Idaho. In a letter to a friend in Seattle, a young man gave the following account:

> At 9 A.M. we stopped in Nampa and there were two Japanese at the station who had left Seattle long before the evacuation. I thought how ironic that we should see two Japanese who were free to do as they pleased while we, by the trainloads, were being herded into camps.[2]

This account points out the presence of an often-overlooked aspect of the lives of Nikkei during the war years, the different experiences of those from the West Coast who were imprisoned and those who, by virtue of living outside Military Area 1,[3] were not. The latter group lived in what came to be referred to as the "free zone," and persons of Japanese ancestry living there were free of most of the restrictions imposed on the former. The two populations had much in common in their histories and considerable intermingling during the war. In fact, those from the West Coast who moved inland during the period of "voluntary 'relocation'" and those who left the camps to work in the region became "free zoners" themselves, thus blurring the distinctions between the two groups.[4]

The so-called "voluntary relocation" began following the first announcement that Nikkei were to be excluded from the West Coast and continued until March 29, 1942, when a proclamation by the head of the Western Defense Command halted it. By that time, almost five thousand people had moved to sites inland, hoping to escape the forced evacuation which was on the horizon. Colorado was the most attractive destination, receiving 1,963. Utah followed with 1,519, Idaho was third with 305, and the eastern portions of Washington and Oregon received 208 and 115, respectively.[5] Those who moved in represent a significant increase in the number of Nikkei already residing in these areas. Those who moved to Idaho equaled about one-fourth of that state's Nikkei population in 1942. New Nikkei coming into eastern Washington and Oregon almost doubled Nikkei populations in those areas. The circumstances between imprisoned people and those who were already residing in the region often made for stresses and conflicts between the groups as they each tried to cope with their wartime situation. Their relationship was complicated by "voluntary evacuation" and by the leave programs of the War Relocation Authority, both of which resulted in considerable numbers of the excluded people working and living in the "Free Zone."

The areas discussed in this paper are primarily the State of Idaho and Malheur County in Oregon, with occasional references to Spokane County, Washington. The latter two areas are contiguous to Idaho on its western border and, as such, have cultural and economic ties to the state. These areas represent "case studies" that vary in important respects from either Colorado or Utah. One important difference is in the character of the political leadership. Idaho's governor, unlike Colorado's, was openly hostile to the presence of Nikkei in the state, either as "voluntary relocatees" or as incarcerated people. In that, he differed even from Utah's governor, who was willing to accept the presence of the relocated people if they were in camps guarded by the military. This difference had a great deal of impact on the nature of the relationship between the Idaho Nikkei and those who came from the West Coast, particularly during the "voluntary" period. Also, unlike Colorado and Utah, Idaho was contiguous to the exclusion area, and this played a significant role, as people were able to leave the camps but were not yet able to return to their former homes. Many of these chose to move as close as they could in anticipation of an eventual return home. Otherwise, the history of the Nikkei in Idaho and the adjacent portions of Oregon and Washington was remarkably similar to that of their counterparts elsewhere in the Rocky Mountain region.

Much of the prewar population in these areas was due to employment of Nikkei in railroad construction in the last half of the nineteenth century and the first part of the twentieth. The development of the sugar beet industry also accounts for some of the early settlement in the region. From those early beginnings, Idaho had about 1,500 Nikkei by 1930. Like their counterparts on the West Coast, they faced a range of discriminations that helped define their status on the eve of World War II. Long before the United States Supreme Court established the principle of no citizenship for the Issei in the 1922 Ozawa case, a federal judge in Boise denied an Idaho Issei's petition for citizenship in federal district court in Boise. In his opinion, the judge cited language from the federal naturalization statute, which held that only Caucasians and persons of African ancestry could be naturalized.[6]

In 1923 Idaho passed an anti-Japanese land law patterned after that of California, which passed its legislation in 1913.[7] The state legislature had considered such a law in every session since 1917 before it was adopted. The year before its adoption, an article in the *Idaho Farmer* sounded the alarm against the "Japanese Invasion." It argued that land laws restricting Japanese ownership of land in other states were driving them to Idaho. "A number of Japanese driven out of Oregon and California and Washington, and some who have been driven off of Indian reservations by a recent ruling of the department of the interior, are coming to Idaho and offering rent that it is claimed white men cannot pay and make a profit. . . . It is hoped to evolve some method of preventing the Japanese from invading the Boise Valley."[8] The 1923 land law was designed to do just that. In debates over this legislation in the previous legislative session, the proposed bill was usually referred to as the "Japanese exclusion bill."[9] While small farmers seemed to support this legislation, the region's sugar companies opposed its passage and were successful for several sessions in killing it. The passage of a similar law in Oregon at that time, coupled with Washington's adoption of an anti-Japanese land bill two years earlier, helped overcome opposition to the bill and add credence to the alarmist rhetoric noted above.

In 1922 the state's anti-miscegenation law was amended to include a prohibition against Japanese marrying Caucasians. The original statute had included prohibition against Caucasians marrying "negroes, mullatoes, and mongolians," the latter seemingly referring to Chinese.[10] These laws were reminders of their second-class status.

Meanwhile the Nisei population was coming of age and becoming more visible in the communities. In the Boise Valley, Nisei students were excelling in school. In 1934 a Nisei was the valedictorian of the state's largest high school. In that year and the one following, the valedictorians at another Boise Valley high school were Nisei, children of long-time families in the area.[11] Other area Nisei were achieving success and acceptance in local colleges, including one young man who was the head of the cheerleading squad at Northwest Nazarene College in Nampa, and several who played on athletic teams at the College of Idaho throughout the 1930s.[12] There is little evidence that these young people had any realistic hopes of moving into careers other than farming, but in 1935, a Nisei woman passed her examination to practice medicine in Idaho. Dr. Kimi Nojima of Idaho Falls attended college at the University of Utah and studied medicine at the University of Michigan. She opened a practice in Pocatello that year, one of the centers of Idaho's limited Nikkei population.[13]

By 1930, although Nikkei resided in almost all of Idaho's forty-four counties, the population tended to be concentrated at opposite ends of the state. More than a third lived in three counties in the upper Snake River region: Bannock, Bingham, and Bonneville, which reflected the influence of Nikkei involvement in railroad work and early sugar beet operations in that area. About two hundred lived in Canyon County, at the extreme western edge of the state, adjacent to Malheur County in Oregon. A decade later, although this population had been reduced somewhat, it maintained the same general pattern. There was some interaction among the Nikkei in different parts of the state, including baseball tournaments, and some with the development of Nisei clubs, forerunners of the Japanese American Citizens League in the region. As early as 1936 the JACL attempted to organize these clubs as part of that organization and had achieved some success on the eve of World War II, with chapters in Boise Valley, Idaho Falls, Pocatello, and Rexburg, all communities with significant Nikkei involvement in farming. The region also saw two chapters in Utah, at both Salt Lake City and Ogden.[14]

Meanwhile, in Oregon, the Nikkei community in Malheur County was growing, due in part to farming opportunities resulting from the building of the Malheur dam in the mid-1930s. That population was at 137 in 1940, barely more than one-half of one percent of the county's total population. But even by 1938, the community was robust and successful enough to build a "Japanese Hall" for community functions.[15] Bimonthly church meetings were held there as well as "dances, parties and occasional Japanese movies or plays."[16]

Even with such advances, the degree of integration into the general community life was limited, and the Nikkei in this area, as elsewhere, were vulnerable at the time of Pearl Harbor. The actions of the United States government against the Nikkei have been judged harshly by history. Justified at the time on the grounds of military necessity, we now know no such necessity existed. But the actions were taken in an atmosphere of hatred and fear undergirded by a history of racism and fanned by the winds of confusion and hysteria in the days following Pearl Harbor. The Commission on Wartime Relocation and Internment of Civilians, in its 1982 report, determined that this unnecessary decision occurred because of three factors: racism, wartime hysteria, and failure of political leadership.[17]

Idaho provided its share of all three. Racism was evidenced by the legal discriminations imposed over the half century of the Nikkei's presence in the state. The general panic that followed the attack at Pearl Harbor contributed to a civil rights disaster of major proportions.

The anti-Japan rhetoric of the West Coast made its way inland and resulted in panic headlines in Idaho's newspapers: "Japs May Fly All the Way to Idaho!" Nationalist fervor got out of hand, with treatment of Idaho's Nikkei population at the hands of their neighbors ranging from expressions of support to acts of violence. In Caldwell, a Japanese American home was hit by gunfire, Japanese American homes were raided by the FBI and local police, and various business, fraternal, and "patriotic" organizations passed resolutions calling for the internment of all enemy aliens for the duration.[18] In Idaho Falls the war brought the closure of the Japanese meeting hall. This building had been used as a Japanese language school and had also served as a meeting place for the community. In Ontario, Oregon, local Japanese signed their community hall over to the city in the hopes that would ensure the safety of the building. They were acting in good faith that, after the crisis, it would be returned to them, which it was. Ontario proved to be a "haven" of sorts for Nikkei relocating during the "voluntary" period, and others arrived on seasonal and later permanent relocation from the camps.[19]

Compounding the problem for Idaho's Nikkei was the capture of over a thousand Idaho employees of the Morrison-Knudson Construction Company, who were working on construction projects for the military in the Pacific. These men were captured in the days and weeks following Pearl Harbor, and no word as to their condition or whereabouts was received until February 19, 1942.[20] Newspaper accounts of atrocities committed by the Japanese military during this period bore a special weight on the families of those captured in the Pacific, and this situation may account for much of the heightened feelings toward Japanese in the area. A business associate of the head of the company, in a letter to a colleague, argued against bringing Japanese to Idaho for fear that some could be killed, which might lead to retaliation against Idahoans being held by Japan. "Better send the Japs that we intern to some state that does not have workers interned in Japan," he wrote.[21] This was taking place during a period when Governor Chase A. Clark's rhetoric against allowing Japanese into the state reached its highest intensity.

The animosity toward persons of Japanese ancestry occurred in other parts of the state as well. Denny Yasuhara, who later served as national president of the Japanese American Citizens League (JACL), was sixteen years old when the war began, living with his family in Bonners Ferry, in northern Idaho. The family was forced to leave their home and relocate to Spokane because of harassment and abuse, including allegations of disloyalty, even from white people who had known the family for years.[22]

Idaho Nikkei were confused and concerned in the early days of World War II. They attempted to show their loyalty to the United States through a variety of means, including a telegram to the governor pledging support and the purchase of savings bonds.[23]

A number of the restrictions imposed on West Coast Nikkei affected them as well, including the freezing of bank accounts of aliens from countries with which the United States was at war. In the week after Pearl Harbor, an official of the First Security Banking Corporation wrote to all branch managers in the region confirming that "the property of all Japanese nationals in the possession of the banks are frozen unconditionally until further order." Further, he indicated they were not

> to pay any checks or allow the transfer of any Japanese nationals' bank accounts in any manner, shape, or form. For instance, supposing you have bonds as collateral to a Jap's note to you. You have no authority to accept the payment of the note and release the security. As a practical matter, collect the money to pay the note if you possibly can, but do not release his security.[24]

Although this position was later modified, some restrictions remained and constituted a hardship on many. This included placing a limit on the amount that could be withdrawn monthly from a bank account.

Another form of discrimination occurred at local ration boards. In Twin Falls, a long-time Issei farmer in the county was denied ration stamps to purchase tires for an automobile. He was rejected by the county ration board, which ruled that "rationing regulations allow only American citizens to acquire rubber for motor vehicles."[25]

Other farmers in the region, particularly in eastern Washington and eastern Oregon, reported difficulty obtaining crop loans in 1942 because of the uncertainty of the status of Nikkei in that area. Nikkei were excluded from the eastern part of California, which was part of Military Area #2, and some feared that that order might be extended to include the eastern portions of Washington and Oregon as well. Those rumors persisted throughout early 1942.

Throughout the region Issei employees of railroads were dismissed, some having put in decades of service. In Idaho Falls, two men who had worked for the railroad for forty-one years lost their jobs a few days after the war broke out. They were detained and eventually placed in Heart Mountain, the camp in Wyoming.[26]

While the Nikkei in the interior were suffering such hardships, those in California and western Oregon and Washington were bracing for even greater difficulties. Demands for their removal began immediately after Pearl Harbor, and those demands turned into official policy by late winter. On February 19, 1942, President Franklin Roosevelt signed Executive Order 9066, which authorized the removal of any or all persons from prescribed military areas for purposes of national defense. This authority was granted to the commander of the Western Defense Command, Lt. Gen. John L. DeWitt. On March 2 he issued Public Proclamation No. 1, establishing the western half of Washington, Oregon, and California, and the southerly half of Arizona as Military Area #1. The initial effort at removal was the so-called "voluntary relocation," and from March 2 to March 29, "nearly anyone who was affected by the proposed evacuation program . . . was encouraged . . . to leave."[27] As that policy was discussed and put in place, the interaction of Nikkei from the two regions became significant. According to a study done in 1946, "When relocatees were sent into this area [eastern Washington] where there had been no evacuation of the few Japanese who had lived here for years, friction resulted with Caucasians and, to some extent, among the resident Japanese and those who came into the area during this period." This friction, together with that which already existed because of the war with Japan, led to occasional outbreaks of violence. Throughout the inter-mountain West, local Nikkei communities found themselves in some peril if they were too aggressive in helping friends and family relocate from the West Coast. In Spokane, leaders of the Nikkei community there publicly took the position that they would "discourage any coast Japanese from coming to the Spokane area."[28]

In early March some groups of Nikkei in the Pacific Northwest were formulating plans to find new homes in the interior. However, they found that "inland communities were giving the voluntary evacuees a cold reception." In Tacoma, a Japanese American community leader said "opposition of Idaho and eastern Washington communities has kept Japanese from evacuating voluntarily."[29]

Meanwhile, in Idaho, Governor Chase Clark continued his crusade to keep Nikkei out of the state. Clark was among the most outspoken and racist public officials over the matter of the removal to the interior, and he was determined to keep the Nikkei out. As West Coast Nikkei sought out opportunities inland, many looked to friends, family, and acquaintances in the intermountain region. But because of intense anti-Japanese sentiment, this proved to be difficult, and it put the region's Nikkei in an awkward position. In early March, Paul Okamura, president of the Pocatello JACL, wrote to Mike Masaoka, the executive secretary of the national organization, telling him that, because of Governor Clark's attitude, the local Nikkei's "hands are tied so far as helping the Pacific coast mass evacuation problem to any great extent." He continued to write "a certain amount of Niseis could come here without causing undue alarm, providing some employment arrangements have been made or that they have relatives here who would be responsible for them." He also deemed it wise "that these people, if they come here, come in as small a group as possible at intervals rather than a large group at one time." He went on to indicate that they were having difficulty locating a home for a local family who had been forced to move, and that "some property owners are reluctant towards leasing ground to the local Japanese."[30]

He had reason to be concerned about Clark, who, less than two weeks later, issued a warning through the press to "American Japanese in Idaho that it is better to refrain from any activity in encouraging other Japanese to come into Idaho, because it might result in the exclusion of all."[31] Idaho JACL presidents, meeting at Caldwell a week later, passed a resolution "pledging all members of the league in Idaho to discourage all evacuee relatives, friends, and others" from coming to Idaho. "While we sympathize with those Japanese who are required to leave California and other restricted districts, we can not look at it from an individual point of view but must consider it from the viewpoint of public welfare," according to a spokesperson for the organization.[32] Paul Okamura wrote to Governor Clark asking that he "make a distinction between 'coast evacuee Japanese Americans and those of us who reside in Idaho permanently.'"[33] There is no record of a response from the governor, who continued his position in opposition to Japanese coming into the state.

Local Nikkei had learned to be wary of Clark, for he was a dangerous man on this topic. In a letter to a Pocatello newspaper, he said: "I am not ready to sell the State of Idaho to the Japanese for a few dollars, while our American boys are dying to prevent Japan from taking the State of Idaho and our entire nation by force of arms. I appeal to every citizen of the State of Idaho not to sell land to the Japanese. If we let them come now, and by

the purchase of land, settle themselves here, we will soon be sick of them."
Later in the letter, Clark continued:

> The ones who were born here are more dangerous than those born in Japan
> because the latter, to some extent, may appreciate their escape from despot-
> ism, but those born here are taught that Japan is heaven and their Emperor
> is the Almighty.[34]

These were strange words from a man who, in November 1941, had been
the guest speaker at a gathering of Nikkei from throughout the intermountain area, the purpose of which was "to impress upon fellow countrymen their loyalty to the United States." Mike Masaoka, who attended
the conference, said that the purpose of the meeting was to explain the policies and objectives of the JACL, a goal he felt to be important because, as
he said:

> In these critical days, when the policies of many organizations representing
> various nationality groups may be viewed with suspicion by certain individ-
> uals not intimately acquainted with the aims, ideals and leadership of such
> associations, it becomes necessary and proper in the public interest that such
> fraternal and educational orders as the Japanese American Citizens League
> make clear their policies and objective.[35]

The purpose of the gathering apparently failed to influence Clark.

In spite of Clark's objections and the lack of full cooperation on the part
of local people, some Nikkei did arrive during the period of "voluntary evacuation," the result of family and friends willing to risk defying the governor.

When that was ended by official order on March 27, 1942, the relationship between the Free Zone Nikkei and the relocatees entered a new phase.
A young woman who had come to Caldwell during the voluntary period wrote
to a friend in Seattle that "The prejudice here has died down immensely since
the voluntary evacuation has been stopped."[36] Part of the new situation
involved the imposition of curfews in a number of towns in Idaho and elsewhere in the region. The "rules" were applied rather spottily, with some area
towns, like Weiser, Idaho, observing them, and others, like Ontario, Oregon, not. These "town" curfews especially affected farmers because some farm
operation activities, such as storage, shipping, equipment repair, and the like,
involved going into towns often at the end of a workday.

Within days following the ending of "voluntary evacuation," announcements were made concerning the placement of large "relocation centers" in the region, to be operated by a new civilian agency, the War Relocation Authority, established by an Executive Order 9102 on March 18, 1942.[37] The news brought additional pressure on local Nikkei in that anti-Japanese feelings became even stronger.

The war was not going well for the United States in the Pacific, and each bit of bad news seemed to fan anti-Japan feelings in the region. Vociferous protests were launched over the placement of one of these camps, the Minidoka Relocation Center, in south-central Idaho, even though a major force in the placement of the camp was the need for laborers for the region's agricultural industry. Some of these protests came from the same farmers who would later benefit from the presence of the camps. Individual farmers and some organizations protested in part because they were uncertain of the impact of the camp on available water supplies for agriculture.

In a number of curious ways, the Minidoka Relocation Center's construction and placement operated against the local Nikkei. Many local employers and some farmers were upset that the construction of the camp would drain the local labor supply and drive up wages, which they would have to pay to get good employees. Others complained that the camp's operation, which depended in part on Caucasian "appointed personnel," might exacerbate the problem of shortages in critical areas. In fact, a number of local teachers and a local doctor went to work in the camp.

Anti-Japanese attitudes and actions increased with the building of the Minidoka camp.[38] Some of these actions did not affect a large number of people directly, but they demonstrated the strong attitudes present. In the election campaign of the fall of 1942, the opponent of the incumbent Twin Falls county treasurer placed a political advertisement in the local newspaper criticizing the incumbent for employing a young Japanese American woman in her office, claiming that the treasurer obviously did not understand the feelings of families of "boys who lost their lives at Pearl Harbor, Wake Island, Midway, Guam and [the] Solomon Islands..., when they have to walk into the county treasurer's office and pay their taxes to a Japanese." In response the treasurer pointed out that the young woman in question was an American citizen, a native of Twin Falls, and a recent honor graduate of the local high school. But this did not satisfy those who chose to make no distinction between Japanese in Japan and Americans of Japanese ancestry. The incumbent lost the election, and the employee in question was dismissed when the new treasurer took office.[39]

In the summer of 1943 the Twin Falls Kiwanis Club passed a resolution protesting against public use of "languages of countries with which the United States is at war." While the language of the resolution would seem to include the German and Italian languages, the only issue was the use of the Japanese language by individuals in town on passes from Minidoka. While the camp newspaper, the *Minidoka Irrigator,* issued a mild protest, it also printed a letter from an officer of the Magic Valley JACL. The writer of the letter acknowledged that some of the behaviors in question were from those of "nisei from other relocation camps, . . . it has been noted that a good many visitors from Hunt, including families, argue and talk in public. . . . There have been complaints of groups of niseis getting intoxicated and making scenes in public. It so happened that on the Saturday night our last officers meeting was held, the largest group of disgraceful drunks were out. After seeing with our own eyes these sights, hearing the course [*sic*] language being used, we feel something must be done about it. This small group is making our public relations work very difficult."[40] The same writer wrote again to the camp newspaper on this topic. He said a prominent local Caucasian businessman who complained about the continuation of this practice had contacted him. "He told me of seeing a group of niseis in an establishment conversing in Japanese. He knew they were able to speak English because they were talking to the proprietor. To some people it makes little difference but to others it serves to create unnecessary suspicion. The [Japanese] residents of Idaho have always realized the necessity of speaking in English. The Issei parents very seldom go out in public unless they would speak English, and when conversing among themselves they do so quietly. However, these people, both issei and nisei, from the relocation center, do not seem to realize that they are doing themselves harm, and making their positions increasingly difficult in the face of growing anti-Japanese sentiment in this state." He went on to write, "We must ask all loyal Japanese Americans to 'be Americans.'"[41]

One issue concerning wartime treatment of the Nikkei centers around their use as agricultural laborers. The enormous demand for farm workers had a lot to do with both the existence and the placement of the camps. Even before the large centers were open, imprisoned Nikkei were urged to leave the assembly centers to work in agricultural areas in the intermountain West. The first group to do so went from the North Portland Assembly Center to Malheur County in May 1942. This continued with the operation of the large permanent centers, and thousands more followed in the next two years.

The movement from the assembly centers to the large camps was essentially complete by late September 1942, just in time to meet the fall labor needs of the agricultural regions in which the camps were located. In the harvest season of 1942, Minidoka led the camps in numbers on seasonal leave, although most of the camps contributed.[42] In fact, in most respects, the contributions made by workers released from the camps went a long way toward created a climate of acceptance for the Nikkei. As one historian has noted, "the Nikkei received praise from nearly all quarters and were credited with saving the beet sugar crop in Idaho, Montana, Wyoming, and Utah."[43] Repeat performances in subsequent years earned a great deal of respect for Japanese Americans.

While the overall experiences of the Nikkei as farm workers were undoubtedly positive, in some instances the tactics of camp officials and employers often created bitterness on the part of workers. They often found that promises made to lure them from camp were not met. The complaints arose very early in the process and centered on poor living conditions, violations of the terms of contracts, and conflicts between workers and local people. This led JACL to dispatch a team of observers into the agricultural areas in October and November 1942 to report on conditions. They traveled throughout the sugar beet areas of the intermountain West, where they found the workers living mostly in Farm Security Administration camps and some living in tents. Their report observed that tents were "adequate for summer housing, but the tenants were not satisfied with them as late autumn domiciles. We found several laid up with colds and a number of women in rather depressed moods." They found it somewhat ironic that "having been accused so often of lowering the living standards on the Pacific coast, these workers were surprised to find quarters and basic facilities provided that even to them are intolerable."[44]

The report included observations on the conflict occasioned by the mixing of populations. In a discussion on this issue at a special JACL meeting in November, Mike Masaoka expressed a strong view on the matter. He believed that "many of these people [the workers] are not aware that the people of this area are not accustomed to seeing so many Japanese who smoke, and drink and conduct themselves in the manner so characteristic, shall we say, of certain Los Angeles elements which we all know."[45] Masaoka, who grew up in Salt Lake City, epitomized some of the cultural differences between the local Nikkei and those who had come from the West Coast, particularly those from urban areas.

One important area of conflict was between long-time Nikkei residents of the region and evacuee workers. An Idaho Falls farmer, Mr. Kasai, expressed the view that there had "been some hard feelings between the evacuee beet workers and our local fellows. The evacuee boys do not measure up to our standards and so the local farmers feel they are not receiving their money's worth. Most of the evacuees are more satisfied to work for Caucasians than for the Japanese."[46]

Some workers also felt pressured into doing agricultural work and felt that the pressure was often unfair. In an effort to encourage camp residents to go out to work in agriculture, camp officials, public officials, and agricultural interests made a specific plea to their "patriotism." An ad for recruiting workers placed in the *Minidoka Irrigator* by a sugar company made an explicit connection between the willingness to work in sugar beet farming and patriotism, calling it "an opportunity to produce more food for freedom, thereby helping America win the war and the peace to follow."[47]

An editorial in the Idaho Farm Labor Camp's *Rupert Laborer* made the connection even more explicit when it expressed the view that beet workers were "soldiers." According to the editor, Arita Ikegami, "The beet knife is your sword and the potato basket is your knapsack. . . . At last 'they' know you want to help; 'they' know you want to see the harvest through. . . . For no one compelled you to do this work. You asked; you even begged for the privilege that is now yours. THIS IS YOUR CHANCE TO DO FOR AMERICA!"[48]

In the discussion over the agricultural "survey" at the November 1942 special meeting of the JACL, an Idaho Free Zone farmer took the side of the employers over the workers. "If these people are to be ambassadors of good will, they should be careful of unjust demands because they will make the caucasian elements bitter and antagonistic. . . . The workers recruited for the beet fields should be men who really want to work and not those who want to go out and have a good time. . . . If we are going to show the American people that we really are going to help out in the labor shortage, we must go out with the idea of helping the war effort as patriotic Americans. We should think of other things than just earning money. We should think in terms of helping this country win this war."[49]

The cautious approach of JACL to the issues facing the Nikkei in this period was also evident in other discussions at the meeting. A delegate from Poston referred to some instances of Nikkei being refused rooms at a hotel in Boise and suggested that such treatment should be challenged. Mike Masaoka cautioned against this: "I wonder if such practices won't add to antagonisms and other measures which will be worse than the present type of prejudice. I know that in my travels it is not uncommon for me to be refused service or rooms, but I've always personally thought that it was better to forget the matter and go look for another place to eat or stay than to create a scene as it were."[50]

While the important contribution to Idaho agriculture the relocated people made brought about a greater degree of acceptance through the war years, this should not be overstated. With the exception of a few counties in the western part of the state, the relocated people did not tend to permanently settle in the state. In contrast, by 1950, both Malheur County in Oregon and Spokane County in Washington saw significant increases to their Nikkei populations over the 1940 figures. Malheur's 1,170 Nikkei accounted for about 5 percent of the total population in the county, and Spokane County's Nikkei population moved from 362 in 1940 to 1,171 in 1950. The counties in Idaho that saw the greatest increase between the two census years were Canyon and Washington, in the western part of the state, adjacent to Oregon. Canyon County grew from 149 to 413, and Washington County, with no Nikkei reported in 1940, had 163 Nikkei ten years later. Jerome County, the site of Minidoka, saw an increase of only one Nikkei in the ten years between censuses, and in Twin Falls County, where hundreds of workers from both Minidoka and the Twin Falls labor camp toiled during the war, the Nikkei population moved from 46 to 78.

Certainly the assistance and good will of Free Zone Nikkei helped make reestablishment in new places possible. But it should not be forgotten that whatever successes were achieved were not without difficulties along the way. The history of the actions of the Free Zone Nikkei created a heavy burden for some of the West Coast Nikkei. More than three decades after the war, there was occasional evidence of bitterness over this. In 1979, during the campaign for redress, a Seattle Nikkei noted that Seattle Japanese Americans "remember that the concentration camps might not have been built if Idaho Japanese Americans had not opposed the immigration of Seattleites from the coast."[51] Whether or not such a view is justified, it reveals the depth of feeling remembered years after the experience. Free Zone Nikkei were under considerable pressure to act exactly as they did even if they knew it was not the right thing to do. And some clearly thought that. Years after the war, an Ontario Nikkei confessed that he was "not too proud of some of the things that went through [his] . . . mind at that time. I never went out of my way to help anybody."[52]

Another area of "humiliation" recalled with some bitterness by some Seattle Japanese Americans was that of "being used as a source of cheap, forced labor in the same sugar beet fields of Idaho farmers who first turned us away."[53]

The bitterness was also reflected in the planning for a service in 1979 at the Minidoka site celebrating its placement on the National Register of Historic Places. As planning for the event proceeded, differences of opinion soon arose over how the site would be memorialized. Some of the former camp residents living in Seattle wanted to build a mock tower that would be burned as part of the service. In the words of one of the planners, the "purifying flames would help lay the past to rest without forgetting or easing the lessons of the internment experience."[54]

Idaho Nikkei had initiated the idea for the memorial and had worked with the Bureau of Reclamation, the agency controlling the site, to organize the event. The Idaho Nikkei refused to go along with the plan to burn a mock tower, essentially telling those in Seattle that if they wanted to do such a thing they would have to organize it on their own. An Idaho JACL member referred to the proposed tower burning as a "worthless publicity stunt that could damage the image of all Japanese Americans." There was nothing new in such caution. In denouncing the position of the Idaho Nikkei, one of those who had proposed the "tower burning" criticized them for their unreasonable fear of a white backlash, an attitude which reflected their position on related issues over three decades earlier.[55]

In speaking of the Nikkei experience in the Pacific Northwest, one would do well to avoid facile generalizations about the population as a whole. While many experiences of those throughout the region are similar, important distinctions mark the different groups. They were shaped by different forces and saw things in different lights. That Free Zone Nikkei had a different perspective on problems related to the removal and imprisonment of the West Coast Nikkei should not be a matter of surprise. What is less clear is just how far one can go in condemning any group for how they cope with a situation. Free Zone Nikkei acted in what they considered their best interests, even when they clashed with the interests of others. I prefer to think that fear and uncertainty also influenced their behavior, even when that behavior was nothing more than standing by and doing nothing. Recently I asked a Nikkei friend who was living near Nampa in the summer of 1942 if he had gone to the train station during the time of the transfer from North Portland to Minidoka. He told me, with great emotion, "I just didn't have the heart."

Notes

1. The term refers to persons of Japanese ancestry, whether aliens or American citizens.

2. Anonymous to Andrews, 24 August 1942, Emery E. Andrews Papers (Accession #1908), University of Washington Libraries, file folder 1–105. The inmates at Minidoka were comprised primarily of former Seattle and Portland residents who earlier had been placed in the Puyallup and North Portland assembly centers.

3. That zone was defined as the area lying to the west of the Cascade and Sierra Nevada Mountains in Washington, Oregon, and California and the southerly half of Arizona. Military Area 2 comprised the eastern halves of Washington, Oregon, and California.

4. Initially these involved farm workers, but when leave programs were expanded in 1943, it involved many other types of employment as well.

5. U.S. War Department, *Final Report: Japanese Evacuation from the West Coast, 1942* (Washington, D.C.: GPO, 1943), 111.

6. *Idaho Register* 10 November 1905, 3.

7. Oregon passed similar legislation in the same year, and Washington had done so in 1921 with an amendment in 1923 to align it more directly with that of California.

8. *Idaho Farmer*, 23 March 1922, 4.

9. *Idaho Statesman*, 22 February 1921, 5.

10. *1921 Idaho Session Laws,* Section 4596, Article I, Chapter 182.

11. *Japanese American Courier,* 12 May 1934, 4; 9 June 1934, 4; 11 May 1935, 4.

12. Ibid., 3 February 1934, 4; 4 May 1935, 3.

13. Ibid., 6 April 1935, 1.

14. *History of IDC-JACL, 1940–1965,* (n.p.; n.d.), 53.

15. *Japanese American Courier,* 24 December 1938, 4.

16. John deYoung, "Japanese Resettlement in the Boise Valley and Snake River Valley, Sept. 1946," Japanese American Evacuation and Resettlement Collection (JERS), W2.04, Bancroft Library, University of California, Berkeley, p. 6 (hereafter, JERS followed by file number).

17. Commission on the Wartime Relocation and Internment of Civilians (CWRIC), *Personal Justice Denied: Report of the Commission on Wartime Relocation and Internment of Civilians* (Washington, D.C.: GPO, 1982), 18.

18. *Idaho Daily Statesman,* 28 December 1941; 1 March 1942; 28 February 1942.

19. deYoung, JERS, W2.04, p. 27.

20. *Idaho Daily Statesman,* 19 February 1942, 1.

21. E. W. Rising to J. W. Crowe, Chairman, Pacific Island Workers Association, Boise, 23 February 1942. Idaho Reclamation Papers, Idaho Historical Society.

22. Laurie Mercier and Carole Simon-Smolinski, "Idaho's Ethnic Heritage," *Historical Overviews* 1 (March 1990), 83–84.

23. *Idaho Daily Statesman,* 10 December 1941.

24. J. L. Driscoll, Executive Vice President, First Security Bank Corporation, "To All Branch Managers," December 12, 1941.

25. *Twin Falls Times-News,* 15 March 1942, 5.

26. Wayne Yamamura, "Notes on Meeting With Idaho Falls JACL," unpublished typescript, 1976.

27. U.S. War Department, *Final Report,* 102.

28. "Survey of Public Opinion in Western States on Japanese Evacuation, Washington, May 18, 1942," JERS, A16.08, 14.

29. Ibid., 15.

30. Paul Okamura, President, Pocatello JACL, to Mike Masaoka, San Francisco, March 3, 1942, box 308, Pocatello JACL Papers, Japanese American Research Project, University of California, Los Angeles Library (hereafter, JARP).

31. *Idaho Daily Statesman,* 18 March 1942, 1.

32. Ibid., 27 March 1942, 6.

33. Paul Okamura to Chase Clark, Pocatello JACL Papers, JARP.

34. *Pocatello Tribune,* 17 March 1942.

35. *Salt Lake Tribune,* 21 November 1941, 10.

36. J. to Andrews, May 1942, Emery E. Andrews Papers, file folder 1–107.

37. U.S. War Department, *Final Report,* 50.

38. The camp was built on land controlled by the Bureau of Reclamation, approximately eighteen miles northeast of Twin Falls, the largest community in that region of the state.

39. *Twin Falls Times-News,* 28 October 1942, 3; 30 October 1942, 4.

40. *Minidoka Irrigator,* 19 June 1943, 4. Area residents also knew Minidoka as "Hunt." There was an existing town named Minidoka approximately thirty miles to the east of the camp; "Hunt" was the designated post-office address of the center.

41. Ibid., 18 December 1943, 2.

42. Robert C. Sims, "'You Don't Need to Wait Any Longer to Get Out': Japanese American Evacuees as Farm Laborers During World War II," *Idaho Yesterdays* 44 (summer 2000): 9.

43. Louis Fiset, "Thinning, Topping, and Loading: Japanese Americans and Beet Sugar in World War II," *Pacific Northwest Quarterly* 90, no. 3 (summer 1999), 134.

44. "Minutes," JACL Special Emergency Conference, November 17–24, 1942, Salt Lake City. Supplement #6, "Beet Field Survey," by G. F. Inagaki and Scotty H. Tsuchiya, box 13, James Y. Sakamoto Papers, Special Collections, Manuscripts, and University Archives Division, University of Washington Libraries (hereafter, Minutes).

45. Ibid., 98.

46. Ibid., 42.

47. *Minidoka Irrigator,* 6 March 1943, 6.

48. *The Rupert Laborer,* 14 November 1942, 3. The *Rupert Laborer* was published by the residents of the Rupert Farm Labor Camp, operated by the Farm Security Administration to house workers engaged in agricultural labor in the region. Although most of the residents were on seasonal leave from Minidoka, the camp contained Nikkei from other camps as well. It was located approximately thirty miles east of Minidoka.

49. Minutes, 57–58.

50. Ibid., 35.

51. Frank Abe, "Pride and Shame: Japanese Americans and the 38 Years' Journey to Justice," *Seattle Sun,* 5 December 1979, 2.

52. J. S., Ontario, Oreg., 4–3–71, University of Washington Library, Special Collections, Tape 216.

53. Abe, "Pride and Shame," 2.

54. Ibid.

55. Ibid.

12 / LESSONS IN CITIZENSHIP, 1945–1949

The Delayed Return of the Japanese to Canada's Pacific Coast

PATRICIA E. ROY

I n the fall of 1945, police in Vancouver, British Columbia, charged John Fow Lung with breaking and entering. They determined that he was really Akhide Otsuji, an eighteen-year-old Japanese Canadian who had been living in the city for about a year. He also pled guilty to a second charge, that "as a Japanese, he unlawfully returned to the protected area." The prosecutor recommended a six-month sentence to ensure that all Japanese realized the penalty for coming to the coast without permission.[1] The sentence may have deterred others, but Otsuji went to jail again for the same offense three years later. In 1945 no one had publicly defended him; in 1948 two Vancouver *Sun* columnists protested. Jack Scott suggested that the order-in-council that kept citizens from moving freely about the country was "every bit as such rank discrimination and hate-breeding as any of those unwritten laws of America's deep south"; Elmore Philpott noted that American Japanese had successfully resettled on the coast for several years but that "this great Christian country—Canada—sends one of its own men to jail for a year for pretending his grandfather was Chinese and not Japanese."[2] Until April 1, 1949, Japanese Canadians could not go within a hundred miles of the coast without a police permit.

The postwar debate about the rights of Japanese residents intertwined with the debate about the Canadian Citizenship Act of 1947, which for the first time identified Canadians as citizens of Canada and not just British subjects. Discussions about the meaning of citizenship and about the effects of the U.S. Constitution—albeit misunderstood—on the wartime treatment of Japanese Americans helped raise public awareness of the failure of the new citizenship law to address civil rights. The discussions did not, however, seem to influence federal political leaders or British Columbia Members of Parliament (MPs, elected members of the House of Commons). In this instance, contrary to traditional lore, national leaders heeded the province's MPs, whose advice was in harmony with their prejudices. Unfortunately, neither group realized that Japanophobia was fading. The delayed return of the Japanese to the coast was caused more by the atavistic ideas of federal politicians than by popular opinion in British Columbia.

Within hours of the Japanese attack on Pearl Harbor, the Canadian government made Japanese Canadian fishermen surrender their boats, imposed a curfew, and encouraged Japanese language schools and newspapers to close. In early January 1942, it announced that it would move male Japanese nationals of military age inland to work on road construction, but its slowness in doing so, combined with Japan's military successes, stimulated British Columbians' long-standing antipathies to local Japanese as well as fears of sabotage. In late February, responding to public pressure from British Columbia and warnings of possible anti-Japanese riots, the government declared that no Japanese could remain within a hundred miles of the Pacific coast. This edict meant that approximately 22,000 people, more than 90 percent of Canada's Japanese population, had to move. The federal government set up a civilian agency, the British Columbia Security Commission, to supervise the move.[3] By the end of October, the commission had placed about 4,000 Canadians of Japanese ancestry east of the Rockies. The remainder stayed in B.C.: about two thousand moved on their own initiative, mainly to self-supporting settlements where they had minimal supervision; 1,500 men were sent to road-building camps; the majority were relocated to former mining towns in the interior, where old buildings were rehabilitated or small cabins hastily built to house them. Residents required police permission to leave, but mountains and a paucity of roads effectively curbed movement.[4]

Both Canadian and American governments had hoped that wartime relocation would break up concentrated settlements of Japanese and scatter them throughout their respective nations. But few Japanese Canadians accepted jobs in eastern Canada during the war, despite official encouragement to do so. In August 1944, Prime Minister W. L. Mackenzie King announced a policy of repatriation and dispersal: Japanese Canadians must "repatriate" to Japan after the war, that is, accept deportation, or move east of the Rocky Mountains. In contrast, since that spring, the U.S. Western Defense Command had let a few Japanese return to the Pacific Coast "to test public reception."[5] Then, in December 1944, after the presidential election and anticipating that a Supreme Court ruling might lead to their unrestricted movement, the army announced that Japanese whose loyalty had been determined were free to go back to the coast as of January 2. The approximately 1,300 who did so by April were the targets of scattered violence, intimidation, and economic boycotts, particularly in rural California, Washington, and Oregon. In Washington State, Governor Monrad Wallgren and Senator Warren G. Magnuson opposed lifting the ban until the war ended. So did Governor Earl Warren of California, who feared anti-Japanese "civil disturbances"; but in late 1944, he urged residents of his state to permit an "orderly return of evacuees."[6]

As in Canada, civil libertarians and church groups helped defuse the situation. By the end of the Pacific War in August 1945, hostile incidents had almost disappeared except in such pockets of resistance as Hood River, Oregon. By January 1946, about half of the Japanese Americans evacuated from the West Coast were back.[7] A Vancouver *Sun* reporter saw them walking "freely about the streets" in Seattle, where "white people appear to pay little, if any attention to them." In May 1946, Humphrey Mitchell, Canada's labor minister, informed his cabinet colleague Ian Mackenzie of Vancouver, the minister of veterans affairs, that the American public had been "friendly" to returnees and that "the few irresponsible individuals who attempted to stir up trouble were quietly repressed."[8]

Canadian officials thought they were well informed on events south of the border, but they knew that the U.S. situation was different from their own. In the United States, not all Japanese property left behind during wartime relocation was sold; in Canada, the government disposed of real property and such capital goods as fishing boats and motor vehicles, often at fire-sale prices. Moreover, the United States clearly distinguished between the American born and immigrants; Canada did not. For example, in the U.S., Japanese immigrants could not become American citizens, and several states would not let aliens ineligible to citizenship own or lease land; in Canada, many Japanese immigrants became naturalized in order to secure commercial fishing licenses, and there were no restrictions on landholding. For the Nisei, the second generation, the situation was reversed. In the U.S., Nisei had the same political rights as other American citizens; in British Columbia, they lacked such a basic right as the federal or provincial franchise.[9] Arthur MacNamara, a federal Department of Labour official, thought that the Japanese south of the border were more "thoroughly Americanized" than their northern counterparts were "Canadianized." Precisely what he meant he did not explain. Finally, Canadians knew that, even though citizenship had not protected Americans of Japanese ancestry, the rights of citizenship in the United States were more clearly laid out constitutionally and in the public mind than in Canada.[10]

While loyal Japanese Americans were resettling in West Coast communities, their Canadian counterparts could only visit the coast for specific purposes, such as specialized medical treatment, and with permission from the Royal Canadian Mounted Police (RCMP). In time, more exceptions were made; for example, a high school soccer player from the Okanagan came to Vancouver for a tournament in 1948, though he told a *Sun* reporter that it gave him a "funny feeling." A young man being ordained in the United Church and his parents were permitted to attend the ceremony in Vancouver in 1947. The appearance of a few Japanese conducting business matters caused little excitement (except in Duncan, where the arrival of one worried the Chinese community). By April 1948, representatives of the Japanese Canadian Citizens Association (JCCA) were so confident of their acceptance that they went to Victoria to seek the provincial franchise.[11] Such visits to the coast were newsworthy, but the lack of comment suggests that they did not arouse antagonism. No newspaper reported on fifteen Nisei who attended the University of British Columbia in the fall of 1948.

The only other Japanese Canadians allowed on the coast were sixty-two Nisei who had enlisted in the Canadian army late in the war to assist British forces in Asia as translators and interpreters. Their training included time at the Japanese Language School in Vancouver. Given concern about public reaction, there was no publicity, and they were encouraged to keep a low profile. When the school moved to West Vancouver in November 1945, despite some agitation fomented by James Sinclair, a Liberal MP, some residents were friendly, and most, indifferent. Prior to the recruitment of the sixty-two, fears that military service would lead to demands for enfranchisement and concerns about mixing Asian and white soldiers—there were not enough Nisei to form a distinct unit—meant that the Canadian armed forces had admitted few Japanese. In the United States, the well-publicized heroics of Nisei army units in Europe helped dispel uncertainties about their loyalty. In retrospect, F. J. Mead of the RCMP thought that enlisting Nisei in the armed forces would have improved both their image in the white community and Japanese morale.[12]

Although Nisei soldiers demonstrated their loyalty to Canada, military service brought no benefits to them or to Japanese veterans of World War I. In the spring of 1946 several men who had served in that earlier conflict were denied permission to return to the coast lest they be "victims of violence."[13] That ruling was made on the advice of Ian Mackenzie. When other veterans sought to return, Mitchell, the labor minister, warned that refusing them might create a legal case and "a good deal of public comment." Nevertheless, he yielded when Mackenzie threatened to resign from the cabinet if any Japanese went to the coast.[14] When the Japanese widow of a Canadian soldier killed in the First World War and her son applied to settle there, civil servants rejected their request. Mackenzie and other British Columbia Liberal MPs remained firm. In the spring of 1947, they opposed the request of a distinguished soldier, S. A. Cato, to settle in the Fraser Valley; they feared that Cato would "be the beginning of a return to the Coast of all Japanese." Despite pressure from Mitchell, the Canadian Legion, and even Cecil Merritt, a war hero and Conservative MP from Vancouver, Mackenzie claimed that "antagonistic feeling from a very large section of the public" would "militate against [Cato's] successful rehabilitation."[15]

Similarly, when Sgt. T. Buck Suzuki, who had "served with distinction" in Malaya, asked to enter the British Columbia fishery in the spring of 1947, he learned that the 1942 order denying fishing licenses to Japanese was still in effect. He had support from prominent members of the left-wing Cooperative Commonwealth Federation (CCF) party, including Premier T. C. Douglas of Saskatchewan, but Tom Reid, the Liberal MP for New Westminster, opposed changing the wartime law. Morris Shumiatcher, a Saskatchewan government lawyer who lobbied Howard Green, the Conservative MP for the Vancouver South riding, on Suzuki's behalf, found that Green was "letting his prejudices and his political aspirations run away with his rationality." At times, a discouraged Suzuki wished he "hadn't served at all in the Armed Forces because it seems so much as if I'm using my service in the Army for bargaining for special privileges."[16]

In reporting how the United States welcomed home bemedaled Japanese veterans, whereas Canada had only "smuggled" a few Nisei into the army as linguists, the liberally inclined Vancouver *News-Herald* observed, "All this makes thinking people wonder how it is that Canada and the United States look differently on citizenship. In a new world, drawn from all races, birth should give the first right of citizenship, no matter what the color of the skin."[17]

The concept of Canadian citizenship was confusing; in law, it did not exist. Canadian nationals were simply British subjects, but as nationalism increased during and after the war, they wanted to establish their own legal identity. As the *Victoria Daily Colonist* put it, "Canada should be in a position to say what a Canadian is."[18] Recognizing growing nationalism and the practical need to define "the fundamental status upon which the rights and privileges of Canadians will depend," the federal government introduced a citizenship bill in April 1946. The measure, however, dealt only with legal definitions of nationality and said nothing about the rights and privileges of citizenship.[19]

In presenting the bill, Paul Martin, secretary of state, referred to European but not Asian immigrants. When questioned, he rightly noted that it had nothing to do with the Japanese question. British Columbia MPs, however, used the debate to honor election promises to oppose the return of the Japanese. During the June 1945 federal election campaign, British Columbia candidates had widely assumed that repatriation and dispersal meant exclusion of Japanese from the province. Speaking as a Conservative, Green summarized the parties' policies: "Our stand is, and always has been, that we won't have Japs in the province. The Liberal policy is to scatter them: the C.C.F. want to scatter them and give them the vote."[20] What Green said about the Liberal policy of scattering was true nationally, but local Liberals such as Reid favored sending *all* Japanese to Japan. Mackenzie, who had long advocated "No Japanese from the Rockies to the sea," wanted to retain the fisheries and farms "for our gallant men who fought at Ortona, at Caen, at Falaise."[21] Liberals and Conservatives claimed that the CCF would return the Japanese to the West Coast, and some Liberals hoped that the CCF position on "the Jap issue" would effectively eliminate it from British Columbia politics.[22] In fact, the CCF advertised itself as "the only party with a policy which will prevent a mass return to the coast."[23] It won five seats, four more than it had had. Three of them, however, were in the interior, where attitudes toward the Japanese often differed from those on the coast.[24]

The 1945 election results gave British Columbia MPs a mandate to fight against the return of the Japanese. In the debate on the citizenship bill, they reiterated shibboleths about Japanese unassimilability and doubtful loyalty to Canada (indeed, some Canadian-born Japanese had registered with the Japanese consulate before the war, and a few had served in Japan's military forces). So insistent were members' demands that the Japanese leave the province that Angus MacInnis (CCF, Vancouver East), his party's chief spokesman on the issue, accused them of discussing a "perpetual racial discrimination act." But even MacInnis, who favored Japanese rights, referred to "the menace of their return."[25]

The citizenship bill promised to give Canadians a legal identity but did not specify what rights ensued from that status. British Columbia MPs feared that the law would grant all Canadians the right to live wherever they wished in the country. That would make dispersal unenforceable. George Cruick-shank, a Liberal from the Fraser Valley, asked, "How can you give all the rights of citizenship to a man when you tell him what province or what municipality he shall live in?" E. Davie Fulton (Progressive Conservative, Kamloops), though disagreeing with the decision to let the Japanese remain in B.C., conceded that if they were fit to become Canadian citizens they must have all of the rights of citizenship. He reconciled his support of antithetical positions by erroneously assuming that none of the deportees were Canadian citizens. Another Progressive Conservative, George Pearkes (Nanaimo), proposed to resolve the perplexities in the principle that "Canadian citizens must live somewhere and not be allowed to live elsewhere" by advising all Japanese to go to Japan as soon as possible "whether you were born there or not." The chairman, however, ruled out of order a motion by J. L. Gibson (Independent, Comox-Alberni) to amend the citizenship bill so that persons of Japanese ancestry could not reside in the coastal security zone for at least twenty years.[26]

The virtually unanimous front of the British Columbia MPs had some effect in Ottawa. While denying that he knew anything about the Japanese, the justice minister Louis St. Laurent accepted their arguments. "Human nature," he said,

> is such that you cannot in an instant make it over; and it is difficult to conceive that a group of persons of the Japanese race, known as our hon. friends from British Columbia who have lived alongside of them say they know them, can become part of a united community here which would respect to the letter every title of this undertaking we have pledged ourselves to carry out under the terms of the charter of the united nations.

The secretary of state, Martin, had already heeded the complaints and amended the bill to ensure that it would not affect the deportation orders. The measure passed the House of Commons in May 1946 and the Senate a short time later.[27]

When Green earlier warned that the new law might prevent deportation of the Japanese, the *Victoria Daily Colonist* claimed that he spoke for the majority of British Columbians.[28] That was not accurate. Many British Columbians believed that if Canadian citizenship were to be worth anything, Canadian-born Japanese must have rights. A columnist in the *Western Miner,* a trade magazine, asked in the fall of 1945, "Is it possible to tell a Canadian citizen that he can inhabit one part of his own country and not another?"

The editors of the *Vancouver Daily Province* noted that to be regarded as a nation Canada must wipe out such racial distinctions as the disfranchisement of Asians in B.C.; the federal government must ensure that "a Canadian is a Canadian however he has acquired his citizenship" and that he has exactly the same rights, privileges, and duties as every other Canadian.[29] Bruce Hutchison, a prominent journalist, warned that if government got "the power to say where any Canadian shall live, then no Canadian will ever be safe again." He called for a bill of rights to preserve liberties.[30] On December 3, 1946, the *Vancouver Daily Province* made a similar argument. A few months later, the Vancouver branch of the Canadian Civil Liberties Union rued "the anomaly of a citizenship that can be arbitrarily stripped of its rights," an anomaly that "did much to take the lustre from the recent ceremonies that accompanied the conferring of Canadian citizenship."[31] Dr. George Ishiwara, president of the JCCA, asked why British Columbia should be the only province not to uphold the new Citizenship Act and let Japanese citizens move freely throughout the province.[32]

Coincidentally, on January 24, 1947, a few weeks after the Citizenship Act came into effect, Prime Minister King yielded to pressure from churches, especially the United Church, and civil liberties groups throughout Canada, including British Columbia, and announced cancellation of the repatriation program even though the courts ruled the policy valid. Few British Columbians objected so long as the Japanese continued to disperse and did not return to the coast. Acting on the advice of civil servants and, no doubt, drawing on his own experience, King retained the wartime restrictions on the movement of Japanese residents—these were necessary, he said, to maintain law and order and ensure successful resettlement. Effective April 14, 1947, the government lifted all travel restrictions on Japanese outside British Columbia.[33]

Although dispersal was largely complete by January 1947, and only 6,776 Japanese remained in the province,[34] British Columbia MPs pursued the old line. In April, when the House of Commons debated continuation of the Emergency Powers Bill, which authorized controls on the movement of Japanese Canadians, Ian Mackenzie warned that interfering with B.C.'s wishes concerning the security of its coastline would strike "a mortal blow at the very heart and soul of Confederation." No one questioned dispersal. Apart from CCF-ers who called for full citizenship rights for Japanese Canadians, the British Columbia MPs differed only in details as they insisted that the ban be extended for a further period.[35]

Liberal and Conservative MPs, recognizing that racism was no longer fashionable, denied it as a motivation but rehashed ancient allegations of Japanese unassimilability, "unfair competition" especially in the fisheries, and immigration that would overwhelm the province. They repeated stories about Japanese spies and reminded Parliament of atrocities committed by Japanese soldiers like the infamous Kamloops Kid, who, though Canadian born, fought for Japan and was especially cruel to Canadian prisoners of war in Hong Kong. Despite the thoroughness of its military defeat, Reid claimed that Japan, when it rose again, would find Canada's Japanese useful "because they will all be back in British Columbia once the restrictions are removed."[36] Without any supporting evidence, some British Columbia MPs warned of violence if the Japanese returned to the coast. Green predicted bloodshed if they reentered the fisheries. In the Senate, S. S. McKeen (Liberal, Vancouver) also suggested that there might be riots. His colleague Senator J. W. de B. Farris (Liberal, Vancouver) agreed.[37] The coastal security zone into which Japanese could not enter without permission remained.

The MPs were guided by their own entrenched ideas and by such advice from home as they selected.[38] Editorials in the *Sun* and the *Daily Colonist* had criticized some eastern newspapers as "holier-than-thou's" for accusing British Columbians of racism while not accepting their share of the "burden" and not understanding the problem.[39] In addition, the provincial attorney general, G. S. Wismer, had privately remarked that the absence of legislation to prevent the Japanese from returning to British Columbia en bloc was "a most serious situation." Wismer's predecessor, R. L. Maitland, had told the Supreme Court of Canada that as late as 1946 British Columbians still sensed "a very great deal of emergency regarding the Japanese" and that the Japanese who had signed for repatriation "might well be a menace to the country."[40] Those doubts about the loyalty of Canadian Japanese explained much prewar hostility and persisted even after Japan's defeat. Early in 1946, the Surrey *Leader,* a weekly published in Reid's riding, had said that a Japanese person, "whether born in Yokohama or Surrey, is still proudly Japanese and even conscious of his race's divine destiny."[41]

Dissatisfied with the order-in-council that excluded all Japanese from west of the Rockies, Vancouver Centre Liberals called for a permanent statutory exclusion; updating an old argument, they warned of "unfair competition with our War Veterans and other residents on the Pacific Coast."[42] Similarly, the Lower Mainland Council of the Army and Navy Veterans in Canada demanded permanent dispersal of the Japanese so they would not return en masse to "menace . . . labour" again.[43] The provincial convention of the Canadian Legion and some Progressive Conservative associations also opposed the Japanese return.[44] Even those sympathetic to Japanese Canadians—including some Japanese Canadians—agreed that "a few Japanese in a community might be regarded as an asset" but "concentration" could pose a threat.[45] The British Columbians who signed dozens of petitions in the spring and summer of 1946 for the lifting of restrictions on "Canadian Residents of Japanese Ancestral Stock Who Are Not Subject to Deportation" said that "for the time being" it might be advisable to retain some control over the return of evacuees to the coast.[46]

By the end of 1946, however, opinion was shifting. Some previous critics moderated their views. For example, in January 1947, the Langley *Advance*, a weekly in Reid's riding that had earlier questioned the loyalty of any Japanese to Canada, favored extending "Canadian courtesy and hospitality" to any who desired "to become a good citizen" and accepted the accompanying responsibilities. Likewise, the New Westminster *British Columbian*, highly skeptical in January 1946, in December said, "The emergency that uprooted coast Japs is over; it would be impossible to justify continuance of special restrictions now." By the spring of 1947, the *Sun* columnist Jack Scott noted, "The hatred of some of our white citizens against our brown citizens has cooled into apathy."[47] Even a spokesman for the Native Sons of Canada conceded that the Japanese would "become citizens too when the emergency powers bill goes." "I suppose," he ruminated, "there's nothing to prevent them coming back."[48]

In April 1947, when Parliament voted to extend the restrictions on the movement of the Japanese for at least another year, the *British Columbian* accepted the decision but argued, "If a Japanese is entitled to be in Canada at all he is entitled to choose his own location in Canada." The *News-Herald* sharply criticized Ottawa's "pandering to the race-baiting politicians of the province." Hutchison, writing in the Winnipeg *Free Press*, suggested that Ian Mackenzie and a number of British Columbia Liberal and Conservative MPs had "blackmailed" Parliament and deliberately written "sheer racialism, the doctrines of Hitler . . . into the laws of Canada."[49]

Since the extensions were made a year at a time, the cabinet considered them again early in 1948 shortly after Prime Minister King appointed Mackenzie to the Senate.[50] That move forced a by-election in Mackenzie's riding, Vancouver Centre, for his seat in the House of Commons. A few days before the cabinet discussed the Japanese question, British Columbia's new premier, Byron Johnson, like King a Liberal, warned the prime minister that repealing restrictions on Japanese movement to the coast would cost the Liberals the seat. Ralph Campney, the Liberal candidate, and the province's Liberal MPs echoed those views. Despite protests from some members, the cabinet accepted King's argument that a government that let itself be defeated would be condemned. The Liberal MPs agreed to extend the orders-in-council restricting the Japanese for another year after King, referring to the pending by-election, asked if the party wanted to protect "the minority constituted by the handful of Japanese, or . . . the minority constituted by the entire population of B.C."[51] Thus, the King government asked Parliament to extend the orders "to insure stability for resettlement elsewhere in Canada" lest the return of even a few Japanese "resurrect racial issues and animosities" that could otherwise disappear.[52] The extension was for one final year. In explaining the delay in letting the Japanese return to the coast, Humphrey Mitchell credited Canada's "evolutionary way" with sparing them "the inconveniences . . . that occurred in the United States, and the bitterness re-engendered in some of the cities on the west coast."[53] He offered no evidence of such bitterness.

Few British Columbia MPs spoke in the relatively brief debate, but they appreciated that opinions were changing. Citing public disapproval of the provincial government's recent attempt to deny Japanese Canadians employment on Crown timberlands, MacInnis tried to disabuse the federal government of its "assumption . . . that there is a tremendous race prejudice in British Columbia against the Japanese." Pearkes, who had told the press that the Japanese should eventually be allowed to return, reported that bitterness was fading; nonetheless he favored an extension of restrictions in order to prevent "crimes of revenge." And, while regurgitating old arguments, Reid said that a year's delay could allay remaining strong feelings and benefit the Japanese.[54] Civil libertarians, on the other hand, were dismayed and complained that continuing to bar the Japanese from the coast contradicted the principle of the Citizenship Act, but the extension of the restrictions aroused little comment in British Columbia, even in the by-election.[55]

A few diehards still tried to stop the inevitable. The *North Shore Press* demanded, for safety's sake, an indefinite ban on the return of the Japanese; some people still doubted their loyalty. The board of trade in Maple Ridge, a rural area that had been home to a number of Japanese berry farmers and lumber workers, unanimously warned of "serious friction" if the government did not "prevent a return to the undesirable state of affairs existing in Japanese infested districts pre-war." Alleging that Japanese had congregated in small areas, worked for lower wages than whites, and were socially unassimilable, the board circulated its resolution.[56] After a "heated" debate, the Associated Boards of Trade of the Fraser Valley and Lower Mainland rejected the Maple Ridge forecast of friction.[57] The Maple Ridge resolution reflected fear of economic competition. But the fishing and lumbering industries indicated how opinion was changing.

Despite widespread beliefs that Japanese Canadian fishermen had been spies ready to assist landing Japanese troops, the main argument against their return was concern that they would again dominate the industry. Even Elmore Philpott noted in 1945 how Japanese "ganged up" on competitors, particularly British Columbia Indians. The postwar industry was overcrowded: veterans were entering it, and new technology let fewer fishermen catch more fish.[58] In a somewhat ambiguous speech in 1947, H. G. Archibald, a CCF MP whose Skeena riding had included many Japanese fishermen, hinted at violence if they returned.[59] Prince Rupert Liberals, however, had already found that not all fishermen opposed their return. In the 1945 provincial election, supporters of the former premier T. D. Pattullo, who was campaigning as an Independent, had tried to use CCF statements "in favour of no restrictions on Japanese" against the CCF, but 80 percent of the fishermen voted for that party's candidate anyway.[60]

Some native fishermen and some locals of the United Fishermen and Allied Workers Union (UFAWU), which represented both fishermen and shore workers, wanted total exclusion of Japanese from the fisheries.[61] The communist leaders of the organization favored bringing "everybody in the industry into the union so we'd have bargaining power," but as late as 1948, members' opinions ranged "from extreme anti-Japanese discrimination to that of complete co-operation, harmony and treatment of Japanese-Canadians as equals and as brother workers."[62] As restrictions against the Japanese were about to lapse in 1949, representatives of the JCCA approached the UFAWU. George Tanaka of the JCCA advised Japanese fishermen to join the union and disperse along the coast. After a lively discussion in which Tanaka refuted allegations about Japanese dual citizenship and acceptance of lower wages, the 1949 UFAWU convention unanimously decided to organize Japanese fishermen.[63] Not all white fishermen approved, and gangs briefly engaged in "terrorist tactics" against the few Japanese who entered the industry that year. But in Steveston at least, fishermen voted 67 to 7 against any discrimination by race, color, or political opinion. The vote indicated that most fishermen would work with their Japanese counterparts.[64]

Change also came in the lumber industry. After the International Woodworkers of America (IWA) district council endorsed dispersal at its January 1945 convention, its communist leaders began organizing Japanese workers in the interior. When coastal members complained, the leaders explained that such organization was in line with "trade union principles, the CIO program and democracy as a whole" and necessary to prevent the Japanese from undercutting the standard of living of other workers.[65] That year, interior locals asked Ottawa to give loyal Japanese full citizenship rights, including the right to vote and work in British Columbia; by early 1948, the provincial IWA convention urged "an immediate and effective removal of each and every restriction against Canadian citizens of Japanese ancestry" as "repugnant to every conception of Canadian citizenship and to the principles of the United Nations Charter."[66]

More indicative of changing opinion was reaction to the provincial government's decision to reinstate its 1902 ban on the employment of Japanese on Crown timberlands. During the wartime labor shortage, the federal government had suspended provincial regulations so that some eight hundred relocated Japanese could work in interior logging and sawmill operations. In January 1948, almost a year after the federal order-in-council expired, E. T. Kenney, provincial minister of lands and forests, announced the restoration of the prewar law effective April 1. Public response revealed that most British Columbians were "not the blindly rabid Jap-haters they have been made to appear."[67] The *Province* called reinstatement "a ruling to make Canadians blush" that violated "the principles of equality which the Citizenship Act seeks to establish" and demonstrated the need for a Canadian bill of rights.[68] More significant, many longtime opponents of the Japanese made similar arguments. On January 28, 1948, the *Sun* complained of "deplorable discrimination" and suggested that the province's six thousand Japanese could be absorbed into its "fast-expanding economy" if they diversified their occupations. Until racist policy is abandoned, "British Columbia will be shamed in the eyes of the whole Dominion." The Victoria *Times* asked if Canada could "risk the hazards of maintaining a second-class citizenship for a minority."[69]

The provincial cabinet quickly realized that public sentiment had changed and decided to consult the legislature before reinstating the ban. But the lawmakers, who regarded the Japanese as a federal responsibility,[70] lifted barriers to employment on Crown lands only in the interior and rejected the call of the CCF leader Harold Winch to remove all restrictions and enfranchise the Japanese. Kenney claimed that giving "the Japs full rights . . . would be a detriment to our own people"; two CCF legislators, Sam Guthrie and Herbert Gargrave, went against Winch and stubbornly insisted that fishermen and miners did not want the Japanese back.[71]

On their part, the Japanese exhibited no great desire to return to the coast.

George Ishiwara of the JCCA told the *News-Herald* that laws banning the Japanese from the coast were unnecessary because they did not want to return. Most exiles had made, or were making, new—sometimes better— lives in the East. A *Sun* photo story on October 4, 1947, showed former British Columbia residents who had established successful businesses in Toronto. Six months later, Tanaka told the *Sun* that Ontario had become a land of opportunity for Japanese who had entered the professions; in B.C., even those with professional qualifications had been largely confined to unskilled work. Only for individuals "not satisfactorily resettled" was returning to the coast attractive.[72] The *New Canadian*, the Japanese Canadian newspaper published in Toronto, had warned early in 1947 that the advantages of the coast were more imagined than real, that the physical climate might be better, but that "deep-rooted discrimination" remained. According to a survey it conducted that year, 80 percent of the evacuees said they would not return to the coast, and those who went there on business "came back with the feeling they just hate the place."[73] Spokesmen for Japanese Canadians stressed the difficulty of reestablishment: their prewar property had been sold, the proceeds spent on living inland, and the cost of new capital goods such as fishing boats was high. Moreover, people in the interior and east of the Rockies were "more friendly than on the coast."[74] Thus, many Japanese campaigned to return to the coast simply to protest a "shameful curtailment of civil liberties" and a law that was contrary "to democratic principles and the precepts of Canadian citizenship."[75]

British Columbia's Japanese residents also lacked another basic right of citizenship, the right to vote. Early in 1947, the legislature readily enfranchised Chinese and East Indians and considered doing the same for the Japanese. Of the groups appearing before the Elections Act Committee in the fall of 1946, only the Japanese Repatriation League, a short-lived group, opposed it. However, after a "bitter argument" within the committee, the chairman cast the deciding vote against recommending letting the Japanese vote.[76] Three legislators (two CCF-ers and W. T. Straith, a Coalition member for Victoria) opposed racial discrimination in the Elections Act. The debate was lively but brief. CCF members described the government's stand as "unchristian, contrary to the Atlantic Charter, Yalta agreement, and Canadian citizenship," but this view did not prevail.[77] The Coalition government denied the franchise to the Japanese. A year later, a legislative committee rejected another CCF proposal to drop racial bars to the franchise.[78]

Then, without debate, in June 1948 the House of Commons amended the federal Elections Act to make "Canadian citizens who are of Japanese race . . . eligible to vote."[79] On June 17, even the *Victoria Daily Colonist* admitted "a Gilbertian situation" if the Japanese could vote federally but not provincially. The gate was open. Some months later, despite protests from Halford Wilson, an alderman who had led the prewar anti-Japanese movement in Vancouver, that "it would be an excuse for the Dominion Government to lift the restrictions banning them from the Pacific coast," the Vancouver City Council extended the municipal franchise to all Asians, including Japanese.[80] In the spring of 1949, the legislature enfranchised the Japanese in other municipalities, and Premier Johnson himself introduced an amendment to the Elections Act to let them vote provincially.[81]

For many observers, this was the last chapter of the wartime story of the Japanese in British Columbia. Even a hostile columnist in the *North Shore Press* commented on the calm reaction to enfranchisement and the pending return of the Japanese to the coast. As the *Sun* observed,

> In the leavening process of a few years, both sides have learned something. . . . The Japanese themselves are scattered all across Canada, instead of being congested in a special area around Vancouver. They are willing and anxious to be Canadian, owing this country first loyalty. We shall do well to accept their resolve at its face value and to remove all obstacles from their path to citizenship.[82]

Yet so few Japanese Canadians came to the coast in 1949 that reporters complained that they could not find any to interview.[83] Two years later, only 2,642 people of Japanese origin lived in census districts that roughly encompassed the defense zone; and most, 2,245, were in the lower mainland and Fraser Valley.[84] In the meantime, the public seemed uninterested. When British Columbians went to the polls for both provincial and federal elections in June 1949, the Japanese were voters, not subjects of debate.

Thus, dispersal seems to have solved British Columbia's "Japanese problem." In 1945 and 1946, except for people who advocated the deportation of *all* Japanese, no one had challenged the wisdom of dispersal. But in 1947 the government canceled its repatriation policy, and most Japanese Canadians had left the coast. Why did the ban survive for another two years?

A simple answer is what Hutchison described as "one of the most successful feats of political blackmail in our history," namely, Ian Mackenzie's persuading the cabinet that coastal British Columbians were not ready to accept the Japanese.[85] Mackenzie is an easy target because he was outspoken and the only British Columbian in the cabinet, and he had the support of provincial Liberal and Conservative MPs led by Tom Reid and Howard Green. Some cabinet colleagues shared his prejudices.

In contrast, by 1947 British Columbia church groups, civil liberties organizations, and the JCCA were urging the government to lift the restrictions on the Japanese. No one suggested a mass return, but most of these civil libertarians stressed citizenship rights in a democracy. The Social Service Committee of the Convention of Baptist Churches, for example, called the restrictions a "violation of democratic principles."[86] Two communist-led unions, the UFAWU and IWA, endorsed the return of the Japanese. In 1948 the Student Liberal Club at the University of British Columbia reminded federal and provincial Liberals that by supporting restrictions on the Japanese they were "in danger of lending a factual basis to the claims of the CCF and the Labour Progressive party [a Communist party], that the 'Left' alone is the true and only protector of minorities."[87] That was not quite true. Although many civil libertarians had links with the CCF, the *Province* was independent, and the *British Columbian* was owned and sometimes edited by members of a prominent Conservative family. Young Conservatives in Vancouver-Burrard called for "unrestricted movement" of the Japanese in Canada.[88] And although the *Sun* opposed the Japanese editorially, its columnists Philpott and Scott favored easing restrictions, and Hutchison, an occasional contributor, called for making Japanese Canadians full Canadian citizens.

In defense of the MPs, messages from B.C. were mixed. In April 1947, the *Victoria Daily Colonist* claimed that "British Columbia will require time to erase the memory of a danger that seemed real enough to its citizens," but the *News-Herald* described continued restrictions on the Japanese as mere "pandering to the race-baiting politicians of the province."[89] Scott wrote of apathy on the Japanese question in 1947 but in early 1948 suggested that hostility "under the surface" could "flare up" if there were a mass return. The man in the street, he said, had a paradoxical attitude of wanting to give minorities full citizenship rights but not wanting "those Japs" back.[90] The misfortune was that, as Muriel Kitagawa, a Nisei, wrote, "far too many" MPs relied on information provided by "the avowed racists from B.C. . . . . The MPs seem to prefer believing the worst, and that worst is but a thin cover for personal prejudices."[91] Liberal and Conservative MPs seemed blind to changes in the province. Wartime prosperity continued into the postwar era with only minor interruptions. The total population grew from 817,861 in 1941 to 1,165,210 in 1951; and about 14 percent of that was due to migration from other parts of Canada.[92] These newcomers and improved communications made British Columbians feel less isolated from the rest of the country than before, and they shared in the new sense of national identity symbolized by the Citizenship Act.

The belief that in the United States the Bill of Rights had to some extent protected Japanese residents during the war helped Canadians to refine their concept of citizenship and alerted them to the desirability of guarantee-ing specific civil rights. If Canadian citizenship were to mean very much, it had to apply to all who were born in Canada or naturalized, including people of Japanese ancestry. Although the American Bill of Rights did not save U.S. Japanese from "arbitrary, unwarranted, and completely unnec-essary security measures," many Canadians believed that it had.[93] Com-paring Canadian and American experiences, Kitagawa wrote that she could "see why more and more Canadians are demanding a Bill of Rights."[94] The *Province* observed that the federal government had violated "the whole conception of Canadian citizenship in order to give effect to its pol-icy of dispersion." It too suggested that Canada needed a bill of rights in part to protect citizenship (it particularly mentioned the Japanese) and to prevent it from being "the plaything of prejudice or violable at the desire of any government, federal or provincial."[95] Alas, in pandering to the prej-udices of MPs, the Canadian government had shown that it needed lessons on a basic principle of citizenship, the right to move freely in one's own country.

Notes

1. *Vancouver Sun,* 15 November 1945.

2. Ibid., 27, 30 October 1948 (Scott), and 12 November 1948 (Philpott). Otsuji received six-month concurrent sentences for both crimes. His subsequent tragic his-tory is recounted in Maryka Omatsu, *Bittersweet Passage: Redress and the Japanese Canadian Experience* (Toronto: Between the Lines, 1992), 112–13.

3. The B.C. Security Commission was disbanded in 1943, and its work was taken over by the federal Department of Labour. Its personnel and letterhead did not change, and "Commission" remained the name associated with the administration of Japanese affairs.

4. Statistics come from: British Columbia Security Commission, *Removal of Japanese from Protected Areas, March 4, 1942, to October 31, 1942* (Vancouver, B.C.: B.C. Security Commission, 1942); Canada, Dept. of Labour, *Report on the Admin-istration of Japanese Affairs in Canada, 1942–1944* (Ottawa: Dept. of Labour, 1944);

and Canada, Dept. of Labour, *Report on the Re-establishment of Japanese in Canada, 1944–1946* (Ottawa: Dept. of Labour, 1947). For details, see Patricia E. Roy, J. L. Granatstein, Masako Iino, and Hiroko Takamura, *Mutual Hostages: Canadians and Japanese during the Second World War* (Toronto: University of Toronto Press, 1990), chaps. 4–6.

5. Audrie Girdner and Anne Loftis, *The Great Betrayal: The Evacuation of the Japanese-Americans during World War II* (New York: Macmillan, 1969), 380, and chaps. 14 and 15. See also Roger Daniels, *Concentration Camps USA: Japanese Americans and World War II* (New York: Holt, Rinehart and Winston, 1971,) 156–57.

6. Louis Fiset, *Imprisoned Apart* (Seattle: University of Washington Press, 1997), 88; Warren quoted in Roger Daniels, *Asian America: Chinese and Japanese in the United States since 1850* (Seattle: University of Washington Press, 1989), 292–93.

7. Kevin Allen Leonard, "'Is That What We Fought For?' Japanese Americans and Racism in California; the Impact of World War II," *Western Historical Quarterly* 21 (November 1990): 468–69; for Hood River, see Lauren Kessler, *Stubborn Twig: Three Generations in the Life of a Japanese American Family* (New York: Random House, 1993), chap. 12.

8. *Vancouver Sun,* 3 December 1945; H. Mitchell to Ian Mackenzie, 25 May 1946, vol. 79, Ian Mackenzie Papers, National Archives of Canada, Ottawa (hereafter, Mackenzie Papers). The prime minister chooses the cabinet from among the elected members of the House of Commons, taking regional representation into account.

9. The handful of Japanese in other provinces could vote if otherwise qualified. Nationally, there was universal suffrage, but the federal government honored provincial racial disqualifications. In British Columbia, about seventy-five Japanese veterans of the Canadian Expeditionary Force in the First World War were enfranchised in 1931 but lost the right to vote in 1942.

10. A. MacNamara to N. A. Robertson, 14 July 1945, vol. 639, Department of Labour Records, National Archives of Canada (hereafter, DLab); A. H. Brown, "Report on Interviews with the U.S. Japanese Relocation Authorities in Washington, November 15, 1945," vol. 658, ibid.

11. T. B. Pickersgill to A. MacNamara, 29 January 1945, vol. 655, DLab; *Vancouver Sun,* 17 May 1947, 17 December 1948; *Cowichan Leader (*Duncan, B.C.), 27 March 1947; *Vancouver Daily Province,* 6 April 1948.

12. F. J. Mead to A. MacNamara, 28 May 1947, vol. 3154, Royal Canadian Mounted Police (RCMP) Records, National Archives of Canada. For details, see Patricia E. Roy, "The Soldiers Canada Didn't Want: Her Chinese and Japanese Citizens," *Canadian Historical Review* 59 (September 1978): 341–58.

13. Ian Mackenzie to Humphrey Mitchell, 20 May 1946, vol. 79, Mackenzie Papers.

14. Humphrey Mitchell to Ian Mackenzie, 18 July 1946, vol. 24, ibid. Also see Ian Mackenzie to Humphrey Mitchell, 23 July 1946, ibid.

15. Thomas Reid to Ian Mackenzie, 4 March 1947 (1st quotation), and Ian Mackenzie to Cecil Merritt, 27 August 1947 (last quotation), vol. 25, Mackenzie Papers.

16. Canada, House of Commons, *Debates,* June 25, 1946, 2844; *Vancouver Sun,* 19 April 1947, 26 November 1947; M. C. Shumiatcher to T. B. Suzuki, 10 February 1947; and T. B. Suzuki to M. C. Shumiatcher, 23 February 1947, file 25–1–10, Japanese Canadian Citizens Association Records (JCCA), National Archives of Canada. The provincial fisheries minister, L. H. Eyres, also objected to granting fishing licenses to Japanese.

17. *Vancouver News-Herald,* 19 July 1946. See also *Vancouver Daily Province,* 29 December 1945.

18. Paul Martin, "Citizenship and the People's World," in *Belonging: The Meaning and Future of Canadian Citizenship,* ed. William Kaplan (Montreal and Kingston: McGill-Queen's University Press, 1993), 67; *Victoria Daily Colonist,* 24 October 1945.

19. Canada, House of Commons, *Debates,* April 2, 1946, 503. The Citizenship Act was part of several postwar measures marking the continuing evolution of Canada's independence from Britain.

20. *Vancouver Daily Province,* 17 May 1945. See also Canada, House of Commons, *Debates,* April 11, 1946, 800, and May 2, 1946, 1157.

21. *Vancouver Daily Province,* 19 September 1944 (1st quotation); *Victoria Daily Times,* 6 June 1945 (2nd quotation).

22. G. G. McGeer to W. L. M. King, 28 July 1945, no. 346331, William Lyon Mackenzie King Papers, National Archives of Canada (hereafter, King Papers).

23. *Vancouver News-Herald,* 31 May 1945.

24. Some interior communities were keen to retain their Japanese populations. See Patricia E. Roy, "A Tale of Two Cities: The Reception of Japanese Evacuees in Kelowna and Kaslo, B.C.," *BC Studies,* no. 87 (autumn 1990): 23–47; and Roy, "If the Cedars Could Speak: Japanese and Caucasians Meet at New Denver," *BC Studies,* no. 131 (autumn 2001): 81–92.

25. Canada, House of Commons, *Debates,* Nov. 21, 1946, 2386 (quotations), May 13, 1946, 1492. Other CCF MPs from B.C. favored granting citizenship rights to the Canadian-born Japanese. If they did not directly endorse the dispersal policy, they implied that they favored it.

26. Canada, House of Commons, *Debates,* April 9, 1946, 704 (Pearkes) and 726 (Cruickshank), April 30, 1946, 1062, May 8, 1946, 1342 (Fulton), and May 3, 1946, 1210 (Gibson).

27. Ibid., May 8, 1946, 1335 (St. Laurent), and May 3, 1946, 1209.

28. *Victoria Daily Colonist,* 9 April 1946. Also Canada, House of Commons, *Debates,* April 6, 1946, 619.

29. D. Badger, "Passing Judgment," *Western Miner* 18 (October 1945): 56; *Vancouver Daily Province,* 28 August 1945.

30. Bruce Hutchison, "This Is No Surprise," *Vancouver Sun,* 21 December 1945. Hutchison admitted that the *Sun* did not endorse his article. John Diefenbaker, a Progressive Conservative MP from Saskatchewan, proposed to amend the citizenship bill to include a bill of rights but did not specifically refer to the Japanese. Neither did his seconder, Davie Fulton. Paul Martin, secretary of state and father of the Citizenship Act, noted that Fulton argued for both a bill of rights and deportation of the Japanese. The main thrust of his own argument was that a bill of rights was unnecessary since common law, the Magna Carta, and the legal system provided such rights. He also suggested that no Parliament could bind its successors. Martin, "Citizenship and the People's World," 75. See also Canada, House of Commons, *Debates,* May 7, 1946, 1310–11.

31. Hunter Lewis, Canadian Civil Liberties Union (CCLU), Vancouver Branch, to W. L. M. King, March 25, 1947, no. 386751, King Papers. The CCLU brief drew favorable comments from the *Winnipeg Free Press,* 20 May 1947, and the *Calgary Herald,* 12 May 1947.

32. G. A. Ishiwara to W. L. M. King, 8 May 1947, no. 385949, King Papers.

33. W. L. M. King, Diary, Jan. 22, 1947, King Papers (microfiche); Cabinet Committee on Japanese Problems, Minutes, Jan. 10, 1947, vol. 639, DLab.

34. According to a government report, between 1942 and 1946 approximately 8,500 Japanese Canadians left B.C. for Canada east of the Rockies; records suggest that a greater number left in 1946, some for Japan. Dept. of Labour, *Report on the Re-establishment of Japanese,* 25–26. Many who remained were the families of people too aged or infirm to leave.

35. Canada, House of Commons, *Debates,* April 22, 1947, 2317. Also see April 23 and 24, 1947.

36. Ibid., April 23, 1947, 2335–36.

37. Canada, Senate, *Debates,* May 8, 1947, 324. See also Canada, House of Commons, *Debates,* April 23, 1947, 2349, May 14, 1946, 1506, March 15, 1948, 2231, and April 5, 1946, 619; *Vancouver Sun,* 9 May 1947.

38. According to an unscientific public opinion poll conducted in September 1947, 87.6 percent of Vancouver-area residents believed that naturalized Canadians of Japanese descent should not be allowed to return to the coast; *Vancouver Daily Province,* 11 September 1947. It said nothing of Canadian-born Japanese. A Gallup poll in December 1947 indicated that 70 percent of British Columbians approved

making it an offense to refuse someone a job on grounds of race, color, or religion. Elmore Philpott commented that if the question had been "Do you believe persons of Japanese ancestry should be allowed back in British Columbia and [to] take any jobs for which they are qualified?" the answers would have been different. Fishermen, he said, would say no, but housewives would be happy to hire a Japanese maid; *Vancouver Sun,* 11 December 1947.

39. *Vancouver Sun,* 11 April 1947. See also *Victoria Daily Colonist,* 10 May 1947.

40. G. S. Wismer to Ian Mackenzie, 6 May 1946, vol. 24, Mackenzie Papers; Maitland quoted in *Vancouver Sun,* 26 January 1946.

41. *Surrey Leader,* 24 January 1946. See also *Vancouver Sun,* 28 January 1946.

42. H. Edwards to W. L. M. King, 14 June 1946, J2, vol. 473, King Papers.

43. Army and Navy Veterans in Canada to W. L. M. King, 3 May 1946, no. 379821–2, King Papers.

44. *Vernon News,* 15 May 1947; see also Saanich and Vancouver South-Point Grey Progressive Conservative associations' letters to John Bracken, vol. 22, John Bracken Papers, National Archives of Canada.

45. *Vancouver Daily Province,* 20 February 1947.

46. Petition to W. L. M. King and the Cabinet (April 1946), no. C1949966, King Papers.

47. *Langley Advance,* 18 October 1945, 3 January 1947; *British Columbian (New Westminster),* 18 January 1946 and 3 December 1946; *Vancouver Sun,* 1 April 1947.

48. *Vancouver News-Herald,* 21 January 1947.

49. *British Columbian (New Westminster),* 26 April 1947; *Vancouver News-Herald,* 28 April 1947; *Winnipeg Free Press,* 9 May 1947.

50. The Canadian Senate is not an elected body; the prime minister appoints its members. A common criticism is that the Senate is a dumping ground for difficult, inconvenient, or ineffective cabinet ministers.

51. W. L. M. King, Diary, 18 February 1948. See also ibid., 3 February 1948; *Vancouver Sun,* 8 March 1948.

52. Canada, House of Commons, *Debates,* March 15, 1948, 2217–19. A paraphrase of this statement about ensuring stability was part of a form letter sent to those who protested the application of the Transitional Measures Act, which replaced the Emergency Powers Bill in 1948, to the Japanese. See, e.g., A. MacNamara to David Owen, 18 May 1948, vol. 657, DLab.

53. Canada, House of Commons, *Debates,* March 15, 1948, 2230.

54. Ibid., 2225 (MacInnis), 2231 (Pearkes), 2233–36 (Reid).

55. *Vancouver News-Herald,* 17 March 1948; Jack Scott, "Why B.C. Draws the Color Line," *Maclean's,* 1 February 1948, 17. The Liberals lost to the CCF for reasons unrelated to the Japanese.

56. *North Vancouver North Shore Press,* 2 April 1948; H. Allen to Louis St. Laurent, 16 February 1949, vol. 657, DLab (quotation).

57. *Vancouver Sun,* 25 March 1949. The Army, Navy and Air Force Veterans Association circulated among veterans' groups a resolution similar to the Maple Ridge one. *Surrey Leader,* 3 March 1949.

58. J. E. Eckman, Canadian Fishing Company, to Humphrey Mitchell, 14 December 1946, vol. 657, DLab; *Vancouver Sun,* 23 November 1945; Geoff Meggs, *Salmon: The Decline of the British Columbia Fishery* (Vancouver: Douglas & McIntyre, 1991), 162–63.

59. H. G. Archibald's main targets were capitalist canners; he proposed solving "the Jap issue" by turning the fishery over to the fishermen; Canada, House of Commons, *Debates,* April 23, 1947, 2348–50.

60. G. W. Nickerson to Reid, 1 May 1947, vol. 25, Mackenzie Papers.

61. *Prince Rupert Daily News,* 7 February 1949; J. Cameron, Pender Island Local, UFAWU, to W. L. M. King, 6 January 1947, vol. 25, Mackenzie Papers; Minutes of Sunbury Local, April 14, 1946, copy in vol. 83, United Fishermen and Allied Workers Union (UFAWU) Records, University of British Columbia Library, Vancouver (hereafter, UFAWU Records).

62. Homer Stevens to George Tanaka, 15 February 1949, vol. 83, UFAWU Records.

63. Tanaka, Address to the Third Provincial Convention of the JCCA, Greenwood, B.C., February 1949, UFAWU Records; JCCA press release by Tanaka, Nov. 28, 1949, vol. 83, UFAWU Records; and transcript of question period, March 22, 1949, copy in vol. 220, UFAWU Records; *Fisherman,* 8 April 1949. (T. Buck Suzuki became the organizer for Japanese fishermen and served for many years on the UFAWU executive board.)

64. *Fisherman,* 21 June 1949; George North, *A Ripple, a Wave: The Story of Union Organization in the B.C. Fishing Industry,* ed. Harold Griffin (Vancouver : Fisherman Publishing Society, 1974), 14.

65. *B.C. Lumber Worker,* 8 October 1945. See also J. Greenall to G. G. McGeer, vol. 1, G. G. McGeer Papers, British Columbia Archives, Victoria; *Vancouver Daily Province,* 26 May 1945; *Vancouver Sun,* 24 September 1945.

66. E. Dalskog to W. L. M. King, 16 February 1948, no. 398184–5, King Papers.

67. *British Columbian (New Westminster),* 3 February 1948.

68. *Vancouver Daily Province,* 30 January 1948. An unscientific public opinion poll indicated that 62 percent of the population disapproved of the ban on Japanese in interior logging camps; *Vancouver News-Herald,* 12 February 1948.

69. *Victoria Daily Times,* 30 January 1948.

70. Under the Canadian constitution, the federal government has power over all matters not specifically assigned to the provinces and can disallow provincial leg-

islation that it deems contrary to the interests of the nation as a whole. In fact, Ottawa had overridden a number of B.C. laws restricting the activities of Japanese residents in the late nineteenth and early twentieth centuries (notable exceptions being the franchise and employment on Crown lands, over which the Constitution granted the provinces control). Thus, before the end of the war, the provincial government said little on the Japanese question. At this time, B.C. was governed by the Coalition, an alliance of Liberals and Conservatives intent on promoting wartime unity and keeping the CCF out of power. During the October 1945 provincial election, individual Coalition candidates had claimed that electing a CCF government would mean the return of the Japanese and their enfranchisement, but both the attorney general, R. L. Maitland, and Harold Winch, the CCF leader, tried to avoid the issue by saying it was a federal matter. The B.C. government favored voluntary repatriation.

71. *Vancouver Daily Province*, 22 April 1948 (quotation); *Vancouver News-Herald*, 22 April 1948. Guthrie represented the Vancouver Island constituency of Cowichan-Newcastle; Gargrave, Mackenzie, a coastal riding that had had few Japanese residents.

72. *Vancouver News-Herald*, 5 February 1947; *Vancouver Sun*, 6 April 1948; *Toronto New Canadian*, 11 January 1947 (quotation).

73. *Toronto New Canadian*, 11 January 1947; *Toronto New Canadian*, quoted in *Kamloops Sentinel*, 7 January 1948.

74. *Nanaimo Free Press*, 26 February 1949. See also *Vancouver Daily Province*, 30 January 1948; Muriel Kitagawa, *This Is My Own*, ed. Roy Miki (Vancouver : Talonbooks, 1985), 237–39.

75. *Toronto New Canadian*, quoted in *Vancouver Sun*, 21 September 1945 (1st quotation); Tanaka to W. L. M. King, 23 January 1948, vol. 657, DLab (last quotation).

76. According to a newspaper report, the Coalition government told its members of the committee that "the Japanese issue is one creating widespread dissension," so the Japanese could not be enfranchised; *Vancouver Sun*, 22 January 1947. See also *Vancouver News-Herald*, 11 January 1947.

77. *Victoria Times*, 3 April 1948. Dissent did not harm Straith politically. When Byron Johnson formed a government in December 1947, he appointed Straith minister of education. See *Victoria Times*, 19 February 1947.

78. *Vancouver News-Herald*, 24 March 1948.

79. Canada, House of Commons, *Debates*, June 15, 1948, 5258.

80. *Vancouver Daily Province*, 1 November 1948.

81. *Vancouver News-Herald*, 8 March 1949.

82. *North Vancouver North Shore Press*, 25 March 1949; *Vancouver Sun*, 11 March 1949. A few barriers remained. For nine more years, Japanese who were not Canadian citizens could not be employed on public works contracts or on Crown tim-

berlands. That restriction was lifted, almost as an afterthought, in 1958. Although there were no regulations against employing Japanese Canadians, as late as 1950 the JCCA complained that the provincial civil service did not employ them. (Proceedings of Fourth Annual Provincial JCCA Convention, 1950, vol. 83, UFAWU Records.)

83. C. V. Booth to A. H. Brown, 14 April 1949, vol. 655, DLab.

84. Canada, *Census,* 1951, vol. 1, table 1.

85. Bruce Hutchison, "The Price of Blackmail," *Winnipeg Free Press,* 9 May 1947.

86. A. J. MacLachlan to W. L. M. King, June 26, 1947, vol. 657, DLab.

87. Frank G. P. Lewis to W. L. M. King, Liberal Senators, and MPs, etc., 13 March 1948, DLab.

88. *Vancouver News-Herald,* 21 February 1947.

89. *Victoria Daily Colonist,* 24 April 1947; *Vancouver News-Herald,* 28 April 1947.

90. Scott, "Why B.C. Draws the Color Line," 17.

91. Kitagawa, *This Is My Own,* 237.

92. Jean Barman, *The West beyond the West,* rev. ed. (Toronto: University of Toronto Press, 1996), 379, table 5. The Asian population fell from 42,472 to 25,644.

93. Edward McWhinney, "The Bill of Rights, the Supreme Court, and Civil Liberties in Canada," in *Canadian Annual Review for 1960,* ed. John T. Saywell (Toronto: University of Toronto Press, 1961), 270.

94. Kitagawa, *This Is My Own,* 259.

95. *Vancouver Daily Province,* 5 February 1948. In 1982 Canada got its version of a bill of rights in the Charter of Rights and Freedoms. Japanese Canadians, who were then beginning their redress campaign, worried that the charter might not prevent the kind of wrongs that they and their parents had suffered during the war. See Roy Miki and Cassandra Kobayashi, *Justice in Our Time: The Japanese Canadian Redress Settlement* (Vancouver: Talonbooks; Winnipeg: National Association of Japanese Canadians, 1991), 10. In the redress settlement the government pledged "to ensure, to the full extent that its powers allow, that such events will not happen again"; Terms of Agreement between the Government of Canada and the National Association of Japanese Canadians, reprinted in Miki and Kobayashi, *Justice in Our Time,* 138.

13 / PECULIAR ODYSSEY

Newsman Jimmie Omura's Removal from and Regeneration within Nikkei Society, History, and Memory

ARTHUR A. HANSEN

I t galled many long-standing Japanese American Citizens League (JACL) members who read the "Millennium New Year's Edition" of the *Pacific Citizen (PC)*, the League's newspaper, to encounter "Influential JA Journalist: James Omura" in an issue commemorating outstanding twentieth-century Nisei.[1] Perhaps no other Nikkei name could so predictably have nettled old-guard JACLers as Jimmie Omura, who was born on Bainbridge Island, Washington, in 1912, and died in Denver, Colorado, in 1994.

Thus, JACL pioneer Fred Hirasuna wrote the *PC*:

> Who named James Omura influential journalist of the past century? Omura . . . did not challenge evacuation by physically resisting evacuation [but avoided it] . . . by leaving the area [West Coast] in March of 1942. His main claim to fame seems to be that he supported the Heart Mountain draft resisters and castigated the JACL for not doing the same.
>
> His record pales when compared with that of Bill Hosokawa . . . [or] Larry Tajiri. . . . If any one person deserves the title of leading journalist, my choice would be Bill Hosokawa, and he would be the choice of the majority of JAs who actually experienced the evacuation and internment.[2]

Certainly a case could be made for Larry Tajiri, the *PC*'s 1942–1952 editor.[3] Possibly, Hirasuna's reason for ranking Hosokawa over Tajiri is tied to his rationale for depreciating Omura. While Seattle-born and bred Hosokawa was imprisoned at Washington's Puyallup Assembly Center and Wyoming's Heart Mountain Relocation Center, Tajiri did not "do time" in a concentration camp. Instead, he departed California on the final day of "voluntary evacuation" to "resettle" in Salt Lake City.

That same day, March 29, 1942, Omura left the Golden State for Denver, the other intermountain mecca for voluntary migrants. A Bay Area florist, Omura was publisher-editor of the Nisei magazine *Current Life*. While his 1930s sidekick and fellow journalist Tajiri planned to convert the *PC* into a weekly,[4] Omura determined to resume publishing the politics and arts monthly he founded two years before in San Francisco.

Likely Hosokawa's stellar *Denver Post* career from 1946 to 1992 made him Hirasuna's choice. Stridently anti-Japanese during wartime, the *Post* afterwards became so liberalized that it embraced Hosokawa and, later, Tajiri.[5]

World War II–era Denver, with 325,000 residents, was a relatively favorable place for Nikkei. Located in the "free zone," near four War Relocation Authority (WRA) camps,[6] Denver attracted voluntary resettlers like Omura as well as those, like Oregonian Nisei curfew resister Minoru (Min) Yasui, who resettled there from a WRA camp. Denver's wartime Nikkei population peaked at five thousand, even though the WRA clamped a 1943 moratorium on resettlement there.[7]

Colorado's prewar population of four thousand Japanese Americans was the largest such population for non-Pacific Coast states, but only seven hundred lived in Denver. There, a several-block transitional area around Larimer Street formed a Japantown. In Denver, racism was not as unremitting as it had been for prewar coastal Nikkei.

Likewise, Denver was a favorable place for Nisei journalism. As David Yoo observes, the expanded readership of Nikkei migrants to the intermountain region "breathed new life into the struggling English-language sections of three . . . papers outside the restricted zones: the *Rocky Nippon, Colorado Times*, and *Utah Nippo*."[8] The first two were published in Denver. The *Rocky Nippon* (later called the *Rocky Shimpo*) inaugurated its English-language section in October 1941, while the *Times* followed suit in August 1942.[9]

The *Rocky Shimpo* appealed more to WRA-camp inmates than did the *Times* (for which Omura wrote in late 1942), and buttressed its masthead claim as the "largest circulated Nisei vernacular in the continental U.S.A." The *Times*, whose publisher-editor was veteran Issei Denverite Fred Kaihara, resonated more with resettlers in burgeoning midwestern cities, namely Chicago, which until mid-1947 lacked a vernacular newspaper with an English-language section. The early postwar addition of columns by Togo Tanaka, the prewar English-section editor of Los Angeles's *Rafu Shimpo* and one of Chicago's twenty-thousand-plus resettlers, and Minoru Yasui helped the *Times* double its Denver rival's subscriber base.

Scattered evidence suggests that the two papers experienced a reversal in popularity from the wartime to the postwar years, probably because the Nikkei readership inside and outside of the Denver region changed from anti-JACL to pro-JACL. Indeed, Omura's shifting journalistic fortunes in Denver between 1942 and 1947, which led to his "banishment" from Nikkei life and letters until the 1980s, dramatized this transformed ideological climate in Colorado and throughout Japanese America.

This essay first treats this World War II and immediate postwar transformation in terms of the Omura-JACL battle. It then fast-forwards three decades to consider Omura's resurrected role as a Nikkei writer and outspoken JACL critic after testifying at the 1981 Seattle hearings of the Commission on Wartime Relocation and Internment of Civilians (CWRIC) and achieving community validation within the Seattle-originated National Council for Japanese American Redress (NCJAR).

By the time of Jimmie Omura's arrival in Denver April 2, 1942, the JACL leadership saw him as their primary nemesis. Their mutual animosity began when a 1934 article in the Omura-edited *New World Daily News* of San Francisco—which seemingly impugned the integrity of a Placer County JACL leader—so provoked JACL founder Saburo Kido, a Nisei attorney for the rival pro-JACL *Hokubei Asahi*, that he threatened to sue Omura for slander.[10] Omura and Kido, later the JACL's wartime president, soon clashed directly when Kido interpreted Omura's editorials criticizing "Nisei leadership" as attacking "JACL leadership."

When the JACL's 1934 national convention met in San Francisco, Omura was an established JACL critic. Omura's newspaper had him welcome incoming JACL president and *Japanese-American Courier* editor Jimmie Sakamoto to the city. The two Pacific Northwest Nisei met four years earlier when Omura sought work on Sakamoto's paper. Then the JACL's founding father had patronized Omura, but now Sakamoto was reproachful. "He said, 'Why did they have to select you?' . . . I felt so insulted that I turned around and walked away."[11]

Relations between Omura and the JACL came to a head in 1935 after the *New World Daily News* and the *Hokubei Asahi* merged into the *New World Sun*. Both English-section editors, Howard Imazeki and Omura, managed a page. Omura wrote his own editorials, but Imazeki deferred to Saburo Kido's "Timely Topics" column. Before long Kido confronted Omura: "I'm being embarrassed. . . . I write an editorial one way on the front page, and my friends say they flip the page and there's an exact opposite editorial on the second page."[12] In early 1936 Omura resigned.

Up until October 1940, when Omura began *Current Life,* journalism and the JACL had figured little in his life. Larry Tajiri, English-section editor of the *Japanese American News* and then staunchly anti-JACL, did get Omura to write editorial features. However, when Tajiri left for a New York post, Omura's writing was censured and then discontinued.[13]

Omura's *Current Life* editorials increasingly chastised the JACL: its leadership was feckless in not preparing Nisei for a probable clash between the United States and Japan, and its membership was reckless in partying at gala bashes instead of promoting social action. Moreover, the JACL's prolonged accommodation to Japanese imperialism and its flamboyant eleventh-hour American flag waving bothered Omura. Finally, according to him, "shortly after or even before Pearl Harbor," JACL leaders fingered him as a potentially dangerous person.[14] While this accusation fell on deaf ears, the Omura-JACL war had heated up considerably.

The boiling point came in February 1942 during meetings of the Bay Region Council for Unity (BRCU). Omura urged this progressive Nisei group's membership to form a coalition with the JACL *on an equal partnership basis* and pitched resistance to the prospective mass eviction policy. The BRCU chair, Larry Tajiri, unsuccessfully sought Omura's expulsion, but argued successfully that the BRCU affiliate as a "Sounding Board" with JACL. This meant BRCU would support JACL Executive Secretary Mike Masaoka's impassioned plea of "constructive cooperation" with the government for "future considerations."[15] Omura was outraged at Masaoka, felt Tajiri had betrayed him, and was convinced he "didn't have a single supporter."[16]

Then, on February 23, Omura testified before the Tolan Committee. Following accommodating, pro-JACL witnesses, Omura registered strong opposition to mass evacuation, and then added: "It is a matter of public record that I have been consistently opposed to the Japanese American Citizens League. . . . I have felt that the leaders were leading the American-born along the wrong channels."[17]

In the *PC* of March 1, 1942, Evelyn Kimura scored Omura's testimony as a grand if worthless gesture by "a magazine with a circulation of 500 more or less," and lamented that "the tragedy of the whole thing is that simply because one puny publisher desired to make a show of himself, all the American citizens of Japanese ancestry are affected." Omura believed Saburo Kido had authored this rebuke. Five days later, at a San Francisco mass gathering, Masaoka named Omura the JACL's "Public Enemy Number One." His had been the sole voice raised against Nikkei cooperation with mass eviction. When Omura left the meeting and brushed past Masaoka, the JACL executive secretary threatened, "We'll get you."[18]

Omura's wife and *Current Life* business manager, Fumiko Caryl Okuma, departed San Francisco on March 14, 1942. Seeking a "free zone" site for their magazine, she stopped in Salt Lake City before reaching Denver on March 18. In both places she found Masaoka at arranged meetings with public officials. Ruling out Salt Lake City as "enemy territory," she recommended Denver as the Omura wartime home. When *Current Life* publishing plans were dashed, Omura established the Pacific Coast Evacuee Employment Placement Bureau in April 1942 to give cost-free employment assistance to area resettlers, and later that year his wife opened Caryl's Malt and Sandwich Shop.

Throughout 1942 discontent toward the JACL for "selling the Japanese community down the river" was widely shared within the Nikkei community, a situation Omura capitalized upon. Likely because Omura was one of Denver's few experienced Nisei journalists, the *Colorado Times,* on October 29, initiated his column, "The Passing Parade." It opened with an ominous entry: "The motto of the Japanese American Citizens League should be 'Let Well Enough Alone,' but if the report that a representative of the organization is to be sent out here to Denver for organizational purposes is correct, the JACL is still meddling where they are neither needed or wanted." Omura promised stiff opposition in Denver.[19]

By the *Times*'s November 17 issue, the paper had taken on JACL coloration. Prefacing Mike Masaoka's lead article was an editor's note explaining how its author "well put forth" the timeliness and urgent need for the JACL's current emergency conference in Salt Lake City. Masaoka's claim that "when the supreme test came for Japanese Americans, the JACL met that challenge nobly, boldly, loyally," must have been tough for Omura to swallow.

Although Omura's *Times* column appeared for the balance of 1942, he said nothing about the JACL. Mostly, Omura commented on labor issues. Occasionally, as on November 24, he celebrated Nikkei community heroes such as Colorado Governor Ralph Carr, who had welcomed Nikkei resettlers but then lost his next bid for elective office. At other times, as on December 10, Omura criticized the U.S. government: "Here in one block [Larimer Street] can be found the evidence of . . . a history of which the nation should be ashamed but is not." By the end of 1942 the *Times* had metamorphosed into a JACL mouthpiece, and when editor-publisher Kaihara censored a couple of Omura's columns, Omura resigned.[20]

Earlier Omura had affiliated with the tri-weekly *Rocky Nippon,* so he retained an interpretive outlet. The prevailing tone of his column for this paper, begun on October 28, 1942, was established when he regretted that "in these times more Nisei are not alert to the grave situation on hand and willing to put their shoulders to the wheels crunching out the weeds of prejudice and racial maltreatment." On December 14, Omura took dead aim at the U.S. government: "The great days of democracy, once an emblem of red-blooded Americans, have gone by the board and the nation is today ruled by the grip of dictatorship and fascism."

Omura came out smoking against the JACL in his 1943 columns. On January 4, he recapped his "war record" for readers, emphasizing his Tolan Committee testimony and invidiously comparing the JACL's performance against it. "Instead of looking at the evacuation from a broader standpoint," wrote Omura, ". . . [national] J.A.C.L. leaders attempted to profit on the distress of U.S. Japanese as individuals and as an organization. It was first J.A.C.L. and second, the cause." Omura then renewed his own pledge to that cause: "Perhaps the Evacuee Placement Bureau will drain me of every red cent I possess, but until that last cent is spent this work will be carried on. And even afterward."

In his February 3 column, Omura vigorously opposed an all-Nisei combat team. But he feared the idea might appeal to many Nisei, for they "are too easily susceptible to the ingenuities of public officials and the trumped-up slogans of American patriotism." His February 8 column reiterated his opposition to the JACL's extension in Colorado and its capital and challenged the newly arrived JACL representatives to confront him in an open hearing on community issues.

Omura filled his columns with his intensifying JACL feud through the August 9, 1943, *Rocky Nippon*—renamed the *Rocky Shimpo* in April after Issei publisher Shiro Toda's removal to an alien internment camp for allegedly pro-Japan writings in the Japanese section. Shiro Toda's family likely approved of these JACL attacks because they believed its leaders behind his arrest.[21]

In 1943, however, Omura was fighting a losing campaign in Denver against the insurgent JACL. Mike Masaoka's brother, Joe Grant Masaoka, who had been driven out of California's Manzanar camp by the anti-JACL December 1942 riot,[22] was thereupon detailed to Denver to drum up JACL recruits. At a local meeting, the JACL field representative's responses to floor questions, as related in Omura's February 10 column, had been "vague, evasive and indirect." But even Omura conceded the audience had thought otherwise and warmly applauded Masaoka, especially after he read aloud his brother Mike's letter saying he had volunteered for the Nisei combat team.

On February 20, 1943[?],Omura published an open letter in the *Rocky Nippon* delineating his ten key differences with the JACL. One point cut to the bone: "The League has failed to uphold freedom of the press, employing pressure on newspaper editors to curtail the expression of critics and to propagandize its own program." Although Omura enjoyed press freedom, he could not prevent the JACL's organizational wave from cresting in Denver. "Michael M. Masaoka, the high sachem of the J.A.C.L.," noted Omura in his March 12[?] column, "is finally coming to Denver." Omura astutely predicted that "Mr. Big's" upcoming appearance at the Japanese Methodist Church should prove "an interesting test of strength in this area for the organization which he represents." But the results were not to Omura's liking. His March 19 column maintained that even Masaoka's presence could not override "the strong opposition which has taken root among the Nisei people of Colorado against the extension of the J.A.C.L. east of the Rockies." However, the same page provided countervailing evidence to readers: "J.A.C.L. Draws Capacity Audience," "Young Buddhists Hail Talk by J.A.C.L. National Secretary," "Ft. Lupton J.A.C.L. Chapter Holds Monthly Meeting," and "Longmont Japanese Gather to Hear J.A.C.L. Talk."

Though surrounded, Omura refused to retreat. Instead, he took the offense. On March 29 the *Rocky Nippon* reported on a public talk Omura gave the previous evening. The text of "Why I Oppose the JACL" occupied the entire subsequent issue. "I have watched for eleven years the gradual expansion of the J.A.C.L.," Omura declared, "[and] I have watched it clutching and grasping for power like the inexorable will of the octopus, relentlessly crushing out the honest criticisms of the ordinary man." After a tedious discussion of his employment service's trials and triumphs, Omura underscored the Nisei's need to resist the JACL's "egoistic," "narrow-minded," and "self-aggrandizing" leadership. "I do not want you to believe that I am alone in this fight," said Omura. "Look to the various relocation centers and you will find a great angered majority who have disowned the J.A.C.L."[23]

The April 2 *Rocky Nippon* was dedicated to Omura and his Pacific Coast Evacuee Employment Placement Bureau, whose doors had just closed. Other Denver doors were slamming in Omura's face. In the April 10 *Colorado Times*, Kaz Oka of Poston, Arizona, denounced Omura. In "Why I Disagree with Mr. Omura," Oka dismissed Omura's recent lecture "on his favorite topic" as more of his rantings. He mocked Omura for devoting half his talk to his placement bureau.

I fail to see what it has to do with his discussion of the JACL and its alleged failings . . . UNLESS he is aware . . . that the JACL may "invade" his territory and encroach upon his private enterprise by offering reasonably better services.

On May 14 Omura waved off Oka as just another JACL hireling who dealt in innuendo and propaganda, declaring that he had never charged a fee for his employment bureau services. On May 28 he returned to Oka in his new *Rocky Shimpo* column, "Nisei America: Know the Facts." Why, Omura agonized, had the JACL tapped such a nothing writer as Oka when their stable had so many capable writers, like "Mr. Tajiri himself, the editorial genius of the Pacific Citizen . . . to employ his prolific pen [in the JACL's defense]." What Nisei needed to know, explained Omura on June 28, was that Tajiri and his *PC* associates were suspected of alleged Communistic leanings, and because of "this fact [it] may go badly for him and the J.A.C.L."[24]

In reality, things were going well for the JACL, leastwise in Denver, and Omura knew it. The main June 4 *Rocky Shimpo* story concerned the JACL district office's opening in downtown Denver to serve the organization's expanding needs in Colorado, Nebraska, and Wyoming. On July 7, the paper conveyed proof of the JACL's growing strength through a story about a meeting at which Joe Grant Masaoka informed potential members of the League's public relations efforts, new credit union, and legislative activities to ameliorate Nisei discrimination.

Omura tried putting a positive spin on his life in Denver. Usually he tried too hard, and it showed in embarrassing ways, as with the August 9, 1943, *Rocky Shimpo* article "Caryl's Is Sold to Virginia Couple." This anonymous contribution was clearly Omura's handiwork. "In the Evacuation Period's most astounding transaction," it ran, "the widely-known Caryl's Malt & Sandwich Shop changed hands on August 2, going to the highest bidder. . . . The sale . . . is unquestionably the shrewdest deal put across by Miss Okuma." Four decades hence Omura recalled what this show of bravado had masked: "With all the problems we were having, we were going downhill financially." Moreover, the Okuma-Omura marriage was "deteriorating." Putting his anti-JACL campaign on hold, Omura took a gardening position and his wife became a "schoolgirl" and enrolled at Denver University.[25]

That 1943 winter, Omura assumed a war industry trainee position that he later described as "killing me physically."[26] So when the *Rocky Shimpo* invited him back at the start of 1944 to be its English-section editor and public contact agent, he readily complied. Soon the draft issue exploded at Heart Mountain, and Omura launched the editorial series constituting arguably the most courageous and significant Nikkei journalistic writing ever produced. Omura relates this complex story in detail within his unpublished memoir, but its contours warrant coverage here.[27]

As noted, a year before he became the *Rocky Shimpo*'s editor, Omura contested the JACL-supported Nisei combat unit. He did so chiefly because it was to be segregated and, therefore, a symbol of racism. Omura's 1944 *Rocky Shimpo* appointment came on the heels of Secretary of War Henry L. Stimson's announcement about Nisei draft resumption. This was another policy Omura believed the JACL had urged upon the government. When it caused the Heart Mountain Fair Play Committee (FPC) to mushroom, Omura opened the *Rocky Shimpo* to the FPC for news releases. Then, on February 28, Omura wrote his first editorial about draft reinstitution and the reaction to it by those detained in WRA camps. His concern at this point was not Heart Mountain, but the actions taken at the Granada, Colorado, and Minidoka, Idaho, centers. There draft resistance had been sporadic and punctuated with denunciations of democracy and avowals of expatriation to Japan. Whereas Omura believed that the government should restore a large share of the Nisei's constitutional rights before asking them to sacrifice their lives in battle, he would not condone impulsive and irresponsible draft resistance.[28]

It quickly became plain to Omura that the FPC represented an organized draft resistance movement dedicated to the principle that citizen Japanese should do their duty as Americans equally but not before being treated equally by the U.S. government. Thereafter his editorials supported the FPC not as an organization but solely on the issue of restoration as a prelude to induction. That the *Heart Mountain Sentinel*, the camp newspaper, was staunchly pro-JACL (and, as such, censorious of the FPC for placing Japanese American loyalty and patriotism at risk) added fuel to Omura's fiery editorials. These gained members for the FPC and dramatically increased *Rocky Shimpo* sales in Heart Mountain and the other camps (where Omura believed the overwhelming majority of those detained there were opposed to the JACL).[29] But Omura's hard-hitting editorials also caused the government, facilitated by the WRA and the JACL, to force his resignation in late April 1944, after which he was replaced by the actively pro-JACL Roy Takeno. Then, on May 10, the grand jurors of Wyoming secretly indicted him along with seven FPC leaders. On July 20 Omura was arrested and jailed for unlawful conspiracy to counsel, aid, and abet violations of the draft. In

early November, at their joint jury trial in Cheyenne, Wyoming, while the
FPC leaders were found guilty and sentenced to federal imprisonment,
Omura was acquitted.

But acquittal did not mean vindication for Omura insofar as the Japanese American community in the Denver region (and even beyond) was
concerned. The community had cold-shouldered him at the time of his arrest
and stymied the defense fund being raised for him. One solicitor was gang-
beaten in a Denver alley at night, while the Fort Lupton JACL chapter president, threatening bodily harm, warned another solicitor against seeking
donations in outlying agricultural areas. Also, when Omura sought employment after the courts cleared him, JACL Nisei harassed and hounded him
so that he had "a hell of a time finding a job."[30] Eventually he settled into
a landscape gardener job, but not before his impoverishment had so damp-
ened his marriage as to bring about divorce in 1947.

During the last half of 1947, Omura did take another stab at editing the
Rocky Shimpo. But his postwar editorial mission to expose and stop the JACL
occurred when their leadership controlled the community, enjoyed the full
support of the U.S. government, and was promoting measures that resonated
within their community and mainstream America. This story has been given
extended treatment,[31] but only one sidebar, Omura's clash of words and
worldviews with Minoru Yasui, will be broached here.

It is ironic that Yasui and Omura, Pacific Northwest Nisei dissidents who
alike championed constitutional and human rights, should have become
mortal enemies within wartime and postwar Denver. Their interaction com-
menced while attorney Yasui was serving a jail sentence in Portland, Oregon, during 1942–43 for violating the army's curfew order so as to provoke
a constitutional test case. Although Yasui was a member of JACL, its leadership opposed test cases by, to quote Mike Masaoka, "self-styled martyrs."[32]
While in solitary confinement, Yasui took exception, by post, to Omura's
published boast that his placement bureau "represent[s] the ONLY people
of Japanese ancestry to demand equal consideration and treatment as citizens of the United States and to fight for these rights."

Their next confrontation was in Denver on April 19, 1944, just before
Omura's resignation as editor. While detained at the Minidoka camp, Yasui
had altered his attitude toward Nikkei who chose the path of most resistance during wartime. Along with two local JACL leaders, Yasui came to the
Rocky Shimpo office to confer with Omura about his Nisei draft position,
but left by snarling at him, "I'm going to see you go to prison one way or
another."[33]

Yasui became a Denver resident in the fall of 1944 and began his law practice two years later. Additionally, he promoted JACL fortunes as the local chapter's vice-president and the national organization's regional representative. In the fall of 1947, he became a *Colorado Times* columnist, and through his "Denver Nisei-Grams" column, Yasui next locked horns with Omura.

On May 16, 1947, Omura promised *Rocky Shimpo* readers in his resuscitated "Nisei America: Know the Facts" column to expect a "progressive type of journalism" that will "freely criticize wherever occasions demand." He further sounded a warning to the JACL leadership: "Those who have disagreed with us in the past and have been unpardonably guilty of working nefariously in the shadows may evince certain misgivings with our return to the Nisei journalistic wars. They have cause to feel uneasy."

Omura's special brand of "liberalism" pervaded his 1947 columns,[34] roughly one-fifth of which criticized JACL leadership and policies. On August 2, for example, Omura blasted the "selfish and arrogant" JACL leadership for denying "the right of any Nisei to hold views contrary to its own."

Min Yasui's initial *Colorado Times* column of September 23, 1947, boosted Denver as a liberal, progressive city that was "fair-minded toward minority groups." Thereafter, Yasui's columns were free of boosterism,[35] except when spotlighting the JACL leadership. "Despite acrimonious criticism to the contrary," declared Yasui on September 30, "[Mike] Masaoka has done an outstanding job in Washington D.C. He has been able to shove through a complete legislative program [naturalization rights for Issei; evacuations claims indemnification; and equality in deportation laws] halfway thru Congress in a single session."

A face-off between Omura and Yasui was catalyzed by Omura's strenuous objection to *Times* editor Fred Kaihara's statement that no discrimination of significance toward Nikkei existed in either wartime or present-day Denver. Wartime discrimination against Japanese Americans, fumed Omura, had been both "widespread" and "bitter," especially in employment, while postwar prejudice extended to public accommodations, education, and housing.

When Yasui charged that Omura's ravings about discrimination were "not borne out by facts," Omura denigrated Yasui as a "whipping boy" for Kaihara and "not conscientious of the truth." Whereas the *Rocky Shimpo*'s policy "pointed up" instances of discrimination, observed Omura, the policy of the *Colorado Times* "pointed down" such behavior.

What differentiated his outlook from Omura's, bristled Yasui, was that "we have tried to DO something actual about discriminatory situations,"

FIG. 13.1 *Jimmie Omura,* Rocky
Shimpo *editor, appeared on radio
station KLZ in Denver on October 12,
1947, to inaugurate a new series,
"Liberty Calling," designed to deepen
public understanding of minority
group issues in Denver.*

while Omura had been negatively fixated on the fact of discrimination. There
was probably a basis for a debate between them, Yasui pondered, "but we
refuse to fight the wind, even as we found that butting our head against a
stone wall during evacuation was fruitless."

Omura's November 24 issue featured a city-commissioned report's
finding that "racial prejudice in Denver was on the rise and had seeped into
virtually every phase of community life." In this same edition, Omura took
Yasui to task for calling him a do-nothing Cassandra while posturing as a
constructive doer in the fight against discrimination.

On December 4, a small *Rocky Shimpo* item announced James Omura's
resignation as editor, effective December 15. Personal finances figured heavily in Omura's decision. So also did fatigue. Throughout much of his edi-
torship, Omura had operated the Omura Landscape Service,[36] and this
double duty exacted its price.[37]

Omura fired parting shots at the JACL, the *Colorado Times,* and Min Yasui.
On December 3 he declared the JACL's liberal element its best reform hope.
But it would have to occur, he wrote on December 9, before the JACL's fanatics destroyed the organization. Unfortunately, he remarked, these fanatics
pervaded the top leadership, demanded other Nisei's unqualified allegiance,
and were virtually immune to constructive criticism.

Omura's December 12 editorial compared his newspaper's approach with
that of the *Times.* Whereas the *Rocky Shimpo* was forthright about the inad-

equacy of the JACL leadership, the *Times* both defended that leadership and shielded it from criticism. A "vicious example" was Yasui attributing to Omura the "patently false and absolutely untrue" allusion that none of Denver's leaders were any good at all. "We have labeled this statement," explained Omura, "a lie. Mr. Yasui has threatened to sue us unless we retract. We have refused to retract. The next move is Mr. Yasui's."

In the December 18 *Times,* Yasui responded to Omura's indictment of the *Times:* The *Times* believed in objective reporting of the news and covering topics of interest to local Nisei residents, including discrimination, but also strove to encourage Nisei and place their activities in "the best possible light." He admitted his having considered suing Omura, but now felt this action pointless. It was quite enough for him that "a disturbing factor in Denver journalism is now gone."

Still, on December 29 Yasui revisited the issue most responsible for the bad blood with Omura—wartime Nisei draft resistance. What provoked Yasui's editorial was President Harry Truman granting amnesty to the 315 convicted Japanese American draft violators. Although charitable toward those resisting "to register a legal protest against evacuation," especially under the extenuating circumstances, Yasui's commentary represented a stinging critique of the Fair Play Committee, Omura, and Nisei draft "evaders."

> When other Nisei boys were slugging against the enemy, reports of draft violation hit the morale of our Nisei GI's. On the home front, refusal to serve was construed by the public as out-right disloyalty. But now . . . we believe that this is the end of that sad and shameful story.

> A moral that we can safely draw . . . is that as citizens and as human beings, we must first fulfill our obligations to the nation and society before we can legally or socially expect that our complete rights will be granted to us.

Thus, by the closing of 1947, a perceptive observer could conceivably have grasped the current power arrangements in Japanese Denver, glimpsed the contours of the emerging collective memory of the Japanese American wartime experience (within both the Nikkei and mainstream American communities), and fathomed the likely trajectory of postwar Japanese American society and history.

Omura's retreat eliminated a formidable counterweight to the JACL's hegemonic hold over Japanese Denver's public life. The existence of a large, active JACL chapter, along with a favorable press to promote its agenda and social gospel, ensured that the organization would prevail. How the immediate Japanese American past would be configured within (and outside of) Denver's Nikkei community was also discernible. The basic lesson for Nikkei to learn from their wartime history, as adumbrated by Yasui, was that, unlike most other Americans, they needed to fulfill obligations like military service before their civil and human rights would be granted to them. This lesson's subtext was that the JACL's policy of "constructive cooperation" had been prudent and patriotic, while those who had advocated and/or practiced resistance on constitutional grounds were misguided, mischievous, or treasonable. The real Japanese American heroes had been those valiant Nisei who had answered their military duty call so that they could "go for broke" for America.

The *Pacific Citizen* disseminated this same JACL-shaped historical narrative throughout Japanese America. One of its two principal interpretive voices was Denver-based columnist Bill Hosokawa, with the other being its editor, Larry Tajiri, who moved to Denver after the *PC*'s transfer in 1952 from Salt Lake City to Los Angeles. The *PC* was the unofficial voice of early postwar Japanese America. Because Mike Masaoka was a veritable one-man gang lobbying Congress for the JACL-crafted program covering Japanese American rights and benefits, he amplified the *PC*'s version of Japanese American history within a strategic national center. During wartime Masaoka had strongly supported Nisei military service, viewing it as the best way of "proving" their loyalty. The all-Nisei 442nd Regimental Combat Team's first volunteer, Masaoka had served as a public relations officer and, in that capacity, was a very effective pitchman for the JACL rendition of Japanese American history.

For over three decades following his *Rocky Shimpo* resignation, Jimmie Omura disappeared from Japanese American society and was erased from Japanese American history. He remained a Denver resident, but lived apart from the Nikkei community. In 1951 Omura remarried another Nisei woman, and together they raised two boys. Omura operated a successful landscaping business until illness in the late 1970s forced him into retirement.

The JACL played a key role in expunging Jimmie Omura's name and memory from Japanese American history and consciousness. While he prospered in landscaping, the JACL thrived as an organization. Its expanding membership encompassed the Nisei elite, and outside of Japanese America it was viewed as that community's representative. This situation crystallized as early as 1948, as can be seen through one of Togo Tanaka's *Colorado Times* columns reprinted in the *Pacific Citizen* on September 25 that year.

Although Tanaka began his column by pointing out how Japanese Americans had been transformed from a despised into an accepted, even respected American minority group, his primary motivation for writing it was to rejoice over the reversed estates of JACLers and anti-JACL resisters since camp days. Then, "pressure boys" within such morally defiled places had intimidated and seduced the Nikkei majority into believing that JACL leaders were informers who had sold out their ethnic community for self-advancement and needed to be punished with beatings and banishment. Having accomplished this objective, resistance "messiahs" were themselves removed from the camps as "troublemakers." Still, as with Harry Yoshio Ueno, whose arrest had sparked the Manzanar Riot and driven Tanaka and his JACL cohorts out of the Manzanar camp, each of the other charismatic resistance leaders had been transformed into "a martyr to his glowing cause."

However, explained Tanaka, posterity would vindicate neither Ueno nor his counterparts. Just three years after the war it was apparent that these individuals had not "contributed anything more than zero to securing the present position of Japanese Americans in U.S. life."

Having punctured the historical pretensions of camp resisters, Tanaka turned his pen to obliterating them, via Ueno, from the collective memory of Japanese and mainstream America: "This ex-fruit-stand clerk has disappeared into the obscurity and oblivion from which he reared his sallow head, and no one seems to care very much if at all. Thus, the story endeth."

Although Yasui and Tanaka were not literally conspiring to oust resisters from the Japanese American World War II story and to refigure the JACL's role in it, they worked in tandem toward those ends. While Tanaka was exorcising those who had resisted the dismantling of the Nikkei community's traditional cultural arrangements by the alliance between the U.S. government, the WRA, and the JACL, Yasui was extirpating those who had resisted that same alliance's compromising of Nisei citizenship rights.

Neither Yasui nor Tanaka presumed to write books about Japanese American history and its defining World War II experience. However, another prominent JACL leader, Bill Hosokawa, did tackle this task, authoring or coauthoring four interrelated publications: *Nisei* (1969),[38] *East to America* (1980),[39] *JACL in Quest of Justice* (1982),[40] and *They Call Me Moses Masaoka* (1987).[41]

Setting aside these books' overall quality, what is instructive here is Hosokawa's erasure of resisters from the Japanese American wartime story. Nowhere appears the name of James Omura. This could hardly have been

simply an oversight. Both Hosokawa and Omura had been born and raised
in the Seattle area, figured significantly in the 1942 Tolan Committee hearings, were associated with Heart Mountain political developments, and resettled in wartime Denver and remained there. Hosokawa does mention draft
resisters in his last three books, but only perfunctorily and as a foil, vari-
ously, to discredit the purported revisionism of historians (like Roger
Daniels),[42] to glorify the compassionate efforts of JACLers (like Minoru Yasui
and Joe Grant Masaoka) to "save" them,[43] and to highlight their meager
number and lack of heroic merit relative to Nisei soldiers.[44] As for Harry
Ueno and other militant anti-JACL resisters, Hosokawa is also silent, with
the single exception of a reference in *Nisei* to Joe Kurihara, "perhaps the
chief agitator in Manzanar."[45]

Between publication of Hosokawa's *Nisei* in 1969 and his *East to America* in 1980, American society and culture, including the Nikkei community,
underwent a tumultuous upheaval. As the mounting protests against the
Vietnam War, racism, and sexism evinced, passivity and obedience to
authority had ceased being admired. Historians were drawn to outspoken
individuals and activist groups who had stood up for social justice and
enlarged democratic rights. Moreover, they used this tradition of dissent
to promote contemporary developments and personalities. Conversely, they
subjected the past's sacred cows—whether individuals, institutions, movements, or events—to rigorous and skeptical scrutiny and, if necessary, strong
criticism, and this legacy, too, was put into the service of present-day politics.

This development vis-á-vis Japanese American history was evident in sem-
inal books by Roger Daniels and Michi Nishiura Weglyn.[46] As Moses Rich-
lin's foreword to Daniels's *Concentration Camps USA* (1971)[47] noted: "[He]
has given special attention to the resistance and protest of the evacuees, an
aspect neglected or glossed over by others."[48] Daniels's acknowledgments
discreetly intimated his break with the JACL interpretation: "The late Joe
Grant Masaoka . . . would not have agreed with some of my strictures about
the Japanese American power structure, but would, I am sure, have defended
my right to make them."[49] Devoting considerable space to the Heart Mountain draft resistance movement and Omura's correlated role, Daniels contrasted his perspective with the WRA-JACL one.

> This account of the "loyal" Japanese American resistance . . . calls into ques-
> tion the stereotype of the Japanese American victim of oppression during
> World War II who met his fate with stoic resignation and responded only with
> superpatriotism. . . . The JACL-WRA view has dominated the writing of the

evacuation's postwar history, thereby nicely illustrating E. H. Carr's dictum that history is written by the winners. . . . [But] there are those who will find more heroism in resistance than in patient resignation.[50]

Community historian Michi Weglyn used similarly bald terminology in her title and text for *Years of Infamy* (1976).[51] That book's dust jacket featured the Manzanar camp's controversial plaque blaming "hysteria, racism, and economic exploitation" for the ten WRA "concentration camps." As Raymond Okamura's review stated, Weglyn wrote "from the perspective of an outraged victim." She relied heavily on primary sources and "discarded preconceptions" such as benevolent administrative-inmate cooperation and invested her data with experiential meaning. Her selection of opening photographs coupled "WRA brutality" and the Nikkei response of "defiance and resistance" to such oppressive actions.[52] Weglyn was mute about the draft resistance movement at Heart Mountain, but for one chapter's epigraph she summoned Omura's Tolan Committee testimony: "Has the Gestapo come to America? Have we not risen in righteous anger at Hitler's mistreatment of the Jews? Then, is it not incongruous that citizen Americans of Japanese descent should be similarly mistreated and persecuted?"[53] Moreover, Weglyn provided copious, empathetic coverage to camp resisters in all of the WRA camps (including the Moab and Leupp isolation centers for "troublemakers" and the Tule Lake Segregation Center for "disloyals"). Even her dedication—"To Wayne M. Collins, Who Did More to Correct a Democracy's Mistake Than Any Other One Person"— conveyed the book's resistance motif. A civil rights lawyer and social crusader, Collins had been instrumental to the notorious Tule Lake stockade's closing,[54] and also spent many postwar years restoring citizenship rights for nearly five thousand Tuleans who had renounced them.

Jimmie Omura was oblivious to this new resistance historiography. But as a 1980s retiree he began reflecting on his journalistic past, including his war against the JACL leadership. Plagued by a cardiac condition, Omura decided to write his memoirs and to emphasize the wartime years. Perhaps, in so doing, he could vindicate the Japanese American community and himself for the damage the U.S. government and the JACL had inflicted on both.

His decision coincided with the Nikkei community's campaign to achieve redress and reparations for its wartime mistreatment. Aware that the congressional Commission on Wartime Relocation and Internment of Civilians (CWRIC) had scheduled hearings in ten U.S. cities, Omura resolved to testify.[55] He chose to bypass Washington, D.C., where Mike Masaoka and Min Yasui (JACL's National Committee for Redress chair) testified, and his prewar journalism beats of Los Angeles and San Francisco, and selected his "home town" of Seattle (where the hearings were sited at his high school alma mater). Seattle also appealed to him because it would allow Omura to visit people and places from his Bainbridge Island boyhood and do background research for his book.

Redress was rooted in Omura (and Seattle). As one redress leader, William Hohri, states unequivocally, "James Omura was the first Japanese-American to seek redress from the United States." Indeed, on May 1, 1942, Omura had written to a Washington law firm seeking their representation, only to discover that the firm's start-up fee was more than he could afford.[56]

Omura was among 150-plus individuals to speak at the three-day hearings.[57] Within a four-person panel addressing "economic loss and harassment," he was granted a five-minute presentation. Hugh Mitchell, chairing the proceedings, twice abruptly cut him off. Omura made two points: 1) CWRIC should broaden its inquiry to encompass "voluntary evacuees" like himself; and 2) he was speaking as "one of the chief targets of the JACL," which he had "fought . . . from start to finish." He requested the opportunity to submit a fuller report to the Commission (which he subsequently did on October 16, 1981).[58]

Testifying in Seattle, too, were several Nikkei destined to play a significant role in Omura's remaining lifetime: Frank Abe, Lawson Inada, Chizu Omori, and Rita Takahashi. Yet, the CWRIC testifier having by far the biggest future impact upon Omura was not any of these second- and third-generation Japanese Americans, but a fifth-generation Chinese American— Frank Chin.[59]

A California native, Chin came to Seattle in the mid-1960s and exploded on the Asian American and mainstream literary scene in the next decade as an innovative dramatist.[60] He was one of four editors—another being Sansei poet Inada[61]—of a landmark Asian American literary anthology.[62] Chin's search for an Asian American literary and historical tradition led him to Nisei writers like Toshio Mori[63] (whose earliest work Omura had published in *Current Life*). But for Chin the most potent Nisei writer had been Seattle-reared John Okada. In his 1957 novel *No-No Boy*, which had been largely neglected, Okada modeled his protagonist on Jim Akutsu. He was a Seattle Nisei who, as a Minidoka camp draft resister, had corresponded with Omura in 1944[64] and who also testified at the Seattle CWRIC hearings. Pronouncing *No-No Boy* the most significant prose ever produced by a Japanese American, Chin and Inada collaborated editorially to have it reprised as a self-published volume.

In the late 1970s, Chin got immersed in the redress movement. Abetted by onetime Sansei actor Frank Abe, Chin in 1978 conceived Seattle's Day of Remembrance and, under the aegis of the Seattle Evacuation Redress Committee, staged a Thanksgiving weekend evacuation reenactment. Although never a member, Chin played a key role in the May 1979 formation of the Seattle-based National Council for Japanese American Redress (NCJAR). Upon Michi Weglyn's urging, he convinced William Hohri of Chicago to assume NCJAR's leadership. Afterwards, NCJAR, to quote Hohri, "gravitated towards Chicago," but it retained a core of Seattle supporters, such as Chizu Omori and Frank Abe. They agreed with Hohri that CWRIC was a "cop-out" and had developed because of "the JACL's unwillingness to demand redress directly from the United States Congress." In spite of NCJAR's 1980 decision to seek judicial rather than legislative redress, Omori and Abe, like Hohri, decided to participate in the CWRIC hearings.[65]

Chin's Seattle CWRIC testimony indicted the JACL for its incriminating role in "the formulation of the infamous loyalty oath" administered at the camps in early 1943 and for its "intention to use the camps to modify Japanese American society, culture, history, and individual behavior." Concluded Chin: "The greatest damage . . . that the government inflicted on Japanese Americans was the imposition of the Japanese American Citizens League as the leaders of the Japanese Americans inside the camps."[66]

Such a position naturally commanded Omura's attention, and he asked Seattle redress activist Henry Miyatake to introduce him to Chin. Hearing Omura's name, Chin remarked, "Not *the* James Omura," to which Omura responded, "The very same." Chin and Lawson Inada then conversed, off tape, with this "long lost uncle" about his remembrance of things past, particularly the Heart Mountain draft resistance movement.[67]

Then, Chin's "The Last Organized Resistance" appeared in the 1981 *Rafu Shimpo's* holiday issue.[68] It led to Chin being contacted in early 1982 by Frank Emi, a surviving Fair Play Committee leader,[69] and in that year Chin and Inada, along with allies, started collecting oral histories about this forgotten historical event.[70] As Chin later recalled, "men who had never spoken of their resistance jail terms, appeared in broad daylight to meet James Omura."[71] These interviews also catalyzed, a decade later, two well-attended resisters' reunions and reader's theater presentations, in San Jose in May 1992 and in Los Angeles in February 1993.

The early 1980s activity had ramifications for Omura, who had been "reborn in Seattle."[72] Hohri invited him to speak in Chicago and there avail himself of research material amassed by NCJAR (for which he, along with other notable wartime resisters like Harry Ueno, became a substantial backer)[73] for his in-progress memoir. San Francisco and Los Angeles vernaculars commissioned Omura to write editorials,[74] while UCLA's Asian American Studies Center wooed his participation in conferences and panels and solicited him to review books for the *Amerasia Journal* (including Hosokawa's *JACL in Quest of Justice*).[75] Scholars elsewhere interviewed him for academic projects, documentary films, and museum collections. Radical historian Richard Drinnon included Omura within his *Keeper of Concentration Camps* dedication for being a Japanese American who had said "no."[76] Even in Colorado, a group calling itself "Making Waves" arranged speaking engagements for him in the Denver region.

Repeatedly, Omura returned to the Pacific Northwest. Hosted in Seattle by Chizu Omori and Frank Abe, among others, he sometimes had Jim Akutsu serve as his chauffeur. His most meaningful return occurred in March 1988, when he participated in the Association for Asian American Studies meeting at Pullman, Washington. Omura presented a paper, as did Frank Emi, at a panel moderated by Frank Chin. After mentioning that since Pearl Harbor, the JACL had been "the voice of Japanese American opinion to the press and the voice of Japanese American history," Chin then mused: "I believe you will agree that Frank Emi of the Heart Mountain Fair Play Committee and James Omura of the *Rocky Shimpo* are honorable men. They have been written out of history. They should never have been forgotten."

Meanwhile, Omura had been working diligently to ensure that the label script being prepared by the JACL- and military-dominated advisory committee for the Smithsonian Institution's National Museum's 1987 exhibition, "A More Perfect Union: Japanese Americans and the United States Constitution," would do the draft resisters justice. Upon traveling to Washington, D.C., to see this exhibition, he was convinced it pretty much did.[77]

Omura tried to set the record straight about another text that to him polluted the truth of the World War II Japanese American historical record—*They Call Me Moses Masaoka* (1987), written by Mike Masaoka with Bill Hosokawa. The opening salvo of Omura's *Rafu Shimpo* review presaged what would follow: "History indeed is infinitely the poorer and literature thereby greatly diminished by publication of this fabricated account of the historic Japanese American episode of World War II."[78] This review's damage was compounded by the finding in JACL-commissioned

researcher Deborah Lim's 1990 report that, at the JACL's March 1942 Special Emergency Meeting in San Francisco, Masaoka allegedly had recommended "Japanese be branded and stamped and put under the supervision
of the Federal government."[79]

In the late 1980s and early 1990s Omura received long-deferred public
recognition and acclaim. Biographical encyclopedia and dictionary entries
honored him,[80] while organizations feted him for his accomplishments. Two
tributes meant most to Omura. In 1989, the Asian American Journalists Association (AAJA), meeting in San Francisco, conferred their Lifetime Achievement Award upon him. Frank Abe, then a KIRO Radio (Seattle) reporter
and an AAJA board member, was instrumental in Omura's selection. Abe
cited Omura's courageous journalistic World War II role upholding constitutional principles and contrasted his behavior with the JACL's capitula-
tion to pragmatic accommodation. Not expecting an Asian American group
to honor him during his lifetime, Omura doubted the award would change
public opinion toward him. Then, in 1992, the National Coalition for
Redress/Reparations (NCRR) recognized Omura in a Day of Remembrance
candle-lighting ceremony, also in San Francisco, on Executive Order 9066's
fiftieth anniversary. Significant for Omura were the other community
benefactors honored (civil rights lawyers Ernest Besig and Wayne Collins,
crusading *Bainbridge Review* editors Walt and Millie Woodward, and the
American Friends Service Committee) and his being the sole Japanese American honoree. "I had no expectation that anyone would be thinking of me
on the 50th Anniversary of the signing of Executive Order 9066," Omura
wrote Michi Weglyn. "I was wrong!"[81]

Meanwhile, the JACL was fighting to retain its righteous place in Japanese American history. But since the CWRIC hearings, and especially after
the Civil Rights Act of 1988 enacting the Commission's recommendations,
it had been battling a defensive war. Having gained a U.S. government apology, a growing number of Nikkei also demanded one from the JACL for its
wartime leaders' community betrayal, a point driven home by the evidence
in the Lim Report (which the JACL attempted to suppress). In Omura's opinion, a rear-guard JACL action to deflect criticism and restore its dignity was
its embracing "the glorification of the trio of failed Supreme Court chal-
lengers [Gordon Hirabayashi, Fred Korematsu, and Minoru Yasui]." These
test cases, argued Omura, had "no relevance to their [Japanese Americans]
sufferings and the tragedy of the Japanese American episode," but instead
"sprang out of personal impulses." What really disturbed Omura was Denver's Mile Hi JACL chapter's fund-raising campaign for a city statue to honor

Minoru Yasui, "unarguably the [Japanese American community's] number one informer, or in cultural terms, *inu.*" The very idea to Omura was a
desecration.[82]

Denver's Nikkei community disagreed with Omura, believing that Yasui
was a deserving Nisei hero. From 1967 to 1983, he headed the city's commission on community relations, and from the 1970s to his 1986 death he
spearheaded the JACL's redress movement. Thus, he was much honored in
Denver. In 1994, the year Omura died, Yasui's image was unveiled on a bronze
plaque memorial (sculpted by Ruth Asawa and relating the Japanese American historical narrative) in the Robert Peckham Federal Building. In 1999
this building was dedicated as Minoru Yasui Plaza, and prominent in its lobby
was a replica of the Yasui bust in Sakura Square at the historic heart of Denver's Japantown. Finally, in 2000, Yasui was one of a very few Denver leaders granted Mayor's Millennial Awards for their extraordinary contributions
to the city.[83]

Bill Hosokawa, another Pacific Northwest native and JACL leader, also
had "monuments" created to his memory within his adopted city. Most came
after Omura's death. In 1996 Hosokawa was inducted into the Denver Press
Club's Media Hall of Fame. In 1999 the Japan America Society of Colorado
and the Japanese Consulate recognized him as honorary consul general for
Japan in Colorado. And in 2000, Hosokawa received the American Civil Liberties Union's Whitehead Award for "lifetime service on behalf of all who
suffer inequality and injustice."[84]

But no similar city and state honors were forthcoming for Omura, before
or after his death. He thus remains in the region where he lived from 1942
to 1994 as an unrecognized hero of Japanese American and U.S. history.
The same general situation still prevails throughout the nation, including
the Pacific Northwest. But the winds are blowing the other direction. In his
Rafu Shimpo obituary for Omura, "Let Us Now Praise Famous Men," Frank
Chin fittingly eulogized him: "He [Omura] had lived to see the resisters he
championed begin to be restored to the community. After 40 years of silence
and obscurity, Jimmie began to be rediscovered and his work recognized
by Asian America. . . . But Japanese America, Asian America never knew Jimmie well enough."[85]

Since Chin's obituary appeared, not only Japanese America and Asian
America have come to know Omura quite well, but even the larger American community has been introduced to him. Chin deepened the first two
audiences' awareness by including a long section on Omura and Heart
Mountain draft resisters in his lead essay ("Come All Ye Asian American

Writers of the Real and the Fake") for a 1991 anthology of Chinese and Japanese American literature.[86] Moreover, Chin's 2002 documentary novel, *Born in the USA,* which valorizes the Heart Mountain draft resistance story and makes Omura a central interpretive voice for the authentic Japanese America legacy, promises to influence a large mainstream population.[87] Two documentary films—Emiko Omori's *Rabbit in the Moon* (1999)[88] and Frank Abe's *Conscience and the Constitution* (2000)[89]—have already reached this larger audience via national public television. The first (co-produced by Omori's sister, Chizu) won major awards, including the American Historical Association's award for the year's best historical documentary. Abe's film claimed top honors at film festivals and competitions, and in 2001, the AAJA recognized it as the year's best film for Unlimited Subject Matter in Television. Whereas *Rabbit in the Moon* was dedicated to Omura and praised camp resisters generally, including those challenging the Nisei draft, *Conscience and the Constitution* focused exclusively on the Heart Mountain draft resistance movement and Omura's support for it.

Two 2001 books, *Resistance*[90] and *Free to Die for Their Country,*[91] both depict Omura within the larger draft resistance story so as to enhance his historical reputation. William Hohri authored the first of these books, with essays by former Fair Play Committee members Mits Koshiyama, Yosh Kuromiya, and Frank Emi. According to Philip Tajitsu Nash's *Washington Journal* review of *Resistance,* "Hohri reminds us of the patriotism of those who chose incarceration, and a subsequent lifetime of ostracism, rather than see the Constitution undermined. . . . [and provides] sometimes gripping accounts of the human cost of standing up for justice."[92] *Free to Die for Their Country,* by University of North Carolina constitutional law professor Eric Muller, is more mainstream-oriented than Hohri's book. This is due to its prestigious publisher, the University of Chicago Press, and its foreword by Senator Daniel K. Inouye, an American as well as a Japanese American icon of patriotism, valor, and justice.

While it will take more time for Omura to gain the iconic stature achieved by Senator Inouye and now almost attained by the draft resisters of conscience, he seems destined to reach this lofty plateau. He had seen and written about fascism's darkening clouds in the prewar United States, he had testified, ominously, about the Gestapo coming to America during the war's early stages, and in the war's fullness he had waged a fearless editorial battle against lawless militarism and for civil, minority, and human rights. At the end of his life, Omura was reliving this past for his own purposes as well as the edification of posterity. "Jimmie," noted Frank Chin in his obituary, "was at work on his book when he was struck with a heart attack and died in Denver, at 6:35 A.M., June 20, 1994."[93] Omura had been laboring over that book, his memoir, for more than a decade. Perhaps when it is published there will be a greater appreciation for why, at the turn of this new millennium, he was honored as Japanese America's (most) influential journalist of the twentieth century.

Notes

The author thanks Louis Fiset and Gail Nomura for editorial assistance; Frank Abe, Frank Chin, and William Hohri for reviewing the manuscript; and Debra Gold Hansen, Rebecca Manley, Martha Nakagawa, Chizu and Emiko Omori, Wayne Omura, Rita Takahashi, Mary Kimoto Tomita, and Steve Yoda for facilitating his ongoing work on James Omura.

1. Takeshi Nakayama, "Influential JA Journalist: James Omura," *Pacific Citizen* 1–13 (January 2000): 6.

2. Fred Hirasuna, "Letters to the Editor," *Pacific Citizen* 7–13 (April 2000): 7.

3. Brian Niiya, ed., *Encyclopedia of Japanese American History: An A-Z Reference from 1868 to the Present* (Los Angeles: Japanese American National Museum, 2001), s.v. "Tajiri, Larry (1914–1965) *journalist*" by David Yoo. See also Bill Hosokawa, "Larry Tajiri, A Better Choice," *Pacific Citizen* 11–17 (February 2000)" 6.

4. Bill Hosokawa, JACL *in Quest of Justice: The History of the Japanese American Citizens League* (New York: Morrow, 1982), 156–57, 178–79.

5. Bill Hosokawa, *Out of the Frying Pan: Reflections of a Japanese American* (Niwat, Colo.: University Press of Colorado, 1998), especially "Hosokawa of the *Post*," chap. 8, 63–79.

6. Minidoka (Idaho), Heart Mountain (Wyoming), Topaz (Utah), and Amache (Colorado).

7. Russell Endo, "Japanese of Colorado: A Sociohistorical Portrait," *Journal of Social and Behavioral Sciences* 31 (fall 1985): 100–110.

8. David K. Yoo, *Growing Up Nisei: Race, Generation, and Culture among Japanese Americans of California, 1924–49* (Urbana: University of Illinois Press, 2000), 129.

9. Ibid., 130.

10. James M. Omura, interview by Arthur A. Hansen, "Resisters," pt. 4 of Arthur A. Hansen, ed., *Japanese American World War II Evacuation Oral History Project* (Munich, K. G. Saur, 1995), 209–11.

11. Arthur A. Hansen, "Interview with James Matsumoto Omura," *Amerasia Journal* 13 (1986–87): 104.

12. Ibid., 104–5.

13. *World Biographical Hall of Fame* (Raleigh, N.C.: Historical Preservations of America, 1992), s.v. "James Matsumoto Omura."

14. Omura to Hansen, "Resisters," 254.

15. Ibid., 261; Jere Takahashi, *Nisei/Sansei: Shifting Japanese American Identities and Politics* (Philadelphia: Temple University Press, 1997), 95–96.

16. Omura to Hansen, "Resisters," 262.

17. U.S. Congress. House. Select Committee Investigating National Defense Migration, San Francisco Hearings, February 21 and 23, 1942, Pt. 28 (Washington, D.C.: GPO, 1942), 11229–30.

18. Omura to Hansen, "Resisters," 263.

19. According to correspondence filed in the James M. Omura Papers (currently in custody of author for eventual deposit at Stanford University's Green Library), Omura became aware of JACL's imminent incursion in Denver shortly after moving there. See Omura's letters to A. Norman Depew dated 9 May and 22 May 1942.

20. This point is discussed in James Omura, "Japanese American Journalism During World War II," in *Frontiers of Asian American Studies: Writing, Research, and Commentary,* ed. Gail M. Nomura, Russell Endo, Stephen H. Sumida, and Russell Leong (Pullman: Washington State University Press, 1989), 72–73. "It was not until the fall of 1942," Omura writes, "that the *Colorado Times* transformed into a pro-JACL organ. . . . This policy switch resulted when the *Colorado Times* agreed to be subsidized by OWI [Office of War Information] and thus subject to its 'propaganda releases.' It was because the *Colorado Times* transformed into a pro-JACL organ that I discontinued writing for them."

21. Omura to Hansen, "Resisters," 284.

22. Arthur A. Hansen and David A. Hacker, "The Manzanar Riot: An Ethnic Perspective," *Amerasia Journal* 2 (fall 1974): 112–57.

23. For a profile of the JACL's predicament in the camps, see Niiya, *Encyclopedia of Japanese American History,* s.v. "Japanese American Citizens League," by Glen Kitayama. "Within several of the camps," explains Kitayama, "JACL leaders were the targets of threats and physical violence and had to be removed from the camps for their own protection. Because of the controversy surrounding the JACL, the wartime president of the organization, Saburo Kido [himself an assault victim at the Poston camp], estimated [in 1946] that the membership 'dwindled down to only about 10 active chapters and about 1,700 members.'"

24. See Omura's revealing letter to his brother, Kazushi Matsumoto, dated 1 January 1945, James Omura Papers: "The F.B.I. is shooting in the dark when it attempts to dress me in the garb of communism. I have been a militant foe of Nisei communism. . . . It wasn't much over a year ago that I attacked the editor of the Pacific

Citizen for his left-wing affiliations. This prompted a threat of a libel suit from Lawrence Tajiri."

25. Omura to Hansen, "Resisters," 284.

26. Ibid.

27. The present author is editing this autobiographical manuscript of Omura's for future publication as "Nisei Naysayer: The Memoir of Japanese American Newsman Jimmie Omura."

28. This editorial, "Let Us Not Be Rash," is reproduced in Omura, "Japanese American Journalism During World War II," 78.

29. According to Omura, a contemporary FBI report noted that "before I [Omura] took over they [the *Denver Rocky Shimpo*] had only about 500 subscribers at Heart Mountain, and that after I took over and started the editorials, the number of subscribers zoomed to 1,200." Omura to Hansen, "Resisters," 287.

30. Ibid., 314.

31. See Arthur A. Hansen, "Return to the Wars: Jimmie Omura's 1947 Crusade Against the Japanese American Citizens League," in Sucheng Chan, ed., *Remapping Asian American History* (Walnut Creek, Calif.: AltaMira Press, 2003), 127–50.

32. See Minoru Yasui's interview in John Tateishi, *And Justice for All: An Oral History of the Japanese American Detention Camps* (New York: Random House, 1984), 80–82.

33. Omura to Hansen, "Resisters," 301.

34. Omura praised the Committee for Industrial Organizations (CIO), urged Nisei to join unions, and called for the abolition of race, sex, and creed-based restrictions in union constitutions.

35. Commonly, Yasui promoted minority rights and civic-minded, liberal organizations and individuals.

36. See "Shimpo Editor to Assume Full Time Duty with Paper," *Denver Rocky Shimpo,* 30 October 1947.

37. See "The Facts and Mr. Tanaka," *Denver Rocky Shimpo,* 12 August 1947.

38. Bill Hosokawa, *Nisei: The Quiet Americans* (New York: Morrow, 1969).

39. Robert A. Wilson and Bill Hosokawa, *East to America: A History of the Japanese in the United States* (New York: Morrow, 1980).

40. Bill Hosokawa, *JACL in Quest of Justice* (New York: Morrow, 1982).

41. Mike Masaoka with Bill Hosokawa, *They Call Me Moses Masaoka: An American Saga* (New York: Morrow, 1987).

42. Hosokawa, *East to America,* 243–44, and Masaoka with Hosokawa, *They Call Me Moses Masaoka,* 179.

43. Hosokawa, *JACL in Quest of Justice,* 273–74.

44. See, especially, Masaoka with Hosokawa, *They Call Me Moses Masaoka,* 179.

45. Hosokawa, *Nisei,* 361–62.

46. See Niiya, *Encyclopedia of Japanese American History,* s.v., "Daniels, Roger (1927–) *pioneering scholar on the history of Japanese Americans,*" 148, and "Weglyn, Michi Nishiura (1926–1999) *historian, activist,*" 411. Also influential were Gary Okihiro's articles on Nikkei; see, "Japanese Resistance in America's Concentration Camps: A Re-evaluation," *Amerasia Journal* 2 (fall 1973): 20–34, and "Tule Lake under Martial Law: A Study of Japanese Resistance," *Journal of Ethnic Studies* 5 (fall 1977): 71–86.

47. Roger Daniels, *Concentration Camps USA: Japanese Americans and World War II* (New York: Holt, Rinehart and Winston, 1971).

48. Ibid., x.

49. Ibid., vii-viii.

50. Ibid., 128–29.

51. Michi Weglyn, *Years of Infamy: The Untold Story of America's Concentration Camps* (New York: Morrow, 1976).

52. See Raymond Okamura, "The Concentration Camp Experience from a Japanese American Perspective: A Bibliographical Essay and Review of Michi Weglyn's *Years of Infamy,*" in *Counterpoint: Perspectives on Asian America,* ed. Emma Gee (Los Angeles: Asian American Studies Center, University of California, 1976), 27–30.

53. See Weglyn, *Years of Infamy,* chap. 3, "'So the Army Could Handle the Japs,'" 67.

54. Niiya, *Encyclopedia of Japanese American History,* s.v., "Collins, Wayne Mortimer (1900–1974) *attorney,*" 140–41.

55. For the summary of the hearings, see Commission on the Wartime Relocation and Internment of Civilians (CWRIC), *Personal Justice Denied: Report of the Commission on Wartime Relocation and Internment of Civilians* (Washington D.C.: GPO, 1982).

56. William Hohri, *Repairing America: An Account of the Movement for Japanese-American Redress* (Pullman, Wash.: Washington State University Press), 30.

57. Yasuko I. Takezawa, *Breaking the Silence: Redress and Japanese American Ethnicity* (Ithaca, N.Y.: Cornell University Press, 1995), 51.

58. See transcription of "Commission on Wartime Relocation and Internment of Civilians" (Wednesday, September 9, 1981, Seattle Central Community College, Seattle, Washington) and email correspondence from Aiko Yoshinaga-Herzig to Arthur Hansen, 15 May 2001, in James M. Omura Papers. The author thanks Yoshinaga-Herzig, a key CWRIC research associate, who supplied both the transcription and the explanation for the context of Omura's panel testimony. See ibid., "Written Submission by James M. Omura, Seattle Hearings, CWRIC, 16 October 1981."

59. For a biographical overview of Chin, see Shawn Wong, ed., *Asian American Literature: A Brief Introduction and Anthology* (New York: HarperCollins, 1996), 15–16.

60. According to Shawn Wong, "Chin's *The Chickencoop Chinaman* was the first Asian American play performed on a legitimate New York stage when it was produced in 1972 by the American Place Theatre." Ibid., 15.

61. See Niiya, *Encyclopedia of Japanese American History,* s.v. "Inada, Lawson Fusao (1938–) *poet, writer,*" by Emily Lawsin, 207–8.

62. See Frank Chin, Jeffrey Paul Chan, Lawson Fusao Inada, and Shawn Wong, eds., *AIIIEEEEE! An Anthology of Asian-American Writers* (Washington, D.C.: Howard University Press, 1974).

63. See Niiya, *Encyclopedia of Japanese American History,* s.v., "Mori, Toshio (1910–1980) *writer,*" 283–84. In 1985, the University of Washington Press republished, in its Asian American series, Mori's 1949 classic collection of short stories, *Yokohama, California,* with a new introduction by Lawson Inada. This edition also included the original introduction by William Saroyan, a staunch supporter and contributor to Omura's *Current Life.*

64. For the context of this wartime contact between Akutsu and Omura, see Omura to Hansen, "Resisters," 300. As recalled by Omura in 1984, the situation forty years earlier was this: "Because he [Akutsu] was searching for an answer [about how to deal with the draft], he went to . . . Min Yasui [at Mindoka], feeling that, since he had violated a curfew, he was a champion of civil rights. He looked up to someone like that, see? Then he talked with Min. . . . He wrote me about this: 'I'm so disappointed.'"

65. See Hohri, *Repairing America,* 48–50, 87, and 83. In Mitchell T. Maki, Harry H. L. Kitano, and S. Megan Berthold, *Achieving the Impossible Dream: How Japanese Americans Obtained Redress* (Urbana: University of Illinois Press, 1999), 122, the authors claim that NCJAR pursued redress via the courts partly because it "and William Hohri in particular were motivated by an intense dislike of the national JACL."

66. See Hohri, *Repairing America,* 125–29.

67. See Frank Chin, "Let Us Now Praise Famous Men," *Los Angeles Rafu Shimpo,* 25 June 1994; this account in Chin's obituary of Omura was amplified by him in personal conversations with the author.

68. See Martha Nakagawa's entry on "draft resisters" in Niiya, *Encyclopedia of Japanese American History,* 153–54.

69. Ibid., 154.

70. The Frank Chin Oral History Collection is in the Manuscripts, Archives, and Special Collections department at Washington State University.

71. Chin, "Let Us Now Praise Famous Men."

72. See Robert Sadamu Shimabukuro, *Born in Seattle: The Campaign for Japanese American Redress* (Seattle: University of Washington Press, 2001).

73. Omura and Ueno were both NCJAR *ronin,* signifying minimal donations of one thousand dollars.

74. In San Francisco, the *Hokubei Mainichi,* and in Los Angeles, the *Rafu Shimpo.*

75. For Omura's review of the Hosokawa volume, see *Amerasia Journal* 11 (1984): 97–102; see also his review of Peter Irons, *Justice at War: The Story of the Japanese American Internment Cases* (New York: Oxford University Press, 1983), *Amerasia Journal* 10 (1983): 127–29.

76. See Richard Drinnon, *Keeper of Concentration Camps: Dillon S. Myer and American Racism* (Berkeley: University of California Press, 1987).

77. Omura's involvement in this process was aided by Aiko Yoshinaga-Herzig, a member of both NCJAR and the exhibition's advisory committee, and his efforts received a critical boost from historian Roger Daniels.

78. James Omura, "Debunking JACL Fallacies," *Los Angeles Rafu Shimpo,* 11 April 1989.

79. See Deborah Lim, untitled report, 1991, p. 9. For an unabridged version of the Lim Report, see Frank Abe's Web site at: www.resisters.com.

80. See J. K. Yamamoto, "Wartime Journalist Recognized," *San Francisco Hokubei Mainichi,* 31 July 1993, published when Omura was named to receive the Twentieth Century Award of Achievement by the International Biographical Association of Cambridge, England.

81. Jimmie Omura, letter to Michi and Walter Weglyn, 7 February 1992, James M. Omura Papers.

82. See Jimmie Omura, "Yasui Statue Would Be Undeserved Honor," *San Francisco Hokubei Mainichi,* 15 June 1980.

83. The information relative to Denver's honoring of Yasui was drawn chiefly from newspaper articles; see *Denver Rocky Mountain News,* 2 March 1999; and *Denver Post,* 5 December 1999 and 11 December 2000.

84. For press accounts of Hosokawa's Denver honors, see the following: *Denver Rocky Mountain News,* 20 April 1996 and 20 August 1998; *Denver Post,* 13 December 1998, 9 February 1999, 14 February 1999, and 25 October 1999; and *Denver Rocky Mountain News,* 28 September 2000.

85. Chin, "Let Us Now Praise Famous Men."

86. Frank Chin, "Come All Ye Asian American Writers of the Real and the Fake," in Jeffrey Paul Chan, et al., *The Big Aiiieeeee! An Anthology of Chinese American and Japanese American Literature* (New York: Meridian, 1991), 52–92.

87. Frank Chin, *Born in the U.S.A.: A Story of Japanese America, 1889–1947* (Lanham, Md.: Rowman & Littlefield, 2002).

88. Emiko and Chizu Omori (prod.) and Emiko Omori (dir.), *Rabbit in the Moon,*

60 mins., 1999 (New Day Films, c/o Transit Media, 22D Hollywood Ave., Hohokus NJ 07423).

89. Frank Abe (prod.; dir.) and Shannon Gee (prod.), *Conscience and the Constitution*, 60 mins., 2000 (Resisters.com Productions, 3811 S. Horton St., Seattle, WA 98144). For a joint review of these two films, see that by Naoko Shibusawa in the *Journal of American History* 88 (December 2001): 1209–11.

90. William Hohri, *Resistance: Challenging America's Wartime Internment of Japanese-Americans* (Los Angeles: The Epistolarian, 2001).

91. Eric L. Muller, *Free to Die for Their Country: The Story of the Japanese American Draft Resisters in World War II* (Chicago: University of Chicago Press, 2001).

92. Philip Tajitsu Nash, "William Minoru Hohri: Visionary, Writer and Activist for Resisters of Injustice," *Washington Journal*, August 17–23, 2001.

93. Chin, "Let Us Now Praise Famous Men."

14 / RECLAIMING AND REINVENTING "POWELL STREET"

Reconstruction of the Japanese Canadian Community in Post–World War II Vancouver

MASUMI IZUMI

In the early months of 1942, a thriving ethnic community disappeared from the map of Vancouver. People gathered at the station with two suitcases per individual. In most cases, whatever they had in those suitcases were the only things they were allowed to keep. Everything else they had left— their houses, furniture, family possessions—was later sold and lost forever. The trains took the people into the mountains.[1]

With this forced mass migration, "Little Tokyo," or the "Japantown" on Powell Street disappeared. Shortly after, in interior British Columbia, small ghost towns were rehabilitated, and new ethnic enclaves appeared. Their existence, however, was temporary. Within several years, people were dispersed again, this time all across Canada. As the Japanese Canadians left their spartan housing centers, government officials told them never to form a community again.

Before the uprooting, Powell Street was a thriving Japanese Canadian community. The 300 and 400 blocks on Powell Street were the commercial and business area. People lived on and around these blocks. There were stores, pharmacies, doctors' and midwives' offices, taxi companies, banks, tofu factories, rooming houses, hotels, and even a department store.[2] In the early years of the city's development, many of the residents were single men, staying in boarding houses. By the 1930s, however, Japanese Canadians owned most of the buildings in the area, which became a lively community of families. A Japanese language school opened in 1928, and there were Buddhist and Christian churches, where children could enjoy cultural and athletic activities. Oppenheimer Park, or the "Powell Ground," lay in the center of the community. Asahi, a semi-professional baseball team, played and practiced in the park, drawing large crowds of people.[3]

In the 1960s, Powell Street was not the vital community it once was. It was an impoverished area, a skid row, whose residents were predominantly disadvantaged by their class, race, and/or age. Run-down rooming houses and cheap apartments, owned often by absentee landlords, were occupied by those who were left behind during the postwar prosperity and development of the city of Vancouver. Among them were a number of Issei, the first generation Japanese Canadians, who had returned to the neighborhood they had cherished before the uprooting.

This paper examines the reconstruction of the postwar Japanese Canadian community in Vancouver with particular focus on the development that took place in the Powell Street area in the 1970s. The process of reconstruction was affected heavily by the Canadian state policy of multiculturalism, and this study will place the ethnic community construction in a dialectic relationship between government policy and community initiatives. The Powell Street community revival occurred at a historical junction where ethnic and governmental politics intersected.

Many past studies on the Japanese Canadian community have been limited to the "cultural" aspect of multiculturalism. These studies list "heritage items" such as heritage language education, religion, sports, and art, and often focus on non-mundane occasions such as festivals and ceremonial rituals.[4] However, as Lisa Lowe has pointed out, the representation of cultural diversity in a multicultural society must be distinguished from the existing structural hegemony that determines the material conditions ethnic individuals experience in everyday life. Criticizing the naïve celebration of multiculturalism in the sixteen-day-long Los Angeles Festival of the Arts, Lowe states:

> The synthetic production of multiculturalism unravels and its crises are best seized and contested at the moments when the contradiction between the representational economy of ethnic signifiers, on the one hand, and the material economy of resources and means, on the other, becomes unavoidably clear. That is, what the claim to "new stories for a new America" made dangerously invisible is that to most African Americans, Asians, or Latinos living and working in Los Angeles today, for the other 349 days of the year, it may be very clear indeed *who* "owns" culture.[5]

Sharing the above critical viewpoint, this study focuses on the pragmatic aspects of life essential for the survival of minority communities and, in many cases, the survival of individual persons in a literal sense. On Powell Street, community activists simultaneously engaged in everyday political and social activities and their own cultural production. Through the reclamation of Powell Street, the once-erased Japanese Canadian community recovered its "ground" and reinvented its psychological "hometown." This is a story of how the Japanese Canadian ethnic landscape reappeared on Powell Street in the 1970s.

The 1960s: Community Resistance to Vancouver Urban Renewal Schemes

The uprooting of Japanese Canadians during World War II was a massive governmental assault on the existence of a visible ethnic community in Canada. On August 4, 1944, Prime Minister W. L. Mackenzie King explained in Parliament the reason for the dispersal of Japanese Canadians. He made it clear that the incarceration was Ottawa's response to British Columbia's concern that the province had "within its borders virtually the entire Japanese population of Canada"—a situation that led to "acrimony and bitterness." The government decided that "it would be unwise and undesirable, not only from the point of view of the people in British Columbia, but also from that of persons of Japanese origin themselves, to allow the Japanese population to be concentrated in that province after the war."[6]

King, in his speech, blamed British Columbians' racism on its victims. As far as the Canadian government was concerned, the problem was the very existence of the visible ethnic community. The hostility towards the Japanese Canadian community resulted in a ruthless policy of dispersal and subsequent pressure for assimilation.[7] During the war, the government sold the property of Japanese Canadians without the consent of the owners, ensuring that nothing was left for them to come back to. Towards the end of the war, those who were interned in interior B.C. were forced to choose between "repatriation" to Japan and relocation to east of the Rockies. The government did not allow Japanese Canadians to return to the West Coast until April 1, 1949. Even after resettlement, the pressure for assimilation was so strong that many Japanese Canadians refrained from speaking Japanese and in many cases started using their Anglicized first names.[8] Their children grew up in predominantly white neighborhoods and did not learn to speak Japanese.[9]

In the 1950s, the governmental assault on ethnic communities again revealed itself in the Urban Renewal Scheme of the city of Vancouver.[10] This time, the target was another visible minority community: Chinatown.

After World War II, Vancouver underwent rapid growth. As was happening generally in North American cities, the land prices of downtown areas rose while the inner city areas started to decline. The city government started to see Chinatown as a problem because of its close vicinity to downtown and the low tax income from the district. In the mid-1950s, the City Planning Department made an urban redevelopment plan in which it declared that Chinatown was one of the city's most "blighted" areas.[11] After the assessment in 1956, the City Technical Planning Board recommended preservation of the commercial area of Chinatown and redevelopment of the residential sections:

> That part of Pender Street between Carrall Street and Main Street forms the most important part of Chinatown. Chinatown is an area which is improving in quality. In fact, it rates more highly than most of the normal retail areas, in the amount of money spent on new retail construction and repairs to stores since the war. This particular part of the whole Chinese quarter is the only one which can be said to be a tourist attraction. The remainder of the Chinese quarter to the east of Main Street is at present of significance only to the people who live there.[12]

For the city bureaucrats, the commercial part of Chinatown was valuable because Chinatown signified the "otherness" that was commodified through tourism since the late 1930s.[13] Chinatown from this aspect was "a treasure of Oriental culture [that] contributes an exotic flavour to Canada's Oriental gateway."[14] However, the residential part of Chinatown was conceived as a "slum," a potential health and fire hazard, and in the mainstream population's mind, it was filled with social vice and moral degeneration.[15]

In the early and mid-1960s, the city government carried out the "slum clearance."[16] The city brought in bulldozers and cleared the areas east of Main Street between Union and East Hastings Streets. Urban redevelopment for Chinatown residents meant demolition of their houses and relocation to high-density modern public housing. Residents who were opposed to the plan established the Chinatown Property Owners Association (CPOA), conducted public hearings, and submitted written appeals to stop the procedure.[17] The city, however, ignored the opposition and proceeded with the plan. By 1966, over 3,300 residents were displaced and relocated under the Urban Renewal Scheme.[18]

In 1967, the city government announced its plan to build a freeway through what remained of Chinatown. This time, however, opposition came not only from local residents but from the mainstream population.[19] A number of architects, social workers, and university students joined the struggle to defend Chinatown, insisting on its historical significance as well as the value of the area as a major tourist attraction. In 1968, a group of local residents formed the Strathcona Property Owners and Tenants Association (SPOTA). SPOTA had some strengths that the CPOA (defunct by the time) had lacked. Although it had predominantly Chinese membership, SPOTA contained some non-Chinese members who were committed to the cause. It conducted a grassroots movement, such as a general survey of the residents in the Strathcona (Chinatown) area and a signature campaign, both of which proved that overwhelming local opposition to the redevelopment plan existed. SPOTA also had connections with the local Liberal Party, which eventually attracted the attention of the Trudeau government. With the successful grassroots opposition campaign and the federal government's intervention, the city abandoned its freeway plan.[20] Vancouver's Chinatown was preserved.

This policy change reflected a shift in Canada vis-á-vis the ethnic diversity of the country from a modernist to multiculturalist stance. The state increasingly came to regard diversity itself as a national asset. Instead of emphasizing progress and efficiency through assimilation, the government started to respect and simultaneously exploit the differences of non-mainstream communities in Canada. The abandonment of the Chinatown highway plan was one of the events that marked the coming of the policy of multiculturalism, which was adopted officially in 1971.

Adjoining Chinatown to the north was the Downtown Eastside Oppenheimer area, or the Powell Street area. After the Japanese Canadian community was uprooted in 1942, the area was reclassified as an industrial zone. Since property owners in industrial zones were not eligible for mortgage money or bank loans for repairs and renewal of residential property, the buildings and streets in this area lay neglected and were left to deteriorate during and after the war.

The poor conditions of this area are described in a technical report of the *Vancouver Urban Renewal Study,* published in 1969.[21] Although the area was zoned as an industrial district, manufacturing industries occupied only 26.28 net acres, or 19.4 percent of the acreage in the district, while 30.17 acres, or 22.2 percent, were used for residences, parking lots, or billboards. Building conditions in the district averaged only 2.65 on the scale between 0 and 5, which meant that most buildings needed substantial repair.[22] This was one of the lowest in all the zoning districts in Vancouver. Of the 248 residential buildings in the district, 55 were hotels or apartments, and 3,200 persons lived in the estimated 1,050 dwelling units. The conditions of the residential buildings averaged 2.12, and 74 percent of the residential buildings were in less-than-average condition, including 42 categorized as dilapidated buildings.

In the 1960s, there were a few ethnic markers in the former Japantown. There were Japanese food stores and restaurants, a Japanese language school, and a Buddhist church. The office of the local Japanese Canadian Citizens Association (JCCA) was located in the language school building one block away on Alexander Street. Nonetheless, Powell Street in the late 1960s was one of the poorest and most badly deteriorating neighborhoods in metropolitan Vancouver.[23]

The 1970s: Sprouting of Ethnic Community Activities

Japanese Canadians in the postwar period worked very hard to rebuild their lives. With the removal of numerous adversarial laws and by-laws and the subsiding of overt racial prejudice, many Japanese Canadians achieved remarkable upward social mobility and structural assimilation within two decades.[24] Tomoko Makabe reported that Japanese Canadians in Toronto in the mid-1970s were better educated than the general population and that a majority of them held white-collar jobs.[25] She also noted the geographic dispersion in their residential pattern and their mobility from the central area of the city toward the suburban areas.

Likewise, in Vancouver, Japanese Canadians never lived in concentration in one area of the city after the uprooting. Following the general pattern of residential mobility in postwar North America, people moved to the suburbs as their economic situations improved. On the other hand, some Issei, particularly those who lacked English language ability and families who could help them, were not able to take advantage of the postwar economic growth of the city. Powell Street became home for many of those disadvantaged Issei.

In the early 1970s, a Nisei called Jun Hamada became aware of the plight of these people.[26] Hamada was born in Vancouver and had been interned in the Tashme Camp during the war. He relocated to eastern Canada, but came back to Vancouver in the early 1960s. He worked at Cedar Cottage Neighbourhood House, through which he developed his skills as a social worker. Seeing the hardships of the seniors living on and around Powell Street, Hamada applied for a federal government grant to develop a social service program for them. He received the grant in late 1974.

Hamada started a survey of the Issei seniors in the area, with the assistance of some young immigrants from Japan, including Takeo Yamashiro, a well-known shakuhachi (bamboo flute) player. They visited run-down hotels and rooming houses to talk to the Issei in order to get information on how many Japanese Canadian seniors actually lived around the area, and what their needs were. After the six-month grant ended, Hamada kept working as a volunteer. They established a connection with the Downtown Eastside Residents' Association (DERA), a neighborhood organization established in the area in 1973.[27] With financial assistance from DERA, Yamashiro was able to stay as a paid staff member for the project. On August 25, 1975, they opened a drop-in center at 573 East Hastings Street to provide social services for Nikkei seniors. This was the start of Tonari Gumi (Japanese Community Volunteers Association).[28]

Tonari Gumi provided social services, such as translation of laws concerning immigration or rental housing, assistance with applications for health care and social welfare, transportation of the infirm to and from hospitals, as well as various kinds of recreational and cultural activities. The staff visited seniors in their homes. The drop-in center also functioned as a place where Japanese Canadian individuals scattered across Vancouver could come and meet each other.

Tonari Gumi became a gathering place not only for seniors but also for the younger members of the community. Some younger-generation Japanese Canadians had become politically active in the 1960s. For example, Tamio Wakayama, a Nisei photographer, was involved in the Civil Rights movement in the United States.[29] A handful of Sansei at the University of British Columbia formed an Asian Canadian study group named the "Wakayama Group."[30] They studied and discussed the issues of racism, imperialism, and discrimination under the guidance of a Japanese American professor, Ron Tanaka, who was teaching at the time at the University of British Columbia.[31] Strongly influenced by the Asian American movement, those Sansei activists started to search for their own cultural and political expressions.

Tanaka taught the importance of community involvement to the young activists in the group.[32] The group did not last very long due to organization problems and Tanaka's return to the United States, but some of the group's ideological principles had a long-term influence. Several years later, former "Wakayama Group" members were joined by Tamio Wakayama and Rick Shiomi, along with other Sansei and postwar Issei. They worked for Tonari Gumi and, at the same time, pursued their cultural expressions through various forms of art and music.[33] Through their community activities, a lot of Sansei rediscovered their community history. Many learned about the wartime internment for the first time in their lives.

As there was a language barrier between Issei seniors and young Sansei, postwar immigrants from Japan played an important role in the process of ethnic community reconstruction in Vancouver. Takeo Yamashiro, who had emigrated to Canada in the early 1970s, became the chief staff member of Tonari Gumi, and still works for the organization almost thirty years later.[34] Another postwar Issei, Michiko Sakata, established a nearby organization called "Language Aid" around the same time.[35] Like Hamada, Sakata also saw the poor living conditions of the Nikkei seniors in the Powell Street area, and she offered translation, interpretation, and counseling services for them. According to Sakata, many Issei on Powell Street were facing health and financial difficulties, and some of them even had mental problems, since they had never recovered from the traumatic experiences during the war.[36] Sakata describes her encounter with an Issei senior in Vancouver:

In the summer of 1973, I met an old Japanese man in a government mental institution. Through his medical record, I found out that he was put there 32 years ago. He was arrested in 1941 and committed to the hospital for not carrying his registration card identifying him as a person of Japanese origin. On my regular visits, I tried to talk to him in Japanese, but he said, "Don't speak Japanese. They are watching us." I tried to talk to him in English, but he could not speak English. His identity had been totally destroyed, and I could not reach him. On one of my visits in 1976, I was told that he had stopped eating and had died.

One day he came to me in a dream and stared at me. Suddenly a horrible thought struck me, and I said to him, "All these years, all you wanted me to say was that you were innocent."[37]

When Sakata and Hamada first started their community activities, they couldn't get cooperation from preexisting community organizations, such as the Vancouver JCCA.[38] Some Nisei leaders were suspicious of outsiders like Sakata and Hamada. Nisei tended to be hesitant to ask for social welfare and did not want to "rock the boat."[39] The Nisei-led JCCA had been inactive for two decades since the resettlement period, after what they called "the Evacuation." Nonetheless, Tonari Gumi and Language Aid attracted Nikkei seniors even from outside the Powell Street area, and people started to come to Powell Street to receive various services and to socialize.

Younger Japanese Canadians also gathered to get involved in the community activities as well as to engage themselves in other activities, such as forming rock bands, creating and inviting theatre productions, collecting historical photos and oral interviews, organizing music concerts with Asian American artists and musicians, etc.[40] Tonari Gumi provided the opportunity for Sansei to literally find each other and to learn the history of their community through stories told by Issei. The *Tonari Gumi News* revealed that the organization was catering to the needs of both Issei seniors and young Sansei. The Japanese language section of the newsletter provided information mostly for seniors and new immigrants from Japan, but the English section offered information mainly for Sansei, such as on concerts, dance parties, and other events.[41] By working for Tonari Gumi as volunteers or hired staff, these Sansei reconstructed their own ethnicity through both social *and* cultural activities.

In 1975, the JCCA also started its own project for the Issei on Powell Street. Some JCCA members created a new organization called the Japanese Canadian Society of Greater Vancouver for Senior Citizens Housing (JCS) so that it would be eligible for the subsidy from the city, specifically for senior housing projects. With financial help from the city, the JCS conducted research on the necessity for housing improvement for Nikkei seniors and started looking for possible buildings in the city to purchase towards this end.[42]

Thus, in the mid-1970s, new Japanese Canadian community organizations established themselves in the Powell Street area. These organizations attracted Japanese Canadians of different generations, creating networks and communication among the people who had been dispersed and scattered throughout the city and suburbs of Vancouver. These new organizations also provided channels through which Japanese Canadians could negotiate with the government, not only to advance the well being of those who lived on Powell Street but also to reclaim the area as their revived ethnic hometown.

The Neighbourhood Improvement Program and the Powell Street Area

While the Japanese Canadian community started to reorganize itself in Vancouver, the government's urban redevelopment initiative was turning its direction from a modernist to multiculturalist approach. In 1975, the city

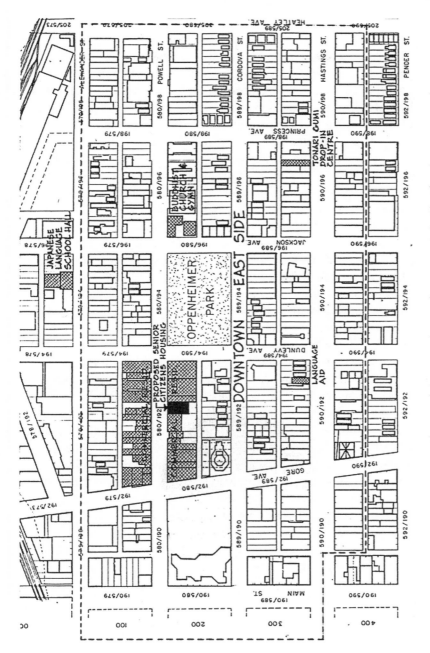

FIG. 14.1 *Downtown Eastside Oppenheimer Area in 1976. (Vancouver, B.C., City Planning Department)*

of Vancouver designated the Downtown Eastside Oppenheimer area for the Neighbourhood Improvement Program.[43] The Neighbourhood Improvement Program was a federal-provincial-city cost-sharing program, which was designed "to conserve and rehabilitate the housing stock (through the companion Residential Rehabilitation Assistance Program—R.R.A.P.); to add to or rehabilitate required municipal services and social or recreational amenities; to remove blighting land use; and to promote the maintenance of the neighbourhood after the N.I.P.[44] project is terminated."

The Neighbourhood Improvement Program had its origin in the abandonment of the Urban Renewal Scheme initiated by the federal government in the late 1960s. As a response to the "local outcry and opposition to Urban Renewal in Vancouver's Strathcona Neighbourhood," the federal government decided to use Strathcona (Chinatown) as a testing ground for the rehabilitation and preservation of local neighbourhoods.[45] This new urban policy later developed into a nationwide Neighbourhood Improvement Program. In Vancouver the program began in Cedar Cottage and Kitsilano in 1974. Downtown Eastside had been zoned as an industrial district, and thus was not eligible for the Neighbourhood Improvement Program as such. To solve this problem, the city government rezoned the area to CD-1 (Comprehensive Development District) on November 25, 1975.[46] In the same year, the city office designated the Downtown Eastside and Mt. Pleasant areas for the Neighbourhood Improvement Program and allocated special assistance to the Strathcona Community Centre. Portions of Grandview-Woodland and Riley Park received assistance in 1976.[47]

The Neighbourhood Improvement Program was basically a liberal policy that formed an alternative to the unpopular Urban Renewal Scheme, which ignored the needs and wishes of local residents in the inner city. In the United States, similar repressive projects had faced strong opposition. In 1966, the Johnson administration introduced the Model City Program in which the government sought more comprehensive redevelopment of disadvantaged areas by combining urban restructuring with improved educational and occupational projects for local residents.[48] The Trudeau government's Neighbourhood Improvement Program was modeled on this American scheme. From the planning stage of the program, committees were formed to reflect the voices of local residents in each area.

On February 10, 1976, the Vancouver City Council approved the Planning Stage Work Program for the Downtown Eastside Oppenheimer area, which "outlined the various studies required and the co-operative efforts of other civic departments" in order to formulate a "Concept Plan."[49] Ten days

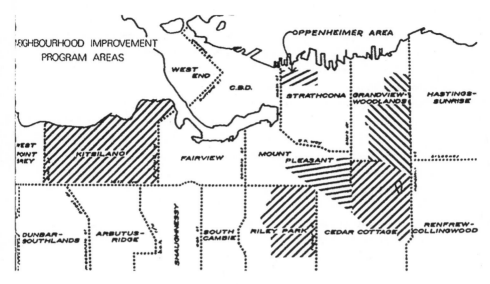

FIG. 14.2 *Neighbourhood Improvement Program Areas in Vancouver (Dan Cornejo, "Vancouver's Neighbourhood Improvement Program," Vancouver City Planning Department,* Quarterly Review, *Jan. 1977, p. 11)*

later, the Downtown Eastside Site Office opened to coordinate the needs of the local community and policy makers. On May 12, members of the Oppenheimer Area Planning Committee were elected. The committee was composed of both owners and tenants from the area's commercial and industrial facilities and residential buildings, as well as employed workers. In addition, a representative was selected from the Chinese and Japanese communities respectively to participate in the Planning Committee. These two positions were created to facilitate local ethnic community involvement, and during the election meetings the entire proceedings were interpreted into both Japanese and Chinese.[50] The budget for the Neighbourhood Improvement Program in Downtown Eastside Oppenheimer was $685,000. Fifty percent of the total budget, or $342,000, came from the federal government, and the province and the city governments covered 25 percent, or $171,250, each.

The Downtown Eastside Planning Office conducted a survey on the characteristics of population in the area in 1976.[51] The population in the area totaled 3,425. The survey found that males outnumbered females by a two to one ratio. Population aged sixty-five and above comprised 39.58 percent (13.50 percent in the city of Vancouver), and 60.51 percent of the residents were living on some sort of pension or fixed income (17.16 percent in the city of Vancouver). Ethnic Chinese accounted for almost two-thirds of the local population. Ethnic Japanese residents comprised 2.24 percent. The high percentage of the population living on pension plans indicated that many of these Chinese and Japanese Canadians were senior citizens. The survey pointed out that in older times this area had housed, in hotels and rooming houses, a large number of single men who had worked in the lumbering and fishing industries, and that these old-timers still lived in the area and wished to remain.[52] To accommodate the characteristics of the population in this neighborhood, the Planning Office emphasized the need for improved low-cost housing and healthcare facilities as well as the creation of employment opportunities and improvement of pedestrian-oriented amenities.

The Planning Committee paid special attention to the Japanese Canadian presence in the area and proposed to encourage Japanese Canadians to preserve their culture and expand their community facilities:

> There are not many Japanese people still living in the area (perhaps 100 senior citizens) but there are many retail outlets and social/cultural facilities catering specifically to the wider Japanese population in the city. Because of the historical importance of this group as well as their intimate relationship with this area encouragement should be extended to them to strengthen their presence in the area for the benefit of the neighbourhood and the city as a whole. Some very positive responses have already been received since the introduction of the Neighbourhood Improvement Program, and indications are that if some N.I.P. funding can be made available for a cooperative Japanese/general community facility, then additional monies will be made available by the Japanese groups.[53]

According to the "Concept Plan," the city carried out a number of projects aimed at the revitalization of the local community through the Neighbourhood Improvement Program between 1976 and 1978. Included in the program in the Downtown Eastside Oppenheimer area were improvements to Oppenheimer Park, the planting of trees on Powell, Cordova, and Main Streets, the improvement of lighting and sidewalks on Powell Street, and a new building for the local health clinic. Smaller grants provided funds to renovate the swimming/wading pool at the Franciscan Sisters of the Atonement daycare, and to purchase carpentry and leatherworking tools to help local residents acquire manual skills.[54] These projects benefited the entire community as well as the Japanese Canadian residents. Indeed, improvements to the neighbourhood encouraged the Buddhist church, which had been considering relocation, to stay in the area.

In addition to these improvements to social and recreational facilities, the program allocated a budget specifically for improving Japanese Canadian community facilities. Fifty thousand dollars was supplied by the government to buy materials and hire people for the Japanese Language School, supplemented by $16,000 raised from the Japanese Canadian community. The Buddhist church built a new gymnasium with $100,000 allocated through the Neighbourhood Improvement Program and a donation of $650,000 raised by the church itself.[55] It should be noted that $150,000, or 22 percent of the total program fund, was allocated to the improvement of two projects involving specifically Japanese Canadian community facilities. Considering the fact that the number of ethnic Japanese residents was less than 3 percent of the local population, the needs of the Japanese Canadian community were substantially over-represented in the Neighbourhood Improvement Program in this area.

Although not specifically targeted for the Japanese Canadian community, the program further brought about an important change that facilitated the success of a new cultural event organized by the Japanese Canadian community. It was the improvement of Oppenheimer Park. Oppenheimer Park, or "Powell Ground," which was a central park in Japantown before World War II, had severely deteriorated after the war. The park was thus chosen to be one of the sites that required major rehabilitation through the Neighbourhood Improvement Program. Part of the park was developed with giant checkerboards, shuffleboards, and horseshoe pits to provide entertainment for senior adults. The baseball field was graded and drained. A children's play area was developed, the field house and lighting were upgraded, twenty-seven park benches were installed, and trees were planted around the park. After the project, Oppenheimer Park became a place where local seniors and children could safely enjoy themselves.[56] To show their appreciation, Tonari Gumi seniors donated and planted cherry trees in April 1977.

The renovation of Oppenheimer Park was finished in time for the first Powell Street Festival, which became one of the Japanese Canadian Centennial events held in Vancouver in 1977.[57] The Powell Street Festival has become an annual community event since then, providing a place for Japanese Canadians not only from Vancouver but from all over Canada to gather every summer. This festival was an "invention of tradition," which signified the reclamation of Powell Street by the postwar Nikkei community.[58] Ken Shikaze, one of the Sansei who got involved with the Japanese Canadian community through Tonari Gumi, explained the significance of the first Powell Street Festival as follows:

> I think most of us from Tonari Gumi felt that Powell Street was very impor-
> tant to the Issei, because it was almost like we were reclaiming the park that
> was theirs, reclaiming that area that was theirs before the wartime. That was
> very significant, that they could walk on Powell Street and see all the banners
> and all the stuff, and say, "Hey, this is our park. This is our street."[59]

During the Powell Street Festival, Japanese Canadians celebrated their ethnic heritage publicly for the first time since the uprooting. The sound of *taiko* (Japanese drumming) and the sight of cherry trees on Powell Street symbolized their regained pride and confidence.[60]

Another project benefited Nikkei seniors on Powell Street in 1977. With a government subsidy, the JCS, which had been working on the senior housing project, purchased a run-down building on Powell Street called the Richmond Hotel.[61] Cooperating with Tonari Gumi, the JCS renovated the building so it would be suitable for senior housing. The building was renamed "Sakura-so" and was opened in 1977.

The fact that these projects materialized in this early period of multiculturalism shows that policymakers as well as local community members acknowledged the importance of the presence of the Japanese Canadian community on Powell Street. This was only possible because the pressure worked from two directions, bottom-up at the grassroots level and top-down at the governmental level, which merged during the implementation of these projects. On the ethnic community's side, a number of Japanese Canadians had been organizing social and cultural activities that aimed towards the improvement of their everyday community lives, and Powell Street was becoming the center of these activities. If it had not been for these community activists, the policymakers would not have catered to the needs of a particular ethnic group that was not significantly dominant in terms of the local resident population. On the other hand, the willingness of the government to acknowledge the importance of the Japanese Canadian presence in the area indicates that, in the collective memory of the city of Vancouver, Powell Street still belonged to Japanese Canadians. The documents and reports on the Neighbourhood Improvement Program repeatedly referred to the historical significance of the area as a Nikkei place. In the late 1970s, the historical memory of the Japanese Canadian community on

Powell Street was reconstructed through community activities and government projects not only for the ethnic community, but also for the city as a whole.

The intention of the government and that of the community, however, did not entirely agree with each other. The gap became apparent when the city government announced the Powell Street Commercial Beautification scheme after the termination of the Neighbourhood Improvement Program in 1978. From 1979 to 1980, city officials met local and ethnic representatives "to determine support for a possible upgrading of a portion of Powell Street with a Japanese theme, partially to recognize the important historic and cultural contributions of Japanese Canadians in the Oppenheimer Area, and partially to provide an impetus for the revival of the commercial retail-restaurant aspect of Japanese-Canadians, tourists and others."[62] The 300 and 400 blocks of Powell Street were decorated with Japanese-theme lighting, banners, and street signs. Storefronts and building facades were upgraded, and sidewalks were repaired. Japanese Canadian organizations basically welcomed the plan, but Ken Matsune, a member of the Oppenheimer Citizen's Committee, described some divergence between the opinions of Japanese Canadians and government officials concerning the purpose of the beautification:

> I remember City staff saying you will return it into a Japanese village and have all the Japanese come back and live there, but that was never our goal. We want to be treated like everyone else. We don't want to be ghettoized.[63]

Japanese Canadians at the time were heavily dispersed throughout the city and suburbs of Vancouver and did not wish to reestablish geographic residential segregation as in the prewar period. The city government also had a similar plan for the commercial part of Chinatown, and wanted to turn the district into a major tourist spot.

All in all, however, the Neighbourhood Improvement Program and the Powell Street Commercial Beautification plan had positive effects on the Vancouver Japanese Canadian community. Although actual residents in the area were limited, many Nikkei people visited the area to shop, participate in community activities, or receive social services. For the senior residents in the area, the street became safer and nicer, a place where they could walk comfortably with pride and dignity. Thus, by facilitating both everyday community survival and symbolic celebration of cultural identity and expression, the multiculturalist urban renewal process in the late 1970s and the early 1980s played a significant role in the revival of the postwar Nikkei community in Vancouver.

Conclusion: Multiculturalism in an Everyday Way

This case study shows that the postwar revival of the Vancouver Japanese Canadian community was achieved through the dialectic of top-down politics and bottom-up multiculturalism. Governments and mainstream societies often attempt to exploit and appropriate the "exotic" ethnic community for their own interests through promotion of tourism and creation of positive national images such as "tolerance" and "diversity." On the other hand, ethnic communities can demand and utilize resources from the government in order to improve their living conditions and to develop their cultural and artistic expressions. The relationship is not always cooperative, but it is also not always adversarial. Analyses of negotiations between government bodies and ethnic communities reveal the complexity of the relationship between the dominant and the marginal. This relation creates, as a whole, a dynamic national history.

It should also be noted that the geographic location of the revived community is an important determinant of the character of the community that is to be developed. In the case of Vancouver, many so-called assimilated middle-class Japanese Canadians live in affluent suburban neighbourhoods.[64] Had the community formed itself in those neighbourhoods instead of the Powell Street area, which was easily accessible by bus, only people with an automobile would have had access to the community facilities. In fact, a variety of activities were taking place in different parts of Vancouver, where a number of Japanese Canadians gathered for sports activities such as kendo and judo, religious activities in various churches, and events and meetings at *kenjin-kai* (prefectural associations). These organizations were self-contained within their membership or catered to people interested in their particular activities regardless of ethnicity.

The community revival that this paper has described, on the other hand, had certain characteristics that were not shared by other ethnic organizational activities *because* it happened on Powell Street. Postwar community activities on Powell Street started as social services for disadvantaged Issei. This fact meant that the activities always involved class/structural issues: How could minorities oppressed by their race, class, and age survive in Canada?[65] What kind of responsibility did the state have for the welfare of the disad-

vantaged in the country? Tonari Gumi, in its letter to the government applying for a grant, wrote:

> Japanese Canadian seniors should be considered a living historical treasure
> in terms of Canadian history. . . . If a provincial ministry of multicultural-
> ism is to have a really positive and constructive impact upon the Japanese
> Canadian community, as well as other ethnic communities, it should address
> itself to needs of organizations such as Tonari Gumi. By channeling funds
> and support into such organizations that function on a daily basis and pro-
> vide a wide spectrum of services and cultural resources, the ministry could
> do much more for ethnic communities than sponsor occasional festivals or
> conferences.[66]

Sansei community activists on Powell Street, who engaged in cultural
activities and symbolic expressions of their ethnicity, were aware of issues
of class, racism, and oppression in concrete terms, thanks to their daily contact with Issei. This affected the orientation of their cultural expressions as
well as their social and political activities.[67]

Last but not least, this study points out the important role that history
played in the community formation and also in government policymaking.
Sansei's social activities and their interactions with Issei induced their
recovery of the erased past of the vital prewar Japanese Canadian community. As Tonari Gumi insisted, Issei are the living history of multicultural
Canada. Sansei, who grew up without knowing about past racism and particularly the wartime internment, learned community history, the history
of Canadian racism, and the stories of human survival through Issei narratives. Their stories provided some answers to the questions that Sansei
had had in terms of the missing links in their family histories and their parents' silence about their wartime experiences.

In 1976, a group of Nisei, Sansei, and postwar Issei who gathered at Tonari
Gumi started to collect historical photos of the community. They collected
over four thousand photographs and interviewed people across Canada. This
collection developed into an exhibition, "The Japanese Canadians 1877–1977,"
which was published as a book in 1978.[68] This photo collection not only contributed to the recovery of community history, but also was instrumental
in bringing dispersed Japanese Canadians together to celebrate the community's pioneers and eventually to organize politically.

History was important not only for the ethnic community but also for
the policymakers. In the Neighbourhood Improvement Program and the

subsequent Powell Street Commercial Beautification plan, historical significance of the area as a Nikkei place was incontestably acknowledged. By creating the visible landscape with ethnic and historic features, the city was able to assume the image of cultural diversity, a representation of successful multiculturalism. This utility of history, however, was a double-edged sword. On the one hand, by inducing a historical imagination of the continuity of Chinatown and Japantown, it whitewashed the memory of the various assaults by past governments on these ethnic communities. On the other hand, urban projects based on multiculturalism contributed to the reconstruction of the collective memory in Vancouver of the existence of a once-thriving Japanese Canadian community in the city. This memory was not contained in the framework of benign multiculturalism, but became essential in the exposure of the past racial injustice, which eventually inspired the general public to support the redress settlement between the government and the Japanese Canadian community.[69]

It seems likely that the physical existence of the Nikkei community on Powell Street is going to fade away as time passes, with Issei passing away and ethnic organizations moving out of the area. In 2000, the National Nikkei Heritage Centre opened in Burnaby, a suburb of Vancouver. The Japanese Canadian Citizens Association and the National Japanese Canadian Museum moved into the building, and the New Sakura-so Senior's Residence stands within the same lot. Sakura-so, which had housed Nikkei seniors for a quarter of a century, was closed and sold due to the diminishing demand from Nikkei seniors for accommodation on Powell Street. A plan for the fifty-nine-unit housing project next to the National Nikkei Heritage Centre is proceeding under the leadership of the Nikkei Seniors Health Care and Housing Society.[70] Tonari Gumi also moved out of the Powell Street area in 2001. Burnaby has no historical connection with the Japanese Canadian community, and how this relocation will affect the community activities and formation is yet to be seen.

However, the Japanese language school on Alexander Street remains in the area and is likely to remain, since it has built a new part adjacent to the old building. Moreover, Powell Street will remain part of the name of the Powell Street Festival and will continue to carry symbolic significance in the Japanese Canadian community, signifying their psychological "hometown."[71] Since the erasure of Japantown in the 1940s, Japanese Canadians have come a long way in reconstructing their ethnic community. The reclamation of Powell Street in the 1970s was an important part of this, and the historical memory of the Japanese Canadian community on Powell Street, shared by the Nikkei community and the city of Vancouver, may last long after the physical evidence of the community disappears from the area. "Powell Street" as an imagined community may continue to be reinvented and re-imagined, while the faces and activities of the community will go through constant changes over time.

Notes

This article is a substantial expansion of my past work published in Japanese, "Paueru Chiku Fukkou Monogatari: 1970 Nendai no 'Chiiki Kaizen Keikaku' to Bankuba Nikkei Kanadajin Komyuniti" (Post-war revival of the Japanese-Canadian community in Vancouver: Neighbourhood improvement program and the Powell Street area in the 1970s), *Imin Kenkyu Nenpo* (Annual Review of Migration Studies) 6 (December 1999): 53–64. I would like to thank the numerous Japanese Canadians who shared their life stories with me in the interviews, particularly Takeo Yamashiro, Michiko Sakata, Tamio Wakayama, Mayu Takasaki, Ken Shikaze, and Gordon Kadota. I am also indebted to Kathy Shimizu, who not only offered information, but provided lodging while I was doing research in Vancouver. I also greatly appreciate the warm friendship from Kathy and other staff members and volunteers of the Powell Street Festival 1998, 2001, and 2002, in which I participated. Last but not least, I would like to acknowledge that this research was made possible by financial assistance from the Canadian Government through the Government of Canada Awards.

1. For details about the Japanese Canadian wartime internment, see Ken Adachi, *The Enemy that Never Was: A History of the Japanese Canadians* (Toronto: McClelland and Stewart, 1976), and Ann Gomer Sunahara, *The Politics of Racism: The Uprooting of Japanese Canadians during the Second World War* (Toronto: James Lorimer & Company, 1981).

2. Audrey Kobayashi, *Memories of Our Past: A Brief History and Walking Tour of Powell Street* (Vancouver: NRC Publishing, 1992). The number of Japanese Canadian stores and organizations in the Japantown area shifted over time. According to the analysis by Toshiji Sasaki, the number of ethnic Japanese stores and organizations in the Japantown area (those on Alexander, Powell, East Cordova, Columbia, Westminster, Gore, Jackson, Dunlevy, and Princess) were 233 in 1908, 262 in 1912, 409 in 1917, 578 in 1921, 413 in 1936, and 378 in 1941. Toshiji Sasaki, *Nihonjin Kanada Imin Shi* (History of Japanese immigrants in Canada) (Tokyo: Fuji Shuppan, 1999).

3. Pat Adachi, *Asahi: A Legend in Baseball, A Legacy from the Japanese Canadian Baseball Team to Its Heirs* (Etobicoke, Ontario: Asahi Baseball Organization, 1992).

4. Wing Chung Ng, in his study of the postwar Chinese community in Vancouver, proposed a study that was not limited to this kind of "heritage items" analysis. Wing Chung Ng, *The Chinese in Vancouver, 1945–80: The Pursuit of Identity and Power* (Vancouver: University of British Colombia Press, 1999), 5.

5. Lisa Lowe, *Immigrant Acts: On Asian American Cultural Politics* (Durham: Duke University Press, 1996), 88.

6. Canada, House of Commons *Debates*, August 4, 1944.

7. Compared with the U.S. government on the equivalent policies, the Canadian government was much more outspoken about its racial motives for the uprooting and internment of Japanese Canadians. See Sunahara, *The Politics of Racism.*

8. In 1956, Elizabeth Wangenheim, who conducted research on the Japanese Canadian community in Toronto, noted that "very seldom does one even find two Japanese families in one block, and there is no sign at all of a concentration of ethnic institutions." Elizabeth Wangenheim, "The Social Organization of the Japanese Community in Toronto: A Product of Crisis" (master's thesis, University of Toronto, 1956), 3.

9. For the nature of the policy of dispersal, see Roy Miki and Cassandra Kobayashi, *Justice in Our Time: The Japanese Canadian Redress Settlement* (Vancouver: Talonbooks; Winnepeg: National Association of Japanese Canadians, 1991), 46–55.

10. Urban Renewal Schemes were developed both in the United States and Canada in the 1950s and 1960s in order for governments to deal with "inner city problems," which, in the case of the United States, were causing riots and major social unrest. Earlier programs targeted impoverished communities of ethnic and racial minorities and involved bulldozing of old buildings and the relocation of residents. Many old ethnic communities, such as Chinatowns and Manilatowns, disappeared or faced the threat of disappearance, which often created severe resistance from the residents and the community. The conflict over the International Hotel in San Francisco was the most notable case of this kind of resistance. Steve Yip, "Serve the People—Yesterday and Today: The Legacy of Wei Min She," in *Legacy to Liberation: Politics and Culture of Revolutionary Asian Pacific America*, ed. Fred Ho et. al. (San Francisco: Big Red Media and AK Press, 2000), 20–22.

11. Kay J. Anderson, *Vancouver's Chinatown: Racial Discourse in Canada, 1875–1980* (Montreal: McGill-Queen's University Press, 1991), 188–89.

12. City of Vancouver, *Downtown Vancouver*, 26, quoted in Anderson, *Vancouver's Chinatown*, 188.

13. Anderson, *Vancouver's Chinatown*, 158.

14. *Beautiful British Columbia Magazine* 3:2 (fall 1961): 27–33, quoted in ibid., 193.

15. For images of Vancouver's Chinatown in a historical perspective, see ibid. Chinatown's images in the United States are researched and discussed in Robert G.

Lee, *Orientals: Asian Americans in Popular Culture* (Philadelphia: Temple University Press, 1999).

16. For details, see Anderson, *Vancouver's Chinatown,* 188–200.

17. Wing Chung Ng points out the fact that some of the English-speaking second-generation Chinese Canadians supported the city's redevelopment plan. Ng, *The Chinese in Vancouver,* 97–99.

18. Anderson, *Vancouver's Chinatown,* 199; Ng, *The Chinese in Vancouver,* 99.

19. Anderson, *Vancouver's Chinatown,* 202; Ng, *The Chinese in Vancouver,* 99.

20. Anderson, *Vancouver's Chinatown,* 202; Ng, *The Chinese in Vancouver,* 101–2.

21. City Planning Department, Vancouver, "Technical Report Number 4, Industrial Districts," *Vancouver Urban Renewal Study* (August 29, 1969), 52–56.

22. The Criteria for the ratings were as follows:

Condition 0—no building, building being demolished or erected

Condition 1—building beyond feasible rehabilitation, building in need of substantial repair and functionally obsolete, or building in need of substantial repair and activity considered a nuisance or detriment to neighbourhood

Condition 2—building in need of substantial repair but with an economic life of more than five years

Condition 3—building in acceptable condition, or in need of only minor repairs

Condition 4—building in better than average condition

Condition 5—building in excellent condition, building well designed and constructed, or site well landscaped.

See, City Planning Department, "Technical Report," 3.

23. Downtown Eastside (Powell Street area) is still an impoverished neighborhood. The prevalence of alcoholism, the high unemployment rate in British Columbia in the last two decades of the twentieth century, and drug problems in particular have contributed to further deterioration of the area.

24. Japanese Canadians who had lived in British Columbia before the war had been disenfranchised from federal and provincial elections. They received the right to the federal vote in June 1948 and to the B.C. vote in March 1949.

25. Tomoko Makabe, "Ethnicity Group Identity: Canadian-born Japanese in Metropolitan Toronto" (Ph.D. diss., Univeristy of Toronto, 1976); Tomoko Makabe, *The Canadian Sansei* (Toronto: University of Toronto Press, 1998), 38–50.

26. Hamada's eulogy, written and read by Tamio Wakayama, is printed in the *Tonari Gumi News,* July 1980, 4–5.

27. DERA was formed to contend with the social problems in the Downtown Eastside Oppenheimer area and was instrumental in the community development projects in the 1970s, which greatly contributed to the improvement in social serv-

ices and law enforcement and to the increased construction of social housing units in the area. Graeme Wynn and Timothy Oke, eds., *Vancouver and Its Region* (Vancouver: University of British Columbia Press, 1992), 237–38.

28. For the history of Tonari Gumi, see Michiko Sakata, "Tonari Gumi," *Rikka* 4:2 (summer 1977): 4–11; Takeo Yamashiro, "Tonari Gumi: Powell Street Positively Revisited," in *Spirit of Redress: Japanese Canadians in Conference,* ed. Cassandra Kobayashi and Roy Miki (Vancouver: JC Publications, 1989), 55–58.

29. Tamio Wakayama, *Signs of Life* (Toronto: Coach House Press, 1969), is a book of photography from Wakayama's Civil Rights movement period.

30. The name "Wakayama group" was chosen because several of the members were from Steveston, a fishing village south of Vancouver, whose population was predominantly Japanese before World War II. Many fishers there had come from Wakayama Prefecture in Japan. Mayumi Takasaki, interview with the author, Vancouver, January 19, 1998.

31. Tamio Wakayama, interview with the author, Vancouver, January 17, 1998; Ken Shikaze, interview with the author, Vancouver, January 18, 1998; and Mayumi Takasaki, interview with the author, Vancouver, January 19, 1998. For the Sansei activities in this period, see also Rick Shiomi, "Community Organizing: The Problems of Innovating and Sustaining Interest," in *Asian Canadians Regional Perspectives: Selections from the Proceedings Asian Canadian Symposium V, Mount Saint Vincent University, Halifax, Nova Scotia, May 23 to 26, 1981,* ed. K. Victor Ujimoto and Gordon Hirabayashi (n.p.: 1981), 339–54.

32. Ron Tanaka, "The Sansei Artist and Community Culture," *Powell Street Review* 1:1 (1971): 4–6.

33. Rick Shiomi became a playwright and leads Theater Mu, an Asian American theatre in Minnesota.

34. Takeo Yamashiro, interview with the author, Vancouver, July 8, 1998.

35. Michiko Sakata, interview with the author, Vancouver, October 6, 1998.

36. Ibid.

37. Michiko Sakata, quoted in Japanese Canadian Centennial Project, *A Dream of Riches: The Japanese Canadians 1877–1977* (Vancouver: Japanese Canadian Centennial Project, and Dreadnaught, Toronto, 1978), 3.

38. Sakata, "Tonari Gumi," 7–8; Sakata, interview; Yamashiro, interview. In the Vancouver Japanese Canadian community, Gordon Kadota played a great role as a liaison between the conservative Nisei and the radical Sansei/Shin-Issei groups. Kadota is a Kika-Nisei (a Canadian-born Nisei who was sent to Japan for education, the equivalent of Kibei in the United States) and completely fluent in both English and Japanese. Kadota had earned great trust from the Nisei, and at the same

time he supported the new organizations and projects and was trusted by the Sansei. He was able to convince the two groups to cooperate with each other in creating community events such as the Powell Street Festival. Wakayama, interview.

39. Nisei in the United States also tended to be hesitant to receive social welfare. Harry H. L. Kitano, *Japanese Americans: The Evolution of a Subculture* (Englewood Cliffs, New Jersey: Prentice-Hall, 1969). In recent years, however, new scholarship is finding evidence that counters the stereotypical image of the Nisei as being "quiet Americans." The author considers that both of these images have truth in them.

40. Numerous Sansei activities are recorded in *Tonari Gumi News* and the JCCA newsletter, the *Bulletin*.

41. Tonari Gumi, *Tonari Gumi News* (1978–1980), Special Collections, University of British Columbia.

42. Greater Vancouver JCCA, "JCCA Senior Citizens Homes & Community Centre: Progress Report," *Bulletin*, February 1975.

43. Dan Cornejo, "Vancouver's Neighbourhood Improvement Program," *Vancouver City Planning Department, Quarterly Review* 4:1 (January 1977): 10–11.

44. Ibid., 10. The acronym of the Neighbourhood Improvement Program, N.I.P., is used throughout the documents prepared by the city government. Japanese Canadians, however, did not use the term, since it reminded them of a derogatory term for people of Japanese descent. Interview with Ken Matsune, quoted in City Planning Department, *Vancouver Neighbourhood Improvement Program Review* (Vancouver: City Planning Department, 1983), 102. In this paper, I do not use the acronym for the same reason, except in direct quotes.

45. City Planning Department, *Review*, 2.

46. Director of Planning Report, "Oppenheimer Area Land Use and N.I.P. Concept Plan," A Report from the City Planning Department to the Standing Committee on Planning and Development, City Manager's Office, September 2, 1976. City Clerk's Department, Residential Funding, N.I.P.—Downtown Eastside, 1975–1977, Vancouver City Archives.

47. The amount of federal, provincial, and municipal assistance to each neighborhood is listed in a table in Cornejo, "Vancouver's Neighbourhood Improvement Program," 10. According to the table, the total budget for the Neighbourhood Improvement Program in Vancouver was $10,187,143. Federal government bore about 50 percent of the cost ($4,825,000), and the provincial and city governments paid approximately 25 percent of the cost respectively (Province—$2,412,500; City—$2,949,643).

48. U.S. Congress. Senate. *The Central City Problem and Urban Renewal Policy:*

A Study Prepared by Congressional Research Service, Library of Congress for the Sub-committee on Housing and Urban Affairs, Committee on Banking, Housing and Urban Affairs, 93rd Cong., 1st sess. (Washington: G.P.O., 1973).

49. Director of Planning Report, "Concept Plan," 1.

50. Director of Planning Report, "Oppenheimer Area Planning Committee," May 28, 1976. City Clerk's Department, Residential Funding, N.I.P.—Downtown Eastside, 1975–1977, Vancouver City Archives. On May 12, eleven elected members and seven alternate members were chosen for the committee. The members included four Japanese Canadians, Sai Moto, Doug Ozaki, Ken Matsune, and Ken Takeuchi; and one Chinese Canadian, Anna Wong.

51. "Director of Planning's Discussion Paper," City Clerk's Department, Residential Funding, N.I.P.—Downtown Eastside, 1975–1977, Vancouver City Archives.

52. Ibid., Appendix III, Part I, 8. City Clerk's Department, Residential Funding, N.I.P.—Downtown Eastside, 1975–1977, Vancouver City Archives.

53. Ibid., 7.

54. City Planning Department, *Review,* 28–9.

55. Ibid., 29–30.

56. City Planning Department, *Downtown Eastside/Oppenheimer Policy Plan* (Vancouver: City Planning Department, 1982), 35.

57. In 1977, Japanese Canadian communities across Canada celebrated the centennial of the arrival of the first Japanese immigrant in Canada. The program of the first Powell Street Festival is available as Japanese Canadian Centennial Society, Arts Workshop, "Powell Street Festival," June 11 & 12, Oppenheimer Park (brochure), Special Collections, University of British Columbia.

58. The notion was borrowed from Eric Hobsbawm and Terence Ranger, eds., *The Invention of Tradition* (Cambridge: Cambridge University Press, 1983).

59. Shikaze, interview.

60. For the significance of the Powell Street Festival in the revival of Japanese Canadian community, see Tamio Wakayama, *Kikyo: Coming Home to Powell Street* (Madeira Park, B.C.: Harbour Publishing Co. Ltd., 1992). As the cherry trees symbolized the reclamation of the park by the Nikkei in the 1970s, totem poles were erected in the park in the 1990s to celebrate the presence of the First Nations people.

61. Japanese Canadian Society of Greater Vancouver, "A Correspondence from the Japanese Canadian Society of Greater Vancouver to the Vancouver City Council, Re: Japanese Canadian Senior Citizens Housing, Downtown East Side, Richmond Hotel, 374–378 Powell St., Vancouver," January 26, 1977, Vancouver City Archives.

62. City Planning Department, *Downtown Eastside/Oppenheimer Policy Plan,* 53.

63. Interview with Ken Matsune, quoted in City Planning Department, *Review,* 103.

64. Tomoko Makabe has interviewed and analyzed the general characteristics of these middle-class Sansei. Makabe, *Canadian Sansei*.

65. It should not be forgotten that the poor living conditions of Issei were the result of the past racism and injustice, the culmination of which was the internment and the confiscation of their property during World War II.

66. Tonari Gumi, "Multiculturalism in an Everyday Way," unpublished paper, April 3, 1979, Special Collections, University of British Columbia, 4.

67. An example of the cultural expression of these activist Sansei was *taiko,* which started in Vancouver in 1979. Members of Katari Taiko, the first *taiko* group formed in Canada, emphasized the group's "left of center" political stance in interviews with the author. For more details, see Masumi Izumi, "Reconsidering Ethnic Culture and Community: A Case Study on Japanese Canadian Taiko Drumming," *Journal of Asian American Studies* 4:1 (February 2000): 35–56.

68. Japanese Canadian Centennial Project, *A Dream of Riches*.

69. About the details of the redress movement, see Miki and Kobayashi, *Justice in Our Time*.

70. Japanese Canadian Society of Greater Vancouver for Senior Citizens Housing (JCS) merged with the Japanese Canadian Health Care Society of British Columbia (JCHCS), and became the Nikkei Seniors Health Care and Housing Society in 2001.

71. Wakayama, *Kikyo*.

CONTRIBUTORS

NORIKO ASATO is assistant professor of Japanese at the University of Nebraska-Lincoln. She is working on a book on the Japanese language school controversy in Hawaii and the contiguous United States from 1919 to 1927.

MICHIKO MIDGE AYUKAWA, born in Vancouver, British Columbia, was incarcerated for four years during World War II in a Slocan Valley camp for Japanese Canadians. A former chemist, Ayukawa obtained a doctorate in history in 1997 at the University of Victoria. She has written numerous articles on Japanese Canadians and is co-author of "The Japanese," in *The Encyclopedia of Canada's Peoples*, ed. Paul Robert Magocsi (University of Toronto Press, 1999).

ROGER DANIELS, Charles Phelps Taft professor emeritus of History, University of Cincinnati, has published widely on Asian American and immigration topics. His most recent book is *Guarding the Golden Door: American Immigration Policy and Immigrants since 1882* (Hill and Wang, 2004).

GAIL LEE DUBROW is a professor in the College of Architecture and Urban Planning at the University of Washington and serves as associate dean for academic programs in the graduate school. She is the author of *Sento at Sixth and Main: Preserving Landmarks of Japanese American Heritage* (Seattle Arts Commission, 2002).

LOUIS FISET is the author of *Imprisoned Apart: The World War II Correspondence of an Issei Couple* (University of Washington Press, 1997) and is currently at work on a history of the Puyallup Assembly Center and on a book focusing on health care in the World War II internment camps, assembly centers, and relocation centers.

ANDREA GEIGER-ADAMS is a Ph.D. candidate in history at the University of Washington, studying Meiji-era Japanese immigrants in the North American West, including both Canada and the United States. She graduated from the University of Washington Law School in 1991 and is a former editor-in-chief of the *Washington Law Review*.

ARTHUR A. HANSEN is emeritus professor of History and Asian American Studies at California State University, Fullerton, where he directs the Center for Oral and Public History and its Japanese American Project. He is also senior historian at the Japanese American National Museum, Los Angeles.

JAMES A. HIRABAYASHI is the chief program advisor at the Japanese American National Museum in Los Angeles. He is professor emeritus of Anthropology and Ethnic Studies at San Francisco State University, where he served as dean of the nation's first School of Ethnic Studies. He has also held research and teaching positions at the University of Tokyo, Japan, and Amadu Bello University in Zaria, Nigeria.

MASUMI IZUMI is associate professor in the Institute of Language and Culture at Doshisha University, Kyoto, Japan. She has studied and published on the postwar political and cultural activities of Japanese Canadians and Japanese Americans.

ERIC L. MULLER is the George R. Ward professor at the University of North Carolina School of Law in Chapel Hill, North Carolina. He holds a J.D. from Yale Law School and worked for a New York law firm and as an assistant U.S. attorney in Newark, New Jersey, before entering academia. He is the author of *Free to Die for Their Country: The Story of the Japanese American Draft Resisters in World War II* (University of Chicago Press, 2001).

GAIL M. NOMURA is assistant professor of American Ethnic Studies and adjunct assistant professor of History and Women's Studies at the University of Washington. She is the co-editor (with Shirley Hune) of *Asian/Pacific Islander American Women: A Historical Anthology* (New York University Press, 2003) and is completing a book on the prewar history of Japanese Americans on the Yakama Indian Reservation. She is a past president of the Association for Asian American Studies.

PATRICIA E. ROY teaches Canadian history at the University of Victoria, Victoria, British Columbia. She is the author of *A White Man's Province: British Columbia Politicians and Chinese and Japanese Immigrants, 1858–1914* (University of British Columbia Press, 1989) and *The Oriental Question: Consolidating a White Man's Province, 1914–41* (University of British Columbia Press, 2003).

ROBERT C. SIMS is professor emeritus of history at Boise State University. He began teaching there in 1970; for ten years, he was dean of the College of Social Sciences and Public Affairs. He serves as an advisor to the National Park Service on the Minidoka Internment National Monument.

INDEX

Illustrations are indicated in boldface type.